REFRAMING GLOBAL SOCIAL POLICY

Social investment for sustainable and inclusive growth

Edited by
Christopher Deeming and Paul Smyth

First published in Great Britain in 2018 by

Policy Press
University of Bristol
1-9 Old Park Hill
Bristol
BS2 8BB
UK
t: +44 (0)117 954 5940
pp-info@bristol.ac.uk
www.policypress.co.uk

North America office:
Policy Press
c/o The University of Chicago Press
1427 East 60th Street
Chicago, IL 60637, USA
t: +1 773 702 7700
f: +1 773-702-9756
sales@press.uchicago.edu
www.press.uchicago.edu

© Policy Press 2018

British Library Cataloguing in Publication Data
A catalogue record for this book is available from the British Library

Library of Congress Cataloging-in-Publication Data
A catalog record for this book has been requested

ISBN 978-1-4473-3249-7 hardcover
ISBN 978-1-4473-3251-0 ePub
ISBN 978-1-4473-3252-7 Mobi
ISBN 978-1-4473-3250-3 epdf

The right of Christopher Deeming and Paul Smyth to be identified as editors of this work has
been asserted by them in accordance with the Copyright, Designs and Patents Act 1988.

Cover design by Hayes Design
Front cover image: Shutterstock
Printed and bound in Great Britain by Clays Ltd, St Ives plc
Policy Press uses environmentally responsible print partners

Contents

List of figures

List of boxes and tables

Boxes

Tables

Acknowledgements

We are grateful to staff at Policy Press for their help with this volume, especially Emily Mew and Laura Vickers.

Notes on contributors

Giuliano Bonoli is Professor of Social Policy at the Swiss Graduate School for Public Administration at the University of Lausanne. His work has focused on pension reform, labour market and family policies, with particular attention paid to the politics of welfare state transformation. He has published some 50 articles and chapters in edited books, as well as a few books. Among his key publications is *The origins of active social policy: active labour market policy and childcare in a comparative perspective* (2013, Oxford University Press).

Marius R. Busemeyer is a Full Professor of Political Science at the University of Konstanz, Germany. His research focuses on comparative political economy and welfare state research, education and social policy, public spending, theories of institutional change and, more recently, public opinion on the welfare state. Busemeyer studied political science, economics, public administration and public law at University of Heidelberg and the Harvard Kennedy School of Government. He holds a doctorate in political science from the University of Heidelberg. He worked as a senior researcher with Wolfgang Streeck and Kathleen Thelen at the Max Planck Institute for the Study of Societies in Cologne and was a postdoc visiting fellow at the Center for European Studies at Harvard before coming to Konstanz. His publications include a book on *Skills and Inequality* (Cambridge University Press, Winner of the 2015 Stein Rokkan Prize for Comparative Social Science Research), an edited volume (with Christine Trampusch) on *The Political Economy of Collective Skill Formation* (Oxford University Press) as well as a large number of articles in leading journals of the discipline.

Sarah Cook is the Director of UNICEF's Innocenti Research Centre. She was Director of the United Nations' Research Institute for Social Development (UNRISD) from 2009–2015 and previously a Fellow at the Institute of Development Studies as well as working for the Ford Foundation in China. Her research has focused on China's social and economic transformations and more broadly on social policy and gender in development contexts.

Christopher Deeming is a Senior Lecturer in Social Policy at the University of Strathclyde. Research interests include inclusive growth and social investment inspired social policy, and comparative social policy. For this work he was supported by a three-year UK Economic and Social Research Council Fellowship ES/K001353/1 and a five-year Chancellor's Fellowship from the University of Strathclyde.

Anton Hemerijck is Professor of Political Science and Sociology at the European University Institute (EUI) and Centennial Professor of Social Policy at the London School of Economics and Political Science (LSE). Trained as an economist at Tilburg University in the Netherlands, he took his doctorate from Oxford University in Social Studies in 1993. At the Vrije Universiteit he was Dean of the Faculty of the Social Sciences between 2009 and 2014 and Professor of Institutional Policy Analysis in the Department of Public Administration and Political Science. Important book publications include *A Dutch Miracle* with Jelle Visser (Amsterdam University Press, 1997), *The Future of Social Europe* with Maurizio Ferrera and Martin Rhodes (CELTA Press Lisbon, 2000), and *Why We Need a New Welfare State* with Gosta Esping-Andersen, Duncan Gallie and John Myles (Oxford University Press, 2002). With OUP he published the monograph *Changing Welfare States* (2013) and most recently the edited volume *The Uses of Social Investment* (2017).

Tim Jackson is Professor of Sustainable Development at the University of Surrey and Director of the newly-awarded Centre for the Understanding of Sustainable Prosperity (CUSP). Funded over five years by the Economic and Social Research Council (ESRC), CUSP aims to explore the moral, cultural, social, political and economic dimensions of prosperity on a finite planet. Tim currently also holds an ESRC Professorial Fellowship on Prosperity and Sustainability in the Green Economy (PASSAGE). He has been at the forefront of academic work on sustainability for over two decades and has undertaken numerous advisory roles on the social and economic dimensions of sustainability for business, government, civil society and intergovernmental agencies. Between 2004 and 2011, he was Economics Commissioner on the UK Sustainable Development Commission, where his work culminated in the publication of *Prosperity without Growth – economics for a finite planet* (Routledge, 2009/2016), which received wide acclaim and was subsequently translated into 17 foreign languages. He was awarded the Hillary Laureate for exceptional international leadership in 2016. In addition to his academic work, Tim is an award-winning dramatist with numerous radio writing credits for the BBC.

Jane Jenson is a Professor Emerita in the Political Science Department, Université de Montréal. In 2001 Jane was awarded the Canada Research

Chair in Citizenship and Governance at the Université de Montréal. In 2004 she was named a Senior Fellow of the Successful Societies programme of the Canadian Institute for Advanced Research (www. cifar.ca/successful-societies). Her research focuses on comparative social policy and European politics as well as social movements (www.cccg.umontreal.ca). Since 1999 she has been following the introduction of the social investment perspective into welfare regimes. Her current work deals with social innovation, social enterprise and social investment.

Stephan Klasen is Professor of Development Economics at the University of Göttingen. He is also the director of the Ibero-America Institute for Economic Research and the Coordinator of the Courant Research Center 'Poverty, equity, and growth in developing and transition countries'. He holds a PhD from Harvard University and has since held positions at the World Bank, King's College (Cambridge, UK) and the University of Munich. His research focuses mostly on issues of poverty, inequality, environment, and gender. He is a member of the UN Committee on Development Policy, President of the European Development Research Network, and was a member of the Intergovernmental Panel on Climate Change for the 5th Assessment Report.

Jon Kvist is Professor of European Public Policies and Welfare Studies at the Department of Social Science and Business, Roskilde University. He was Professor at the Centre for Welfare State Research at the University of Southern Denmark, Odense from 2008 to 2014 and has also worked at SFI – The Danish National Institute of Social Research. Kvist has published widely on the Nordic welfare model, Europeanisation and set-theoretic methods. He has chaired international research projects and been a member of the Norwegian Research Council's welfare, work and migration programme, the Scottish Government working group on welfare and the Danish Government Commission on Unemployment Insurance, and is national coordinator in the European Commission's new Expert Network on Social Policy. Recent publications include 'A framework for social investment strategies: Integrating generational, life course and gender perspectives in the EU social investment strategy' (*Comparative European Politics*), 'Three Worlds of Welfare Capitalism: The making of a classic' (co-author, *Journal of European Social Policy*) and *Fighting Poverty and Exclusion Through Social Investment* (European Commission, 2016). See www.jonkvist.com for more.

Huck-ju Kwon is Professor at Graduate School of Public Administration, and the Asia Development Institute, Seoul National University. He is also the Editor of the *Korean Public Administration Review* and Co-editor of *Global Social Policy*. His research interests are comparative social policy and international development policy. He was Director of the Global Research Network on Social Protection in East Asia and Visiting Scholar at the Harvard Yenching Institute (2013–14). Previously he worked as the Research Coordinator at the UNRISD (2002–05). His publications include 'Poverty Reduction and Good Governance' (*Development and Change*, 2014), *Transforming the Developmental Welfare State in East Asia* (Palgrave, 2005), and the *Korean State and Social Policy* (Oxford University Press, 2011).

Guillem López-Casasnovas is Professor of Economics at the Pompeu Fabra University of Barcelona, since June 1992. He is currently Director of the Centre for Research in Health and Economics (CRES-UPF). Since 2005 he has been a member of the Governing Council of the Bank of Spain and member of the Advisory Council of the Ministry of Health (since 2000). He was President of the International Health Economics Association between 2007 and 2013 and has also served as an expert adviser for the World Health Organization on health inequalities in the EU.

Laia Maynou is a Research Officer at the London School of Economics (LSE) – Health and Social Care, Researcher at the Centre for Research in Health and Economics (CRES-UPF) and Adjunct Lecturer at the Department of Economics and Business at Pompeu Fabra University. Her research focuses on Health Economics, in three areas in particular: 1) Economics and Health Inequalities, 2) Health Technology Assessment (HTA) and 3) Public Policy Evaluation. All these fields of research are analysed from an empirical perspective.

James Midgley is Harry and Riva Specht Professor of Public Social Services and Professor of the Graduate School, University of California, Berkeley. He previously served as the Dean of the School of Social Welfare. He has published widely on issues of social development, international social welfare and social policy. Among his most recent books are *Social Policy and Social Change in East Asia* (Lexington, 2014, with James Lee and Yapeng Zhu), *Social Development: Theory and Practice* (Sage, 2014), *Social Welfare for a Global Era: International Perspectives on Policy and Practice* (Sage, 2017), *Future Directions in Social Development* (Palgrave, 2017, with Manohar Pawar) and *Social Investment and Social*

Welfare: International and Critical Perspectives (Edward Elgar, 2017, with Espen Dahl and Amy Conley Wright). He is a Fellow of the American Academy of Social Work and Social Welfare and has held honorary professorial appointments at Nihon Fukishi University in Japan, the University of Johannesburg, South Africa, Hong Kong Polytechnic University, and Sun Yat-sen University in China.

Günther Schmid is retired Professor of Political Economy at the Free University Berlin and he is also Director Emeritus at the WZB Berlin Social Science Centre. He published – among others – the *International Handbook for Labour Market Policy and Evaluation* (Edward Elgar, 1996) and *Full Employment in Europe: Managing Labour Market Transitions and Risks* (Edward Elgar, 2008). He was member of various advisory committees, in particular the Committee preparing the German Labour Market reforms under Chancellor Schröder. He holds degrees in political science and economics and honorary doctorates at the Universities Aalborg (Denmark), Växjö and Linnaeus (Sweden); www.guentherschmid.eu

Paul Smyth is Honorary Professorial Fellow in the School of Social and Political Sciences at the University of Melbourne, Australia. From 2003 to 2013 he held the joint position of Professor of Social Policy at the University of Melbourne where he was the Founding Director of the Master of Social Policy programme and also the General Manager of the Research and Policy Centre at the Brotherhood of St Laurence, a prominent welfare non-government organisation. His numerous writings on Australian social policy include three editions of *Australian Social Policy Understanding for Action* (2014) and *Inclusive Growth in Australia* (2013).

Robin Webster is a researcher and writer on environmental issues. She was Friends of the Earth's senior campaigner on climate and energy for two and a half years. In 2010 Robin helped start up the climate blog Carbon Brief, where she worked as a fact checker and policy analyst until 2014. She has written extensively on UK energy policy and food sustainability issues. Robin has a Masters from University College London in conservation and a Bachelor's degree in biology.

Introduction and overview

Christopher Deeming and Paul Smyth

As uncertainty in the global economy continues we find there is already underway a new worldwide movement away from the 'neoliberal' policy models and frameworks of the late 20th century. Policymakers and epistemic communities are in search of a new understanding of society which has at its core the quest for a better integration of economic development with social and environmental policy, in order to promote what Barack Obama has called 'shared prosperity' (White House, 2011) and Christine Lagarde (2014) at the IMF has termed 'inclusive capitalism'.

Certainly the idea of the social investment welfare state has attracted significant critical attention but the new ideas about inclusive economic growth and development have not been held up to such critical scrutiny within the academic social policy discipline even though the central problem of promoting economic development while reducing inequality is fast becoming the characteristic political desideratum of our time.

We now find a constellation of international organisations like the OECD, the IMF and the World Bank (key actors in the global social policy arena, see Deacon, 2007; Béland and Orenstein, 2013; Kaasch and Martens, 2015) constructing new 'policy ideas' (Béland, 2009, 2016) and alternatives for social investment, inclusive growth and sustainable development out of neoliberalism. Global social policy is now being reframed to promote inclusion and cohesion.[1] Rebuilding solidarity across countries and regions continues to be a challenge, however. After the global economic crisis, the shock of Brexit and the rise of 'populism' in Europe and the US, with the rhetoric of protectionism and parties on the right promising to stop job competition through migrants and refugees, the politics of any post-neoliberal policy settlement has become impossible to predict. Growing inequality, however, presents the major threat to environmental sustainability, to equity and to the world economy, and needs to be tackled now. According to the economist and Nobel laureate Joseph Stiglitz, capitalism does not have to produce inequality (Stiglitz, 2015: 75–6, 105–13, 300–05). With the right policies, it is possible to choose both efficiency and fairness, he argues.

This volume takes stock of the major changes that are already underway in the global policy arena – the neoliberal period having reached its social policy limits. We find that this changing policy perspective based on the new and emerging ideas about investment and the inclusive economy have yet to be captured, formulated, defined or held up to critical scrutiny in any systematic fashion. Here we chart new ground by looking at how global social policy is being reframed by policy actors and institutions shaping global social governance for the remaking of economy and society for after-neoliberalism. Broadly speaking, and at the risk of over-simplification, this movement in many of the advanced economies can be followed in the transition from the 'welfare state' towards the 'social investment welfare state', now incorporating some of the latest thinking about inclusive or shared prosperity. While in development economics, it is generally recognised as the move from the 'Washington Consensus' to what the World Bank has termed 'inclusive growth' because of the way in which this emerging concept emphasises social inclusion with economic growth.

Increasingly, it is evident that international organisations and domestic policy communities are using ambiguous and contested notions relating to 'social investment' and 'inclusive growth' as quasi-concepts in order to make them both more deployable for policymaking purposes (Jenson, 2017). For these reasons, we have chosen to incorporate these terms and perspectives in the title of the volume. Part of our aim here then is to critically consider the present policy logic of integrating and unifying ideas about inclusive growth and social investment – and some of the social, economic and environmental opportunities and challenges ahead – as international organisations and policy communities around the globe seek to forge a new policy consensus for the 21st century based on sustainable development and human rights.

Social investment and inclusive growth perspectives are held up to critical scrutiny throughout the volume. The social investment approach was always much stronger on the need for a modernised welfare system adapted to the labour market flexibility associated with the globalised economy. While the inclusive growth approach has certainly emphasised the need for a broad-based, employment centred, pattern of development as the foundation of any welfare regime. Arguably, this was neglected in the social investment approach but must now be addressed in the wake of the global economic crisis.

In the book we take very seriously the fact we are witnessing a policy shift of deep importance, towards a new 'inclusive' model of economy and society for the 21st century. This shift is now forcing us to rethink past policy legacies (for example, Hemerijck, 2017), and with ever increasing integration and interdependence some old and familiar divisions are now beginning to fade and diminish. Referring to this 'new multi-polar' world, in which notions of a 'First World' and a 'Third World' are no longer meaningful, World Bank President Robert Zoellick (2010) observed that 'as economic tectonic plates have shifted, [policy] paradigms must shift too'. The fundamental renewal of policy logic is already underway. This book captures these emergent trends and seismic shifts in policy perspectives and holds them up to critical scrutiny. The years ahead will differ markedly for social policy than those defining moments of Keynesianism and neoliberal capitalism that went before.

The volume and plan of the book

As a contribution to the evolving debate for the reframing of global social policy, this volume brings together some of the leading scholars in the field to critically engage with the new and emerging policy frameworks and perspectives that are now being designed by policy actors for the remaking of global social policy for the 21st century.

Part I: Theoretical frameworks addresses the emerging theoretical frameworks. The opening chapter by Christopher Deeming and Paul Smyth provides an introduction to the discourses on 'social investment', 'inclusive growth and development' in key documents in three respects: it draws the lines of the discourses back to their origins, shows the limits of the concepts and examines the potential of these concepts in developing a synthesis, which brings together the protective and productive functions of social policy at the micro level (institutions, enterprise), meso-scale (nation) and the macro level (world, climate-natural environment). In Chapter Two, Anton Hemerijck examines the strengths and weaknesses of the social investment approach before looking at how it can be enhanced by the inclusive growth framework which has been the subject of a major dialogue between the OECD itself with the World Bank. Here Hemerijck reflects on how well the social policy discipline is responding to the challenge of reintegration with economic policy identifying some of the key challenges which lie ahead.

Chapter Three by Sarah Cook looks at the new integration of social with economic policy from the developing economies perspective. It provides a brief overview of post-war perspectives on social policy in development thinking from the Keynesian framework to radical political economy and then the Washington Consensus. It highlights the key social policy instruments in what were seen as 'pre-welfare state' economies, before surveying the 'social policy spring' occurring notably in Latin America and in Asia. Her chapter draws out the main learnings for social policy research from the new productivist models associated with the perspective of inclusive growth.

Remaking the relationship between paid work and welfare looms as the central challenge for an inclusive growth regime. In the Keynesian period, the policy of full employment meant that paid work did in fact underpin the welfare state regime. Subsequent neoliberal economic policies created a legacy of high unemployment and precarity that was not addressed by the social investment approach, with its purely supply-side focus. An inclusive growth approach insists that paid work must underpin a sustainable welfare regime. But how can this be done given the state of current labour markets? In Chapter Four, Huck-ju Kwon examines developmental welfare and inclusive growth and reconsiders the paid work welfare nexus.

One of the biggest challenges for developing a new more 'productivist' social policy approach has been the apparent absence of a new, post-neoliberal, economic model – even after the global financial crisis. Across the post-war period, scholars have tended to conceive of the options in terms of the contest between the Keynesianism of the neoclassical synthesis and neoliberal economics. While the resilience of neoliberalism is still evident in some European welfare states, as austerity economics lingers, the inclusive growth framework associated with the 'post-Washington Consensus' or 'Beijing Consensus' appears to abandon neoclassical fundamentalism without a simple return to the neoclassical synthesis.

Next, Part II: Policy applications looks more closely at some theoretical and policy applications. Inclusive growth has been proposed as another approach to ensuring that economic growth promotes well-being for all. At the same time, the precise definition and measure of inclusive growth is not totally clear, nor is the relationship with other concepts, such as 'pro-poor' growth. These issues are taken up by Stephan Klasen in Chapter Five. Here Klasen examines the ways in which inclusive growth has been defined and measured in developing and advanced economies using different types of income and non-income indicators. He goes on to propose a way to define inclusive growth, differentiated from related concepts, and proposes particular indicators that can be used to monitor inclusive growth effectively within developing and advanced economies.

As Günther Schmid makes clear in Chapter Six, the inclusive growth agenda prioritises a broad-based, employment centred pattern of growth as a foundation of social development. Welfare goals cannot be pursued solely through taxes and transfers 'after the economic event'. The focus must also be on the predistribution of economic endowments such as human capital, and the distribution of opportunities within the labour market, as well as the wages and conditions of employment. This means raising the general level of education and training in the workforce, promoting inclusion of marginalised and vulnerable groups, encouraging transitions between various employment relationships over the life course, and ensuring the potential of social mobility. It also requires an agenda for innovation and the promotion of entrepreneurship that is also inclusive. Schmid explores the challenge of developing a competitive and innovative 'knowledge economy' which is employment rich but also avoids labour market exclusion and polarisation; and advancing what he calls the 'virtuous circle of flexibility and security'.

Inclusive growth that benefits all and to which everyone contributes has major implications for purely passive, redistributive policies. 'Active labour market policies' or ALMPs (understood broadly to also encompass in-work benefits) now pose a range of issues and fresh challenges from an inclusive growth perspective. ALMPs require some rethinking according to Giuliano Bonoli in Chapter Seven. In his chapter Bonoli explores how ALMPs might now be 'intelligently' redesigned in order to promote the notion of inclusive growth at the interface between employment and benefits in a way that encourages and rewards participation in productive processes by those who contribute.

High investment in human capital is the signature of the social investment approach embracing both education and skills. Education was the great catalyst for the rediscovery of the economically productive value of social policy at the turn of the century. Initially focussed on the importance of the 'early years' it has been elaborated into a policy concern for skills over the life course. Quickly taken up in to the concept of the 'social investment welfare state' (Morel et al, 2012) it is yet to be fully integrated into inclusive growth policy practices unused to accounting for the productive as well as the protective value of social services. In Chapter Eight, Marius Busemeyer explores their integration through an examination of the complex relationships which exist between skills, growth and social inequalities. More specifically, it expands the conventional perspective taken up in the social investment literature by systematically discussing the potential contribution of vocational education and training and lifelong learning to promoting inclusive growth and social investments.

Globally, policymakers promote social investments as a reform strategy to increase individuals' capacities and national economic growth. However, to take full advantage of social investments, the strategy needs a more coherent framework that takes into account the dynamic and multidimensional nature of social issues and social investments. Chapter Nine by Jon Kvist considers such a framework consisting of generational, life course perspectives on social investments and inclusive growth. The generational perspective brings out that social investments involve horizontal redistribution, underpin the productive and reproductive social contract between generations, and the increased diversity within generations. The life course perspective demonstrates how social issues and social investments in one life stage depend on the situation in prior life stages and affect the situation in later life stages and, possibly, in multiple dimensions.

The links between health and development are complex but sufficiently well-established for policy development purposes as Guillem López-Casasnovas and Laia Maynou argue in Chapter Ten. The whole idea that health is not a burden on the economy, but is an active partner in fostering economic growth and tackling health inequalities is now widely acknowledged. Inclusive growth, less unequal wealth creation, better-distributed incomes must lead to more health and health equity. However, they demonstrate that to test this affirmative sequence, with all the assumed linkages, proves to be very difficult indeed.

One of the key learnings from the recent revival of the 'social investment state' in OECD countries has been the challenge of promoting a new interpretation without disparaging the old. Thus, productivist social policy has often been taken up as a substitute for, rather than a complement to, policies for social protection. In Chapter Eleven, James Midgley shows how we can avoid the unwanted polarisation between 'investment' and 'protection'. While certain trends in post-war social policy may have encouraged that bifurcation from economic policy which allowed space for social protection to be cast as 'passive' and a 'cost' on the economy his chapter revisits some of the classic analyses of social protection (Keynes, Beveridge and Myrdal to James O'Connor) to show how nearly all social policies in fact have a dual function: both productive and protective. Even unemployment benefits – often seen as prime examples of 'passive welfare' – are shown here to be important economic stabilisers in periods of downturn while also allowing workers to achieve employment transitions that are more productive both for themselves and the wider economy. Beyond this economic rationale the chapter reasserts the importance of social protection for societies seeking to revive strategies for equality in the new inclusive model of growth.

Analysts of social policy often pay more attention to the content of social policy than to its governance. It is important to assess both, as Jane Jenson argues in Chapter Twelve. International organisations and domestic policymakers, moving beyond neoliberalism, are now embracing new forms of governance and have become enthusiastic for 'social entrepreneurship'. States and other public authorities now call on various kinds of social entrepreneurs to create jobs locally and make investments in human capital. This is a very different model of governance than in the previous eras of Keynesianism and market-making neoliberalism according to Jenson. While there is clearly an emphasis on promoting inclusion and cohesion here as Jenson observes, we are left mourning the loss of a different kind of social politics agenda based on notions of equality and social rights.

Inclusive growth is better than non-inclusive growth. Social investment is better than anti-social investment. However, as Tim Jackson and Robin Webster argue neither approach confronts what is the single most critical question faced by economics on a finite planet. In Chapter Thirteen, Jackson and Webster consider what prosperity might possibly look like in a world of environmental and social limits. They show how critical the question of limits is for our thinking about social justice and the roles of social policy. In the final chapter, Paul Smyth and Christopher Deeming critically reflect on learning and insights from the contributions as a whole. Here we consider what we have learned about the new policy perspectives and the challenges ahead for strengthening social welfare systems, and for shared prosperity for all. Finally, we need to know if we are now talking about a coherent shift in policy perspective, a new global social policy framework in the making, as international organisations and domestic policy communities move further away from neoliberalism. This is the subject of discussion in Chapter Fourteen.

Notes

[1]   G-20 Finance Ministers, Central Bankers' Communique issued 24 July 2016: www.bloomberg.com/news/articles/2016-07-24/g-20-finance-ministers-central-bankers-communique-full-text (accessed 14 June 2017).

References

Béland, D. (2009) 'Ideas, institutions, and policy change', *Journal of European Public Policy*, 16(5): 701–18.

Béland, D. (2016) 'Ideas and Institutions in Social Policy Research', *Social Policy and Administration* 50(6): 734–50.

Béland, D. and M.A. Orenstein (2013) 'International organizations as policy actors: An ideational approach', *Global Social Policy* 13(2): 125–43.

Deacon, B. (2007) *Global Social Policy and Governance*, Thousand Oaks, California: Sage.

Hemerijck, A. (ed.) (2017) *The Uses of Social Investment*, Oxford: Oxford University Press.

Jenson, J. (2017) 'Modernising the European Social Paradigm: Social Investments and Social Entrepreneurs', *Journal of Social Policy*, 46(1): 31–47.

Kaasch, A. and K. Martens (eds) (2015) *Actors & Agency in Global Social Governance*, Oxford: Oxford University Press.

Lagarde, C. (2014) 'Inclusion and Financial Integrity—an Address to the Conference on Inclusive Capitalism', Speech by the Managing Director, International Monetary Fund, 27 May, www.imf.org/external/np/speeches/2014/052714.htm (accessed 14 June 2017).

Morel, N., B. Palier and J. Palme (eds) (2012) *Towards a social investment welfare state? Ideas, policies and challenges*, Bristol: Policy Press.

Stiglitz, J.E. (2015) *The Great Divide: Unequal Societies and What We Can Do About Them*, New York, NY: W. W. Norton & Company.

White House (2011) 'Fact Sheet: The President's Framework for Shared Prosperity and Shared Fiscal Responsibility', 13 April, Washington, DC: The White House, Office of the Press Secretary, www.whitehouse.gov/the-press-office/2011/04/13/fact-sheet-presidents-framework-shared-prosperity-and-shared-fiscal-resp (accessed 14 June 2017).

World Bank (2010) 'Old concept of "Third World" outdated, Zoellick says', Press release, 14 April, www.worldbank.org/en/news/press-release/2010/04/14/old-concept-of-third-world-outdated-zoellick-says (accessed 14 June 2017).

Part I
Theoretical frameworks

Social investment, inclusive growth that is sustainable and the new global social policy

Christopher Deeming and Paul Smyth

Introduction

Over the past two decades, there has been a fundamental reappraisal of the economic value of social policy, coming from a number of different directions. The first is the adoption of the 'social investment perspective' (OECD, 1997a: 14) in the advanced economies, as the old post-war welfare states were reformed in an attempt to address the 'new social risks' associated with post-industrial society. The social investment perspective in social policy appeared to offer a plausible alternative to neoliberalism and the neoliberal critique of welfare (and the discussions about 'permanent austerity' and 'welfare state retrenchment' that proliferated during the 1990s and early 2000s). The second major shift was the transition from the so-called 'Washington Consensus' towards 'pro-poor growth' policies and 'inclusive growth' policy frameworks for reducing poverty in developing country contexts in the Global South (with an 'emphasis on increasing the opportunities for the poor to contribute and benefit from the growth process', as the World Bank observes, 2008: 7). Third, and related, is the shift in policy perspective at the OECD in response to rapidly rising inequality in the advanced economies (OECD, 2008, 2011a, 2015b), as international organisations and epistemic communities began to diffuse ideas for inclusive growth (OECD, 2013a). Finally, there is the environmental imperative of 'sustainability' that is shaping the new global development agenda (Sachs, 2015). Today, we find that socially inclusive models for sustainable growth and development offer policymakers in the Global North (as well as the South) a plausible remedy to address rising social inequality. Although initially quite independent, these intellectual movements and literatures, orientated towards investment and inclusion, have now begun to converge and coalesce and are increasingly seen to contribute towards a single analytical framework and shared policy agenda for human development and flourishing.

In this chapter we consider the emerging global social policy frameworks for inclusive growth and social investment, and draw out the sometimes similar and sometimes quite distinctive insights that these two policy perspectives now bring to our understanding of the relationship between economy and society in the 21st century, and for the future development of global social policy more generally. While global social policy is in the process of being reframed, this chapter, and the other contributions to this volume, make clear some of the key challenges that collectively all societies now face, but we also hope that readers of this volume find some grounds for fresh optimism in today's efforts to humanise global market capitalism, to the benefit of all.

The social investment perspective

The idea of 'social investment' (Midgley, 1999) and the 'social investment perspective' (Jenson and Saint-Martin, 2003) in social policy represent the latest justification for social spending of the investment type to guide the development of the economy and society in the 21st century. With the emphasis on investment it refocuses attention on the productive function of social policy for economic development, as James Midgley (1999) notes, eclipsed for some time by the emphasis on 'welfare state' building and the focus on social protection and compensation roles. Social spending in the post-war period had been insufficiently focused on anticipated investment returns, or so it was claimed (Smyth and Deeming, 2016). A core defining feature of the social investment perspective then is the focus on the 'productive' contribution that social policy can make to the economy, that is social policy as a 'productive factor' (European Commission, 2000: 5). From this perspective, the 'challenge is to ensure that the returns to social expenditures are maximised' (OECD, 1997b: 5). The definitions of social investment in Box 1.1 by some of the leading international organisations show how social policy is being reframed for the 21st century.

Box 1.1 Definitions of 'social investment' in the work of international organisations

The Organisation for Economic Co-operation and Development (OECD) advocates a social investment approach when assessing social programmes. The challenge, according to the OECD, is to ensure that the returns to social expenditures are maximised, in the form of social cohesion and active participation in society and the labour market. This approach stresses interventions that take place early in the life cycle or that support those contributing to their own welfare. Particular attention needs to be directed to supporting those who have low earnings but are working or in training, and to those who are caring for others. A social investment approach also requires a realistic assessment of whether provision of welfare services through public sector institutions are always appropriate. Other social and economic agencies may fulfil the same functions at lower cost, the OECD notes.

The European Commission argues that 'social investment is about investing in people. It means policies designed to strengthen people's skills and capacities, and to support them to participate fully in employment and social life. Key policy areas include education, quality childcare, healthcare, training, job search assistance and rehabilitation'.

The Economic Commission for Latin America and the Caribbean (ECLAC) defines public sector social investment – unlike compensatory policies, which address the effects of an incident or a hazard that has already occurred – as aims to help prevent or prepare for adverse events, and to support and equip people for coping with them, rather than to compensate those affected by, for example, market deregulation. From this perspective, public spending is not a cost for the economy but rather a series of investments that are necessary to ensure strong, lasting and shared growth, meet new social needs and safeguard economic, social and cultural rights. Social investment strategies set priorities with a view to supporting people throughout their life cycle, focusing on groups that are subject to social exclusion (including women, young people and children) in fundamental areas of human development (such as education, health, employment and housing). Social investment can encompass spending in both the public and the private sectors. However, public spending, particularly public social expenditure, makes up the bulk of it.

Sources: Adapted from OECD (1997b: 5–6), the European Commission website (http://ec.europa.eu/social/main.jsp?catId=1044) and ECLAC (2014: 50).

In Chapter Twelve, Jane Jenson examines some of the ideational work behind these 'quasi-concepts' (see also Jenson, 2010, 2015) – 'social investment' and 'inclusive growth' – and explores their ideational linkages. Having entered the language stream of the social sciences, these emerging concepts and policy perspectives have clearly gained traction in recent years. Figures 1.1 and 1.2, for example, show the number of 'hits' retrieved from the Social Science Citation Index after entering these terms. Despite growing popularity, these emerging concepts are subject to many interpretations, because like all 'concepts' in the social sciences they are dynamic historical constructions, as Béland and Petersen (2014) observe.

Figure 1.1 'Social investment' as a key phrase within the social sciences, 1998–2016

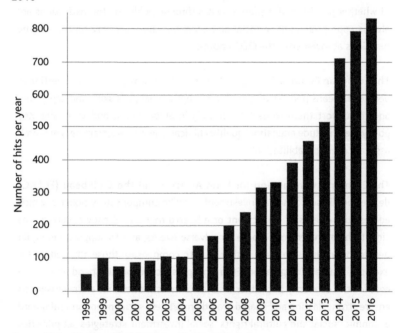

Source: Web of Science (Social Science Citation Index)

Jean-Claude Barbier argues that social investment is a problematic concept with an ambiguous past (Barbier, 2014), that is open to alternative interpretations, and with ongoing uncertainty about what social policy inspired by social investment thinking might or might not encompass (see detailed reviews by Morel et al, 2012; Hemerijck, 2013, 2017; Leibetseder, 2017; Midgley et al, 2017). Nevertheless, we find certain core defining features that may be observed in the

Figure 1.2 'Inclusive growth' as a keyword within the social sciences, 1998–2016

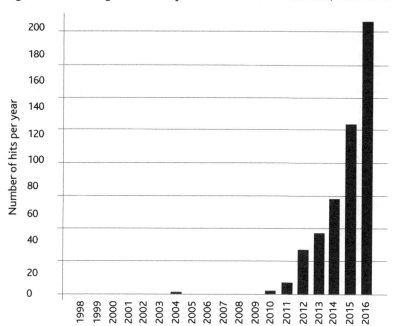

Source: Web of Science (Social Science Citation Index)

development and dissemination of policy ideas and reports from the leading international organisations:

- a child-centred focus, exemplified in OECD policy documents and work streams such as 'Babies and Bosses' (OECD, 2002, 2003, 2004, 2005a, 2007; see Mahon, 2008, 2009), involving publicly funded early childhood education and care policies and programmes (OECD, 2011b) as well as UNICEF and World Bank documents (Jenson, 2010; Mahon, 2010).
- state-led investment in human capital policies for skills and lifelong learning (OECD, 2006a, 2013b).
- active labour market programmes and policies (ALMPs) to increase employment and boost employment growth (OECD, 1994, 2006b, 2013c), and employment policies that invest in human capital, remove obstacles to employment and prevent the depletion of human capital during long periods of unemployment (European Commission, 2016).
- supporting innovation systems and learning in the knowledge-based service economy (OECD, 2015a).

Some of these themes and ideas behind social investment thinking in social policy may be observed in works from the late 1980s (some point to the work on the 'enabling state' for example; Gilbert and Gilbert, 1989). However, the new 'investment' perspective in social policy began to be more formally identified with the work of Anthony Giddens (1998) advocating the 'social investment state' and that of Gøsta Esping-Andersen, Duncan Gallie, Anton Hemerijck and John Myles, who also argued that welfare states needed to adopt a child-centred perspective in order to adapt to the new social and economic conditions associated with the transition to economic globalisation and a shift from industrial to the post-industrial knowledge-based economy (Esping-Andersen et al, 2002). These changes in the economy and society had created 'new social risks', adversely affecting the opportunities of low-skilled workers, women, young adults and children (Armingeon and Bonoli, 2006). As Anton Hemerijck claims in Chapter Two, this now demands a new social investment welfare state architecture based on three functions to cope with the new risks: raising human capital 'stock', easing labour market 'flow', supported by a safety net 'buffer'.

Thus, ideas about the 'productive' role of social policy and a 'social investment' approach to policymaking began to be diffused by international organisations from the late 1990s onwards (Jenson, 2010; Mahon, 2010; 2013). The new thinking inspired political platforms across many of the advanced nations and developing economies (for example, Lister, 2002, 2004; Jenson and Saint-Martin, 2003; Taylor-Gooby, 2004, 2008; Dobrowolsky and Jenson, 2005; Jenson, 2010; Deeming and Smyth, 2015; Hemerijck, 2017). Social investment initiatives were embraced by policymakers at the European Parliament (European Commission, 2000, 2013, 2015) who also saw the promising future of the social investment approach now being reflected in notions of 'active social policy' (OECD, 2005b: 27–40) and the OECD (1988, 1989) watchword of an 'active society' more generally (Jenson and Saint-Martin, 2006). Giuliano Bonoli has also mapped the 'active social policy' turn (Bonoli, 2013). The overall perceptions then of 'new welfare' (Lister, 2002; Taylor-Gooby, 2004), 'new welfare states' (Powell, 1999; Esping-Andersen et al, 2002; Taylor-Gooby, 2008), and 'changing welfare states' (Hemerijck, 2013), fashioned out of a new welfare state architecture for 'preparing' society rather than 'repairing' it, are still relatively recent as Anton Hemerijck (2015) suggests.

The strength of the social investment approach, or so it is claimed, is the successful redefinition of key social service expenditures as investments in human capital; something that was said to be lacking in the social policy tradition, at least in the British tradition of social policy analysis established by Richard M. Titmuss and T.H. Marshall. It was also thought to be largely absent in the preceding period of R.H. Tawney, when in fact the productive value of social policy was keenly appreciated (for a reappraisal see Smyth and Deeming, 2016, and Morel et al, 2015, who focus on the early origins of social investment thinking in the work of Alva and Gunnar Myrdal). In the post-war period of the 'neoclassical' synthesis in economics, the rationale for state intervention was understood primarily in terms of a macroeconomic imperative to maintain full employment. Today, the economic arguments for social investment hinge more on arguments about the potential, future returns on human capital spending. Here the work of the American economists and Nobel Laureates Gary Becker (1964) and James Heckman (for example Heckman and Masterov, 2007) on human capital and education investment in the early years of child development is very important and has lifelong effects, as Jon Kvist illustrates in Chapter Nine. However, this particular view of social policy, largely defined by the logic of 'returns' and 'investment', has attracted critics.

Jane Jenson and Ruth Lister were prominent early critics of 'the social investment state' associated with a 'third way' politics that was increasingly future-orientated and accepting of 'equality' of 'opportunity' as a political ideal, rather than any notion of fairness in the here and now (Jenson, 2001; Jenson and Saint-Martin, 2003; Lister, 2003, 2004; Dobrowolsky and Jenson, 2004, 2005, 2008). The political rhetoric of social investment (framed in terms of 'human capital' development in children, as future workers) has increasingly masked or diminished the equality claims of women (Jenson and Saint-Martin, 2003; Dobrowolsky and Jenson, 2004; Jenson, 2009), people with a disability (Cantillon and Van Lancker, 2013), and older workers in ageing OECD societies who now appear to lack a productivity argument in the 'Heckman Equation' that underpins social investment thinking (Deeming and Smyth, 2016). A second critique acknowledged the legitimacy of social investment orientated social policy but saw it as crowding out traditional redistributive and compensatory functions of social policy and social protection. A number of studies have noted the coexistence of social investment strategies with rising poverty and inequality (Cantillon, 2011; Vandenbroucke and Vleminckx, 2011; Pintelon et al, 2013). Social investment policies appear to have benefited those who are least disadvantaged (the so-called 'Matthew effect'), and so run counter to the goals of the social investment approach.

Then, as Brian Nolan (2013) observes, there is the near impossibility of separating out social policies that are about 'investment' (those looking for rates of 'return'), from those about some form of consumption with little or no 'return' – not to mention the causal uncertainty and issues involved in calculating the social return on social investment (also see Anton Hemerijck's discussion on the economics of social investment, Hemerijck, 2012: 51–56). The notion that compensatory social policies like unemployment benefits are 'passive' with little or no social return is highly problematic. For example, out-of-work benefits help to support livelihoods, aid workers in their search for new employment, and are straightforward crises management instruments during a downturn (Starke et al, 2013). Unemployment benefits as much as education then have a dual social and economic function as James Midgley argues in Chapter Eleven. But, of course, to affirm their productive value is not necessarily to diminish their social protection function. As Hemerijck observes of Nolan in Chapter Two, the latter's main case against the social investment approach appears to be rather that an emphasis on justification in terms of mainstream economic arguments will diminish the case based on progressive social values.

These criticisms, however, draw our attention to the major question in the literature regarding the future of the social investment perspective: namely the possibility of a trade-off between the new investment agenda to raise economic participation and productivity and the traditional emphasis of social policy on social security and social protection. This issue has shadowed the social investment agenda since its early articulation by Anthony Giddens where investment policies could indeed be read as substitutes for income maintenance. Gøsta Esping-Andersen's alternative case argued the success of investment initiatives actually required a strong welfare state with an emphasis on social protection (Esping-Andersen, 2001). Social protection is of paramount importance even in the most productivist of welfare states he argues. The human capital based investment strategy will inevitably leave some citizens behind and, thus, it remains imperative to have a secure welfare safety net of minimum income support underpinning the social investment strategy. As Midgley writes in Chapter Eleven, achieving the right balance between the protective and investment functions of social policy remains a critical issue for the future of global social policy after neoliberalism.

In conclusion, the social investment perspective has been very much about reconnecting social policy and economic policy after several decades when their roles had been seen as either delinked or economically harmful. While the economic case for social investment in human capital is growing, the project remains far from complete (Hemerijck, 2017). It remains highly ambiguous around the relationship between social investment and social protection, and there is something of a silence around broader social objectives to tackle social inequality in the here and now, while the market (and market failure) remains un(der)critiqued. The approach basically took for granted continuing economic growth while assuming 'old social risks' have all but disappeared, assumptions undone by the global economic crises that resulted in rapidly growing unemployment and the declining value of pensions (Crouch and Keune, 2012). The longer-term integration of social with economic policy will require a more comprehensive understanding of their interrelationship. It is here that we turn to examine the parallel debate in development policy over inclusive growth. Importantly, the starting point here is not a social policy model lacking an economic rationale but rather the opposite: an economic growth model lacking a social policy rationale (see the discussions by Anton Hemerijck and Sarah Cook in Chapters Two and Three).

Inclusive and sustainable growth

The idea of a fairer economy, based on the goals of inclusive growth and inclusive development that is sustainable, goes well beyond traditional economic thinking about 'growth' (Commission on Growth and Development, 2008), evident in some of the working definitions of the international organisations, such as the World Bank, OECD (see Box 1.2). Pragmatically, this political economy perspective involves creating the institutions and conditions necessary for managing a broad-based, employment centred pattern of economic growth and inclusion (Khan, 2012). While there can be no definitive list of inclusive development inspired social policies and practices, many innovative solutions (and policy challenges) are discussed in this volume. Including, for example, the new broad-based, employment centred patterns required for inclusion (Chapter Six) and challenges facing ALMPs for an inclusive growth (Chapter Seven), education and skills strategies (Chapter Eight), and fresh thinking on the institutional architecture and governance arrangements for fostering social innovation in order to achieve inclusive growth (Chapter Twelve), to highlight just a few.

A feature of the emerging inclusive growth approach in social policy is that it reopens some old and familiar questions about the governance of economic uncertainty and the scope of intervention in the market to influence social welfare – vis-à-vis policies for 'full employment' (Schmid, 2008), 'job guarantees' (Murray and Forstater, 2014), 'employment insurance' (Schmid, 2015) and other strategies that are available to help individuals and families to mitigate social risks and manage critical transitions over the life course (Chapter Nine). Because inclusive growth focuses social policy attention on the distribution of resources, opportunities and outcomes (and the potential for redistribution), it can be viewed as a complement to a social investment and predistribution agenda (see Huber and Stephens, 2015, on the complementarities of predistribution and redistribution policies). As a result, this dramatically expands or broadens the focus of much contemporary social and economic thinking towards new possibilities, as the 2015 *Inclusive Growth and Development Report* from The World Economic Forum makes clear (Samans et al, 2015).

Box 1.2 Definitions of 'inclusive growth' in the work of international organisations

The World Bank inclusive growth strategy emerged out of the work of the Commission on Growth and Development (2006–10). Inclusive growth (IG) is used to denote both the pace and pattern of economic growth, which are interlinked and assessed together. In the World Bank approach, rapid pace of economic growth is necessary for reducing absolute poverty. But, for this growth to be sustainable in the long run, it should be broad-based across sectors, and inclusive of the large part of a country's labour force. This definition implies a direct link between the macro and micro determinants of growth. From this perspective, inclusive growth focuses on productive employment, rather than on income redistribution per se. Employment growth generates new jobs and income, while productivity growth has the potential to lift the wages of workers and the returns of the self-employed. The World Bank's approach adopts a long-term perspective and is concerned with sustained growth, where inclusiveness refers to equality of opportunity in terms of access to markets, resources and unbiased regulatory environment for businesses and individuals.

The Asian Development Bank's (ADB) corporate strategy (Strategy 2020) aims to promote inclusive economic growth as one of its main objectives. In this framework, inclusive growth is a concept that goes beyond broad-based growth. It is 'growth that not only creates new economic opportunities, but also one that ensures equal access to the opportunities created for all segments of society' (Ifzal and Hwa Son, 2007: 1–2). An income growth episode is considered 'inclusive' when: (1) it allows participation of (and contribution by) all members of society, with particular emphasis on the ability of the poor to participate in growth (the 'non-discriminatory' aspect of growth), which implies a focus on the 'process' of growth; and (2) is associated with declining inequality in those non-income dimensions of wellbeing that are particularly important for promoting economic opportunities, including education, health, nutrition and social integration (the 'disadvantage-reducing' aspect of inclusive growth), which implies a focus on the 'outcomes' of growth.

The United Nations Development Programme (UNDP) recently changed the name of its International Poverty Centre in Brasília, Brazil, to International Policy Centre on Inclusive Growth (IPC-IG), whose work is based on the premise that more equal societies perform better in development. In the UNDP perspective, IG is seen as both an outcome and a process. On the one hand, it ensures that everyone can participate in the growth process, both in terms of decision-making as well as in terms of participating in growth itself. On the other hand, inclusive growth is one whose benefits are shared equitably. Inclusive growth thus implies participation and benefit sharing.

The European Commission launched 'The Europe 2020 Strategy' with the notion of inclusive growth at its core (European Commission, 2013, 2014). In this Strategy, inclusive growth is understood as empowering people through high levels of employment, investing in skills, fighting poverty and modernising labour markets, training and social protection systems so as to help people anticipate and manage change, and build a cohesive society. It is also essential that the benefits of economic growth spread to all parts of the Union, including its outermost regions, thus strengthening territorial cohesion. It is about ensuring access and opportunities for all throughout the lifecycle.

The Organisation for Economic Co-operation and Development (OECD) launched its 'Inclusive Growth Initiative' in 2012 to help governments address rising inequalities (OECD, 2017). It starts from the premise that GDP per capita may not be sufficient to generate sustained improvements in societal welfare. Promoting across-the-board improvements in wellbeing calls for a broader conception of living standards than that contained in traditional measures. Beyond income and wealth, people's wellbeing is shaped by a range of non-income dimensions – such as their health, educational, and employment status – that are not adequately captured in a measure like GDP per capita. Likewise, wellbeing at the societal level cannot be gauged solely by looking at averages. Only by looking at the evolution of living standards for different segments of the population, such as the median or the poorest, can it be seen whether economic growth benefits all groups in society or just the lucky few. Thus, the OECD's 'Inclusive Growth Framework' includes a measure of 'multidimensional living standards' designed to track societal welfare and analyse the extent to which growth – in a given country and over a given period – translates into improvements across the range of outcomes that matter most to people's lives.

It includes income dimensions, and non-income dimensions that matter for wellbeing, such as health inequality and education.

Sources: Adapted from OECD (2014a: 8–9; 2014b: 80) and Samans et al (2015: 5)

As Box 1.2 illustrates, the emerging definitions of inclusive growth all now imply direct links between macroeconomic demand management policies and supply side social investment strategies in order to foster inclusion. As Angel Gurría, OECD Secretary-General, notes:

> tackling inequalities in incomes, health outcomes, education and well-being, requires breaking down the barriers to inclusive growth and reaching new frontiers in policymaking and implementation. Everyone should be able to realise their potential and to share the benefits of growth and increased prosperity.[1]

Discourses highly relevant to thinking about 'inclusion' and inclusive growth in particular include the recognition of universal human rights in the 1940s, women's rights (CEDAW, UN, 1979), children's rights (UNCRC, UN, 1989) and disability rights (CRPD, UN, 2008) for example, but also development theories that have a long history in the Global South: for instance 'social development' (Midgley, 2014), 'inclusive development' (Gupta et al, 2015), and 'sustainable development' (Sachs, 2015). In many ways then the ideational emergence of inclusive growth is not entirely new, the World Bank, for example, published a study in the early 1970s looking at 'redistribution with growth' which set out similar arguments that have since been recapitulated many times (Chenery et al, 1974). Today, what Arjan de Hann calls the reclaiming of social policy in development also reveals some very similar debates to those surrounding the rise of the social investment perspective in the advanced economies (de Haan, 2007). In parallel with the social investment approach then we find a search for 'pro-poor growth' (Ravallion and Chen, 2003; DFID, 2004; Ravallion, 2004); which became more broadly defined as 'shared growth' (World Bank, 1993) or 'shared prosperity' (World Bank, 2014, defined as growth in the income of the bottom 40%), then 'inclusive economic growth' (Kakwani and Pernia, 2000: 3), one of the key objectives set out in the 2008 Asian Development Bank (ADB) corporate strategy (Klasen, 2010), before the 'inclusive growth' concept was finally firmed up at the World Bank and IMF (Ianchovichina and Lundstrom, 2009a;

Ianchovichina and Lundstrom Gable, 2012) as a model that better integrates social and economic policies for the 21st century (Ranieri and Ramos, 2013; Ramos et al, 2013).

Until relatively recently, development studies itself had a separate history to social policy (Devine et al, 2015). As Hall and Midgley (2004) write, both matured as academic disciplines in the post-war period with social policy focusing on the 'welfare state' in the industrialised countries while development was concerned with the growth process in the so-called 'Third World'. Thandika Mkandawire (2011) also discusses the lack of interface between the two disciplines. Social policy, he writes, suffered from an 'OECD bias' (Mkandawire, 2011: 152–3) which was partly to do with a paucity of data but also to a 'static' approach to comparative welfare measures which focused on distribution and protection to the neglect of the role of social policy in growth and structural change. He also finds a 'normative dissonance' in the OECD outlook which discounted the 'productivist' orientation of 'developmental states' with the restricted focus on taxes and transfers in social policy.

There are numerous accounts of what inhibited a greater focus on social policy within development studies (Midgley, 2015, provides a review). The first wave of post-war development policy was based on Keynesianism and understandings of a staged approach to modernisation beginning with the so-called 'big push' towards industrialisation. This involved state coordination of large scale investment projects and public ownership of key sectors. As Amartya Sen emphasises, welfare (including education and health services) was understood as consumption and needing to be reframed to allow for capital accumulation (Sen, 1997). In a similar chronology to welfare state policies, social issues came to the fore in development thinking during the 1960s and 1970s when it had become apparent that in spite of rapid economic growth, poverty and inequality still characterised many societies. This period saw the development of the 'basic needs' strategies in development (Ghai et al, 1977), which was also reflected in the World Bank's policy position (Chenery et al, 1974). In parallel to social policy in the advanced nations this reform optimism was soon overshadowed: first, by the left-wing critiques of capitalism and then by the neoliberal or 'New Right' critique of the welfare state in the 1980s and 1990s. While social policy in the Global North was caught up in the 'crisis' of the welfare state; development policy in the Global South entered the 'structural adjustment' phase of the Washington Consensus.

The Washington Consensus and subsequent transition to the post-Washington Consensus – and Beijing Consensus – is of course a major subject in development economics and not something we wish to canvass here (see Saad Filho, 2005; Serra and Stiglitz, 2008a; Fine and Saad Filho, 2014). However, it is important to observe that unlike the origins of the social investment approach which was very much a reinterpretation of the role of welfare from a social policy perspective, inclusive growth priorities emerged as much from an economic as a social critique of the Washington Consensus. Again, for our purpose it is not necessary to revisit the technical debates around the original definition of the Washington Consensus coined by John Williamson (1990), and how it differed from subsequent usages of the term (Williamson, 2008). Here we simply follow Nobel Prize winning economist Joseph Stiglitz's proposal that for:

> most people around the world' it came to refer to 'development strategies that focus on privatization, liberalization, and macro stability (meaning, mostly, price stability) ... a set of policies predicated upon a strong faith ... in unfettered markets and aimed at reducing, or even minimizing, the role of government (Stiglitz, 2008: 41).

Economic policies described under the Washington Consensus had the most serious, severe (and well documented) repercussions on the poorest families and children in the 'developing' world (Jolly, 1999; Gore, 2000). The economic policy critiques of the Washington Consensus highlighted recognition of poor growth outcomes in numerous African and Latin American countries which had followed the neoliberal doctrines and the Washington Consensus mantra: 'stabilize, liberalize and privatize'. Neoliberalism's failures stood in sharp contrast to the spectacular growth success stories in East Asia that had involved various forms of state 'developmentalism' (Huck-ju Kwon, 2005, also writing on the challenges of inclusive growth for the developmental welfare state in Chapter Four of this volume). Initially, what emerged in the post-Washington Consensus period, as Alfredo Saad Filho observes, was a reflection of the institutionalist perspective of economists, which was largely concerned with 'getting the institutions right' (Saad Filho, 2011). However, a new post-Washington Consensus consensus was emerging as Stiglitz (2008) himself writes, on the understanding that if all citizens do not share in the fruits of growth then inclusive growth cannot be considered a success. Social policy would not aim for a 'one-size-fits-all' approach to inclusion, he suggests, but encourage experimentation and self-determination in an evidence-based way in a more balanced mixed economy for markets and government. Finally, and importantly for social policy, measures of social progress should be broader than GDP and include social and environmental sustainability (Stiglitz et al, 2009, 2010).

The emphasis on social and environmental goals brings social policy designs back into the development frame (Serra and Stiglitz, 2008b). It picks up on the tradition reaching back to the 'basic needs' approach of the 1970s, which re-emerged in the 1990s with Sen's work (Sudhir and Sen, 1994) on the Human Development Index (HDI), culminating in the Millennium Development Goals (MDGs) of the United Nations (which have now been superseded by the Sustainable Development Goals, SDGs). Although the inclusive growth perspective in social policy is much more than an economic policy agenda its economic underpinnings are clearly evident, since all of the evidence suggests that income inequality hinders growth and its sustainability, as economists at the IMF (Dabla-Norris et al, 2015) and the OECD (2015b) have shown. Social inequality is not just bad for society; it is also bad for the economy. Societies that are more equal appear to work better for everyone, as Wilkinson and Pickett (2009) demonstrate. Not only do more equal societies perform better by promoting social wellbeing for everyone, but all of the evidence now suggests that there are benefits for the economy and long-term growth as well. Income inequality is found to have a negative and statistically significant impact on growth (Cingano, 2014).

The debates around the end of the Washington Consensus (Serra and Stiglitz, 2008a) and 'pro-poor growth' (Ravallion and Chen, 2003) were of course hotly contested amid the development research and policy communities but by the end of the first decade of the 21st century the shape of the new post-Washington Consensus was beginning to emerge. Highly significant are the publications from the IMF and the World Bank enunciating the new policy perspectives which have become associated with the 'inclusive growth' approach and the closer integration of economic and social policy (Ianchovichina and Lundstrom, 2009b; Anand et al, 2013). Compared to other policy frameworks, these versions are rather conservative. Nevertheless, they do help to define a new era for development thinking in relation to global social policy. By comparison, the anti-poverty strategy of the United Nations Research Institute for Social Development (UNRISD), for example, has much more emphasis on tackling inequality, especially through the provision of universal services and social protection to address 'inequality traps', but it also calls for an 'employment centred growth' approach (UNRISD, 2010). The more expansive role for social policy in the UNRISD framework is also linked to the broader understanding and measures of development associated with Amartya Sen and the United Nations Development Programme (UNDP) and the '2030 Agenda for Sustainable Development' by addressing the following aspects:

- create opportunities for good and decent jobs and secure livelihoods
- support inclusive and sustainable business practices
- promote better government policies and fair and accountable public institutions (UNDP, 2014).

Little over a decade ago, ideas for a shared prosperity and inclusive economic growth were being formulated by international agencies, for addressing extreme poverty and social inequalities in the Global South. Today, that policy perspective now offers policy communities a plausible remedy to address rising social inequality resulting from wealth creation in the rich economies (amid growing concerns from the OECD [2008, 2011a, 2015b] and the publication of major studies [Marmot, 2008; Wilkinson and Pickett, 2009; Stiglitz, 2012. 2015b; Nolan et al, 2014; Piketty, 2014; Standing, 2014; Atkinson, 2015; Bourguignon, 2015]). The OECD began to set out a new political economy framework to support inclusive growth (OECD, 2013a), while the EU's *Europe 2020 Strategy* states the priorities for smart, sustainable and inclusive growth (European Commission, 2014). Clearly then, policy instruments that were developed to meet the needs of the Global South have moved northward, as Jane Jenson (2015) remarks. There is also now a significant and growing body of policy writing on inclusive growth priorities and strategies to set alongside the growing European literature on social investment (de Mello and Dutz, 2012; Hasmath, 2015a).

Thus, the OECD's work on gender equality (OECD, 2014c), wellbeing (OECD, 2011c), inequality (OECD, 2008, 2011a, 2015b), structural policy reform (OECD, 2005a), development (OECD, 2010), institutions (OECD, 2009), cities and new models for placed-based investment and growth (OECD, 2016a), and ecosystems (OECD, 2011d) all point towards a new and emerging global social policy architecture for understanding, measuring and monitoring the relationship between growth and inclusiveness (see OECD, 2016b). As Stephan Klasen argues, aggregate living standards and social wellbeing outcomes are dependent on both income and non-income dimensions (see Chapter Five), and the sorts of social policies that effect their distributions, as Figure 1.3 suggests.

Figure 1.3 The OECD 'inclusive growth' framework for policy analysis

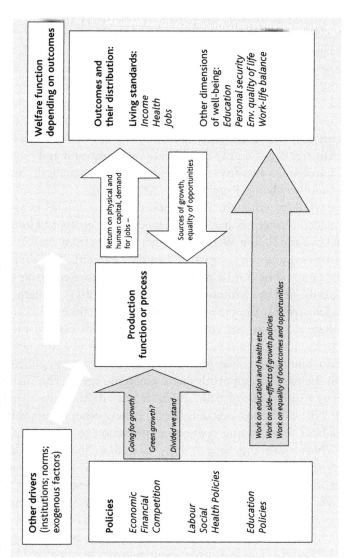

Source: OECD (2014d: 35) (Reproduced with permission of the copyright owner)

While an inclusive growth approach has much to commend itself for addressing widening income inequality; the approach is clearly open to different political agendas, as Hasmath (2015b) observes. Perhaps more so because of its appeal to pragmatism in national policy rather than a firm theoretical basis of the social sciences (see the critical assessments and review of challenges facing the emerging national and regional inclusive growth policy frameworks in Africa [Ncube, 2015] and India [Nagaraj, 2012], Australia [Smyth and Buchanan, 2013], Latin America [ECLAC, 2015], and Scotland [Wilson, 2016] for example). Some critics have questioned the ideological fetishisation of productivity growth as they seek to move the debate beyond 'productivism' or GDP growth: instead there should be more of a focus on social priorities such as 'care' and how 'care' is addressed by society (with regard to the work of UNRISD on the 'Political and Social Economy of Care', see Razavi, 2007). Tony Fitzpatrick (2004) calls for more of a focus on 'reproductive value' and 'sustainability' which is required in an increasingly 'post-productive' world. Important here will be the development and strengthening of policy frameworks based on human rights and equity considerations (Nussbaum and Comim, 2014), frameworks that foster 'social justice', 'sustainability', 'human welfare' and 'wellbeing' (Stiglitz et al, 2009; 2010).

While GDP growth in the world's poorest nations still has an appeal, the advanced economies may have reached their 'ecological limits' as Tim Jackson and Robin Webster suggest, resulting from the relentless pursuit of consumption growth (Chapter Thirteen). The emphasis of social policy should now perhaps focus on a more equitable form of prosperity, perhaps without 'growth' (Jackson, 2017). Whether we are headed towards the end of 'growth' (itself a contested concept) for ecological reasons, or any other reason, is not easy to predict, but as Jackson and Webster argue in Chapter Thirteen, the new age of sustainability and social justice clearly calls for new policies to come to the fore, to support this new emerging agenda for 'inclusive prosperity' (Summers and Balls, 2015) or 'shared prosperity' (Stiglitz, 2015a). This will almost certainly mean, among other things, shifting the emphasis from valuing economic production to valuing 'quality of life' (Nussbaum and Sen, 1993), 'societal wellbeing' (Stiglitz et al, 2009, 2010), notions of 'decent work' (UNDP, 2012), which is broader and deeper than that of jobs or employment alone (UNDP, 2015), encompassing care and caring roles (such as shifting some of the focus away from the current obsession with 'paid employment' and 'production' in tradable goods and services). This emerging agenda for global social policy is simply about putting 'life-first' as Hartley

Dean (2014) suggests. It is likely to involve rethinking the field of 'paid work' and working times (Coote and Franklin, 2013), supporting participation in processes of social value which is likely to further blur the traditional boundaries between paid work and productive welfare (Atkinson, 2015), with a renewed focus on rights in social policy that are designed to foster inclusion and participation (Van Parijs and Vanderborght, 2015).

The inclusive growth perspective appears optimistically orientated towards a social policy future beyond the safety net paradigm, according to Arjan de Haan (2015). However, our rationale for analysing the relationship between globalisation and social policy ('global social policy' as a socially constructed policy perspective and developing research arena, see Yeates, 2002; Deacon and Stubbs, 2013) derives from the theoretical consideration that welfare provision, which is often seen as 'passive', often fulfils important productive and protective functions (see Chapter Eleven). Increasingly, from a global social policy perspective, it seems important to canvass the marriage of protective universalism and productive employment, by rejecting the argument that claims all transfers – especially unemployment benefits – are necessarily 'passive'. New policies for employment and ALMPs should be 'intelligently' designed according to Bonoli (Chapter Seven) and Schmid (Chapter Six) in order to avoid or reduce the problem of 'moral hazard' and to induce or enhance the potential of ensurance (see Table 6.5, Chapter Six). In this context, 'moral hazard' concerns exploiting or misusing protection. While moral 'ensurance' means encouraging individuals to legitimately use protection and to take calculated investment orientated risks (for example, moving jobs, investing in continuous vocational education and training, thus contributing to mobility, innovation, structural change and productivity) where protection is available in case of misfortune (such as in the case of involuntary lack or loss of income, health, or employment).

To date, social policies orientated towards 'virtuous circles' of 'flexibility' and 'security' over the life course, as articulated by the European Commission (2004) for example, have been insufficient to address deeply entrenched societal problems (relating to exclusion and poverty) that now requires a more progressive agenda for protection, social distribution and investment (Cantillon, 2013; Kvist, 2015; Schmid, 2015). In this context we note the growing policy synergy and cooperation between international organisations within the field of social protection (for example, ILO, UNICEF, UNDP, World Bank). The ILO (2011) and UNDP (2011, 2013), for instance, have called on all countries to establish social protection floors which could guarantee income security for millions of people around the world, as Bob Deacon (2015a, 2015b) observes. In Europe, the EU Parliament (European Parliament, 2009) has called on the European Commission and EU Member States to guarantee the right to a Guaranteed Minimum Income safety net irrespective of individuals' chances in the labour market in order to prevent poverty and not just alleviate it (Deeming, 2017).

In summary, the inclusive growth agenda appears to have created more space for a new articulation of the role of social policy in economic thought. Thus, the goals of development should value social wellbeing and environmental sustainability, rather than simply focus on GDP (Stiglitz et al, 2009, 2010; Sachs, 2015). Second, we find that policies should not be residual or 'after the event' but be integrated and hard-wired into economic strategy. Therefore, reliance on taxes and transfers to achieve social goals is insufficient. Rather, the centre piece should be the management of 'shared prosperity' or 'inclusive prosperity' which can support not only 'productive' employment processes but also the 'reproductive' values of care and sustainability. Human capital spending is understood as investment and becomes a critical factor in fostering equality of opportunity, but clearly this should not imply that policymakers abandon social welfare protection altogether, while the inclusion agenda forces us to think more about equality and outcomes in the present. Broadly speaking then, it is increasingly possible to think about the social investment perspective in social policy in terms of a supply side strategy complementing the demand side emphasis of the inclusive growth and development perspective, and the formulations of new strategies for 'shared prosperity' within ecological limits (see Chapter Thirteen).

Reframing global social policy

The perspectives of social investment and inclusive growth now being deployed by key actors in the global social policy arena display two significant policy movements to reintegrate social and economic policy after the one sided economism of the neoliberal period. While these emergent policy perspectives have different contextual origins, they nevertheless share significant commonalities and complementarities that point towards a more unified understanding of the role of social policy within a 'one world' or a 'whole world' approach. Thus, old distinctions are breaking down as social policies and political priorities are reframed, forcing us to search for new meaning: between developed and developing nations, between productive and unproductive processes in the economy, between welfare investment and protection, and between labour supply and demand. The new emerging global social policy agenda implies direct links between macroeconomic governmental strategies, supply side investment for a 'fairer economy' and 'shared prosperity' for just and sustainable goals if consumption and production is squeezed or constrained across the advanced economies with climate change (see Chapter Thirteen).

As we saw, the early logics of their development were quite different. The social investment approach deployed by the OECD was, initially at least, about finding an economic case for social spending albeit within dominant neoliberal policy frameworks. Moreover, it had distinctive policy emphases on child-centred investment and ALMPs with a longer-term impetus towards refurbishing welfare systems in response to the new social risks of post-industrial society. The inclusive growth approach deployed by the World Bank on the other hand emerged within a more general economic as well as social critique of the Washington Consensus. This led to inclusive growth thinking being less about 'welfare' and much more about the interdependent roles of social and economic policy in addressing poverty and inequality and managing economic uncertainty beyond the social investment agenda inspired by thinking about new social risks. There was also the basic assumption of a more 'mixed economy' approach, with an active state managing this interdependence. At the same time there are significant points of convergence and complementarity.

Thus, both perspectives critique the formerly narrow understanding of the role of social policy in terms of 'protection' emphasising instead its value for economic productivity, although the new and emerging notions of 'inclusive prosperity' and 'shared prosperity', in light of ecological and sustainability concerns, are forcing international organisations and epistemic communities to rethink present conceptions of 'productivity' and 'social contribution' within society. While not discounting the redistributive role of taxes and transfers in reducing poverty and inequality they stress the importance of redistributing those resources which will equip individuals to participate in the market economy and new interventions to address market failures and the problems generated by capitalism from an inclusive growth perspective. That growth needs to be employment centred is also a shared understanding. At the same time human capital investments are thought to be more successful when wider inequalities are not present. Indeed, the inclusive growth perspective is much more explicit on the need to redress social inequalities.

Reflecting its origin, the inclusive growth agenda is very much focused on the economy as a whole and whether it works for everyone. While the social investment perspective on the other hand was always much more restrictive, focused on equipping and preparing individuals for their participation in the market economy. Thus, the former emphasises the importance for achieving growth as a basis of inclusion and actively canvasses policies to promote broad-based, employment centred development. The social investment perspective had taken shape in social policy long before the economic crisis following 2008 and tended to assume continuous economic growth (which may no longer be desirable, or even feasible for all nations). We also find that social investment thinking is now being integrated into a broader, new inclusive economic growth framework developed by international organisations and global social policy actors like the World Bank, IMF, OECD and their leaders, which have issued us with the call to action to tackle poverty and growing inequality on a scale that is unprecedented in human history.

These developments in social and economic thought offer us clear points of reflection for thinking about the development of a global social policy strategy for after neoliberalism. They encourage us to think about how welfare regimes are being reformed to enhance their productive and protective functions within social and environmental limits. In addition, and importantly for global social policy, these new and emerging policy perspectives and complementarities point to the importance of looking beyond the welfare regime itself as our authors show.

Acknowledgements
We thank Günther Schmid and Jane Jenson for helpful comments on an earlier draft.

Note
1   Addressing growing inequality through inclusive growth: A conversation with OECD Secretary-General Angel Gurría, www.brookings.edu/events/addressing-growing-inequality-through-inclusive-growth-a-conversation-with-oecd-secretary-general-angel-gurria/ (accessed 14 June 2017).

References

Anand, R., S. Mishra and S.J. Peiris (2013) *Inclusive Growth: Measurement and Determinants*, IMF Working Paper WP/13/135, Washington, DC: IMF.

Armingeon, K. and G. Bonoli (eds) (2006) *The Politics of Post-Industrial Welfare States: Adapting Post-War Social Policies to New Social Risks*, Oxford and New York, NY: Routledge.

Atkinson, A.B. (2015) *Inequality: What Can Be Done?*, Cambridge, MA: Harvard University Press.

Barbier, J.-C. (2014) 'Languages of "Social Policy" at "the EU level"', in D. Béland and K. Petersen (eds), *Analysing Social Policy Concepts and Language: Comparative and Transnational Perspectives*, Bristol: Policy Press, 59–79.

Becker, G. (1964) *Human Capital: A Theoretical and Empirical Analysis with Special Reference to Education*, Chicago, IL: University of Chicago Press.

Béland, D. and K. Petersen (2014) 'Introduction: social policy concepts and language', in D. Béland and K. Petersen (eds), *Analysing Social Policy Concepts and Language: Comparative and Transnational Perspectives*, Bristol: Policy Press, 1–11.

Bonoli, G. (2013) *The Origins of Active Social Policy: Labour Market and Childcare Policies in a Comparative Perspective*, Oxford: Oxford University Press.

Bourguignon, F. (2015) *The Globalization of Inequality*, translated by Thomas Scott-Railton, Princeton, NJ: Princeton University Press.

Cantillon, B. (2011) 'The paradox of the social investment state: growth, employment and poverty in the Lisbon era', *Journal of European Social Policy* 21(5): 432–49.

Cantillon, B. (2013) *Virtuous Cycles or Vicious Circles? The Need for an EU Agenda on Protection, Social Distribution and Investment*, GINI Discussion Paper 52, Antwerp: Herman Deleeck Centre for Social Policy, University of Antwerp.

Cantillon, B. and W. Van Lancker (2013) 'Three Shortcomings of the Social Investment Perspective', *Social Policy and Society* 12(4): 553–64.

Chenery, H., M.S. Ahluwalia, C.L.G. Bell, J.H. Duloy and R. Jolly (1974) *Redistribution with Growth*, Oxford: Oxford University Press.

Cingano, F. (2014) *Trends in Income Inequality and its Impact on Economic Growth*, OECD Social, Employment and Migration Working Papers, No. 163: OECD Publishing.

Commission on Growth and Development (2008) *The Growth Report: Strategies for Sustained Growth and Inclusive Development*, Washington, DC: The International Bank for Reconstruction and Development/ The World Bank.

Coote, A. and J. Franklin (eds) (2013) *Time on Our Side: Why We All Need a Shorter Working Week*, London: nef.

Crouch, C. and M. Keune (2012) 'The Governance of Economic Uncertainty: Beyond the "New Social Risks" Analysis', in G. Bonoli and D. Natali (eds), *The Politics of the New Welfare State*, Oxford: Oxford University Press, 45–67.

Dabla-Norris, E., K. Kochhar, N. Suphaphiphat, F. Ricka and E. Tsounta (2015) *Causes and Consequences of Income Inequality: A Global Perspective*, Washington, DC: SDN/15/13, International Monetary Fund.

de Haan, A. (2007) *Reclaiming Social Policy: Globalization, Social Exclusion and New Poverty Reduction Strategies*, Basingstoke: Palgrave.

de Haan, A. (2015) 'Inclusive Growth: Beyond Safety Nets', *European Journal of Development Research* 27(4): 606–22.

de Mello, L. and M.A. Dutz (eds) (2012) *Promoting Inclusive Growth: Challenges and Policies*, Paris: OECD Publishing.

Deacon, B. and P. Stubbs (2013) 'Global social policy studies: Conceptual and analytical reflections', *Global Social Policy* 13(1): 5–23.

Deacon, B. (2015a) 'The International Labour Organization and Global Social Governance – The 100 Year Search for Social Justice within Capitalism', in A. Kaasch and K. Martens (eds), *Actors & Agency in Global Social Governance*, Oxford: Oxford University Press, 3–17.

Deacon, B. (2015b) 'The ILO and Social Protection Policy after the Global Financial Crisis', in S. McBride, R. Mahon and G.W. Boychuk (eds), *After '08: Social Policy and the Global Financial Crisis*, Vancouver: UBC Press, 105–20.

Dean, H. (2014) 'Life-first welfare and the scope for a 'eudemonic ethic' of social security', in M. Keune and A. Serrano (eds), *Deconstructing Flexicurity and Developing Alternative Approaches: Towards New Concepts and Approaches for Employment and Social Policy*, Abingdon: Routledge, 152–72.

Deeming, C. (2017) 'Defining Minimum Income (and Living Standards) in Europe: Methodological Issues and Policy Debates', *Social Policy and Society* 16(1): 33–48.

Deeming, C. and P. Smyth (2015) 'Social Investment after Neoliberalism: Policy Paradigms and Political Platforms', *Journal of Social Policy* 44(2): 297–318.

Deeming, C. and P. Smyth (2016) 'Reassessing the 'Social Investment Perspective' for 'Inclusive Growth': Where do Older Workers Fit?', *Social Policy and Society* 15(4): 659–74.

DFID (2004) *What is Pro-Poor Growth and Why Do We Need to Know?* Pro-Poor Growth Briefing Note 1, London: Department for International Development.

Devine, J., S. Kuhner and K. Nakray (2015) 'Meeting emerging global policy challenges: positioning social policy between development and growth?', *Journal of International and Comparative Social Policy* 31(2): 95–9.

Dobrowolsky, A. and J. Jenson (2004) 'Shifting Representations of Citizenship: Canadian Politics of "Women" and "Children"', *Social Politics: International Studies in Gender, State & Society* 11(2): 154–80.

Dobrowolsky, A. and J. Jenson (2005) 'Social investment perspectives and practices: a decade in British politics', in M. Powell, L. Bauld and K. Clarke (eds), *Social Policy Review 17: Analysis and debate in social policy*, Bristol: Policy Press, 203–30.

Dobrowolsky, A. and R. Lister (2008) 'Social investment: the discourse and the dimensions of change', in M. Powell (ed.), *Modernising the welfare state: The Blair legacy*, Bristol: Policy Press, 125–42.

ECLAC (2014) *Social Panorama of Latin America*, 2014, LC/G.2635-P, Santiago, Chile: United Nations.

ECLAC (2015) *Education, Structural Change and Inclusive Growth in Latin America*, LC/L.3974, Santiago, Chile: United Nations.

Esping-Andersen, G. (2001) 'A Welfare State For The 21st Century', in A. Giddens (ed.), *The Global Third Way Debate*, Cambridge: Polity, 134–56.

Esping-Andersen, G., D. Gallie, A. Hemerijck and J. Myles (eds) (2002) *Why We Need a New Welfare State*, Oxford: Oxford University Press.

European Commission (2000) *Communication: Social Policy Agenda*, COM(2000)379 final, Brussels: European Commission.

European Commission (2004) *Joint Report on Social Inclusion*, Luxembourg: Office for Official Publications of the European Communities.

European Commission (2013) *Towards Social Investment for Growth and Cohesion – including implementing the European Social Fund 2014–2020*, COM(2013) 83 final, Brussels: Communication from the Commission.

European Commission (2014) *Taking stock of the Europe 2020 strategy for smart, sustainable and inclusive growth*, Brussels: European Commission.

European Commission (2015) *Policy Roadmap for the implementation of the Social Investment Package*, Brussels: European Commission.

European Commission (2016) *Active Labour Market Policies*, European Semester Thematic Fiche: http://ec.europa.eu/europe2020/pdf/themes/2016/active_labour_market_policies_201605.pdf (accessed 14 June 2017).

European Parliament (2009) *Active Inclusion of People Excluded from the Labour Market*, 2008/2335(INI), Brussels: European Parliament.

Fine, B. and A. Saad Filho (2014) 'Politics of Neoliberal Development: Washington Consensus and post-Washington Consensus', in H. Weber (ed.), *The Politics of Development: A Survey*, London: Routledge, 154–66.

Fitzpatrick, T. (2004) A Post-Productivist Future for Social Democracy?, *Social Policy and Society* 3(3): 213–22.

Ghai, D.P., A.R. Khan, E.H. Lee and T. Alfthan (1977) *The Basic Needs Approach to Development: Some Issues Regarding Concepts and Methodology*, Geneva: International Labour Organisation.

Giddens, A. (1998) *The Third Way: The Renewal of Social Democracy*, Cambridge: Polity Press.

Gilbert, N. and B. Gilbert (1989) *The Enabling State: Modern Welfare Capitalism in America*, New York, NY: Oxford University Press.

Gore, C. (2000) 'The Rise and Fall of the Washington Consensus as a Paradigm for Developing Countries', *World Development* 28(5): 789–804.

Gupta, J., N.R.M. Pouw and M.A.F. Ros-Tonen (2015) 'Towards an Elaborated Theory of Inclusive Development', *European Journal of Development Research* 27(4): 541–559.

Hall, A. and J. Midgley (2004) *Social Policy for Development*, London: Sage Publications.

Hasmath, R. (ed.) (2015a) *Inclusive Growth, Development and Welfare Policy: A Critical Assessment*, New, NY York: Routledge.

Hasmath, R. (2015b) 'The Paradigms of Inclusive Growth, Development and Welfare Policy', in R. Hasmath (ed.), *Inclusive Growth, Welfare and Development*, New York, NY: Routledge, 1–9.

Heckman, J.J. and D.V. Masterov (2007) 'The Productivity Argument for Investing in Young Children', *Applied Economic Perspectives and Policy* 29(3): 446–93.

Hemerijck, A. (2012) 'The political economy of social investment', in L. Burroni, M. Keune and G. Meardi (eds), *Economy and Society in Europe: A Relationship in Crisis*, Cheltenham: Edward Elgar, 40–60.

Hemerijck, A. (2013) *Changing Welfare States*, Oxford: Oxford University Press.

Hemerijck, A. (2015) 'The Quiet Paradigm Revolution of Social Investment', *Social Politics: International Studies in Gender, State & Society* 22(2): 242–56.

Hemerijck, A. (ed.) (2017) *The Uses of Social Investment*, Oxford: Oxford University Press.

Huber, H. and J.D. Stephens (2015) 'Predistribution and Redistribution: Alternative or Complementary Policies?', in C. Chwalisz and P. Diamond (eds), *The Predistribution Agenda: Tackling Inequality and Supporting*, London and New York, NY: I.B.Tauris & Co, 67–78.

Ianchovichina, E. and S. Lundstrom (2009a) *What is Inclusive Growth?*, PRMED, Washington, DC: World Bank.

Ianchovichina, E. and S. Lundstrom (2009b) *Inclusive Growth Analytics: Framework and Application*, Policy Research Working Paper No. 4851, Washington, DC, World Bank.

Ianchovichina, E. and S. Lundstrom Gable (2012) 'What Is Inclusive Growth?', in R. Arezki, C. Pattillo, M. Quintyn and M. Zhu (eds), *Commodity Prices and Inclusive Growth in Low-Income Countries*, Washington, DC: International Monetary Fund, 147–60.

Ifzal, A. and H. Hwa Son (2007) 'Measuring Inclusive Growth', *Asian Development Review* 24(1): 11–31.

International Labour Organization (ILO) (2011) *Social Protection Floor for a Fair and Inclusive Globalization*, Report of the Advisory Group chaired by Michelle Bachelet, Convened by the ILO with the collaboration of the World Health Organization (WHO), Geneva: ILO.

Jackson, T. (2017) *Prosperity without Growth: Foundations for the Economy of Tomorrow*, Second Edition, London and New York, NY: Routledge.

Jenson, J. (2001) 'Rethinking equality and equity: Canadian children and the social union', in T.E. Broadbent (ed.) *Democratic Equality: What went wrong?*, Toronto: University of Toronto Press, 112-129.

Jenson, J. and D. Saint-Martin (2003) 'New Routes to Social Cohesion? Citizenship and the Social Investment State', *The Canadian Journal of Sociology / Cahiers Canadiens de Sociologie* 28(1): 77–99.

Jenson, J. and D. Saint-Martin (2006) 'Building blocks for a new social architecture: the LEGOTM paradigm of an active society', *Policy & Politics* 34(3): 429–51.

Jenson, J. (2009) 'Lost in Translation: The Social Investment Perspective and Gender Equality', *Social Politics: International Studies in Gender, State & Society* 16(4): 446–83.

Jenson, J. (2010) 'Diffusing Ideas for After Neoliberalism: The Social Investment Perspective in Europe and Latin America', *Global Social Policy* 10(1): 59–84.

Jenson, J. (2015) 'Broadening the Frame: Inclusive Growth and the Social Investment Perspective', in S. McBride, R. Mahon and G.W. Boychuk (eds), *After '08: Social Policy and the Global Financial Crisis*, Vancouver, BC: UBC Press, 40–58.

Jolly, R. (1999) 'Adjustment with a Human Face: A UNICEF Record and Perspective on the 1980s', *World Development* 19(12): 1807–21.

Kakwani, N. and E. Pernia (2000) 'What is Pro-Poor Growth?', *Journal Asian Development Review* 18(1): 1–16.

Khan, M. H. (2012) 'The political economy of inclusive growth', in L. de Mello and M.A. Dutz (eds) (2012), *Promoting Inclusive Growth: Challenges and Policies*, Paris: OECD Publishing, 15–52.

Klasen, S. (2010) *Measuring and Monitoring Inclusive Growth: Multiple Definitions, Open Questions, and Some Constructive Proposals*, ADB Sustainable Development Working Paper Series, No. 12. Mandaluyong City, Philippines, Asian Development Bank.

Kvist, J. (2015) 'A framework for social investment strategies: Integrating generational, life course and gender perspectives in the EU social investment strategy', *Comparative European Politics* 13(1): 1472–4790.

Kwon, H.-J. (ed.) (2005) *Transforming the Developmental Welfare State in East Asia*, Basingstoke: Palgrave Macmillan.

Leibetseder, B. (2017) 'Social Investment Policies and the European Union: Swimming against the Neoliberal Tide?', *Comparative European Politics*, DOI: 10.1057/s41295-016-0086-2.

Lister, R. (2002) 'Towards a new welfare settlement?', in C. Hay (ed.), *British Politics Today*, Cambridge: Polity Press, 127–56.

Lister, R. (2003) 'Investing in the Citizen-workers of the Future: Transformations in Citizenship and the State under New Labour', *Social Policy & Administration* 37(5): 427–43.

Lister, R. (2004) 'The Third Way's social investment state', in J. Lewis and R. Surender (eds), *Welfare State Change: Towards a Third Way?*, Oxford: Oxford University Press, 157–81.

Mahon, R. (2008) 'Babies and Bosses: Gendering the OECD's Social Policy Discourse', in R. Mahon and S. McBride (eds), *The OECD and Transnational Governance*, Vancouver: University of British Columbia Press, 260–75.

Mahon, R. (2009) 'The OECD's Discourse on the Reconciliation of Work and Family Life', *Global Social Policy* 9(2): 183–204.

Mahon, R. (2010) 'After-Neoliberalism? The OECD, the World Bank and the Child', *Global Social Policy* 10(2): 172–92.

Mahon, R. (2013) 'Social Investment According to the OECD/ DELSA: A Discourse in the Making', *Global Policy* 4(2): 150–59.

Marmot, M. (2008) *Commission on Social Determinants of Health Final Report. Closing the gap in a generation: health equity through action on the social determinants of health*, Geneva: World Health Organization.

Midgley, J. (1999) 'Growth, Redistribution, and Welfare: Toward Social Investment', *Social Service Review* 73(1): 3–21.

Midgley, J. (2014) *Social Development: Theory and Practice*, Los Angeles: Sage.

Midgley, J. (2015) 'Social Investment, Inclusive Growth and the State', in R. Hasmath (ed.), *Inclusive Growth, Welfare and Development*, New York, NY: Routledge, 91–107.

Midgley, J., E. Dahl and A.C. Wright, (eds) (2017) *Social Investment and Social Welfare: International and Critical Perspectives*, Cheltenham: Edward Elgar.

Mkandawire, T. (2011) 'Welfare regimes and economic development: bridging the conceptual gap', in V. FitzGerald, J. Heyer and R. Thorp (eds), *Overcoming the Persistence of Inequality and Poverty*, Basingstoke: Palgrave Macmillan, 149–71.

Morel, N., B. Palier and J. Palme, (eds) (2012) *Towards a social investment welfare state? Ideas, policies and challenges*, Bristol: Policy Press.

Morel, N., B. Palier and J. Palme (2015) 'The Long Road towards a Social Investment Welfare State', in R. Hasmath (ed.), *Inclusive Growth, Welfare and Development*, New York, NY: Routledge, 124–41.

Murray, M.J. and M. Forstater (eds) (2014) *The Job Guarantee: Toward True Full Employment*, Basingstoke: Palgrave Macmillan.

Nagaraj, R. (ed.) (2012) *Growth, Inequality and Social Development in India: Is Inclusive Growth Possible?*, Basingstoke: Palgrave Macmillan.

Ncube, M. (2015) 'Inclusive Growth in Africa', in C. Monga and J.Y. Lin (eds), *The Oxford Handbook of Africa and Economics, Volume 1: Context and Concepts*, Oxford: Oxford University Press, 154–74.

Nolan, B. (2013) 'What use is 'social investment'?', *Journal of European Social Policy* 23(5): 459–68.

Nolan, B., W. Salverda, D. Checchi, I. Marx, A. McKnight, I.G. Tóth and H.G. van de Werfhorst (eds) (2014) *Changing Inequalities and Societal Impacts in Rich Countries: Thirty Countries' Experiences*, Oxford: Oxford University Press.

Nussbaum, M.C. and A. Sen (eds) (1993) *The Quality of Life*, Oxford: Clarendon Press.

Nussbaum, M.C. and F. Comim (eds) (2014) *Capabilities, Gender, Equality: Towards Fundamental Entitlements*, Cambridge: Cambridge University Press.

OECD (1988) *Employment Outlook 1988*, Paris: OECD Publishing.

OECD (1989) *Employment Outlook 1989*, Paris: OECD Publishing.

OECD (1994) *The OECD Jobs Study: Facts, Analysis, Strategies*, Paris: OECD Publishing.

OECD (1997a) *Societal Cohesion and the Globalising Economy: What Does the Future Hold?*, Paris: OECD Publishing.

OECD (1997b) *Beyond 2000: The New Social Policy Agenda*, OCDE/GD(97)66, Paris: OECD Publishing.

OECD (2002) *Babies and Bosses – Reconciling Work and Family Life*, Volume 1: Australia, Denmark and the Netherlands, Paris: OECD Publishing.

OECD (2003) *Babies and Bosses – Reconciling Work and Family Life*, Volume 2: Austria, Ireland and Japan, Paris: OECD Publishing.

OECD (2004) *Babies and Bosses – Reconciling Work and Family Life*, Volume 3: New Zealand, Portugal and Switzerland, OECD Publishing.

OECD (2005a) *Economic Policy Reforms, Going for Growth*, Paris: OECD Publishing.

OECD (2005b) *Extending Opportunities: How Active Social Policy Can Benefit Us All*, Paris: OECD Publishing.

OECD (2006a) *Skills Upgrading: New Policy Perspectives*, Paris: OECD Publishing.

OECD (2006b) *Boosting Jobs and Incomes: Policy Lessons from Reassessing the OECD Jobs Strategy*, Paris: OECD Publishing.

OECD (2007) *Babies and Bosses – Reconciling Work and Family Life: a Synthesis of Findings for OECD Countries*: OECD Publishing.

OECD (2008) *Growing Unequal? Income Distribution and Poverty in OECD Countries*, Paris: OECD Publishing.

OECD (2009) *Government at a Glance 2009*, Paris: OECD Publishing.

OECD (2010) *Perspectives on Global Development 2010: Shifting Wealth*, Paris: OECD Publishing.

OECD (2011a) *Divided we stand: why inequality keeps rising*, Paris: OECD Publishing.

OECD (2011b) *Doing Better for Families*, Paris: OECD Publishing.

OECD (2011c) *How's Life?: Measuring well-being*, Paris: OECD Publishing.

OECD (2011d) *Towards Green Growth*, Paris: OECD Publishing.

OECD (2013a) *OECD Workshop on Inclusive Growth*, Paris: OECD Publishing.

OECD (2013b) *OECD Skills Outlook 2013: First Results from the Survey of Adult Skills*, Paris: OECD Publishing.

OECD (2013c) 'Activating jobseekers: Lessons from seven OECD countries', *OECD Employment Outlook 2013*, Paris: OECD Publishing

OECD (2014a) *Changing the Conversation on Growth: Going Inclusive, Background Note*, New York, NY: Ford Foundation.

OECD (2014b) *All on Board: Making Inclusive Growth Happen*, Paris: OECD Publishing.

OECD (2014c) *Women, Government and Policy Making in OECD Countries: Fostering Diversity for Inclusive Growth*, Paris: OECD Publishing.

OECD (2014d) *Report on the OECD Framework for Inclusive Growth*, Meeting of the OECD Council at Ministerial Level, Paris 6-7 May 2014, www.oecd.org/mcm/IG_MCM_ENG.pdf (accessed 14 June 2017).

OECD (2015a) *Social Impact Investment: Building the Evidence Base*, Paris: OECD Publishing.

OECD (2015b) *In It Together: Why Less Inequality Benefits All*, Paris: OECD Publishing.

OECD (2016a) *Inclusive Growth in Cities Campaign: A Roadmap for Action, The New York Proposal for Inclusive Growth in Cities*, Paris: OECD Publishing.

OECD (2016b) *The Productivity-Inclusiveness Nexus*, Paris: OECD.

OECD (2017) *Time to Act: Making Inclusive Growth Happen*, Paris: OECD Publishing.

Piketty, T. (2014) *Capital in the Twenty-First Century*, translated by Arthur Goldhammer, Cambridge, MA and London: The Belknap Press of Harvard University Press.

Pintelon, O., B. Cantillon, K. Van den Bosch and C.T. Whelan (2013) 'The social stratification of social risks: The relevance of class for social investment strategies', *Journal of European Social Policy* 23(1): 52–67.

Powell, M. (ed.) (1999) *New Labour, New Welfare State: The 'Third Way' in British Social Policy*, Bristol: Policy Press.

Ramos, R.A., R. Ranieri and J.-W. Lammens (2013) *Mapping Inclusive Growth*, Working Paper number 105, Brasília: International Policy Centre for Inclusive Growth www.ipc-undp.org/pub/IPCWorkingPaper105.pdf (accessed 14 June 2017).

Ranieri, R., and R.A. Ramos (2013) *Inclusive Growth: Building Up A Concept*, Working Paper number 104, Brasília: International Policy Centre for Inclusive Growth (IPC-IG), www.ipc-undp.org/pub/IPCWorkingPaper104.pdf (accessed 14 June 2017).

Ravallion, M. and S. Chen (2003) Measuring pro-poor growth, *Economic Letters* 78(1): 93–99.

Ravallion, M. (2004) *Pro-poor Growth: A Primer*, Development Research Group, Washington, DC: World Bank.

Razavi, S. (2007) *The Political and Social Economy of Care in a Development: Context Conceptual Issues, Research Questions and Policy Options*, Gender and Development Programme Paper Number 3, Geneva: UNRISD.

Saad Filho, A. (2005) 'From Washington to Post-Washington Consensus: Neoliberal Agendas for Economic Development', in A. Saad Filho and D. Johnston (eds), *Neoliberalism: A Critical Reader*, London: Pluto Press, 113–19.

Saad Filho, A. (2011) 'Growth, Poverty and Inequality: Policies and Debates from the (Post-)Washington Consensus to Inclusive Growth', *Indian Journal of Human Development* 5(2): 321–44.

Sachs, J.D. (2015) *The Age of Sustainable Development*, New York, NY: Columbia University Press.

Samans, R., J. Blanke, G. Corrigan and M. Drzeniek (2015) *The Inclusive Growth and Development Report 2015*, Geneva: World Economic Forum.

Schmid, G. (2008) *Full Employment in Europe: Managing Labour Market Transitions and Risks*, Cheltenham: Edward Elgar.

Schmid, G. (2015) 'Sharing Risks of Labour Market Transitions: Towards a System of Employment Insurance', *British Journal of Industrial Relations* 53(1): 70–93.

Sen, A. (1997) 'Development and Thinking at the Beginning of the 21st Century', in L. Emmerij (ed.), *Economic and Social Development into the XXI Century*, Washington, DC: Inter-American Development Bank, 531–51.

Serra, N. and J.E. Stiglitz (2008a) *The Washington Consensus Reconsidered: Towards a New Global Governance*, Oxford: Oxford University Press.

Serra, N. and J.E. Stiglitz (2008b) 'Introduction: From the Washington Consensus Towards a New Global Governance', in N. Serra, S. Spiegel and J.E. Stiglitz (eds), The *Washington Consensus Reconsidered: Towards a New Global Governance*, Oxford: Oxford University Press, 3–13.

Smyth, P. and J. Buchanan (eds) (2013) *Inclusive Growth in Australia: Social Policy as Economic Investment*, Sydney: Allen & Unwin.

Smyth, P. and C. Deeming (2016) The 'Social Investment Perspective' in Social Policy: A Longue Durée Perspective, *Social Policy and Administration*: 50(6): 675–90.

Standing, G. (2014) *A Precariat Charter: From Denizens to Citizens*, London and New York, NY: Bloomsbury.

Starke, P., A. Kaasch and F. Van Hooren (2013) *The Welfare State as Crisis Manager: Explaining the Diversity of Policy Responses to Economic Crisis*, Basingstoke: Palgrave.

Stiglitz, J.E. (2008) 'Is there a Post-Washington Consensus?', in N. Serra and J. Stiglitz (eds), *The Washington Consensus Reconsidered: Towards a New Global Governance*, Oxford: Oxford University Press, 41–56.

Stiglitz, J.E. (2012) *The Price of Inequality: How Today's Divided Society Endangers Our Future*, New York, NY: W. W. Norton & Company.

Stiglitz, J.E. (2015a) *Rewriting the Rules of the American Economy: An Agenda for Growth and Shared Prosperity*, New York, NY: W.W. Norton & Company.

Stiglitz, J.E. (2015b) *The Great Divide: Unequal Societies and What We Can Do About Them*, New York, NY: W. W. Norton & Company.

Stiglitz, J.E., A. Sen and J. P. Fitoussi (2009) *Report by the Commission on the Measurement of Economic Performance and Social Progress*, http://ec.europa.eu/eurostat/documents/118025/118123/ Fitoussi+Commission+report (accessed 14 June 2017).

Stiglitz, J.E., A. Sen and J.-P. Fitoussi (2010) *MIS-Measuring Our Lives: Why GDP Doesn't Add Up, The Report of the Commission on the Measurement of Economic Performance and Social Progress*, New York, NY: The New Press.

Sudhir, A. and A. Sen (1994) *Human Development Index: Methodology and Measurement*, Human Development Report Office Occasional Papers, New York, NY: United Nations Development Programme.

Summers, L.H. and E. Balls (2015) *Report of the Commission on Inclusive Prosperity*, Washington, DC: Center for American Progress.

Taylor-Gooby, P. (ed.) (2004) *New Risks, New Welfare: The Transformation of the European Welfare State*, Oxford: Oxford University Press.

Taylor-Gooby, P. (2008) The New Welfare State Settlement in Europe, *European Societies* 10(1): 3–24.

United Nations (UN) (1979) *Convention on the Elimination of All Forms of Discrimination against Women*, New York, NY: United Nations.

UN (1989) *Convention on the Rights of the Child*, New York, NY: United Nations.

UN (2008) *Convention on the Rights of Persons with Disabilities*, New York, NY: United Nations.

United Nations Development Programme (UNDP) (2011) *Human Development Report 2011: Sustainability and Equity: A Better Future for All*, New York, NY: United Nations Development Programme.

UNDP (2012) *Decent Work Indicators: Concepts and Definitions*, ILO Manual First Edition, Geneva: ILO.

UNDP (2013) *Humanity Divided: Confronting Inequality in Developing Countries*, New York, NY: United Nations Development Programme.

UNDP (2014) *Human Development Report 2014. Sustaining Human Progress: Reducing Vulnerabilities and Building Resilience*, New York, NY: UNDP.

UNDP (2015) *Human Development Report 2015: Work for Human Development*, New York, NY: United Nations Development Programme.

UNRISD (2010) *Combating Poverty and Inequality*, UNRISD Research and Policy Brief 10, Geneva: UNRISD.

Van Parijs, P. and Y. Vanderborght (2015) 'Basic Income in a Globalized Economy', in R. Hasmath (ed.), *Inclusive Growth, Development and Welfare Policy: A Critical Assessment*, New York, NY: Routledge, 229–47.

Vandenbroucke, F. and K. Vleminckx (2011) 'Disappointing poverty trends: is the social investment state to blame?', *Journal of European Social Policy* 21(5): 450–71.

Web of Science, Social Sciences Citation Index (SSCI), Clarivate Analytics, https://clarivate.com/products/web-of-science/ (accessed 14 June 2017).

Wilkinson, R. and K. Pickett (2009) *The Spirit Level: Why More Equal Societies Almost Always Do Better*, London: Allen Lane.

Williamson, J. (2008) 'A Short History of the Washington Consensus', in N. Serra and J. Stiglitz (eds), *The Washington Consensus Reconsidered*, Oxford: Oxford University Press, 14–30.

Williamson, J.B. (ed.) (1990) *Latin American Adjustment: How Much Has Happened?*, Washington, DC: Institute for International Economics.

Wilson, D. (2016) 'The challenge of inclusive growth for the Scottish economy', *Fraser of Allander Economic Commentary* 39(3): 131–40.

World Bank (2008) *What Are the Constraints to Inclusive Growth in Zambia? A Policy Note*, Report No. 44286-ZM, Washington, DC: World Bank.

Yeates, N. (2002) 'Globalization and Social Policy: From Global Neoliberal Hegemony to Global Political Pluralism', *Global Social Policy* 2(1): 69–91.

TWO

Taking social investment seriously in developed economies

Anton Hemerijck

Introduction

This contribution is about taking social investment seriously. It delineates the intellectual background conditions in politics and social policy analysis against which social investment ideas have encountered difficulties in being heard since the 1990s. The chapter then reviews the slow, contained but progressive, evolution of social investment ideas from the metaphoric notion of 'social policy as a productive factor' in the second half of the 1990s to the more fundamental paradigmatic rethink of welfare provision over the 2000s. The chapter concludes by considering how social investment reform can contribute to 'inclusive growth', as advocated today by practically all international organisations and think tanks in the global marketplace of economic ideas.

Social investment taken seriously

Over the past two decades, the notion of social investment has gained considerable traction in scholarly debates, especially with international think tanks. In domestic policy making arenas social investment precepts have also been taken increasingly taken seriously. However, it is fair to say that social investment has not assumed paradigmatic primacy in 21st century welfare provision, for reasons to be explored here.

At the level of the European Union (EU), the idea of social investment, building on the pioneering work of the Dutch Presidency of the EU in 1997 on 'social policy as a productive factor', became a foundation for the Lisbon Agenda, launched in 2000 with the ambition to turn Europe into the 'most competitive and dynamic knowledge-based economy in the world, capable of sustainable economic growth and more and better jobs and greater social cohesion' (European Council, 2000). The EU's more recent and most assertive endorsement of social investment is the *Social Investment Package for Growth and Social Cohesion* (henceforth SIP), launched by the European Commission in February 2013, urging EU member states to advance post-crisis welfare reform strategies that help 'prepare' individuals, families and societies to respond to the changing nature of social risks in advanced economies, by investing in human capabilities from early childhood through to old age, rather than pursuing policies that merely 'repair' social misfortune after moments of economic or personal crisis (European Commission, 2013a; 2013b).

Over the past two decades, a fair number of European welfare states enacted what can be described as social investment reforms by aligning their existing social policy repertoires with novel services in the areas of early childhood education and care, active labour market policies (ALMP), work–life balance reconciliation, lifelong learning and elderly care (Bonoli, 2013; Hemerijck, 2013; Kersbergen and Hemerijck, 2012; Bouget et al, 2015). The European diffusion of social investment travelled south from the Scandinavian heartland of the 'active' welfare states to the traditionally passive and male-breadwinner oriented Bismarckian welfare systems in the Benelux countries, Austria and Germany. To wit, mainland Continental European welfare states all expanded childcare alongside more generous parental leave provisions for dual-earner families (Palier, 2010). In a westward direction, social investment policy prescriptions made inroads on the Anglo-Irish Isles, combining 'in-work' benefits and family credits with strong activation requirements. Across the new member states, including Estonia, Poland, Slovenia, Hungary, the Czech Republic, minimum income protection became universal and education systems were modernised, after entry into the EU in 2004 (Bouget et al, 2015). Rather surprisingly, the Mediterranean member states, presiding over Europe's most rigidified, insider-biased labour markets and pension-heavy welfare systems seemingly took little interest in social investment reform over the Lisbon era between 2000 and 2010, except for Spain (Hemerijck, 2013; 2017b).

Although the social investment impetus originated in the context of European integration, we are today able to observe far wider global intellectual support for social investment, progressing on the banner of 'inclusive growth', championed by the OECD and the World Bank. Within the OECD, Canada, especially its province of Quebec, has become the new poster child of social investment, based on a comprehensive reform package of income and family support with considerable success in raising labour market participation and forestalling poverty increases (Banting and Myles, 2013; Noël, 2017).

In 2015, Barack Obama placed social investment on the US political agenda in his State of the Union Address, promising better access to high-quality early care and education as a 'must-have' for middle-class American families, saying: 'It's times we stop treating childcare as a side issue, or a women's issue, and treat it like the national economic priority for all of us' (Obama, 2015). Meanwhile, social investment innovation has taken roots in Australia (Smyth and Buchanan, 2015), while in South East Asia, in South Korea, Japan and Taiwan, welfare provision is undergoing a far-reaching transformation with an impressive expansion of family policy to address the post-industrial challenge of low fertility (Fleckenstein and Lee, 2017; Brinton, 2016).

As social investment policy prescriptions are progressively being taken seriously, I would hesitate to conclude that social investment has become the overarching early 21st century welfare policy paradigm. The proliferation of social investment policy priorities across the globe remains imbalanced and uneven. Across Europe, Scandinavian nations continue to approximate a Pareto-optimal solution to the knowledge-based dual-earner economy; however, recent reforms have made Nordic welfare states decidedly less universal and more unequal. And although Germany significantly upgraded its childcare and parental leave provisions over the past decade, it continues to preside over a dualised labour market, hardened by an incipient growth in atypical and poorly-paid (mini-)jobs since the Hartz IV reform of 2004 (Palier and Thelen, 2010; Emmenegger et al, 2012). In quite a few social investment vanguard countries, such as Finland and the Netherlands, fiscal imbalances after the global credit crunch of 2008 pressed policymakers to backtrack on dual-earner family support provisions (Bouget et al, 2015; Van Kersbergen et al, 2014).

The European Commission's current position on social investment is contradictory. Under the helm of Jean Claude Juncker, the Commission, on the one hand, presents itself as the global social investment cheerleader, in line with the 2013 SIP. But, on the other hand, it demands strict fiscal rectitude from its member states, as prescribed by the Six-Pack, Two-Pack, and the Fiscal Compact, enacted in the wake of the euro crisis after 2009. This effectively trumps social investment progress in countries in fiscal dire straits, especially in the southern periphery, which perhaps most need a social investment impulse to overcome long-term economic stagnation.

The ambivalent reception of social investment ideas, not only in policymaking circles, but also with leading social policy researchers, is the product of intellectual inertia. Social investment ideas came to fruition over the 1990s and early 2000s when the neoliberal 'Washington

Consensus' was riding high (Williamson, 1990). Descending from the stagflation crisis of the 1970s and early 1980s, the neoliberal consensus was firmly grounded in a negative appreciation of public welfare provision and its associated risks of 'moral hazard', 'displacement', 'substitution effect' and administrative 'deadweight', together with a rejection of Keynesian demand management and the use of deficit fiscal spending to counter economic recessions and mitigate social hardship. In Europe, the architects of the Economic and Monetary Union (EMU) believed that a single currency, layered on top of the internal market, would discipline member states to hold their 'wasteful' welfare states in check, by inadvertently adopting liberalising 'structural' reforms of removing job protection legislation, retrenching social security benefits, privatising pensions, healthcare and education and deregulating capital markets. Despite the growing lip service paid to social investment ideas and policies by centre left politicians since the 1990s, the 'default' policy paradigm of market liberalisation and fiscal austerity time and time again relegated social investment innovation to the world of fair–weather politics.

Post-crisis management continues to be riddled with ambiguity. While the dominant inclination veers towards cuts, savings and liberalisation, times are slowly changing. Policy attention is shifting considerably to accumulating evidence, brought forth by a host of OECD studies since the mid-2000s, bringing to the fore that well-calibrated social (investment) policies 'crowd in' inclusive growth and social progress in tandem. The recent re-appreciation of social investment is also helped by a growing recognition that austerity alone, underwritten by the heterodox monetary policy interventions, will not suffice to restore economic growth and social and political stability. Conceivably, a halfway social investment paradigm shift is underway (Hemerijck, 2015; Kvist, 2015). As we know from the seminal writings on the political power of economic ideas from Peter Hall (1989; 1993), alternative policy paradigms really only become practically relevant when they provide solutions to mainstream politics. The pressing *political* reason for taking social investment truly seriously is that, close to a decade after the global credit crunch, OECD countries are in dire need of a growth strategy that is – all at once – economically viable, politically legitimate and seen as socially fair. Where stagnation prevails, high unemployment and rising poverty and inequality become breeding grounds for xenophobic populism. Electorates continue to hold national politicians accountable for socioeconomic (mis-)fortune and this is bound up with popular welfare programmes. The failure to resolve the euro crisis in recent years been met by rising EU sceptic domestic pressures to water down ruling governments' commitments to European solutions. Betwixt intrusive austerity and anti-establishment populism, unsurprisingly, a 'political-institutional vacuum' is looming. This begs the question whether the political centre, from the greens to social democracy, Christian democracy, and social liberalism, together with enlightened business elites and farsighted trade unionists, are able to muster an overlapping consensus on a transformative reform agenda of social investment welfare recalibration, against the rising tides of welfare chauvinist populism and the call for deficit and debt reduction, based on the mantras of balanced budgets, low taxes, and less regulation?

Confronting intellectual inertia

The folk wisdom that generous welfare provision inescapably 'crowds out' private entrepreneurship, employment, productivity and consequently, economic growth, runs deep. Chancellor Angela Merkel, who efficaciously stood at the helm of important German social investment reform, is never tired of dramatising the European crisis predicament by underscoring that the embattled continent 'represents 7% of the world's population, 25% of the world's GDP and 50% of the world's social spending' (Merkel, 2012), intimating that such a ratio is hard to sustain in an era of intensified global competition. This is the moral of her much cited speech given at the 2013 World Economic Forum in Davos (Merkel, 2013). On close inspection, however, we have to acknowledge that the EU's share of global welfare spending is less than 40%, and in relative terms broadly in sync with the US and Japan. Moreover, simply because of catch-up growth in the developing economies, the EU's share in global social spending is destined to fall in the future (Begg et al, 2015). More erroneous in Merkel's diagnosis of the European competitiveness malaise of overgenerous welfare provision is that her conjecture does not stand up to empirical scrutiny. Four out of the ten most successful economies, according to the Global Competitiveness Index of the World Economic Forum (WEF, 2014), are among the world's most generous welfare states, including Germany, with levels of social spending hovering between 25% and 30% of GDP. Should we not consider the causal arrow run in reverse with proactive welfare provision adding to the long-run economic success of Finland, Sweden, Germany and the Netherlands, respectively spending 30.6%, 28.2%, 25.6% and 24.2% of their national income on social protection in 2013? To be sure, with France and Italy in places 18 and 43 of the Global Competitiveness League (WEF, 2014), with social spending levels of 28.7% and 32% of GDP respectively, Merkel obviously has a point. If there is a causal link, socioeconomic disparity between Finland, Germany, the Netherlands and Sweden, on the one hand, and France and Italy, on the other, seemingly suggests that what really matters is the *quality*, not the *quantity* of social spending. To wit, this is the key message of the SIP, published by the Commission a month after Chancellor Merkel gave her provocative address in Davos. Social spending directed to raise and protect human capital investment and to ease employment and life course transitions seemingly fosters social progress and economic competitiveness in tandem.

That said, the nuanced policy message of the SIP that family support, employment policy and protective social security provision together enhance socioeconomic resilience, prepared by the Directorate-General of Employment, Social Affairs and Inclusion (DG EMP) under Commissioner Lazslo Andor, was effectively cast aside in the aftermath of the euro crisis of 2009 and 2010. In a conservative reflex, a majority of Eurozone Finance Ministers, led by German colleague Wolfgang Schauble, and intellectually supported by the Commission's Directorate-General for Economic and Financial Affairs (DG ECFIN), the Economic and Financial Affairs Council (ECOFIN), and the European Central Bank (ECB), by 2013, trumpeted – in unison – that there really was no alternative to austerity, harking back to Arthur Okun's formulation of a 'big trade off' between social equity and economic efficiency of 1975, reigning supreme across the OECD world for decades (Okun, 1975).

In the early 1990s, the OECD received a mandate to examine the labour market performance of its member countries. The *OECD Jobs Study*, first published in 1994, launched a critical attack on the 'dark side' of double-digit unemployment of many European OECD members (OECD 1994, 1997, 2006a). Already in 1987, Blanchard and Summers offered the paradigmatic explanation of unemployment as a problem of supply side 'hysteresis', in particular low search intensity and poor motivation, because of disincentives produced by generous welfare provision and stiff job protection legislation (Blanchard and Summers, 1987). Hereby, job preservation for already employed workers was achieved at the expense of labour market outsiders, preventing real wages from falling sufficiently to restore full employment. In addition to the 'market distorting' of generous welfare provisions and rigid labour markets, there is the conjecture of low (public) service productivity, often associated with so-called 'Baumol cost disease' (Baumol, 1967). When public service pay increases follow wage developments in the more dynamic capital-intensive private sector, low productivity services become relatively more expensive, thereby triggering a predicament of secular stagnation. The 1994 and 1997 *OECD Jobs Study* reports proved highly influential in terms of the debate on welfare state reform. Hovering around 10% with few signs of improvement, unemployment rates in France, Germany, and Italy were twice as high as in the USA, while the European employment rate was about 12 points below the US rate. The OECD economists argued that Europe's generous welfare states, with job security, high minimum wages and generous unemployment benefits, heavy taxation, and an overriding emphasis on coordinated wage bargaining and social dialogue, had raised labour costs above market clearing levels. Strong 'insider–outsider' cleavages with unfavourable employment chances for the young, women, the old and the unskilled prevented the European labour markets from achieving employment rates on a par with the US and New Zealand (Lindbeck and Snower, 1989).

Although the Anglophone world spearheaded the rise of neoliberalism with the elections of Margaret Thatcher in the UK (1979) and Ronald Reagan (1980) in the US, the Single European Act (SEA) of 1986 and the Economic and Monetary Union (EMU) of 1999 were negotiated at a time when the 'supply side' revolution in micro- and macroeconomic theory was riding high. Designed as the natural complement of the Single Market, the EMU was firmly grounded in a rejection of Keynesian demand management and the use of deficit fiscal spending to manage economic recessions and mitigate social hardship. The architects of EMU effectively believed that the single currency would force member states to adopt liberalising 'structural' reforms, including breaking down job protection, retrenching welfare benefits, and privatising pensions. EMU was designed to discipline member states to hold their 'wasteful' welfare programmes in check by fast-forwarding market-conforming economic convergence (Jones, 2013). Hence, the fight against unemployment and the attainment of economic convergence was redefined as the quest for labour market flexibility by removing restrictions on wage bargaining, minimum wages, job protection, and cuts in non-wage labour costs, unemployment benefits and pensions.

In the conclusion to the *General Theory of Employment, Interest and Money* (1936 [1973]), John Maynard Keynes famously wrote that:

> the ideas of economists and political philosophers, both when they are right and when they are wrong, are more powerful that is commonly understood. ... Practical men who believe themselves to be quite exempt from any intellectual influence, are usually the slaves of some defunct economist. (1936 [1973]: 383)

Today this applies to the very practical Angela Merkel, warning against high levels of social spending as a brake on competitiveness, ignorant of how her reform success in social investment-oriented work–family policy spending, in part breaking with male-breadwinner biased welfare policy legacy. The result has been major employment hikes for working mothers, generating an element of 'endogenous' economic growth on top of German industry external competitiveness prowess.

The intellectually muted ascendance of the social investment perspective over the past two decades, however, is not only a story about the tenacity of neo- and ordo-liberal hegemony; it is also a tale of rising scepticism against social investment recipes from within the academic community of social policy research. Many social policy scholars have come to frown on the 'economic' subordination of social protection to productive employment in the social investment literature, starting with research on welfare reform agenda on New Labour in the UK (Lister 2003; 2004). More recently, as social investment gained leverage in EU policy circles, social investment criticisms began to feature in important academic social policy journals (Cantillon, 2011; Nolan, 2013). Jean-Claude Barbier is of the opinion that social investment scholars dodge the issue of poverty and redistribution (Barbier, 2012; 2017). The economic rationale of social investment is most forcefully criticised by feminist scholars (Lewis, 2006; Jenson, 2009). As a case in point, Chiara Saraceno argues that the instrumentalisation of female employment in the social investment perspective is rooted in a deeply biased normative understanding of gender equity that effectively delegitimises mothers' unpaid caring roles as valuable activities in their own right (Saraceno, 2015; 2017). The most pertinent empirical critique of social investment perspective is that social services – in family policy, care, education, activation, training and reintegration policies – are plagued by a plethora of so-called perverse 'Matthew Effects'. The middle and upper classes benefit from social investment services at the expense of more vulnerable segments of societies, triggering adverse redistribution, in correspondence with the proclamation that 'unto every one that hath shall be given' in the Gospel of Matthew (Cantillon and Van Lancker, 2013; Bonoli et al, 2017). In her seminal 2011 article *The paradox of the social investment state: growth, employment and poverty*, Bea Cantillon (2011) holds the social investment paradigm partially responsible for disappointing poverty trends over the Lisbon Agenda decade between 2000 and 2010.

In his much cited article 'What use is social investment?', Brian Nolan (2013) argues that social investment policy analysis lacks a coherent analytical conception and operationalisation of social investment.

Nolan is especially critical of the implicit normative bias of some social investment writings by scholars, seemingly privileging 'capacitating' social investment spending over protective social security, who thereby inadvertently blur the boundaries of proper empirical policy analysis and normative political advocacy. Although Nolan holds nothing per se against bringing out the productive portent of social policy interventions, he fears that by trying to justify social policy interventions in instrumental economic terms, social investment policy analysis easily falls prey to a self-defeating venture of taking on mainstream economists on their own turf. Losing this battle will allow mainstream economists to continue to 'frame the debate' on social protection and welfare spending as a break on competitiveness to the detriment of the normative political case for social policy in terms of social justice. I find Nolan's position unnecessarily defensive. To the extent that mainstream economists venture conjectures and recommendations (which are increasingly difficult to corroborate, as their axiomatic models are ill equipped to make sense of the interaction of gendered labour markets, family demography and the role of welfare provision in a life course perspective), it is imperative for honest social science research, including economics, to expose the anomalies and inadequacies that prevent mainstream economics from seriously probing the productive contemporary portent of active welfare states. This is an academic endeavour in its own right, but no less important is to enlighten self-acclaimed practical policymakers, unperturbed by pre-existing policy beliefs, of the Pareto-optimal potential of social investment as a fully-fledged policy paradigm, based on available evidence.

From 'social policy as a productive factor' metaphor to the social investment policy paradigm

The notion social investment emerged in political and academic discourse around the mid-1990s on the wing of the ambition to modernise the welfare state and ensure its long-term sustainability, in the face of demographic ageing and the rise of the knowledge economy (Giddens, 1998; Ferrera et al. 2000; Jenson and Saint-Martin, 2003; Jenson, 2010; Morel et al, 2012; Bonoli, 2013; Hemerijck 2013; Hemerijck, 2015; Deeming and Smyth, 2015). Quite unexpected, the OECD organised a conference on rethinking social policy as positively contributing to economic output in 1996, at a time when the Paris-based think tank was still allied to the Washington Consensus (Jenson, 2010). The EU followed suit: under the Dutch presidency in 1997, the term 'social policy as a productive factor' was coined, so as to underline that a fair number of social policy interventions do not always adversely affect economic competitiveness and employment (Morel et al, 2012). These ideas were subsequently anchored in the EU's Lisbon Agenda of 2000, when 13 out of the 16 countries that made up the European Union at the time were governed from the centre left. Most of the early attempts to underscore the fortuitous economic impact of welfare provision under the banner of social investment were based on rather isolated policy evaluations with positive effects on the active labour market and work–family policies, vocational education and training policies, often underwritten by social partnership wage coordination, for only a small subset of EU member countries (Hemerijck, 1997).

The policy theory underpinning the social investment was given a more generic impetus with the publication of a collective book by Gøsta Esping-Andersen, Duncan Gallie, Anton Hemerijck and John Myles – *Why We Need a New Welfare State* (2002) – commissioned by the Belgian Presidency of the EU in 2001. The central argument of *Why We Need a New Welfare State* was that economic competitiveness and demographic ageing increasingly fostered suboptimal life chances for large parts of the population. Esping-Andersen et al contended that Europe's welfare states faced a genuine – paradigmatic – 'Gordian knot' of how to sustain a deep normative commitment to social justice while aspiring to create a robust and competitive knowledge-based social market economy. In terms of policy theory, *Why We Need a New Welfare State* not only took issue with the prevailing neoliberal myth that generous welfare provision inevitably implies a loss of economic efficiency, harking back to Okun's formulation of a 'big trade off' between equality and efficiency. Esping-Andersen et al were equally critical of the staying power male-breadwinner social insurance and insider job protection dysfunctions in the face of the emerging 'new social risks' of atypical employment, long-term unemployment, in-work poverty, family instability and labour market exclusion, resulting from obsolete skills and informal care obligations (see also Taylor-Gooby, 2004; Esping-Andersen, 1999; Huber and Stephens 2001; Leoni, 2015). Unlike Anthony Giddens (1998), who at the time continued to critique the protective functions of the welfare state, as they incurred 'moral hazard' contingencies, Esping-Andersen et al. were adamant in reiterating that the 'minimization of poverty and income security is a precondition for any effective strategy of social investment' (Esping-Andersen et al, 2002: 5).

The policy analysis of *Why We Need a New Welfare State* in a shorthand fashion is based on a rather simple cost-benefit equation, whereby social expenditures are effectively born by the quantity and quality of employed workers:

$$\frac{number\ of\ welfare\ recipients}{number\ of\ paid\ workers} \times \frac{average\ consumption\ of\ welfare\ recipients}{average\ productivity\ of\ workers}$$

On this reading, the economic sustainability of advanced welfare states hinged on the number and productivity of future employees and taxpayers (Myles, 2002). Welfare reform should therefore aspire to contribute to mobilising citizens' productive potential. To the extent that social policy is geared towards maximising employment (number of paid workers) while raising the productivity of those in employment, this would better sustain 'carrying capacity' of the welfare state and, by implication, economic competitiveness. Whereas the neoliberal critique of the welfare state narrowly targeted the numerator of the equation through lower benefits and higher eligibility thresholds, *Why We Need a New Welfare State* astutely shifted focus radically towards the denominator side of the equation. Employment and employability are signalled out as important objectives behind the overarching aim of breaking the intergenerational transmission of poverty, as empirical evidence overwhelmingly shows that employment is key to effective poverty mitigation.

The work–family nexus is the 'lynchpin' of the social investment policy paradigm. Female participation rates have increased conspicuously in most OECD countries, in part to compensate for declining incomes of male workers. However, major asymmetries in job intensity, employment stability and the quality of work continue to marginalise women in many countries (Esping-Anderson, 2009). More flexible labour markets and skill-biased technological change, but also higher divorce rates and lone parenthood, make female economic independence essential. Absent possibilities of externalising child and elderly care, a rising numbers of female workers face 'broken careers' and postponed motherhood, resulting in lower fertility, thereby intensifying the ageing burden in pensions and healthcare. In this respect, the feminist critique of social investment mentioned above, is somewhat misconstrued. The important insight that emerges from the empirical studies of quality childcare in combination with easy access to parental leave arrangements is that normative aspirations of gender equity, employment and family formation are compatible with Pareto superior economic outcomes, and, therefore, within reach of practical policy. There is no question of trading off economic efficiency against gender equity. However, a worrisome trend, according to

Esping-Andersen, is the rise of marital homogamy in the new era of high female employment with highly educated and dual-earning couples doing well and low-skill and low-work intensity households falling behind. Highly educated dual-earners are well positioned to 'race ahead' by making additional investments into the human capital of their offspring, whereas low income and single-earner families face higher risk of child poverty (Esping-Andersen, 2015). Working families at the top end of the social ladder have the resources to transition to a dual-earner model and adapt to the challenges of the knowledge society *in spite of* effective policies, while for those 'at the low end' are far more dependent on early childhood education and good quality childcare provision to foster high female labour market participation. For these reasons, *Why We Need a New Welfare State* urged for 'social investment' renewal aimed at resilience over the family life course, with the eradication of child poverty taking pride of place. The life course perspective is fundamental. People are particularly vulnerable: (1) when they move from education into their first job; (2) when they aspire to have children; (3) when they – almost inevitably – experience spells of labour market inactivity; and, finally, (4) when they move to retirement. To the extent that policymakers are able to identify how economic wellbeing and social problem at one stage of the life course impinge on later conditions, preventive policies can be advanced to forestall cumulative social risk reproduction (Hemerijck, 2013).

By reframing the welfare conundrum from redistributive bargain here and now to making sure that popular welfare provision can be sustained for the future under quite adverse economic and demographic conditions, Esping-Andersen et al radically transcended the popular dichotomy of hard-working 'contributors' to the welfare state and inactive 'beneficiaries'. Faced with the increased volatility of modern post-industrial labour markets, many people will occasionally, at various stages in their lives, find themselves in transitions between different jobs and caring obligations. But all in all, the majority of youngsters in schools will become productive workers, most ill people return to the labour market after medical treatment, and also the unemployment usually return to paid work (Hills, 2014; see also Atkinson, 2015; Piketty, 2014).

By the end of the first decade of the 21st century, we are able to observe in hindsight how the social investment perspective matured in a taciturn manner from the benign but underspecified metaphor of social policy as a 'third way' productive factor into a coherent welfare policy paradigm, anchored in a policy theory, specifying in how the changing of social risks is to be understood, what objectives are to be privileged and what sort of policy instruments and institutions have to be put to use to mitigate and contain the changing nature of social risks in the competitive knowledge-based economy and ageing societies. As such, the social investment perspective stands out on its own, also in comparison to the two antecedent, more generally accepted, welfare policy paradigms of the Keynesian-Beveridgean mid-20th century mixed-economic compromise and the late 20th century neoliberal critique of welfare state interventionism.

The mid-20th century breakthrough of the modern welfare state built on the Keynesian revolution in macroeconomics, anchored in an understanding of volatile financial markets and the cyclical nature of industrial capitalism. In his *General Theory* (1936 [1973]), Keynes exemplified how the political objective of (male) full employment can be upheld by countercyclical macroeconomic demand management and fine-tuning. In the event of recession, comprehensive unemployment insurance and adequate job protection, for which the 1942 and 1944 Beveridge reports gave the necessary intellectual ammunition, were to operate as 'automatic stabilisers', thereby protecting families from demand deficient cyclical unemployment and economic hardship (Beveridge, 1942; 1944). In the fortuitous event of full employment, corporatist wage coordination between employers, trade union organisations and the state was required to mitigate inflationary pressures.

If Keynesian macroeconomics was the brainchild of the Great Depression, the revival of 'new' classical microeconomic theory and rational-expectations macroeconomics was the intellectual product of the crisis of stagflation, the malignant combination of cost-push price inflation, economic stagnation, and structural unemployment in the 1970s and 1980s (Scharpf, 1991). In neoclassical economics, cyclical fluctuation is best understood as outcomes of exogenous shocks – the oil shocks of the 1970s being cases in point – combined with the slow transmission through the real economy, as the result of labour market impediments, including 'moral hazard' distortions related to generous welfare transfers. To foster full employment, following this diagnosis, labour market deregulation, welfare retrenchment, low taxation and a rules-based fiscal and anti-inflationary monetary policy regime were deemed imperative.

Social investment is not to be understood as an updated synthesis of fundamental importance of Keynesian macroeconomic stabilisation and neoclassical microeconomic labour market allocation. Akin to the Keynesian-Beveridgean welfare compromise, social investment policy prerogatives underscore the importance for strong social security and minimum income arrangements. With neoliberalism, the social investment paradigm shares a concern with the 'supply side'. However, social investment deviates from the passive male-breadwinner social security, bent on income compensation for consumption and income smoothing and aggregate 'demand side' stabilisation as socioeconomic 'shock absorbers', by privileging the role of human capital, from early childhood education and care, general education, vocational training and adult learning, for enhancing life course employability. And in contrast to the neoclassical obsession with market-conforming 'level playing fields', social investment policy is rooted in a far 'contextualised' understanding of families in relation to the labour market, with a far more positive theory of state and especially social services, alongside activating social security and ALMP, in comparison to the more 'decontextualised' neoliberal solution of the perfectly deregulated labour market, unburdened with social protection and high taxation.

Under both Keynesian 'demand management' and neoclassical 'supply side' economics, social policy interventions remained subservient to private economic production as the prime engine of prosperity. In the social investment paradigm, ex ante preventive and proactive family, employment and training policies are conclusively drawn into the 'productive function' of the knowledge-based economy. With its strong focus on prevention of harm rather than compensating for damage done, the social investment policy paradigm is emblematically *future-oriented*, bent on 'preparing' individuals, families and societies to respond to the new risks of a competitive knowledge economy, by investing in human capital and capabilities from early childhood through old age, rather than in policies that 'repair' damage after moments of economic or personal crisis. By comparison, Keynesian-Beveridgean welfare intervention is principally *reactive*, coming into play in times of demand–deficient recession, until male full employment is restored, whereas the neoliberal policy agenda is essentially *ahistorical*: free markers and indiscriminate fiscal austerity should prevail under all circumstances. In terms of target population, the social investment paradigm is concerned with all age cohorts, as social risks are no longer exclusively connected with unemployment but also with augmented vulnerability due to critical life course transitions, whereas in both Keynesian–Beveridgean and neoliberal paradigms, the adult working-age population is the axial target population. With its strategic concern with work–life balance and reconciliation, the social investment paradigm also radically transcends the *maternalist* bias in the Keynesian male-breadwinner welfare state and the *gender-blind* neoliberal critique of the post-war welfare state. *Gender equity* is critical to allow working families with children to prosper in the knowledge economy in times of adverse demography. The 'full' employment objective is replaced by a concern of high employment levels over the life course to service the 'carrying capacity' of the welfare state, on the one hand, and to enable parents to engage in gainful employment without career interruptions, improve career prospects especially for mothers, while at the same time getting their offspring to a strong start, on the other.

Like any notion of 'investment', the concept of social investment begs the question of measurable 'returns' or 'discount rates' (Begg, 2017; Burgoon, 2017). Conjecturing and testing social investment returns, however, is still in its infancy (De Deken, 2014; 2017; Verbist, 2017). Based on extensive literature research, I have in recent publications attempted to develop a better understanding of the economics of social investment by way of a taxonomy of three complementary and interdependent social investment policy functions: (1) easing the 'flow' of contemporary labour market and life course transitions; (2) raising and upkeeping the quality of the 'stock' of human capital and capabilities; and (3) maintaining strong minimum income universal safety net 'buffers' for micro-level income protection and macroeconomic stabilisation in support of high employment levels in ageing societies (Hemerijck, 2014; 2015; 2017a). In the taxonomy, the 'buffer' function alludes to at securing adequate and universal minimum income protection, thereby also stabilising the business cycle and buffering economic shocks, operative as a kind of Keynesianism through the back door. Next, the 'stock' function has to do with productivity and is focused on developing and maintaining human capital from early childhood all the way to old age. The 'flow' function, finally, bears on the easing of labour market and life course transition to achieve a more efficient and optimal allocation of labour and employment over the lifespan. In this context, Manfred Schmid (2015; 2017) aptly speaks of a shift from 'making work pay' to 'making transitions pay' through 'life course insurance' provision. In actual policy practice there is ample functional overlap between the policy functions of 'stocks', 'flows' and 'buffers'. Policy provision that seemingly addresses only one of the three functions often helps to back up other functions in an interconnected fashion. For example, poverty alleviation is principally a 'buffering' policy, but more adequate financial security can facilitate smoother labour market 'flow' as a consequence of mitigated pressure to accept any job on offer, with the potential overall benefit of better job matching and less skill erosion. By the same token, family income 'buffer' stability is an important background factor for effective learning, human capital 'stock' development, of youngsters. Social investment progress, in other words, hinges on important synergy effects across the policy functionalities of 'stock', 'flow' and 'buffer'. The point about functional synergy is particularly persuasively brought to the fore by the OECD (2015a) report *In It Together; Why Less Inequality Benefits All*. According to the OECD, one of the main transmission mechanisms between inequality and growth concerns human capital. While there is always a gap in education outcomes across individuals with different socioeconomic backgrounds, the cognitive divide is particularly wide in high inequality countries where disadvantaged households disproportionately struggle to gain access quality education for their offspring. Any reduction of inequality between the rich and poor citizens thus requires the mobilisation of a whole range of policies, from turning female employment into good quality careers ('flow'), to proactive early childhood development, youth and adult training policies ('stock'), and the expansion of effective and efficient activating tax and transfer systems ('buffers') in times of dire need (see also OECD, 2006b; 2007; 2008; 2011; 2012; 2015b).

In an ideal-typical fashion a bold conjecture on social investment returns or positive externalities, anchored in a substantial body of available evidence, can be made: *ceteris paribus* the availability of well-designed inter-temporal and transversal complementarities, effective combinations of 'stock', 'flow' and 'buffer' policies 'crowd in' employment, productivity and economic growth following the logic of a 'social investment life course multiplier' for individuals, families and societies at large (Hemerijck, 2017a; Dräbing and Nelson, 2017). With more disadvantaged children having access to early education, overall levels of skill attainment improve, resulting in higher employment and labour productivity and more upward social mobility. Quality childcare and preschool programmes, alongside effective parental leave arrangements and other family benefits and services, supported by appropriate tax and benefit incentives, ALMP and vocational rehabilitation programmes, enable more parents to engage in gainful employment without lengthy (gendered) career interruptions. The more parents, especially mothers, work, the broader the tax base, with even a positive effect on fertility, at higher levels of demand. Dual-earner families often use additional household income to ease chores of work–life balance by relying more on public and private services, thereby creating extra jobs, further boosting economic output. Longer and less interrupted working careers incur lower gender gaps. Higher maternal employment rates are associated with less child poverty. Over the mature phases of the life course, lifelong learning and active ageing policies help secure older worker's employment participation, resulting in a high exit age, and, by implication, lower outlays for unemployment, pensions and health care 'buffers'. The ideal-typical social investment multiplier effect is illustrated in Figure 2.1.

Figure 2.1 Social investment life course multiplier

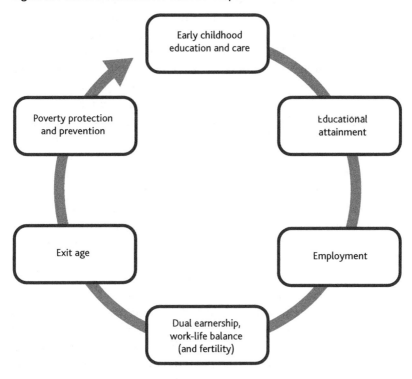

All in all, the available social investment evidence suggests that effective 'stock', 'flow' and 'buffer' policies reinforce the proficiency of each other. But there is no such thing as an optimal social investment policy mix. National welfare states with their varied policy legacies, institutional capabilities and economic challenges require different combinations of 'stock', 'flow' and 'buffer' policies to foster economic progress and social wellbeing, depending on initial economic conditions and prevailing work, care and welfare arrangements (Hemerijck, et al, 2016). That said, social investment policies are most effective when the chain of temporal and transversal complementarities is maintained by cross-department policy coordination, from early childhood education and care to active ageing, by highly competent professionals. With no one-size-fits-all social investment policy package on offer, however, elementary policy coherence between the welfare functions – 'stocks', 'flows', and 'buffers' – is imperative.

The explicit focus propagated above on temporal synergies, interdependencies, and interaction effects between the policy functions of 'stocks', 'flows' and 'buffers', and how policy interventions have to be tailored to meet specific needs of various groups at different stages of the life course, warrant novel methodological tools to better gauge current and future returns on social investment and the institutional prerequisites of effective social investment policy mixes. This methodological point carries enormous political weight: where social policy budget allocation is merely informed by isolated trials and case studies, longer, interdependent and cumulative wellbeing returns will remain under-examined and, as a consequence, under-developed in policy practice, due to an ingrained reluctance to query alternative insights in an age 'evidence based' policymaking. Inadvertently, this requires policymakers to think in terms 'institutional complementarities' of how different policies cohere as multifunctional policy repertoires, and where additional measures are required to better align the three social investment policy functions in the overall welfare policy portfolio (Dräbing and Nelson, 2017; Nelson and Stephens, 2012).

Surely, the elusive conceptualisation of social investment in terms of interconnected policy interventions across the policy areas skill formation, labour market allocation and social protection has left the social investment perspective under-understood as a coherent economic policy theory, in the sense that it lacks a solid anchor in prevailing macro- and/or microeconomic theorising. For reasons of intellectual honesty, I believe this is a strength rather than a weakness. To wit, recent publications of the World Bank and the OECD on poverty and inequality, work–life balance, early childhood development, literacy and skills, and access to public services, already testify to a reappraisal of mid-range policy theorising in attempts to rethink policy interventions that can contribute 'inclusive growth', away from general 'pars-pro-toto' Keynesian or neoclassical macro- and microeconomic modelling (Rodrik, 2006).

In terms of institutional capacity, integrated social transfer provision together with tailored social service delivery, from preschool to activation, require collaborative governance structures that are able to orchestrate mutually reinforcing provisions and ensure effective coordination and feedback learning across multiple layers of policy execution and social concertation. Integrated welfare service and benefit provision is a far cry from governance mode of the Keynesian-Beveridgean welfare state, wherein national social insurance systems, employment services and education and training provision operated as functionally demarcated and independent policy silos under hierarchically organised administrative structures.

In contradistinction to neoliberalism, the positive theory of the state in the social investment policy paradigm places the Baumol cost predicament of the shift to services leading to secular stagnation, in a different light. Publicly financed social investments may create extra private output at less public cost, as parenting services, education, active labour market policy interventions, and long-term care in effect contribute to higher employment (Wren, 2013; 2017). The antithetical neoliberal theory of the state simply (axiomatically) assumed public officials and 'greedy' organised interests, especially trade unions, to pursue monopoly 'rent-seeking' in the absence of market pressures, in line with to public choice models of collective action, principle-agent and New Public Management Theory.

With the progressive diversification of social risks and increased differentiation in social policy provision, it is finally imperative to reflect how normative orientations expanded beyond the classic orientations of full employment and fair income distribution of Keynes and Beveridge and the extremely individualist and anti-collectivist free market conceptions of society of radical free market liberal thinkers, like Milton Friedman and Friedrich von Hayek, judging welfare state intervention as the enemy of both individual freedom and economic efficiency. At the normative heart of the social investment paradigm lies a fundamental reorientation, away from *freedom from want* towards *freedom to act*, based a far richer and more context specific discourse of human flourishing, associated with 'capability approach' of economics Nobel Laureate Amartya Sen (2001; 2009) and Martha Nussbaum (2011) (see Morel and Palme, 2017). The diversity of social risks, together with gendered life course contingencies of modern familyhood, call for a responsibility sensitive 'rights-based' approach to social citizenship, in which the potential of turning citizenship rights into manifest 'functionings' are provided for through differentiated welfare provisions, combining income support for basic economic security and more active preventive and employment-centred (re-) integration and family services to further of 'human flourishing', undergirded by the Rawlsian principle of distribution in favour of the least well-off.

Prioritising high levels of employment for both men and women is the overriding policy objective to foster social inclusion, under the proviso of work–family reconciliation arrangements, access to good education and healthcare, and a guaranteed *social minimum* for basic economic security, serving citizens to pursue fuller and more satisfying lives. Following the 'capability approach' perspective, social benefits and services should enable individuals to act as autonomous agents to allow multiple choices between different employment and family statuses according to shifting preferences and changing circumstances across critical transitions in the life course.

By bringing the positive role of 'capacitating' social policy and the re-appreciation of social protection into a richer and more contextualised understanding of policy intervention in a life course perspective, critically informed by the changing – increasingly erratic and heterogeneous – nature of social risks, and the (incomplete) gender revolution in demography and labour markets, it is my contention that the slow but steady intellectual maturation of the social investment perspective over the past two decades adds up to nothing less than a quiet but fundamental paradigmatic rethink of the welfare state for the 21st century, departing fundamental ways from the political priorities, policy theories, instruments, governance structures, and time-frames, from the preceding Keynesian–Beveridgean welfare state compromise and the neoliberal critique of the interventionist welfare state (see Table 2.1 for an analytical overview).

Table 2.1 Three welfare policy paradigms

	Keynesian-Beveridgean welfare compromise	Neoliberal critique of the welfare state	Social investment welfare state
Political objective	Full (male) employment (fighting unemployment)	Optimal labour market allocation (countering hysteresis and stagflation)	Raising employment over the life course for 'inclusive growth' (to sustain inclusive welfare provision)
Policy problem	Mass unemployment	Cost-containment	Heterogeneous life course risks in relation to welfare state's carrying capacity in times of adverse demography
Policy theory	Volatile capitalism requires counter-cyclical management through strong welfare 'buffers'	Generous welfare provision 'crowds out' private economic initiative because of 'moral hazard', 'displacement' and 'deadweight' inefficiencies (capital markets assumed hyper-efficient)	Social investments 'crowd in' private initiative and competitiveness through higher employment and human capital use and basic economic security across life course – *local optima* – to foster 'inclusive growth'
Policy instruments	Macroeconomic fiscal and monetary demand management but also through comprehensive social insurance and employment protection	Labour market deregulation, privatisation of social services, and targeted minimum poverty protection ex post Pro-cyclical balanced budgets orientated fiscal policy as an effective enforcer of liberalisation and structural reform	Mitigate gender sensitive life course contingencies ex ante through human capital 'stock' upgrading, labour market 'flow' desegmentation, with strong universal safety net 'buffers' in 'institutional complementarity'
Theory of the state (and institutions)	Orchestrate 'class compromise' and 'social partnership' to master inflationary pressures under conditions of full employment	Take out market impediment through contracting out, while disciplining low-trust, rent-seeking 'distributive coalitions' (trade unions and inefficient public bureaucracies) through New Public Management	Governance institutions as both *constraints* and *resources* (public regarding social partners), 'productive coalitions' and quality public services mitigating Baumol cost problems. State key role in investing in skill formation, easing life course transitions, while providing for basic economic security
Gender	Male bias	Allegedly gender neutral, but in effect gender blind	Gender sensitive with strong orientation on family life course resilience
Political discourse	Full employment in a free society without want, disease, ignorance and squalor	TINA (there is not alternative) Inequality is inevitable and fair in more open economies	Capacitating social justice to encourage responsibility-sensitive 'human flourishing'

Source: Adapted from Hemerijck (2017b)

Social investment and inclusive growth

The protracted, however constrained, maturation of the social investment policy paradigm and its piecemeal diffusion across rich OECD democracies, with notable exceptions, was rudely interrupted by the onslaught of the global financial crisis. Nowhere has this predicament been more despondent than in Europe, the birthplace of social investment. In the aftermath of the euro crisis in 2012, the 'default' policy theory of fiscal austerity cum benefit cuts and labour market deregulation made a forceful comeback, relegating social investment reform – once again – to the world of fair-weather policy utopias. Ongoing retrenchments not only disproportionately affect vulnerable families with deep poverty and unemployment problems, they are likely to result in lower employment and employability erosion, which in turn adversely affect European welfare states' capacities to shoulder the upcoming ageing burden in pensions and healthcare. Also politically it is questionable whether pro-cyclical austerity, underwritten by the heterodox monetary policy to counter deflation, will suffice to curb the rise of anti-EU populism and xenophobic welfare chauvinism in times of mass unemployment and large cohorts of youths not in employment, education or training. As political accountability continues to be bound up with widely cherished national welfare states, EU sceptic political mobilisation – including Brexit – presses ruling governments to dilute their commitments to European solutions.

The post-crisis predicament surely begs the question whether social investment is really still relevant economically and politically. I think it is still highly relevant, especially for policymakers and electorates wishing to pursue strategies of 'inclusive growth', understood as growth equitably shared across society and based on a broader concern for socioeconomic wellbeing in terms of human flourishing (Stiglitz et al, 2009). This contribution has taken social investment seriously by exploring its origins, its paradigmatic foundations, its conceptualisation as a policy theory, including methodological metric for dynamically assessing multidimensional returns in socioeconomic wellbeing broadly understood. Within a span of two decades, the notion of social investment matured from an intuitively appealing metaphor of 'social policy as productive factor' to nothing less than a paradigmatic rethink of active welfare states for the 21st century knowledge economy. In the process, the evidence base of social investment policy change and associated socioeconomic returns has only become stronger, with much wider geographic bearing than originally anticipated in the 2002 volume *Why We Need a New Welfare State* (by Esping-Andersen et al).

With the publication of the SIP communication, the paradigmatic genie of the social investment has come out of the bottle fully fledged and with fairly strong evidential corroboration of 'capacitating' welfare provision 'crowding in' economic growth and social progress in tandem.

The challenges of economic globalisation, skill-biased technological innovation, family and gender change, the service economy, population ageing, fiscal austerity, economic crisis management, job polarisation, high unemployment, low growth, increased poverty and inequality and large scale migration, affecting vulnerable citizens through highly personalised life course disruptions for which there is no simple actuarially neutral solution, are not subsiding. In terms of welfare performance, the achievements of social investment vary across countries as different welfare regimes rely on differentiated policy mixes in addressing country specific socioeconomic predicaments in their interdependent systems of skill formation, labour regulation and family servicing. A principal driver in the emancipation and subsequent maturation of the social investment policy paradigm is that many European welfare states, facing demographic ageing and rather subdued levels of growth, have been hard pressed to develop policy strategies to raise levels of employment, of women and older workers in particular. This is apparent in measures to raise the official retirement age through active ageing and important progress in early childhood education care and paternal leave provisions, as important measures to keep older workers on the payroll and lure mothers into the labour market, to have them bolster the 'carrying capacity' of comprehensive welfare systems.

While the more critical literature underscores that social investment is no miracle policy paradigm, the evidential record tells us Matthew Effects are not inevitable (Ghysels and Van Lancker, 2011; Hemerijck et al, 2016). They can be addressed, but their resolution lies in the devilish detail of institutional complementarities between income support and more active preventive integration policies, together with the professional proficiency of policy actors in aligning inter-temporal and transversal synergies. For social investment policy to survive politically in the new hard times ahead, it must break with the policy legacy of being the 'third way' 'handmaiden' to neoliberalism – wise to pursue when the economy expands, but forbidden when the chips are down.

There is no denying that a social investment strategy in the context of today's fragile economic recovery and dire budgetary pressures generates immediate economic trade-offs and political tensions. In the face of accelerated demographic ageing, on the other hand, it is imperative to recoup the social investment momentum lost in the aftermath of the global financial crisis. Social investment reform has proved to be able to contribute to inclusive growth by leveraging on effective policy mixes of 'stocks', 'flows' and 'buffer' in different modalities across countries capable of governing positive-sum externalities prior to the crisis. The post-crisis austerity reflex has thus far not been proficient in jump-starting growth and in terms of inclusion the track record of austerity politics is even more questionable (OECD, 2016; Ostry et al, 2016). Social investment is no 'silver bullet' policy, but compared the post-crisis austerity reflex, it has a better track record of maintaining real economic growth in terms of productivity, employment and greater equality. The gravest threat to economic stability and political cohesion is when mass youth unemployment translates into permanent labour market hysteresis. Given the magnitude of asymmetric overhang of the sovereign debt crisis, and – not to forget – the poor track record of social investment reform in Southern Europe prior to the euro crisis, there are no quick fixes (Hemerijck and Vandenbroucke, 2012). In the context of the Eurozone, my favourite solution is to discount social investment 'stock' policies from the fiscal criteria of the Stability and Growth Pact and the Fiscal Compact, in order to clear the necessary fiscal space for pursuing them in the context of the Europe 2020 Strategy, closely monitored through the European Semester in terms of appropriate alignments of 'stocks', 'flows' and 'buffers' under different economic and institutional conditions (Hemerijck, 2016). For the EU, struggling with the aftershock of fateful the EU referendum in the UK, the governments of which have always been the most vocal critics of 'Social Europe', it is of truly existential importance to explicitly present itself as a 'holding environment' within which 'active' social investment orientated European welfare states can prosper, in an attempt to re-coalesce the silent majorities to Europe's fractured political centre and stand up to rising xenophobic populism.

References

Atkinson, B. (2015) *Inequality. What Can Be Done?*, Cambridge, MA: Harvard University Press.

Banting, K. and J. Myles (eds) (2013) *Inequality and the Fading of Redistributive Politics*, Vancouver: UBC Press.

Barbier, J.-C. (2012) 'Social investment, a problematic concept with an ambiguous past: a comment on Anton Hemerijck', *Sociologica* 1: 1–10.

Barbier, J.-C. (2017) "Social investment': with or against social protection?' in A. Hemerijck (ed.), *The Uses of Social Investment*, Oxford: Oxford University Press, 51–58.

Baumol, W.J. (1967) 'The Macroeconomics of Unbalanced Growth', *American Economic Review*, 57(3): 415–26.

Begg, I, F. Mushoevel and R. Niblett (2015) 'The welfare state in Europe – visions for reform', in Bertelsmann Stiftung (ed.), *Vision Europe Summit. Redesigning European Welfare States – Ways Forward*, Guetersloh, 12–37.

Begg, I. (2017) 'Social Investment and its Discount Rate', in A. Hemerijck (ed.), *The Uses of Social Investment*, Oxford: Oxford University Press, 174–83.

Beveridge, W.H. (1942) *Social Insurance and Allied Services, Presented to Parliament as Command Paper 6404. Report by Sir William Beveridge* [The Beveridge Report]. London: HMSO.

Beveridge, W.H. (1944) *Full Employment in a Free Society: A Report*. London: Allen & Unwin.

Blanchard, O. and L. Summers (1987) 'Hysteresis in Unemployment', *European Economic Review* 31: 288–95.

Bonoli, G. (2013) *The Origins of Active Social Policy. Labour Market and Childcare Policies in Comparative Perspective*, Oxford: Oxford University Press.

Bonoli, G., B. Cantillon and W. Van Lancker (2017) 'Social investment and the Matthew effect: limits to a strategy', in A. Hemerijck (ed.), *The Uses of Social Investment*, Oxford: Oxford University Press, 66–76.

Bouget, D., H. Frazer, E. Marlier, S. Sabato and B. Vanhercke (2015) *Social Investment in Europe: A Study of National Policies*, European Social Policy Network (ESPN), Brussels: European Commission.

Brinton, M.C. and Dong Ju Lee (2016) 'Gender-Role Ideology, Labor Market Institutions, and Postindustrial Fertility', *Population and Development Review* 42(3): 405–33.

Burgoon, B. (2017) 'Practical Pluralism in the Empirical Study of Social Investment: Examples from Active Labour Market Policy', in A. Hemerijck (ed.), *The Uses of Social Investment*, Oxford: Oxford University Press, 161–73.

Cantillon, B. (2011) 'The paradox of the social investment state: growth, employment and poverty in the Lisbon era', *Journal of European Social Policy* 21(5): 432–49.

Cantillon, B. and W. Van Lancker (2013) 'Three Shortcomings of the Social Investment Perspective' *Acta Sociologica* 55(2): 125–42.

De Deken, J. (2014) 'Identifying the skeleton of the social investment state: Defining and measuring patterns of social policy change on the basis of expenditure data', in B. Cantillon, and F. Vandenbroucke (eds), *In Reconciling work and poverty reduction. How successful are European welfare states?*, Oxford: Oxford University Press, 260–85.

De Deken, J. (2017) 'Conceptualising and Measuring Social Investment', in A. Hemerijck (ed.), *The Uses of Social Investment*, Oxford: Oxford University Press, 184–93.

Deeming, C. and Smyth, P. (2015) 'Social investment after neoliberalism: policy paradigms and political platforms', *Journal of Social Policy* 44(2), 297–318.

Dräbing, V. and M. Nelson (2017) 'Addressing Human Capital Risks and the Role of Institutional Complementarities', in A. Hemerijck (ed.), *The Uses of Social Investment*, Oxford: Oxford University Press, 128–39.

Emmenegger, P., S. Haüsermann, B. Palier and M. Seeleib-Kaiser (2012) *The Age of Dualization. The Changing Face of Inequality in Deindustrializing Societies*, New York: Oxford University Press.

Esping-Andersen, G. (1999) *Social Foundations of Postindustrial Economies*, Oxford: Oxford University Press.

Esping-Andersen, G. (2009) *The Incomplete Revolution: Adapting to Women's New Roles*, Cambridge: Polity Press.

Esping-Andersen, G. and F. Billari (2015) 'Re-theorizing Family Demographics', *Population and Development Review* 41(1): 1–31.

Esping-Andersen, G., D. Gallie, A. Hemerijck, and J. Myles (2002) *Why We Need a New Welfare State*. Oxford: Oxford University Press.

European Commission (2013a) *Towards Social Investment for Growth and Cohesion – including implementing the European Social Fund 2014–2020*, COM(2013) 83 final, Brussels.

European Commission (2013b) *Evidence on Demographic and Social Trends Social Policies Contribution to Inclusion, Employment and the Economy*, SWD (2013) 38 final, Brussels.

European Council (2000) 'Lisbon European Council 23 and 24 March: Presidency Conclusions', www.europarl.europa.eu/summits/lis1_en.htm

Ferrera, M., A. Hemerijck, and M. Rhodes (2000) *The Future of Social Europe: Recasting Work and Welfare in the New Economy*, Report prepared for the Portuguese Presidency of the EU, Oeiras: Celta Editora.

Fleckenstein, T. and C. Lee (2017) 'Social Investment in East-Asia', in A. Hemerijck (ed.), *The Uses of Social Investment*, Oxford: Oxford University Press, 266–77.

Ghysels, J. and W. Van Lancker (2011) 'The unequal benefits of activation: an analysis of the social distribution of family policy among families with young children', *Journal of European Social Policy* 21(5): 472–85.

Giddens, A. (1998) *The Third Way: The Renewal of Social Democracy*, Cambridge: Polity Press.

Hall, P.A. (1989) *The Political Power of Economic Ideas: Keynesianism across Nations*, Princeton, NJ: Princeton University Press.

Hall, P.A. (1993) 'Policy Paradigms, Social Learning, and the State: The Case of Economic Policy-making in Britain', *Comparative Politics*, 25(3): 275–93.

Hemerijck, A. (1997) *Social Policy as a Productive Factor*, The Hague: Ministry of Social Affairs and Employment; Brussels: European Commission.

Hemerijck, A. (2013) *Changing Welfare States*, Oxford; Oxford University Press.

Hemerijck, A. (2014) 'Social Investment 'stocks', 'flows' and 'buffers'', *Politiche Sociali* 1(1): 6–22.

Hemerijck, A. (2015) 'The Quiet Paradigm Revolution of Social Investment', *Social Politics: International Studies in Gender, State & Society*, 22(2): 242–56.

Hemerijck, A. (2016) 'Making Social Investment Happen for the Eurozone', *Intereconomics: Review of European Economic Policy* 51(6): 200–06.

Hemerijck, A. (2017a) 'Social investment and its Critics', in A. Hemerijck (ed.), *The Uses of Social Investment*, Oxford: Oxford University Press, 3–39.

Hemerijck, A. (2017b), The Uses of Affordable Social Investment and the Great Recession, in A. Hemerijck (ed.), *The Uses of Social Investment*, Oxford: Oxford University Press, 379–412.

Hemerijck, A. and F. Vandenbroucke (2012) 'Social Investment and the Euro Crisis: The Necessity of a Unifying Concept', *Intereconomics: Review of European Economic Policy* 47(4): 200–06.

Hemerijck, A., B. Burgoon, A. Dipietro, and S. Vydra (2016) *Assessing Social Investment Synergies (ASIS), A project to Measure the Returns of Social Policies* Report for DG EMPL, European Commission Brussels.

Hills, J. (2014) *Good times, bad times: The welfare myth of them and us*, Bristol: Policy Press.

Huber, E. and J.D. Stephens (2001) *Development and Crisis of the Welfare State: Parties and Policies in Global Markets*, Chicago: University of Chicago Press.

Jenson, J. (2009) 'Lost in translation. The Social Investment Perspective and Gender Equality', *Social Politics* 16(4): 446–83.

Jenson, J. (2010) 'Diffusing ideas for after-neoliberalism: The social investment perspective in Europe and Latin America', *Global Social Policy* 10(1): 59–84.

Jenson, J. and Saint-Martin, D. (2003) 'New routes to social cohesion, Citizenship and the social investment state', *Canadian Journal of Sociology* 28(1), 77–99.

Jones. E. (2013) 'The Collapse of the Brussels-Frankfurt consensus and the structure of the euro', in V.A. Schmidt and M. Thatcher (eds), *Resilient Liberalism in Europe's Political Economy*, Cambridge: Cambridge University Press, 145–70.

Keynes, J.M (1936)[1973] *The General Theory of Employment, Interest and Money*, London: Macmillan for the Royal Economic Society.

Kvist, J. (2015) 'A framework for social investment strategies: Integrating generational, life course and gender perspectives in the EU social investment strategy', *Comparative European Politics* 13(1): 131–49.

Leoni, T. (2015) *Welfare state adjustment to new social risks in the post-crisis scenario. A review with focus on the social investment perspective*, WWWforEurope Working Paper (No. 89).

Lewis, J. (2006) *Children, Changing Families and Welfare States*, Cheltenham: Edward Elgar.

Lindbeck A. and D.J. Snower (1989) *The Insider-Outsider Theory of Employment and Unemployment*, Cambridge, MA: MIT Press.

Lister, R. (2003) 'Investing in the citizen-workers of the future: transformations in citizenship and the state under New Labour', *Social Policy and Administration* 37(5), 427–43.

Lister, R. (2004) 'The Third Way's social investment state', in J. Lewis and R. Surender (eds), *Welfare State Change: Towards a Third Way?* Oxford: Oxford University Press, 157–81.

Merkel, A. (2012) Speech by Dr Angela Merkel, Chancellor of the Federal Republic of Germany, at the World Economic Forum Annual Meeting 2012, Davos, www.bundeskanzlerin.de/ContentArchiv/EN/Archiv17/Reden/2012/2012-01-25-bkin-rede-davos.html

Merkel, A. (2013) Speech at the World Economic Forum Annual Meeting 2013, Davos, www.bundesregierung.de/ContentArchiv/EN/Archiv17/Reden/2013/2013-01-24-merkel-davos.html

Morel, N., B. Palier and J. Palme (eds) (2012) *Towards a social investment welfare state? Ideas, policies, challenges*, Bristol: Policy Press.

Morel, N. and J. Palme (2017) 'A Normative Foundation for the Social Investment Approach?', in A. Hemerijck (ed.), *The Uses of Social Investment*, Oxford: Oxford University Press, 150–57.

Myles, J. (2002) 'A new contract for the elderly', in G. Esping-Andersen, D. Gallie, A. Hemerijck, and J. Myles (2002) *Why We Need a New Welfare State*, Oxford: Oxford University Press, 130–72.

Nelson, M. and J.D. Stephens (2012) 'Do Social Investment Policies Produce More and Better Jobs?' in N. Morel, B. Palier and J. Palme (eds), *Towards a social investment welfare state? Ideas, policies and challenges,* Bristol: Policy Press, 205–34.

Noël, A. (2017) 'Social Investment in a Federal Welfare State: The Quebec Experience', in A. Hemerijck (ed.), *The Uses of Social Investment,* Oxford: Oxford University Press, 254–65.

Nolan, B. (2013) 'What Use is 'Social Investment'?', *Journal of European Social Policy* 23: 459–68.

Nussbaum, M. (2011) *Creating Capabilities. The Human Development Approach,* Cambridge, MA: Belknap Press.

Obama, B. (2015) State of the Union Address, 20 January, https://obamawhitehouse.archives.gov/the-press-office/2015/01/20/remarks-president-state-union-address-january-20-2015

OECD (1994) *The OECD Jobs Study: Facts, Analysis, Strategies,* Paris: OECD.

OECD (1997) *The OECD Jobs Strategy: Making Work Pay: Taxation, Benefits, Employment and Unemployment,* Paris: OECD.

OECD (2006a) *OECD Employment Outlook: Boosting Jobs and Income,* Paris: OECD.

OECD (2006b) *Starting Strong II: Early Childhood Education and Care,* Paris: OECD.

OECD (2007) *Babies and Bosses, Reconciling Work and Family Life – A Synthesis of Findings for OECD Countries,* Paris: OECD.

OECD (2008) *Growing Unequal,* Paris: OECD.

OECD (2011) *Doing Better for Families,* Paris: OECD.

OECD (2012) *Divided We Stand: Why Inequality Keeps Rising?,* Paris: OECD.

OECD (2015a) *In It Together; Why Less Inequality Benefits All,* Paris: OECD.

OECD (2015b) *All on board: Making inclusive growth happen,* Paris: OECD.

OECD (2016) *Interim Economic Outlook,* Paris: OECD.

Okun, A.M. (1975) *Equality and Efficiency: The Big Trade off,* Washington, DC: The Brookings Institution.

Ostry, J.D., P. Loungani and D. Furceri (2016) 'Neoliberalism: Oversold?', *Finance & Development* 53(2), Washington: IMF.

Palier, B. (ed.) (2010) *A Long Goodbye to Bismarck? The Politics of Welfare Reforms in Continental Europe,* Amsterdam: Amsterdam University Press, 45–72.

Palier, B. and K. Thelen (2010) 'Institutionalizing Dualism: Complementarities and Change in France and Germany', *Politics and Society* 38(1): 119–48.

Piketty, T. (2014) *Capital in the Twenty-First Century*. Cambridge, MA, and London: Belknap Press of Harvard University Press.

Rodrik, D. (2006) 'Goodbye Washington Consensus, hello Washington confusion? A review of the World Bank's economic growth in the 1990s: learning from a decade of reform', *Journal of Economic Literature*, 44(4): 973–87.

Saraceno, C. (2015) 'A critical look to the social investment approach from a gender perspective', *Social Politics*, 22(2): 257–69.

Saraceno, C. (2017) 'Family relationships and gender equality in the social investment discourse: a too reduced view?' in A. Hemerijck (ed.), *The Uses of Social Investment*, Oxford: Oxford University Press.

Scharpf, F.W. (1991) *Crisis and Choice in European Social Democracy*, Ithaca, NY: Cornel University Press, 59–65.

Schmid, G. (2015) 'Sharing Risks of Labour Market Transitions: Towards a System of Employment Insurance', *British Journal of Industrial Relations* 63(1): 70–93.

Schmid, G. (2017) 'Towards Employment Insurance', in A. Hemerijck (ed.), *The Uses of Social Investment*, Oxford: Oxford University Press, 108–17.

Sen, A. (2001) *Development as Freedom*, Oxford: Oxford University Press.

Sen, A. (2009) *The Idea of Justice*, Cambridge, MA: Harvard University Press.

Smyth, P. and J. Buchanan (2015) *Inclusive Growth in Australia. Social policy as economic investment*, Crows Nest: Allen & Unwin.

Stiglitz, J., A. Sen, and Fitoussi, (2009) *Report of the Commission on the Measurement of Economic Performance and Social Progress*, CMEPSP Technical Report.

Taylor-Gooby, P. (ed.) (2004) *New Risks, New Welfare: The Transformation of the European Welfare State*, Oxford: Oxford University Press.

Van Kersbergen, K. and A. Hemerijck (2012) 'Two Decades of Change in Europe: The Emergence of the Social Investment State', *Journal of Social Policy* 41(3): 475–92.

Van Kersbergen K., A. Hemerijck and B. Vis (2014) 'The Great Recession and Welfare State Reform. Is Retrenchment Really the Only Game Left in Town?', *Social Policy and Administration* 48(7):883–904.

Verbist, G. (2017) 'Measuring Social Investment Returns: Do Publicly Provided Services Enhance Social Inclusion?', in A. Hemerijck (ed.), *The Uses of Social Investment*, Oxford: Oxford University Press, 194–204.

WEF (World Economic Forum) (2014) *The Global Competitiveness Report 2014–2015*, Davos: WEF, www.weforum.org/reports/global-competitiveness-report-2013-2014.

Williamson, J. (1990) 'What Washington means by policy reform', in J. Williamson (ed.), *Latin American Adjustment: How Much Has Happened?*, Washington, DC: Institute for International Economics, 7–20.

Wren, A. (ed.) (2013) *The Political Economy of the Service Transition*, Oxford: Oxford University Press.

Wren, A. (2017) 'Social Investment and the Service Economy Trilemma', in A. Hemerijck (ed.), *The Uses of Social Investment*, Oxford: Oxford University Press, 97–107.

THREE

Making growth inclusive: perspectives on the role of social policy in developing economies

Sarah Cook

The current focus on 'inclusive growth' seems to offer a renewed promise of integration between social and economic concerns in development processes. This relationship has been turbulent: major shifts in mainstream economics since the launch of the development project in the post-war period have determined or constrained the space for social policy ideas and practice. This paper reviews the ways in which dominant economic development paradigms have dealt with the social question alongside debates around social policies and their role in the changing development landscape. It provides a brief overview of post-war perspectives on social policy in development – from post-war Keynesian macroeconomics, through debt crisis and the neoliberal 'Washington Consensus' years, towards a renewed attention to social concerns as reflected in global development goals and an emerging focus on making growth 'inclusive'.

The role social policies have played in development contexts – and how they are understood – has varied across time and place: from complementarity in supporting growth and determining long-term developmental possibilities (as in the Nordic countries and developmental states of East Asia), to the minimalist provision of safety nets as residual to the core economic growth agenda epitomised by the Washington Consensus years. This ambiguous relationship is frequently presented as a trade-off – between economic growth or efficiency on the one hand, and equity (or broader social welfare outcomes) on the other. As a field of inquiry, social policy has itself remained on the margins of mainstream development debates – a field generally dominated by the economic orthodoxy of the moment, and in which GDP rather than any social indicator retains its primacy as the development metric of choice whether for national growth or individual wellbeing. Relatedly, developing country contexts have until recently remained outside the growing body of scholarship on comparative social policy and welfare regimes which has focused largely on rich countries, reinforcing the notion that social policy is the domain of the wealthy, and an aspiration for poor countries only at a later stage of their development.

After reviewing the historical record on social issues in development thinking and policy, this chapter examines current debates around inclusive growth in the context of the new 'universal' agenda of equitable and sustainable development set by the Sustainable Development Goals, and asks whether this offers opportunities for rediscovering the complementary roles that social policy must play in order for development to deliver inclusive and equitable outcomes.

From Bretton Woods to Washington Consensus: the changing fortunes of social policy in development thinking

A synergistic relationship between economic and social policies was a key feature of mainstream Keynesian economic thought. Shaped by the Depression of the 1930s, Keynes saw that 'macroeconomic policy had to be sensitive to its social impact and that social expenditures could be an instrument for addressing macroeconomic problems' (Mkandawire, 2004: 6). More specifically, macroeconomics was 'driven by the social objectives of full employment and the social welfare regimes associated with it' (Mkandawire, 2006: xv). Keynes' economic arguments applied to poor as well as rich countries: economic growth and structural change were seen as instruments to achieve the social objectives of raising the incomes and welfare of populations in low income countries.

For many of the 'pioneers' of economic development – including the Nobel Laureates Myrdal and Tinbergen – social policy concerns were core to economic development: poverty elimination was the central preoccupation of development, and economic growth an instrument for achieving it. Such leading thinkers recognised that the dominant growth models of economists such as Solow and Kuznets, which focused on capital accumulation and 'big' push industrialisation as routes to modernisation, needed to be augmented by social policies that directly addressed the problem of poverty – including the expansion of social services, public investment and service provision and the redistribution of income (Townsend, 2004: 43). The social policies of the then new welfare states, which aimed at stimulating growth and employment to address economic crisis in industrialised countries, informed the emerging 'social development approach that was subsequently formalized in development thinking in the global South' (Midgley, 2014: 22).

Arguments for the contribution of social policy to growth were reinforced by increasing empirical evidence of the returns to investment in social policies, particularly in childhood health, nutrition and education – represented in particular by the work of the Nobel prizewinning economist, Theodore Schulz. Myrdal, drawing on Sweden's experience, was adamant that social expenditure was not merely public consumption but an important instrument for development, with higher consumption a condition for more rapid and stable growth (Mkandawire, 2004: 2). Recognition of the role of these social investments which, alongside other basic infrastructure and investment in human capital and skills (for example through vocational training) could have lifelong effects on productivity, shaped the early agendas of a number of United Nations agencies such as UNICEF, FAO and WHO (Jolly, 2011), and were reflected in the goals of the early UN Development Decades and in Declarations such as the 1978 Alma Ata Health for All agenda. Such elements of what have been termed 'productive' social policies were also an essential component of the 'miracle' success stories of the East Asian developmental states (see Kwon, Chapter Four in this volume).

By the 1970s, redistributive social policies had become more prominent in the development agenda in response to the failure of capital intensive industrialisation and modernisation benefits to 'trickle down' to the poor. World Bank President McNamara's goal to redefine the World Bank as a poverty-focused development agency, along with the influential employment missions of the International Labour Organization (ILO), placed employment and 'basic needs' at the centre of the new development agenda articulated as 'redistribution with growth' (Chenery et al, 1974). The basic needs approach, promoted by UN agencies and the World Bank, set targets for the achievement of defined needs and calculated the rates of growth required to achieve them over a 25-year period (1975–2000). As the estimated growth rates were high by historical standards, an estimate was also made of the level of redistribution of the increase in income required to meet defined needs (Emmerij, 2010: 1). This thinking contributed to the shift away from large scale infrastructure projects and towards promotion of labour intensive industries, investment in basic infrastructure and agriculture, transfers of land and other assets, and provision of health, education and other basic services (Saad-Filho, 2010: 3). As Emmerij (2010: 1) notes:

By the middle of the 1970s it looked as though a more appropriate development strategy had been designed that effectively combined economic growth, productive employment creation, and basic needs. At the core of the strategy was a shift to a pattern of economic growth that is more employment-intensive, more equitable, and more effective in the battle against poverty.

A range of more radical critiques of the development project were also emerging at this time, particularly from political and social development scholars for whom the incremental growth with equity approach ignored structural obstacles to development. The failure of poor countries to converge with the rich 'core', and problems of unequal, distorted or unbalanced development – between countries, sectors, or population groups – were taken up by radical political economists: for dependency theorists, unbalanced development was a manifestation of unequal relations that perpetuated underdevelopment in the periphery, with the solution being delinking, import substitution and autarkic growth. Others called for asset redistribution, particularly land reform, and for greater community participation in decision making, and inclusion of marginalised groups, such as indigenous peoples whose natural resource-dependent livelihoods were often threatened by 'modernisation'. Feminist scholars were likewise exposing the inattention to unequal social relations that led to the neglect of the needs and interests of women in the development process, while the negative environmental and ecological consequences of resource intensive industrialisation strategies were also coming under increasing scrutiny.

Before the agenda laid out in 'Redistribution with Growth' could be seriously pursued, however, countries that might have benefited were caught up in the international debt crisis. The overthrow of Keynesian macroeconomics by monetarism and the shift of the economics profession towards a concern with supply side and neoclassical economics ended this phase of the development project (Saad-Filho, 2010: 3). Development economics abandoned its concerns with structural change, poverty and inequality. The trade-off between efficiency (achieved through competitive markets) and equity (through state intervention in the economy) returned as a core proposition of development. The foundations were laid for a return to ideas of trickle-down growth, with development failures equated with the failure of states – as sources of inefficiency, rent-seeking and corruption; and solutions found in adherence to the operation of the market, in which rational individuals would respond optimally to appropriate incentives. Social policy – in which the state intervened to achieve more equitable social outcomes – effectively lost its autonomous place in the development agenda.

Social policy in disarray: the Washington Consensus years

The links between social and economic policy were strained, if not completely severed, by the rise of neoliberalism and the imposition of 'Washington Consensus' policies on developing countries. At the core of the new agenda was a reliance on macroeconomic policies of stabilisation, liberalisation and privatisation as key instruments to achieve growth. Benefits would eventually 'trickle down' once the market conditions were right, with safety nets available to protect the most vulnerable in the process. Success or failure was assessed not in terms of outcomes (such as poverty reduction), but rather in terms of the implementation of policies designed to re-establish the preconditions for growth (Cornia, 2006: 4). Failure to reduce poverty or achieve other social development goals, rather than being the result of the failure of the new policies, was instead an indication of insufficient or inadequate reform.

The policy agenda of stabilisation and adjustment left little room for the state in social provisioning, protection or redistribution. Government intervention was viewed as a key source of inefficiency and thus a constraint on growth. Social provisioning should occur through the market which would determine the supply of necessary services; social expenditures were reframed from investment to consumption (and thus neither essential nor productive); household demand should be determined as a response to prices; and user fees should apply even to basic health and education services to ensure households would value them appropriately. Apart from the immediate social costs of these policies (which quickly became visible in indicators such as infant mortality, nutrition and school enrolment), and the long-term human disinvestments in terms of lost education and learning, the approach also ignored the microeconomic determinants of aggregate demand, and the role of social policy or welfare institutions in a wider set of insurance, consumption smoothing and crisis management functions. These policy shifts had their parallels in the neoliberal assault on welfare states across the industrialised world, as welfare responsibility and risk were shifted from state to individuals and households, and the public institutions that had provided some means of security to vulnerable populations were weakened.

Reaction against the Washington Consensus agenda came from a number of directions. Evidence of the devastating price that reforms were extracting from the poorest people and countries, as well as the disinvestment in the future, was gathered in a landmark publication by UNICEF. *Adjustment with a Human Face* (Cornia et al, 1987) brought the issues of social costs and investments back to the agenda, asking how one could believe that 'the economy of a country was being strengthened if its children, the human capital of the future, were being weakened by cutbacks in expenditures on nutrition and education?' (Jolly et al, 2009: 145). A debate was also emerging at this time over the reasons for the remarkable success of the newly industrialised East Asian 'developmental states'. Despite efforts to present this experience as 'market conforming' (Fine, 2005: xviii), it was clear that the state, institutional development, strong redistributive social investments and productive social policies had played a fundamental role in the success of the Asian Tigers (see Kwon, Chapter Four in this volume).

A renewed focus on market failures and imperfections was also influencing the development economics field. The new institutional economics, associated in particular with Joseph Stiglitz, justified a greater role for the state in development as compensation for imperfect markets. Investment in institutions and service provision, as well as stronger safety nets, became part of the modified policy prescriptions of the World Bank, with Stiglitz as its new Chief Economist, in what came to be known as the 'post-Washington Consensus'.

The post-Washington Consensus: continuing neoliberalism and the cautious return of the social

While the softer brand of neoliberalism that emerged in the 1990s was less antagonistic to the state and more focused on poverty reduction, the existing macroeconomic agenda of the key Washington institutions remained essentially unchanged (Jomo and Fine, 2006). New policy aims addressing corruption, governance, labour market flexibility and targeted poverty reduction were added to the core Washington Consensus policies of deficit reduction, liberalisation and privatisation (Saad-Filho, 2010: 7). An initiative to reduce the debt of the most affected Highly Indebted Poor Countries (HIPC) was introduced in 1996, with accompanying Poverty Reduction Strategy Papers (PRSPs) aimed at integrating poverty concerns into national plans to ensure that resources freed up by debt relief would be used for poverty reduction. These papers laid out the economic and social policies low income countries should pursue to achieve growth and reduce poverty within the limitations of the existing macroeconomic framework (UNRISD, 2010: 3). The pursuit of equity or social goals should not compromise efficiency or growth.

In this context, social programmes principally took the form of safety nets targeted to the poorest, or interventions aimed at incentivizing community-led investments in basic infrastructure – such as the World Bank's 'Social Investment Funds'. Given the hollowing out of state institutions over the previous decade, social programmes were most often delivered as non-governmental organisation (NGO) or as donor-managed projects. While such initiatives helped to bring issues of poverty and employment back on to the agenda, they generally remained residual to mainstream economic policy, with limited impacts on the poor or on wider welfare (Siri 2000: 1). The return to growth in many parts of the world during the early 1990s created a renewed optimism that 'trickle-down' could still benefit the poor in the absence of more comprehensive social policies. This optimism was, however, quickly dispelled by the Mexican and Asian crises, which demonstrated that even those benefiting from growth remained vulnerable to economic shocks. In response, the World Bank expanded the range of its social programmes through its 'social risk management' framework – still prioritising market instruments but recognising the need to address pervasive market failures through interventions that would insure or mitigate against risks, and help households cope with the adverse effects of shocks (Holzmann and Jorgensen, 2000).

The idea that social protection was principally about risk management and protection against shocks in turn came under criticism for neglecting the chronically poor or those disadvantaged by status or identity (gender, caste) and other structural factors, as well as its inattention to policies to promote wellbeing, productive capacities or other capabilities (Cook and Kabeer, 2010: 5). Space had opened up in the post-Washington Consensus period for a wide range of actors to mobilise in bringing ideas of social development, justice and inclusion, human rights and participation back into the development discussion. United Nations agencies, academics and NGOs, supported by some bilateral development agencies, were generating evidence for alternative approaches, including for an expanded role of social policy in development contexts.

A significant advance was made with the concept of 'human development'. Building on the capabilities approach of Amartya Sen and reflecting earlier work on basic needs, this was popularised through UNDP's Human Development Report and associated index. Launched in 1990 it became an important counterweight to the use of GDP as a monetary measure of wellbeing. The 1995 World Summit for Social Development was another landmark effort to raise the 'social question', with117 heads of state or government committing to 'creating an economic, political, social, cultural and legal environment that will enable people to achieve social development' (Commitment 1 of the Copenhagen Declaration). Under the leadership of Juan Somavia, the Summit brought to the fore issues of social inclusion and cohesion, as well as participation and empowerment including for women and marginalised groups, while also recognising the importance of economic growth and structural change, and social policies that could affect the distribution of the benefits of growth. In returning to pre-Washington Consensus themes of employment and distribution, the Summit drew attention to the neglected links between economic and social policy. Like the Human Development approach, however, these ideas did not offer an alternative to the supply side macroeconomic framework that would give them policy traction. Assessing the situation in 2000, UNRISD noted that:

> what emerges is a fairly disturbing picture of initiatives that remain more at the level of agency rhetoric than effective implementation: and patterns of economic growth, liberalisation and inequality that continue to obstruct rather than facilitate progress in the field of social development. (UNRISD, 2000: i)

Social issues and policies, while finding new spaces in academia and among some international development actors, were unable to escape the residual role to which the dominant economic paradigm had relegated them.

By the turn of the millennium, the new agenda set by the global community in the form of the Millennium Development Goals (MDGs) effectively mobilised the global community around the reduction of poverty. Through a series of social goals, poverty reduction was elevated as a central pillar of development policy and states were held responsible for delivering improvements in wellbeing through increased social spending and basic infrastructural investments. The economic policy environment that could support such objectives was not, however, part of these goals, although targets related to productivity and employment were added in 2003. What emerged in practice was thus a limited needs-based agenda, still lacking a strategy or a macroeconomic framework that would relink social and economic policies (Emmerij, 2010; UNRISD, 2010). In short, social interventions targeted at the poorest remained divorced from the economic processes and structures that generated or perpetuated poverty.

Consolidating the social turn in development debates

A more critical conversation was nonetheless taking place reflecting the tensions between the dominant economic model and social goals. This was informed by growing attention among scholars to social policies in low income contexts, a field that was largely under-theorised and lacked a sound evidence base for policy (Mkandawire, 2004). New academic research was facilitated by improved data that enabled better analysis of comparative and longitudinal patterns of growth, distribution and wellbeing, and were complemented by alternative policy ideas and practices in the developing world where social protection coverage was increasing dramatically. The impact of the global financial crisis and the attention this drew to inequality in the public discourse further consolidated this shift.

Significant contributions were made by scholars aiming to bring developing countries into a comparative social policy framework, examining political and institutional arrangements, welfare regimes or social policy choices that affect development outcomes. Comparative social policy scholars started to pay more attention to lower and middle income countries, with particular attention to the situation in emerging economies including the newly-labelled 'BRICS'. Drawing on Esping-Andersen's work on welfare regimes, some researchers applied a historical-institutional approach to the analysis of social policies of low income countries, characterising them as regimes of insecurity and informality (Gough et al, 2004). The United Nations Research Institute for Social Development (UNRISD), under the direction of Thandika Mkandawire, undertook a historical and comparative study of the role of social policy under a range of policy regimes, and particularly focused on understanding lessons from cases of developmental success. The studies demonstrated varying roles for social policy under different conditions – as essential complements to economic policies, in promoting production and essential investments, contributing to protection, redistribution and reproduction, as well as in ensuring political stability and cohesion. By helping to shape the conditions in which markets operate, social policies enabled growth to be inclusive and thus sustainably to enhance wellbeing. By contrast, when treated as a residual measure to treat the symptoms of poverty or to ameliorate the social costs of mainstream economic policies, social policies were seen to function poorly (Mkandawire, 2004; UNRISD, 2010).

Greater availability of internationally comparable data also allowed researchers to analyse relationships between growth, poverty, inequality and other social outcomes (de Haan, 2015). From the turn of the century a growing concern with 'pro-poor growth' reflected the emerging consensus that growth is not inherently pro-poor, but the question of how this should be defined and measured remained unresolved – whether as growth that improves the absolute or relative condition of the poor (Ranieri and Ramos, 2013). Greater availability of data and a growing concern with inequality shifted debates from conceptual or definitional questions of what constituted pro-poor growth to empirical questions of the relationship between growth and distribution, whether growth was distribution neutral (as argued by Dollar and Kraay, 2002), and how inequality affected growth. Evidence increasingly supported arguments that, while growth was undoubtedly important for reducing poverty, high levels of poverty could be a constraint on growth. Furthermore, in contexts of rapidly rising inequality, evidence was accumulating to show that high levels of inequality impacted the pace of growth, whether growth could be sustained, and the way growth translated into poverty reduction (Besley and Cord, 2007; Berg and Ostry, 2011; UNRISD, 2010).

The growing global anti-poverty consensus that marked the first decade of the 21st century, as well as the recognition that high levels of inequality impeded poverty reduction, could hinder growth and also generated political stability, did not, however, lead to any particular social policy prescriptions (Jensen, 2015: 44). World Bank documents point to a shift away from offering development blueprints and towards more pragmatic and experimental policy making (Saad-Filho, 2010: 10). UN agencies, non-governmental organisations (NGOs) and many low income countries were experimenting with new social protection interventions with a focus on cash as an instrument of choice. Overall, however, the international financial institutions remained cautious about interventions to reduce inequality, including even mildly redistributive social protection programmes, concerned that such interventions might distort incentives and compromise growth.

It took financial crisis and its consequences in the Global North, and the publication of major works on inequality by economists such as Piketty, Stiglitz and Atkinson to refocus global policy attention on the issue of inequality, to see the concentration of wealth as the other side of the problem of poverty, and thus to slightly change the calculus regarding the efficiency/equity trade-off. Uprisings across the Arab world also forged the link between inequality and political instability, presenting an additional impetus to rethinking the connection between social and economic policy. For some, these events were optimistically interpreted as signalling an opportunity for 'post-neoliberalism'. Some saw the possibility of a shift away from supply side macroeconomic policies, towards an alternative development model that would give greater weight to employment generation, strengthen institutions that could mitigate market failures and tackle inequality, and refocus attention on issues of social justice, rights and equity (Utting et al, 2012; Farnsworth and Irving, 2011).

A separate – and potentially more durable – impetus to rethinking the links between economic and social policy has come from the dramatic expansion of social programmes introduced by governments in a number of developing economies. The dominant instrument behind a global expansion of social protection has been non-contributory social cash transfers, generally targeted to the poor and often with associated conditionalities. Starting with municipal experiments in Brazil from the mid-1990s, and the launch of Mexico's *Progresa* in 1997, conditional cash transfer programmes (CCTs) spread first across the region, and were then adopted in varying forms (often without conditions) globally. Initially CCTs were received cautiously by institutions including the World Bank which saw them as potentially distorting economic incentives (Hall, 2015); they were also critiqued by those favouring more universal approaches over targeting and conditionalities (Mkandawire, 2005). However, the conditions, which related in particular to investments in child health and education, helped create acceptability of transfers among those concerned about welfare programmes as a potential drain on growth or as creating dependency. Many countries in Latin America, Asia and sub-Saharan Africa have adopted similar or modified conditional or unconditional social transfer programmes. Other mechanisms of social protection have also expanded: India's employment guarantee scheme (NREGA) provides a minimum number of paid work days per year to all households, while a number of Asian economies including Thailand and China are strengthening more comprehensive social insurance coverage for health, unemployment and pensions, alongside basic income transfers.

This significant expansion of social protection across the developing world has been enhanced by support from development actors. Work by the ILO to demonstrate the affordability of a minimum level of protection helped build support for the idea of a universal 'Social Protection Floor'. The ILO's Social Protection Floor Recommendation (no. 202) in 2012 provided the normative basis for a global consensus around 'building inclusive, productive, responsive social protection and labour programmes and systems tailored to country circumstances' (ILO, 2012), with many international agencies strengthening their support to effective social protection systems. A growing evidence base on the impact of such programmes demonstrates benefits in relation to welfare (protection), human capital investment (promotion) as well as links with productivity and local economic growth. Nonetheless, concerns about their possible negative impacts on growth persist, as Alderman and Yemtsov (2012: 2) writing for the World Bank note: 'Distortions created by fragmented and poorly coordinated social protection interventions may influence the behavior of economic agents, discourage efforts and lock beneficiaries into low productivity-low growth equilibrium'.

Inclusive growth: room for a new accommodation between social and economic policy?

The rethinking of social issues within development policy that began during the 1990s and was consolidated through the MDGs undoubtedly contributed to a reduction in poverty globally and the achievement of social goals. Nonetheless, social policy remained on the fringes of mainstream development policy. A renewed attention to inequality and inclusion may provide a new opportunity for rebalancing the relationship. In the years following the global financial crisis, a level of inequality viewed as politically destabilising and economically unsustainable helped to coalesce 'mainstream' debate around the idea that inequality matters for growth and poverty reduction, and may indeed require different policy responses – including those in the social sphere – in order to make growth inclusive. The goal of more equitable development is also reflected in the Sustainable Development Goals (SDGs), signed up to by the global community in 2015 and aiming for a better alignment of social and economic alongside environmental goals. Promoting economic growth and productive employment and reducing inequality thus complement many of the social goals carried over from the MDGs.

The notion of 'inclusive growth' reflected in the SDGs entered the development discourse around the turn of the century. The Asian Development Bank became the first major institution to adopt the term, noting that:

> In many countries, rising incomes, while reducing overall poverty, have been associated with rising disparities. These

> disparities, left unchecked, could threaten the fragile
> political consensus for economic reforms, or even political
> stability. ... The solution lies in the continuation of pro-
> growth economic strategies—but with a much sharper focus
> on ensuring that the economic opportunities created by
> growth are available to all—particularly the poor—to the
> maximum extent possible. (ADB, 2007: 13–14)

The idea has been taken up by the Bretton Woods institutions, UN agencies and NGOs and used by heads of states at global leadership meetings, responding to concerns that global economic recovery is failing to benefit the poorest. As with the related notion of pro-poor growth, debates exist over definition, measurement and the policies needed to achieve it.

A number of recent reviews have explored definitions, measures and policies associated with the term (Ianchovichina and Lundstrom, 2009; de Haan, 2015; Klasen, 2010; Ranieri and Ramos, 2013; Saad-Filho, 2010). Definitions may be concerned with the process of growth or with outcomes (see Table 5.1, Chapter Five). Outcomes may be measured along various dimensions from monetary income to multi-dimensional poverty and wellbeing, and incorporating other aspects of social identity (gender, ethnicity and so on). Inclusion may relate to different social groups, to economic sectors, to location (where the poor live and work), or be concerned with employment and opportunities, access to credit (financial inclusion) and other institutions, or with the prices of goods that affect the poor. In some cases definitions are interchangeable with relative versions of pro-poor growth whereby inclusive growth is concerned with including the poor in the benefits of growth, in order to reduce disadvantage; for others inclusion is focused on the distribution of benefits among all groups in society (Klasen, 2010; Ranieri and Ramos, 2013). Definitions emphasising the inclusiveness of the growth process focus on the distribution of opportunities, in terms of non-discriminatory access to productive employment, requiring both job creation and productivity growth in low wage employment. The World Bank has translated the idea of inclusive growth into its agenda of 'shared prosperity' focusing on access to opportunities and increased incomes for the bottom 40%. For others, the ability to participate and benefit from growth should tackle structural inequities, including social structures and relations, the economic power of elites, and patterns of stratification related for examples to class, gender, ethnicity or location that lock people into positions of disadvantage and constrain their choices and agency (Kabeer, 2012; Stewart, 2014).

Policies to achieve inclusive growth inevitably vary across this range of perspectives and definitions. In practice, the standard package of supply side macroeconomic policies continues to prevail, along with the additional post-Washington Consensus focus on governance, institutions and safety nets. This has been complemented by a stronger focus on employment creation, active labour market policies and expanded opportunity, as well as investments in human capital to address problems of low productivity. Greater emphasis is placed on institutional arrangements that can facilitate economic participation by the poor, such as labour and credit markets. Social protection – particularly through cash transfers – has been geared more strongly towards productive social investments and in some cases towards facilitating women's labour force participation. Safety nets remain the residual mechanism to address the needs of those unable to benefit from market inclusion. As the limits of the cash-led demand side approach to social protection have become apparent, more attention is gradually being paid to investment in the supply of services, from affordable and better quality health and education, to (less prominently) childcare and social infrastructure that reduces demands on time particularly of women.

Conceptually, the notion of inclusive growth provides new opportunities for rethinking the relationship between social and economic policies in development. In keeping with a Keynesian approach that saw social policies as having a role in crisis management and domestic demand expansion, some developing and emerging economies have taken up the idea of 'inclusive growth' to justify more expansive social policies in support of economic development objectives. China's former President Hu Jintao, for example, has used the term to refer to how the benefits of economic growth can be shared in order to realise balanced economic and social progress. Policies include prioritising human capital investments, implementing a strategy of full employment, improving the quality and competence of workers and building a social security system that ensures sustainable development (Cook and Lam, 2015). Social policies are thus recognised as playing multiple roles – including protection and distribution, enhancing productivity, expanding domestic demand, as automatic stabilisers in crisis management, and in helping to constitute future development paths. Indeed, the potential future returns to growth from Keynesian-style stimulus packages and counter-cyclical fiscal policies was recognised by countries from the USA to China in response to crisis, but is not yet a core part of the policy package for achieving inclusive growth recommended to low income countries.

A number of alternative solutions are being proposed by scholars and activists to resolve the tension between economic and social policies in development. For some, inclusion requires the decommodification of labour with a growing movement in favour of a guaranteed minimum level of security provided through a basic income delinked from work. Others caution against the possibility of delinking employment and social protection while acknowledging the limited capacity of contemporary social policies to protect individuals against risks associated with the current structure of employment (Heintz and Lund, 2012). Instead, they suggest the need for a better understanding of links between processes of social reproduction and production at both the household and macroeconomic levels, with social policies designed to address insecurities related to employment, to balance reproductive and productive roles (through attention to care provision and family policies, for example), as well as addressing the vulnerabilities of those unable to work.

Another strand of research and practice emphasises voice and representation, recognising that civic and democratic participation plays a significant role in shaping the new social policy agenda in the developing world, through electoral politics and rights activism. In contrast to the 'golden age' of the welfare state, where social rights derived principally from labour market participation, the changed nature of the economy suggests that social rights may need to derive from other sources, such as citizenship or universal human rights. Latin America, the region that has made greatest progress towards universalising social protection during this period, has done so based on acceptance of an increasing role for the state in social matters, recognising rights as a basis of public policy, and linked to efforts to strengthen solidarity and the progressive construction of social citizenship (Cecchini et al, 2015). This quest for social citizenship is reflected also in political and social movements, in Latin America and elsewhere, where alternative ways of balancing economic and social goals to achieve inclusion is seen in ideas such as 'buen vivir' and 'social and solidarity economy' (Cook et al, 2012).

The major expansion of social protection across the developing world provides one key channel in the search for greater inclusion; another is employment related – through job creation, increasing productivity and active labour market policies. Beyond these channels, fiscal and macroeconomic policies, and an enabling global environment will be additional key elements in balancing growth and inclusion. Demand side cash transfers, while important for poverty reduction, provide a limited instrument for inclusion in contexts characterised by high rates of poverty, informality and jobless growth, and where economic slowdown or crisis may jeopardise or reverse gains. The international financial institutions and other major development agencies have however moved cautiously to alter the supply side macroeconomic policies to allow for a better integration of economic and social policies. Earlier critiques of post-Washington Consensus social policies may thus still apply: that the mechanisms for inclusion integrate the poor or otherwise marginalised into an economic and financial system that itself creates and perpetuates high rates of inequality. Redistributive policies (including more progressive tax and transfer systems) that could tackle poverty and inequality directly are not core to the new agenda. Instead, the period during which 'inclusive growth' has risen on the policy agenda has coincided with slow post-crisis growth and economic instability in much of the developed world. Commodity price declines and weak demand have been passed on to many lower income countries. The result is an expansion rather than a decline in the number of developing countries implementing 'austerity' policies (Ortiz et al, 2015), with Brazil becoming a significant recent case. Such measures limit the potential for job creation as well as the fiscal space needed for more expansionary social policies – the key channels of inclusion.

In this context, and as boundaries of developing/developed economies and the fields of (economic and social) development become less clearly demarcated, some global convergence is seen in the language of debate on welfare policies. The similarities in the discourse around social investment and inclusive growth have been explored by a number of authors (Jensen, 2015; Midgley, 2015). In welfare states, the rediscovery of social investment policies provides a justification for protecting some level of state welfare spending during periods of contraction. In development contexts, a similar justification has been used for safety net interventions, which has in turn opened space for a return to more expansive productivist social policies.

A key distinction between social investment and inclusive growth in high versus low income contexts, however, is the critical *developmental* role of social policy in the latter – not only in ensuring marginalised groups share in the benefits of growth, but also in supporting processes of structural change associated with economic development. As pursued for example in East Asia, such developmental or productive social policies involved a focus on human capital investment, supply side interventions to universalise provision of basic services, some redistributive mechanisms, and social insurance policies to protect workers against employment related risks. Strengthening the critical pathways to inclusion through increased investment in individual capabilities to take advantage of employment opportunities will however require complementary policies. These should include active labour market and social insurance mechanisms alongside renewed attention to marcroeconomic policies that generate employment while supporting a more equitable distribution of assets and incomes.

Conclusion: towards inclusive societies

There is undoubtedly a pressing need to rethink social development approaches for low income countries in the 21st century. This need arises from a range of new risks and challenges that have substantially changed the context for development – from the degree of global integration and the nature of global inequality, changes in skills required in a post-industrial knowledge economy, to the climate-related challenges of an unsustainable carbon-led growth model (Cook and Dugarova, 2014). The greater frequency of economic crisis, volatility associated with the global financial system and the commodity dependence of many low income countries contributes to the instability of growth processes and in many cases to jobless growth. Climate-related environmental pressures add to the sources of human insecurity, fuelling natural resource conflicts, mobility and displacement.

In this context, the attention to 'inclusive growth' has expanded the space for dialogue around appropriate policies for equity and inclusion. Renewed attention to inequality globally and a sustainable development agenda that aspires to be universal, together with expanding social protection initiatives pursued by governments across the Global South, provide a context in which more transformative policies for inclusive development become possible. The policy agenda articulated to date – with its stronger focus on employment and opportunity alongside human capital investment – starts to relink processes of production with those of social reproduction. At a minimum, an expanded set of social protection and insurance mechanisms together with an improved regulatory framework for wages and employment protection will be needed to address the insecurity of labour, given the structure of informal and precarious employment in low income countries. The additional functions of social policy in contributing to macroeconomic stability and crisis management, by smoothing consumption and maintaining aggregate demand, as well as in overcoming current levels of exclusion through redistributive (tax and transfer) mechanisms, remain insufficiently recognised by those shaping macroeconomic policies, while the risk remains that ongoing austerity programmes will limit progress in both social protection and job creation.

Sustainable and equitable economic growth in developing countries will increasingly depend on resolving tensions in the social and political domains arising from inequality and exclusion, as well as finding ecologically sustainable pathways. Progress across the economic, social and ecological domains also requires policy coherence to ensure that progress in one domain is not undermined by consequences and reactions in another. This demands that the distribution of benefits, costs and opportunities are equitable, and perceived as being so – whether among individuals, groups, countries or regions; that pro-growth policies and technological or efficiency gains do not crowd out welfare and sustainability objectives, and that environmental sustainability goals are balanced with human welfare considerations (Cook and Dugarova, 2014: 35). Social policies will need to play an enhanced role not only as a mechanism for social investment, but more importantly in managing the distribution of costs, benefits and opportunities related to economic, social and environmental change, in order to ensure that growth is a means to the creation of inclusive and stable societies.

References

ADB (2007) *Toward a New Asian Development Bank in a New Asia: Report of the Eminent Persons Group*, ADB97, July, Manila: Asian Development Bank.

Alderman, H. and R. Yemtsov (2012) *Productive Role of Social Protection*, Background Paper for the World Bank 2012–2022 Social Protection and Labor Strategy, Washington DC: World Bank, http://siteresources.worldbank.org/SOCIALPROTECTION/Resources/SP-Discussion-papers/430578-1331508552354/1203.pdf (accessed 14 June 2017).

Berg, A.G. and J.D. Ostry (2011) 'Inequality and Unsustainable Growth: Two Sides of the Same Coin?', Washington, DC: IMF Staff Discussion Note, 8 April.

Besley, T. and L. Cord (eds) (2007) *Delivering on the Promise of Pro-Poor Growth: Insights and Lessons from Country Experiences*, Basingstoke: Palgrave Macmillan.

Cecchini, S., F. Filgueira, R. Martínez and C. Rossel (2015) (eds) *Towards universal social protection: Latin American pathways and policy tools*, ECLAC Books, No. 136 (LC/G.2644-P), Santiago: Economic Commission for Latin America and the Caribbean (ECLAC), www.cepal.org/sites/default/files/events/files/eclac-un-towards_universal_social_protection.pdf (accessed 14 June 2017).

Chenery, H., M. Ahluwalia, C. Bell, J. Duloy and R. Jolly (1974) *Redistribution with Growth: Policies to improve income distribution in developing countries in the context of economic growth*, Oxford: Oxford University Press.

Cook, S. and F. Dugarova (2014) 'Rethinking social development for a post-2015 world', *Development: Special Issue on Shared Societies* 57(1): 30–5.

Cook, S. and N. Kabeer (2010) (eds) *Social protection as development policy – Asian perspectives*, New Delhi, India: Routledge.

Cook, S. and W. Lam (2015) 'In the shadow of crisis: Change and continuity in China's post-crisis social policy' in S. McBride, R. Mahon and G.W. Boychuk (eds), *After '08: Social Policy and the Global Financial Crisis*, Vancouver: UBC Press, 216–34.

Cook, S., K. Smith and P. Utting (2012) 'Green Economy or Green Society? Contestation and Policies for a Fair Transition', UNRISD Occasional Paper 10, Geneva.

Cornia, G. (ed.) (2006) *Pro-Poor Macroeconomics: Potential and Limitations*, Basingstoke: UNRISD/Palgrave Macmillan.

Cornia, G.A., R. Jolly and F. Stewart (1987) (eds) *Adjustment with a Human Face. Volume 1, Protecting the Vulnerable and Promoting Growth*, Oxford: Clarendon Press.

de Haan, A. (2015) 'Inclusive Growth: Beyond Safety Nets?', *European Journal of Development Research* 27: 606–22.

Dollar, D. and A. Kraay (2002) 'Growth is good for the poor', *Journal of Economic Growth* 7(3): 195–225.

Emmerij, L. (2010) 'The Basic Needs Approach to Development', Background paper for *UNDESA World Economic and Social Survey 2010*, New York: UNDESA.

Farnsworth, K, and Z. Irving (eds) (2011) *Social Policy in Challenging Times: Economic crisis and welfare systems*, Bristol: The Policy Press.

Fine, B. (2005) 'Introduction: The Economics of Development and the Development of Economics', in K.S. Jomo and B. Fine (eds), *The New Development Economics: After the Washington Consensus*, New Delhi: Tulika Books.

Gough, I., G. Wood, A. Barrientos, P. Bevan, P. Davis and G. Room (2004) *Insecurity and Welfare Regimes in Asia, Africa and Latin America: Social Policy in Development Contexts*, Cambridge: Cambridge University Press.

Hall, A. (2015) 'It Takes Two to Tango: Conditional Cash Transfers and the Globalizing Role of the World Bank' in S. McBride, R. Mahon and G.W. Boychuk (eds), *After '08: Social Policy and the Global Financial Crisis*, Vancouver: UBC Press, 140–58.

Heintz, J. and F. Lund (2012) 'Welfare Regimes and Social Policy: A Review of the Role of Labour and Employment', UNRISD Research Paper No. 2, July, Geneva.

Holzmann, R. and S. Jorgensen (2000) 'Social Risk Management: A new conceptual framework for social protection and beyond', Social Protection Discussion Paper no. 0006, Washington, DC: World Bank.

Ianchovichina, E. and Lundstrom S. (2009) *What is Inclusive Growth?*, World Bank, http://siteresources.worldbank.org/ INTDEBTDEPT/Resources/468980-1218567884549/ WhatIsInclusiveGrowth20081230.pdf (accessed 14 June 2017).

International Labour Organization (ILO) (2012) 'The Social Protection Floor Initiative', ILO Factsheet, Geneva, www.ilo.org/wcmsp5/ groups/public/---ed_protect/---soc_sec/documents/publication/ wcms_207781.pdf (accessed 14 June 2017).

Jensen, J. (2015) 'Broadening the Frame: Inclusive Growth and the Social Investment Perspective' in S. McBride, R. Mahon and G.W. Boychuk (eds), *After '08: Social Policy and the Global Financial Crisis*, Vancouver: UBC Press, 40–58.

Jolly, R. (2011) 'UNICEF, Economists and Economic Policy: Bringing Children into Development Strategies,' UNICEF Social and Economic Policy Working Briefs, October, www.unicef.org/ socialpolicy/files/Jolly_PolicyBrief_October2011_Final.pdf (accessed 14 June 2017).

Jolly, R., L. Emmerij and T.G. Weiss (2009) *UN Ideas that Changed the World*, Bloomington and Indianapolis, Indiana University Press.

Jomo, K.S. and B. Fine (eds) (2006) *The New Development Economics: After the Washington Consensus*, New Delhi: Tulika Books.

Kabeer N. (2012) 'Women's economic empowerment and inclusive growth: labour markets and enterprise development', SIG WORKING PAPER 2012/1, www.idrc.ca/sites/default/files/sp/ Documents%20EN/NK-WEE-Concept-Paper.pdf (accessed 14 June 2017).

Klasen, S. (2010) *Measuring and Monitoring Inclusive Growth: Multiple Definitions, Open Questions, and Some Constructive Proposals*, Asian Development Bank, http://hdl.handle.net/11540/1404 (accessed 14 June 2017).

Midgley, J. (2014) *Social Development: Theory and Practice*, London: Sage.

Midgley, J. (2015) 'Social Investment, Inclusive Growth and the State', in R. Hasmath (ed.), *Inclusive Growth, Development and Welfare Policy: A Criticial Assessment*, New York: Routledge, 91–107.

Mkandawire, T. (2004) (ed.) *Social policy in a development context*, Basingstoke: UNRISD/Palgrave Macmillan.

Mkandawire, T. (2005) *Targeting and universalism in poverty reduction*, Social Policy and Development Programme Paper Number 23, December, Geneva: UNRISD.

Mkandawire, T. (2006) 'Foreword', in G. Cornia (ed.), *Pro-Poor Macroeconomics: Potential and Limitations*, Basingstoke: UNRISD/Palgrave Macmillan.

Ortiz, I., M. Cummins, J. Capaldo and K. Karunanethy (2015) *The Decade of Adjustment: A review of austerity Trends 2010-2020 in 187 countries*, ESS Working Paper No. 53, New York and Geneva: The South Center, Initiative for Policy Dialogue and ILO, www.social-protection.org/gimi/gess/RessourcePDF.action?ressource.ressourceId=53192 (accessed 14 June 2017).

Ranieri, R. and R. Almeida Ramos (2013) *Inclusive Growth: Building Up A Concept*, Working Paper number 104, Brasilia: International Policy Centre for Inclusive Growth (IPC-IG), www.ipc-undp.org/pub/IPCWorkingPaper104.pdf (accessed 14 June 2017).

Saad-Filho, A. (2010) *Growth, Poverty and Inequality: From Washington Consensus to Inclusive Growth*, DESA Working Paper No. 100, ST/ESA/2010/DWP/100, November, www.un.org/esa/desa/papers/2010/wp100_2010.pdf (accessed 14 June 2017).

Siri, G. (2000) *Employment and Social Investment Funds in Latin America*, Socio-Economic Technical Paper (SETP no 7), Geneva: ILO, www.ilo.org/wcmsp5/groups/public/---ed_emp/---emp_policy/---invest/documents/publication/wcms_asist_7591.pdf (accessed 14 June 2017).

Stewart, F. (2014) 'Why horizontal inequalities are important for a shared society', *Development: Special Issue on Shared Societies* 57(1): 46–54.

Townsend, P. (2004) 'From Universalism to Safety Nets: The Rise and Fall of Keynesian Influence on Social Development', in T. Mkandawire (ed.), *Social policy in a development context*, Basingstoke: UNRISD/Palgrave Macmillan, 37–62.

UNRISD (2000) *Visible Hands: Taking Responsibility for Social Development*, an UNRISD Report for Geneva 2000, Geneva: UNRISD.

UNRISD (2010) *Combatting poverty and inequality: Structural change, social policy and politics*, Geneva: UNRISD.

Utting, P., S. Razavi and R. Buchholz (eds) (2012) *The Global Crisis and Transformative Social Change*, London: Palgrave.

FOUR

The challenges of inclusive growth for the developmental welfare state

Huck-ju Kwon

Introduction

The emerging idea of social investment is an important rationale for constructing the welfare state (Deeming and Smyth, 2015). It sees social policy as policy instruments to prepare people for new social risks. Nevertheless, such a perspective is not an entirely new idea. Bismarkian social insurance was introduced in order to serve the needs of industrial workers in Prussia. In the modern era, some East Asian countries have designed social policy programmes and institutions in such a way that they facilitate economic growth. Under such welfare state arrangements, the costs of social policy programmes were kept minimal so that financial resources could be diverted to the investment projects directly serving economic growth. The arrangements also discouraged people from being dependent on state welfare and encouraged them to rely more on support from families, firms and community (Goodman and White, 1998). The welfare state gave priority to the social protection of those who were considered as strategic for industrialisation. The notion of the 'developmental welfare state' captures well such an institutional arrangement of social policy programmes (Kwon, 2005). From the perspective of social investment, the developmental welfare state is a policy regime that places emphasis on the strategic allocation of social protection resources at the macro level, while the recent view of social investment emphasises investment in people at the individual level (see the EU definition for instance, Box 1.1, Chapter One).

In contrast to the idea of social investment, inclusive growth provides a different perspective to welfare state construction. It places much emphasis on inclusion and equity in the process of economic growth and, in terms of social policy therefore, highlights social policy programmes that would bring about equality and inclusion such as social assistance for the poor and the marginalised groups. In the wake of growing inequality in many industrialised countries, inclusive growth has emerged as an alternative model of growth and social protection. This chapter poses a question regarding these different perspectives on social welfare: are they mutually exclusive so that we must choose one over the other, or can they complement each other so that we can balance the emphasis of welfare state construction?

This chapter will argue that the developmental welfare state, which puts a great emphasis on contribution to economic growth in a similar way to social investment, was sustained on the social basis of inclusion and integration, using the Republic of Korean (hereafter Korea) experience as a case study. This chapter will also examine the recent policy debates and the underlying dynamics regarding a transition towards a universal welfare state with the emphasis on inclusion and equality.

The development welfare state: characteristics and changes

The developmental welfare state essentially refers to a policy arrangement of state welfare in which social programmes are primarily utilised as instruments for economic development while social protection for citizens is relegated to being the secondary concern for social policy (Goodman and White, 1998). The efforts of the developmental welfare state were successful in those countries, such as Japan, Korea and Taiwan, who recorded impressive economic growth in the 1980s and 90s. However, it is important to note that the developmental welfare state in its typical form is not particularly inclusive, but rather selective in terms of provision of social protection. It divides citizens into different categories and prioritises certain groups of them over others. Different groups of citizens get different social contingencies. For instance, when public health insurance was introduced in East Asian countries, public officials and industrial workers working in large scale workplaces were covered first by the programme. Later, other groups of people such as farmers and urban informal sector workers came to be included in the programme but their health insurance funds were organised separately. In this separate system of public health insurance, risks were not pooled between people with high and low risks, and redistribution could not take place between high and low income earners.

The developmental welfare state may have been growth orientated but at the same time it was fragmented and selective. It was certainly not inclusive. With such characteristics, the impacts of social policy can be hardly redistributive if not regressive. Nevertheless, social outcomes of the developmental welfare state were impressive in the East Asian countries. Income inequality has been kept minimal in the East Asian economies compared to other economies. Other social indicators such as the Human Development Index (HDI) have pointed out that East Asian societies equipped with developmental welfare state principles performed much better than countries in other regions with similar levels of economic development. So, how were the developmental welfare states, which are selective and fragmented, able to produce inclusive growth? This is the first main question this chapter will seek to answer. This is a very pertinent question, since it will enable us to see whether a welfare state with a strong propensity for social investment and economic growth can be also socially inclusive.

In the wake of the East Asian economic crisis in 1997–98, many East Asian countries strengthened social policies and institutional arrangements. In the case of Korea, a country hit hard by the economic crisis, unemployment benefits were strengthened, not only in terms of monetary levels but coverage was also extended to wider section of the labour force. Public assistant programmes were also upgraded based on the idea of social rights rather than social relief. In other words, the developmental welfare state became more inclusive (Kwon, 2005). At the same time, however, society became more unequal partly because many of those irregular workers were left outside the social protection system despite the changes that were brought about by the welfare reform.

Nevertheless, factors relating to the developmental welfare state cannot explain all of the deepening inequality and increasing precariousness in the labour market. It will be necessary to examine effects of labour market changes since the labour market reforms of the late 1990s. We need to see the impacts of a dramatic shift in the demographic structure towards an ageing society with very low fertility. Once typical family structures of four, including father, mother and two children, are no longer the predominant norm. There is now a wide range of family living arrangements and care cannot be provided by the family as it used to. Will the developmental welfare state be able to contribute to inclusive growth in this post-industrial society? What challenges lie ahead for the developmental welfare state and what are the possible policy alternatives? Can the universal welfare state be the way forward for the Korean society? These are the second group of questions this chapter will seek to answer. In so doing, this chapter will examine the case of Korea in order to discuss the evolution of the developmental welfare state. In particular, this chapter will analyse the underlying social and economic structure in which the welfare state is established and implemented. As Ringen (1987) points out, the welfare state is a state intervention to re-distribute what has been distributed in the market. For this reason, social investment and inclusiveness are not only dependent on the welfare state but also the social and economic structure of the society which exerts the influence on distribution of economic resource and social protection at the first instance.

The social basis of the developmental welfare state

Social policy in East Asia and Korea in particular has been an effective tool for economic development (Holliday, 2000; Ku, 1997; Kwon, 1999). Social protection was first provided to those workers employed in strategic industries so that they could be mobilised for economic development; however, the poor and other vulnerable groups of people were left outside the system of state welfare. Because of these characteristics, social policies tended to have little impacts on poverty reduction and income inequality (Kwon, 2001). Nevertheless, Korea was able to reduce poverty quite impressively during the rapid period of economic growth (see Table 4.1). Given that economic growth does not necessarily reduce poverty, and that social policy had such selective characteristics, it is important to understand the social dynamics which led to inclusive economic growth in Korea.

The apparent paradox can be understood if we pay attention to the social basis of the developmental welfare state in Korean society. The land reform that was undertaken from 1946 to 1955 in Korea was the most significant event that determined the social basis of Korean society. The land reform transformed Korea into a fairly equal society and changed state–society relations as it brought an end to the landowning class as the dominant force in society. Land reform was implemented in three waves from 1946 creating small independent farmers who had been tenant farmers of Korean and Japanese landlords under the Japanese rule (1910–45). After the Second World War, Korea was divided into two halves with a communist regime in the North and liberal government in the South. In the North, the communist government backed by Soviet Russia confiscated farming land from the landlords and distributed it to the collectives of farmers. The land reform in the North created huge social pressure in the South since farmers who constituted the majority of the population had suffered most under Japanese rule and wanted social change after independence. The US military interim government (1945–48) took a first step towards land reform: putting a limit on rent of tenant farming land and selling the land that belonged to Japan's Oriental Development Company to Korean tenants at a price equivalent in value to the average yields for three years. The subsequent land reform was implemented by the Korean government (established in 1948) by 1955. It was based on three principles: first, farmland can only be owned by farmers who actually work in the land; second, each farmer can own farm land up to 3 hectares; and third, farmers cannot contract out their land to others for farming (Sin, 1988). Based on these principles, the government bought land from those who owned more than the limit, or did not farm it themselves, and sold it to people who had been working on the land.

Government managed to buy 60% of the land and sold it to farmers. While the landowners were paid by the government bonds, farmers paid for their land a price equivalent to 1.5 times its average annual production, payable over three years (Kim, 1997). Land reform in Korea was successful in that it created small independent farmers who owned their land and reduced inequalities in landownership (Cho, 2003). The land reform also increased farmers' income simply because they did not have to pay punishing rent to landlord. Further, the access to land transformed the social and economic conditions for many farmers. Farmers tended to make investments in their soils and also established perennials to increase productivity when they owned their own land. In the longer term they would be able to accumulate assets for future investment. In other words, the land reform undertaken in Korea after the Second World War was significant and powerful in social policy terms, in that it increased the level of income and security for farmers who constituted the majority of the population at that time.

With higher income and improved economic security, farmers were able to send their children to school, instead of work (Seokgon Cho, 2003). The Korean government also invested heavily in the education system; the education sector received the largest chunk of the budget, next to defence which had the lion's share. There was an astonishing increase in primary and secondary education in Korea compared to other developing countries in the 1950s and 1960s. By 1959, the number of students in liberal arts secondary schools from both rural and urban areas had increased by 370% on the 1945 level. The number of students who studied in vocational high school increased by 299% and in tertiary education by 1,293% (Cho, 2003). By the late 1950s, the literacy rate reached 90% among the entire population (Cho and Oh, 2003).

As a consequence Korea was a relatively equal society in terms of income and land compared to other developing countries (Rodrik, 1995). For instance, according to the World Bank estimate (Deininger and Squire, 1995), the Gini index was 0.34 in Korea, while it was 0.51 in the Philippines in 1965. A rural population with a high level of education began to form a hugely significant reservoir of labour force well before the Korean government embarked on its industrialisation drive in the 1960s. In other words, the land reform in the 1950s and subsequent education expansion were very powerful drivers of inclusive economic policy and social investment. It is fair to say that their impacts would be stronger than other typical social and economic policy programmes. Table 4.1 shows that poverty was steadily reduced with economic growth.

Table 4.1 Incidence of absolute poverty, South Korea, 1980–91 (%)

	1965	1970	1976	1980	1991
Urban households	54.9	16.2	18.1	10.4	8.7
Rural households	35.8	27.9	11.7	9.0	2.8
All households	40.9	23.4	14.8	9.8	7.6

Note: the absolute poverty line = 121,000 won (1981 price) a month for a five person household.
Source: Adapted from Kwon (1998: 34)

There were other efforts to reduce poverty. For instance, the government implemented policy measures to prevent usurious loans in rural area in 1961. Usury was a widespread practice in rural areas, and was often a route into poverty. The government imposed a rule that the existing loan should be registered and new loans were prohibited (SCNR, 1963: 1104). The existing lenders received a bond from the agricultural co-operatives and farmers could pay back the debt to them with much lower interest. The agricultural co-operatives began to play a role as financial institutions in the rural areas. They supported farmers when they failed to have good harvest and needed access to credit. Elimination of rural usury practice and set-up of rural financial institutions were very effective in preventing poverty.

Another important social basis of inclusive growth was the investment in public health systems. Sudden illness as well as other social contingencies plays a critical role for people to fall into poverty because of the loss of income earning power and the heavy cost burden of medical care in many developing countries. Further, the overall health condition of the population determines the potential for economic growth. In this context it is very important to maintain public health systems to control communicable disease and to prevent unhealthy practices in daily lives in order to achieve economic growth that is also inclusive and reduces poverty. From the 1960s, the Korean government tried to establish public health centres throughout the country. Such efforts continued through the 1970s when most rural areas were covered by public health centres. These public health centres were equipped with simple medical facilities and a small number of junior doctors, who served there instead of mandatory military service.

Although the land reform, the expansion of education and the establishment of public health centres were not implemented as 'social policy' measures per se, they did create the social basis of a relatively equal society in terms of income as well as opportunity. It is very important to see that the developmental welfare state was established within such equal social basis and embedded in social investment.

The evolution of the developmental welfare state

The modern welfare system in Korea began to take its shape in the 1960s under the military government which took power in a coup d'état in 1961. The first social insurance implemented was Industrial Accident Insurance in 1963. It started to cover workers in workplaces with more 500 employees. Industrial Accident Insurance was chosen as the first programme because the Korean government at that time embarked on its first five-year economic development plan and protecting workers in large industrial plants was the priority for the policymakers. National Health Insurance, another main contour of the welfare state, originated from a pilot programme in 1965, and became a compulsory social insurance in 1977. Just like Industrial Accident Insurance, it started with people working in large scale industrial enterprises. The third main programme was the National Pension Programme, which was first legislated in 1972 and implemented later in 1988.

These programmes were all social insurance programmes in which employers and employees each paid 50% of contributions while the government did not take financial responsibility for the programme other than a small amount of administration cost. For this reason, the government was not forced to spend large amounts of the national budget on social protection. In the 1960s and 1970s, the government took fiscal responsibility only for public assistance, which was based on very strict means test. There was no income support programme for unemployed people until 1993.

In a nutshell the developmental welfare state established in the period of rapid economic development aimed to provide protection for those workers strategic for industrialisation. These programmes were slowly extended to wider sections of the population as Korea made good progress in terms of economic development, but the basic nature of social policy remained the same; social protection for the people with gainful work. The poor, the disabled, the elderly and children were supposed to be cared for by their families. The authoritarian government under President Park Chung-hee (in office 1961–79) ruthlessly oppressed political voices that criticised the selective nature of the developmental welfare state. Although President Park believed that the Korean government should 'provide all the people in this country with decent lives as human beings' (Park, 1962: 224), he made it clear that this would be possible only after economic development. He set out an overall policy strategy seeking out 'economy first'. What this chapter argues is that it was possible to maintain the developmental welfare state because it was based on notions of equality and a firm social basis. It is also important to note that industrialisation in Korea coincided with poverty reduction due to universal primary education and expansion of higher education.

In the late 1970s, the social and political basis of the developmental welfare state was slowly but steadily undermined. As the Korean government placed a strong emphasis on heavy-chemical industries for economic growth, which were led by big *Chaebols*, more public resources were diverted to those sectors than others such as small and medium enterprises. There was also a clear trend of inequality as the fruits of economic development were distributed unevenly across the society. As seen in Table 4.2, income inequality actually rose in the late 1970s.

Table 4.2 Income inequality (Gini Index), South Korea, 1965–78

	1965	1970	1972	1974	1976	1978
Korea	0.3365	0.3125	0.312	0.382	0.389	0.369

Source: Ahn (1995)

In this period of time, there were increasing demands from workers for better working conditions and higher wages. The workers' demands were intensified further as the labour supply from rural areas to urban and industrial places dwindled, while working conditions did not improve (Im 1987). Instead of listening to the growing demands, the Park government opted for further political oppression. In consequence, political opposition grew, and calls for democratisation were on the rise. Opposition parties took uncompromising positions, and student and workers unions became involved in political protest against the authoritarian government. In 1979, amid political unrest in many cities, especially in Busan, Korea's second largest city, President Park was assassinated by his security chief in the middle of a brawl among his close political lieutenants.

Amid political uncertainty and turmoil, military general Chun Doo-hwan took over power, using martial law and bloody oppression against democratisation protests. The Chun government implemented a two-pronged policy to consolidate power. First, on the economic front, it pursued a vigorous structural adjustment programme for economic stabilisation and adopted heavy-handed oppression towards trade unions (Haggard and Moon, 1990). Government exercised strong control over fiscal and monetary policy, which led to economic deflation in 1979–81, but the policy appeared to be successful as the Korean economy recovered and got back on course for economic growth. Second, with respect to social policy, the Chun government pledged to establish a welfare state in which citizens would be guaranteed a minimum standard of living. His government set a higher official line of poverty than the previous one, which led to an increase in the number of people receiving public assistance. The government also changed institutional rules for the public health insurance programme so that those who were outside programme could join in the programme.

The welfare state was further extended in the wake of the 1987 presidential election, the first democratic election in 25 years. National Health Insurance became universal, covering all the population and the National Pension Programme was introduced as promised during the election campaign. In 1993, the Employment Insurance Programme was introduced, which included training schemes for the unemployed and cash benefits for income support, but it only started with large scale enterprises. Despite the changes and extension, the developmental welfare state was mainly for those employed in enterprises, considered as part of ongoing policy efforts for economic development rather than for the sake of social protection.

The important changes in terms of rationale and programmes took place in the wake of the East Asian economic crisis in 1997–98. The long-time opposition leader Kim Dae-jung was elected as president in the middle of the economic crisis in 1997 and he convened a tripartite committee in order to push through policy measures to overcome the economic crisis. The tripartite committee was able to forge a social compact in which the government would carry out structural reforms such as labour market, public sector and corporate governance reforms while social protection for the unemployed, the poor and elderly would be strengthened. Based on the social compact the government swiftly extended the coverage of unemployed benefits and relaxed the conditions for entitlements (Kwon, 2003). A range of training programmes were introduced and many job centres were open across the country in order to support the unemployed to search for new jobs. On top of these institutional changes, provision public work projects were implemented to create jobs for those in need of work, although these jobs were often only for the short term.

The most important changes under the Kim government's welfare reform was the introduction of the Minimum Living Standard Guarantee, which is a programme of public assistance for the poor. The previous public assistance programme was based on the concept of poor relief and provided cash or in-kind support to the poor, as officially defined. The poverty line was very low based on a concept of 'absolute' poverty and cash benefits were minimal. In 1997, before the introduction of the new programme, 3.1% of the population received benefits (Ministry of Health and Welfare, 2005). The Minimum Living Standard Guarantee was introduced in 2000 after a long social policy debate, and it set the poverty line based on relative need: a decent standard of living in the context of Korean society, which raised the level of cash and in-kind benefits for the poor. More importantly it brought a new rationale of public assistance: the poor receive support either in cash or in kind as their social right – not as poor relief. In order to implement the new public assistance programme, public officials needed to change their ways of working at the front line: they should serve the citizens' needs. This created a huge demand for public officials and social administrators.

In 2008, the Long-term Care Insurance for the Elderly was introduced alongside the Earned Income Tax Credit for those families with income just over the poverty line. These programmes added new dimensions to the developmental welfare state as social services began to play a major role. Long-term Care Insurance began to provide care service to the elderly, who used to be at the margin of the welfare state. The middle class families can also access long-term care since it is an insurance programme. At the same time it gives affordable options for the welfare state and the healthcare service. Earned Income Tax Credit, which is intended to provide income support, reflects further changing rationale in which the welfare provision is based on notions of social rights.

Figure 4.1 Public spending on social protection, South Korea, 1999–2009 (won, trillion)

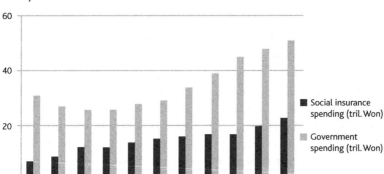

It was extraordinary that Korea strengthened its existing social policies and introduced a new programme in the wake of the East Asian economic crises. Figure 4.1 shows that social expenditure has been steadily increasing. In the past, many developing countries tried to retrench social policy programmes in order to reduce spending on social welfare. At present, many European countries have chosen to implement austerity policies in the aftermath of the global economic crisis. Korea chose to strengthen the developmental welfare state for two reasons. First, the Kim Dae-jung government was elected based on political support from those on low incomes, including those who had been left outside the welfare system. The civil society groups that had argued for reform of public assistance were mainly supporters of President Kim and some members of those civil society groups joined the government. Second, the extension of the developmental welfare state was carried out in order to facilitate the structural reform of the economy. In the wake of the East Asian economic crisis, the Korean government carried out labour market reform as well as public sector and banking sector reforms. The labour market reforms sought flexibility and allowed firms to lay off their workers easily and to employ people on non-regular contracts, which meant short-term and non-renewable contracts. In other words, the extension of the developmental welfare state made itself more inclusive but still developmental.

Dualisation of the labour market and demographic shift

The labour market reforms implemented under the Kim Dae-jung government made the labour market much more flexible than before. The firms could employ workers on short-term contracts and use workers employed via agencies. With the increase in flexibility employment became more precarious, especially for those with non-regular contracts. In 2008, the National Assembly passed a bill that would enforce employers to give regular contracts to those workers with non-regular contracts, if employers wanted them to continue in work after the first two years. It was intended to bring security and pave the way for workers with non-regular contracts to secure work with regular contracts. However, it created a dual labour market structure in which the entrance to the secured employment with regular contract was increasingly difficult. Table 4.3 shows that the proportion of wage earners with non-regular workers has steadily declined but stayed around 32% in 2013 and 2014. It shows that the dual labour market structure has consolidated very firmly. Also, the working conditions are quite different between workers with regular contracts and non-regular contracts. In terms of wages, non-regular workers get on average a wage 11% lower than regular workers, taking into consideration working hours or worker qualifications and other working conditions (National Statistical Office, 2014). A crude comparison (based on averages) shows that a non-regular worker receives only 56% of a regular worker's wage. In terms of the duration of employment in the same firms, regular workers remain much longer than non-regular workers (7 years and one months for regular workers on average compared with 2 years and 7 months for non-regular workers). All in all, non-regular workers are paid less for their employment than regular workers.

Table 4.3 Regular and non-regular workers by employment status, South Korea, 2007–14

	2007	2008	2009	2010	2011	2012	2013	2014
Regular workers	15,731	15,932	16,076	16,617	17,065	17,421	17,743	18,397
Non-regular workers	5,773	5,638	5,374	5,498	5,771	5,809	5,732	5,911
% of non-regular workers	36.7	35.2	33.4	33.1	33.8	33.3	32.3	32.1

Source: National Statistical Office (2014)

The dual labour market structure has exerted downward pressure on the wage levels of non-regular workers and low-waged earners. Regular workers are better organised through trade unions, while firms have been able to take advantage of flexibility in employment contract with non-regular workers. According to OECD statistics, the Korean economy has one of the highest proportion of low wage workers in the world – which is defined as less than two-thirds of the median wage (see Figure 4.2). Such a high proportion is only comparable to that of the US economy.

Dualisation in the labour market together with a rise in income inequality have made Korean society more fragmented, if not polarised, than in the past. Considering that such a trend has taken place in the context of the expansion of the welfare state, an inclusive social policy will need to emphasise employment with job security if further social inequality and fragmentation is to be avoided. Recent studies point out that there has been an increase in conflicts about public policy issues in general and distributional matters in particular (Kwon, 2016).

Another important structural change that has taken place in Korean society is population ageing and the demographic shift to an aged society. It is taking place very rapidly because ageing is combined with very low fertility. It is worth noting that rapid economic growth in the 1970s and 1980s in Korea was also due to demographic shifts. The baby boom generation born in the late 1950s and early 1960s gave a double boost to the economy with higher productivity in large numbers. They are now retiring from work in large numbers, while at the same time the size of the working population has dwindled because of the smaller inflow of the younger population into the labour market. In 2010, people aged over 65 accounted for 10% of the population, and this proportion will increase to 20% in the near future according to the Korea National Statistical Office (KNSO, 2016).

Figure 4.3 shows an international comparison of the size of the working age population, aged 15 to 64, as a percentage of the whole population in three East Asian countries and the USA. As of 2015, Korea still had the highest working age population (as a proportion of the population as a whole) compared to many other OECD nations. Nevertheless, due to the demographic shift to an ageing society with low fertility, the working age population will decline rapidly and it will be one of the lowest in terms of the proportion of the whole population by 2060. The declining size of the workforce presents a challenge to economic expansion and continued increases in GDP, which policymakers now acknowledge can only be offset by increases in the productivity of the labour force. This suggests that Korea must

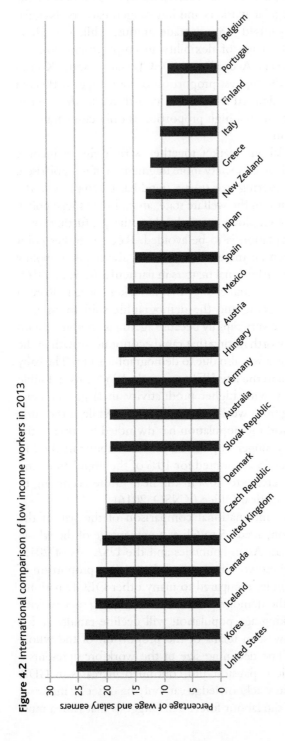

Figure 4.2 International comparison of low income workers in 2013

Source: OECD data (wages and earnings) https://data.oecd.org/earnwage/wage-levels.htm

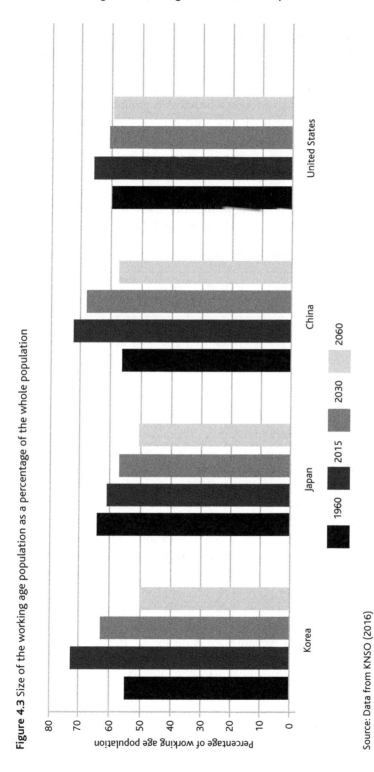

Figure 4.3 Size of the working age population as a percentage of the whole population

Source: Data from KNSO (2016)

move towards an economic growth strategy based on a high increase in productivity. We now see the rising significance of social investment paradigm in Korea, as policymakers consequently seek to step up investments in education and skills. This contrasts with the previous development strategy that focused heavily on production factors.

Together with the demographic shift it is very important to note dramatic changes in household structure. As shown in Table 4.4, there have been two separate transitions in household structure. First, along with industrialisation and urbanisation the traditional household structure comprising extended family of three generations gave way to the nuclear family, including young couple and small children. This transition took place from the 1980s up until the early 2000s.

Table 4.4 Households by number of persons, South Korea (% of all households)

	One	Two	Three	Four	More than five	Average
1980	4.8	10.5	14.5	20.3	49.9	4.55
1990	9.0	13.8	19.1	29.5	28.7	3.71
2000	15.5	19.1	20.9	31.1	13.4	3.22
2010	23.9	24.3	21.3	22.5	8.1	2.70

Source: Data from KNSO (2016)

The second transition, which took place in the 2000s, shows a diversification of household structure. There is no predominant type of households. It can be also interpreted as the separation of the extended family and nuclear family household. Family members do not live with extended family members in the same households. Many elderly people now live alone in one-member households. Young married couples often live in separate households for many reasons, one typical reason being employment in different locations. The diversification of household structure suggests that family members cannot provide social protection including care for the elderly and children as they did in the past.

All in all, dualisation of the labour market and demographic shifts, together with changing family structures, indicates that the social basis of the developmental welfare state is no longer the same as before. There is also the growing need for social protection for the elderly, young families, unemployed and other people with specific social risks. These social changes show that social investment strategy and inclusive growth are a dual imperative for Korean society.

Towards a universal welfare state?

In the run up to the presidential election in December 2012, there was a series of debates between political parties focused on social policy issues. The opposition party, the Democratic Party, explored different social policy in various elections before the 2012 presidential election. It first flagged up the idea of universal welfare in the local educational authority elections in relation to school meals in 2010. The candidates from the Democratic Party promised that they would provide all school children with free school meals for lunch, which appealed to many parents. After the successful campaign for local elections the Democratic Party went further, promising 'free welfare' such as free healthcare and free university education in the general election for the National Assembly in April 2013. Such promises did not sit well with the electorate, with many public and political commentators seeing them as populist.

While the Democratic Party was keen to make social protection its main election programme, the Saenuri Party candidate, Park Geun-hye, also gave social welfare high priority in her campaign. The main idea of her programme was to provide all citizens with social protection to meet their specific needs. Welfare benefits should be tailored to each citizens' needs according to their position in the life cycle. It was a bold move for a candidate from the Saenuri Party since the incumbent President Lee (in office 2008–13) did not give social protection policy priority.

During the election campaign, the governing party pledged that it would introduce new non-contributory public pensions for the elderly over 65 and state-financed universal kindergarten programme for children aged two to five. These new programmes signified an important landmark in the evolution of the developmental welfare state. It was a recognition that those who did not have pension entitlements, despite old age, nevertheless deserve a public pension as their social right.

What emerged from the political debate during the presidential election was a wide political recognition about social risks and the growing need for social protection. It is not difficult to understand why the two major political parties were so keen on making pledges for social protection for social needs and risks, given the underlying demographic shift towards an ageing society and the dualisation of the labour market.

The expansion of childcare programmes was a social investment orientated policy response to demographic ageing with low fertility. Extensive childcare programmes would support families with children so that young mothers could participate in the labour market. It was also expected that early childhood education would increase children's cognitive capability, which would in turn increase productive potential for the future: a typical feature of social investment thinking. Although social risks and needs for social protection have not been effectively addressed by the developmental welfare state perspective in Korea, policymakers are now shifting the emphasis towards the social investment perspective in social policy. At present, however, it is difficult to argue that the developmental welfare state has moved fully towards a more inclusive universal welfare state.

Despite the policy promises, the Park Geun-hye government, once in office, backtracked about old age public pensions and childcare programmes in order to reduce estimated social expenditure on those programmes. For instance, the number of the elderly who would receive public basic pensions was reduced and the level of pensions was reduced to that received for other public benefits. The government also wanted to share the financial burden for childcare programmes with local governments. More importantly the existing social insurance programmes, such as the National Pension Programme and Employment Insurance Programmes, have not covered all the targeted population. For example, only 42.5% of the working population actively contribute to the public pension programme, becoming entitled to the pension on retirement (Kang, 2011).

Considering the Park government's change of policy stance it would be difficult to see the developmental welfare state giving way to the universal welfare state. It will take time for the universal welfare state to take shape in Korean society. Not only because a universal welfare state will need new social programmes, as well as the strengthening of existing programmes, but also the concept of the universal welfare state has yet to be clarified in Korea's political discourse. The future welfare state must be based on a social investment strategy in the context of demographic shift.

The discussion so far in this chapter indicates that a strategy of inclusive growth is necessary for Korean society to sustain economic growth. Dual labour market and polarised income distribution may lead to short-term economic gains but social conflicts, which will inevitably increase in the context of rising inequality, will certainly cost more in the longer term. On the contrary, the present Korean government has pursued further flexibility in the labour market for the past couple of years, but have not made any significant progress. It would take time to create a universal welfare state combined with an inclusive growth strategy in the labour market.

Concluding remarks

From a comparative perspective, the evolution of the developmental welfare state in Korea shows a significant relationship between social investment and inclusive growth. The social investment strategy emphasises the investment credentials of the welfare state, while the policy orientation of inclusive growth places a strong emphasis on equity and inclusion in the market economy. They are both an antidote to the intrinsic goal of the systems that they are concerned with. The idea of social investment demands consideration of the effect of economic growth on the welfare state, with the primary goal of social protection, while the notion of inclusive growth emphasises inclusion in the capitalist market economy, which pursues economic growth. At the same time social investment and inclusive growth seem to contradict each other. This discussion of the evolution of the developmental welfare state indicates that social investment and inclusive growth should complement each other for the effective implementation of each strategy. The relentless pursuit of economic development in combination with the developmental welfare state was possible in Korea in the 1970s and 1908s on the basis of the social basis of equality and inclusion. Since the late 1990s, when the labour market reforms were carried out, labour market idealisation together with population ageing resulted in increases in inequality and fragmentation among the population. Such social trends undermine social investment credentials, as well as the social protection capability of the development welfare state, despite the rapid increase in social spending in recent years. Among policy remedies is the universal welfare state, but policy changes for inclusive growth such as increase in job security and reduction of low wage jobs are necessary. Social investment and inclusive growth are an odd couple but they should remain married.

References

Ahn, K. (1995) 'Economic Development and Income Distribution in Korea', *Journal of Korean Economic Development* 1(1): 53–76 (in Korean).

Cho, S. (2003) 'Land Reform and Capitalism in Korea', in C. Yoo (ed.), *The History of the Korean Development Model and its Crisis* (in Korean), Seoul: Cobook.

Cho, S. and Oh, Y. (2003) 'The Formation of Some Preconditions for the Condensed Growth in the 1950s', *Donghyanggwa Chonmang* 59: 258–302 (in Korean).

Deeming, C. and Smyth, P. (2015) 'Social Investment after Neoliberalism: Policy Paradigms and Political Platforms', *Journal of Social Policy* 44(2): 297–318.

Deininger, K. and Squire, L. (1995) *Measuring income inequality: A new data base*, Washington DC: World Bank.

Goodman, R. and White, G. (1998) 'Welfare Orientalism and the Search for an East Asian Welfare Model', in R. Goodman, G. White, and H.J. Kwon (eds), *The East Asian Welfare Model: Welfare Orientalism and the State*, London: Routledge, 3–24.

Haggard, S. and Moon, C.I. (1990) 'Institutions and Economic Policy: Theory and a Korean Case Study', *World Politics* 42 (2): 210–37.

Holliday, I. (2000) 'Productivist welfare capitalism: Social policy in East Asia', *Political Studies* 48(4): 706–23.

Im, H. (1987) 'The Rise of Bureaucratic Authoritarianism in South Korea', *World Politics* 39(2).

Kang, S. (2011) 'Estimation of the Blind Spot of the National Pension Programme and the Impact on Old age Poverty in relation to the Maturity of the Programme', *Fiscal Studies* 4(2) (in Korean).

Kim, S. (1997) 'A Study of the Land Reform in Korea', in K. Kim (ed.), *Essays on Korean Economic History*, Seoul: Areum.

KNSO (Korea National Statistical Office) (2016) 'General Survey of Population', http://meta.narastat.kr/metasvc/svc/SvcMetaDcDtaPopup.do?orgId=101&confmNo=101001&kosisYn=Y

Ku, Y.-W. (1997) *Welfare Capitalism in Taiwan: State, Economy, and Social Policy*, London: Macmillan.

Kwon, H.J. (1999) *The Welfare State in Korea: The Politics of Legitimation*. London: Macmillan.

Kwon, H.J. (2001) 'Income transfers to the elderly in Korea and Taiwan', *Journal of Social Policy* 30: 81–93.

Kwon, H.J. (2003) 'Advocacy coalitions and the politics of welfare in Korea after the economic crisis', *Policy & Politics* 31(1): 69–83.

Kwon, H.J. (2005) 'Transforming the Developmental Welfare State in East Asia', *Development and Change* 36(3): 477–97.

Kwon, H.J. (2016) 'Social Conflicts and Policy Options for Social Integration in Korea: a structural perspective', *Korea Public Administration Review* 54(2): 93–116 (in Korean).

Kwon, S. (1998) 'The Korean experience of poverty reduction: lessons and prospects', in *UNDP, Combating Poverty: The Korean Experience*, Seoul: United Nations Development Programme, 158–56.

Ministry of Health and Welfare (2005) *Yearbook of Health and Statistics*, Seoul: MoHW.

National Statistical Office (2014) 'Extra Survey on Employment by Employment Status', Seoul: National Statistical Office (in Korean).

Park, C.H. (1962) *Our Nation's Path: Ideology of Social Reconstruction*, Seoul: Hollym.

Ringen, S. (1987) *The Possibility of Politics: a study in the political economy of the welfare state*, Oxford: Clarendon Press.

Rodrik, D. (1995) 'Getting Intervention Right: How South Korea and Taiwan Grew Rich', *Economic Policy* 10(1): 55–107.

SCNR (1963) *History of the Korean Military Revolution*, Volume 1, Seoul: Supreme Council for National Reconstruction.

Sin, P. (1988) 'Comparative Research on Land Refrom in Korea and Taiwan', *Korea and World Politics* 4(2) (in Korean).

Part II
Policy applications

FIVE

Measuring and monitoring inclusive growth in developing and advanced economies: multiple definitions, open questions and some constructive proposals

Stephan Klasen

Introduction

Inclusive growth has been coined as a new approach in the discourse on economic development to ensure that economic growth reaches broader social and economic objectives, beyond higher per capita incomes. At the same time, there exists no clear definition or indicators to monitor progress in inclusive growth at the country, project or programme level. This chapter reviews existing definitions of inclusive growth and proposes an approach to defining and measuring inclusive growth as non-discriminatory and disadvantage-reducing growth.

Despite high overall economic growth rates in many developing countries in the past two decades, increasing concern has been voiced by many policymakers and in international organisations that this growth has been too uneven and was often accompanied by rising income inequality. In addition, it appeared that disadvantaged groups, including members of ethnic minorities, people in remote rural locations and women, were not benefitting proportionately from this rapid economic growth. This question of growth leaving poor and disadvantaged people behind was of considerable relevance in political debates in India surrounding the national election in 2004. There the new government called for 'inclusive growth' as a strategy to overcome these inequalities and disadvantages and, in fact, India's 11th five-year plan (2007–12) was entitled 'inclusive growth' and included concrete strategies to promote wellbeing and participation of disadvantaged groups (Government of India, 2008).

This call for inclusive growth was taken up by the Eminent Persons Group charged by the Asian Development Bank (ADB) to advise on its future strategy. There it recommended a shift from a focus of poverty reduction to a shift on inclusive growth.

> In many countries, rising incomes, while reducing overall poverty, have been associated with rising disparities. These disparities, left unchecked, could threaten the fragile political consensus for economic reforms, or even political stability. … The solution lies in the continuation of pro-growth economic strategies—but with a much sharper focus on ensuring that the economic opportunities created by growth are available to all—particularly the poor—to the maximum extent possible. (ADB, 2007: 13–14)

Since then, inclusive growth has been discussed as a central development paradigm at the World Bank, OECD and UNDP, among other organisations. While this emphasis is thus broadly shared, there are many ways to view this concept. Some of these concepts are rather vague and do not lend themselves to easy quantitative operationalisation, while other are quite specific but may not capture the essence of the concept. To make matters worse, the World Bank has also produced definitions of inclusive growth that are at odds with the ADB concept of inclusive growth. Moreover, there is a range of policy documents from the World Bank, OECD, UNDP and academia on closely related concepts, such as pro-poor growth or equality of opportunities. Given the lack of clarity of the concept, UNDP helpfully invites users of its website to propose a definition themselves (UNDP, 2016).

Inclusive growth has, however, not only been a concept used in the discourse on economic development, but its relevance is seen in the context of advanced economies as well. For example, the OECD (2014) has provided an inclusive growth framework for its membership (of advanced industrialised nations). The World Economic Forum (WEF, 2015) has generated an inclusive growth diagnostic that can be used for all countries of the world and the Scottish Government has chosen inclusive growth as one of its pillars for its economic strategy (Scottish Government, 2015). More recently, inclusive growth has also been used as a key goal for sub-national entities, in particular cities where inequalities, including spatial inequalities, can be quite large and particularly worrying (OECD, 2016; Beatty et al, 2016).

This chapter will briefly discuss different concepts of inclusive growth, highlight the most important content and differences in definitions, and finally proposes a working definition and indicators to measure and monitor inclusive growth. I will start with some conceptual questions, then examine existing definitions in policy documents and policy research documents of the ADB, the first international organisation to engage in detail with the concept, and other organisations before moving towards some proposals for a working definition of inclusive growth, including some approaches to measurement.

What could inclusive growth mean? Some conceptual discussion[1]

To be meaningful and add a new dimension, inclusive growth (IG) must be more than broad-based economic growth. While (economic) growth itself is a well-defined narrow concept (increase in economic output or income), 'inclusive' growth is, by implication, focusing on a *subset* of such growth episodes: not all growth episodes are inclusive and the task is to see which ones are (and which ones are not). This also means that growth is a *necessary* condition for 'inclusive growth'; there is, by implication, no such thing as an 'inclusive contraction'.[2] So the question becomes what characterises those episodes that qualify for the label 'inclusive'? Here two options are possible. One is a focus on *process* in the sense that the actual growth 'included' a lot of people as active participants in that growth; that is, IG is growth based on inputs from a large number of people. In this sense, it is somewhat related to the much older terms of 'broad-based' or the even older term 'labour intensive' growth. These concepts have recently been resuscitated in a slightly amended form in the World Bank's new goal on 'shared prosperity', measured as the growth rate of the poorest 40%. These terms are not quite the same, since 'inclusive' carries with it the notion of non-discrimination among the participants in it, while this is less clear with the other terms. Thus in this sense 'inclusive growth' is broad-based growth where *non-discriminatory participation* in that growth is a key characteristic of that growth.

The second option is a focus on *outcomes* of the growth process; thus IG is growth that includes many people as its beneficiaries. This is closely related to the concept of pro-poor growth about which there has been much discussion in recent years (see, for example, Klasen 2008 for a summary of these discussions). Pro-poor growth, in its (weak) absolute definition, refers to growth that leads to income growth of the poor; in its relative definition, it refers to growth that leads to disproportionate increases in incomes among the poor – so it is accompanied by declining inequality.

IG goes beyond the people below the poverty line, but this makes the concept very broad. IG (interpreted in terms of outcomes) is not quite the same as pro-poor growth either for two reasons. First, there is the question whether it is related to the absolute or relative definition; if it was related to the absolute definition of pro-poor growth, it would merely be growth that is poverty reducing. But logically this cannot be the case: the call for IG (both in the documents from India, the ADB and other actors) emphasises that recent growth episodes in Asia and other parts of the developing world that were accompanied by falling poverty (but rising disparities) were not inclusive; thus the call for IG must be more than pro-poor growth in the absolute definition. Thus IG ought to be related to the relative definition of pro-poor growth, an issue that is taken up below.

But there could be a second difference to pro-poor growth: pro-poor growth focuses on people below the poverty line, while IG is arguably more general; it wants growth to benefit all stripes of society, including the poor, the near-poor, middle income groups, and even the rich. In the extreme, one could argue that 'inclusive' growth is growth that benefits all, a rising tide that lifts all boats, or a trickling down to all. Interpreted in this broad sense (growth for all), it becomes rather meaningless. Of course, one might want to redefine what is meant by 'inclusive' and not mean 'all'. For example, one could limit the 'inclusiveness' to the poor under the respective national or international poverty line (then we are back to pro-poor growth). On the other hand, IG could be defined as benefitting mainly those groups that are otherwise disadvantaged; the latter should more appropriately called 'disadvantage-reducing' growth. Here one could particularly think about growth that reduces regional, ethnic or gender disadvantages and this might be one useful way to differentiate an outcome focus of IG from pro-poor growth. Thus in the outcome dimension, IG could be termed 'disadvantage-reducing' growth. The quote from the ADB cited earlier suggests an emphasis in this direction.

An approach that considers both process and outcome aspects is particularly useful for defining IG. It appears to me that including the process aspect of IG has considerably more bite and novelty and moves the debate forward, particularly also vis-à-vis debates on poverty reduction and pro-poor growth. If one considers outcomes, IG should not just focus on (income) poverty reduction; interpreting it in terms of 'disadvantage-reducing growth' is potentially more interesting. Thus a conceptual approach to IG could be 'non-discriminatory' growth, thus granting equal *non-discriminatory access to growth, plus disadvantage-reducing growth*, thus reducing disparities of disadvantaged groups.

Viewed in this way, IG can easily be extended to non-income dimensions of wellbeing. In all of this discussion, growth itself was limited to the income dimension. Now one could easily expand the focus to improvements in non-income dimensions of wellbeing, such as health and education. Following others, let us call this inclusive development (see McKinley, 2010, and Rauniyar and Kanbur, 2010). Also here one could have a process and an outcome orientation; for example, was growth in education based on non-discriminatory participation of all versus did the growth of education benefit all? Here an outcome focus is just as interesting and novel as a process focus and possibly even more so. In fact, a process focus, interpreted narrowly in the sense of the production of these non-income dimensions of wellbeing, asks some rather narrow and unusual (but not uninteresting) questions (such as did the growth of education make non-discriminatory use of educators from all stripes of society?). In contrast, an outcome focus in non-income dimensions makes a lot of sense: did improvements in education and health benefit all, particularly the most disadvantaged? Thus inclusive development as 'disadvantage-reducing' improvements in non-income dimensions of wellbeing appears to be a particularly promising concept. Thus if we are to consider IG in non-income dimensions – inclusive development – an outcome orientation has much to recommend itself. While this is conceptually interesting, it is quite far from the basic approach taken by many actors, including ADB, to IG which is focused on characterising *income* growth episodes. Thinking about process and outcomes and improvements during episodes of expansion in non-income dimensions would go beyond this focus and would be well worth examining in future work.

A case study: IG in ADB's Strategy 2020

To illustrate how IG has been used, it is useful to study the ADB's Strategy 2020, one of the first users of the term inclusive growth. Asian Development Bank's Strategy 2020 calls for IG as one of the three strategic pillars of ADB engagement (the other two are environmental sustainability and regional integration). While IG is not precisely defined in the document, it will lead to two 'strategic focuses: first, high sustainable (income) growth will create and expand economic opportunities. Second, broader access to these opportunities to these opportunities will ensure that members of society can participate in and benefit from growth' (ADB, 2008: 11). A few items are notable about this approach to IG. First, it is entirely forward-looking. It focuses on what future growth can achieve in terms of being more inclusive, not on how inclusive (or not) current growth is or has been.[3] Second, it has a strong emphasis on the *process* aspect of growth, particularly in the first strategic focus, which emphasises the broadening of opportunities to participate. Third, the second strategic focus on broadening access is quite close to the twin ideas of non-discriminatory participation and disadvantage-reducing growth and thus here it combines both a process as well as an outcome focus. In this sense, it goes a bit further than the proposal by the Eminent Persons Group which focused largely on disadvantage-reducing growth.

Also, ADB emphasises the process aspect of IG. Contrary to the conceptual foundation for IG which ADB lays in the first four chapters of its Strategy 2020, a closer inspection on the priority interventions and core areas of operations reveals that the operational part of Strategy 2020 is very much focused on the process aspect of IG, with strong emphasis on improvements in infrastructure, market access, education and financial intermediation. Safety nets, redistribution and disadvantage reduction is limited to some basic social protection, safety nets to prevent extreme deprivation, measures to promote gender equity, and initiatives that promote human capacities (and thus their potential to participate in growth). Also, there is strong primacy of economic growth as the foundation of all efforts to promote IG is not questioned.[4]

At the same time, the ADB does not have clear indicators to monitor its contribution to IG. This discussion suggests that at the overall strategic level, ADB basically proposes a largely process-oriented approach to IG, emphasising growth that enhances opportunities and equalises access to these opportunities.[5] It is also notable that the Strategy 2020 does not include any clear indicators to monitor its performance in terms of IG. This is somewhat surprising since ADB developed a set of indicators in its so-called Results Framework that is intended to monitor its progress towards Strategy 2020. In this Results Framework, IG does not figure, while regional cooperation and environmental sustainability as well as private sector development have target indicators (albeit at the output and not the outcome level). At the highest level (level 1), outcomes are monitored using Millennium Development Goals (MDGs), GDP, and outcomes in infrastructure, business environment, governance, regional integration, and trade;[6] at the next level, the contribution of ADB to country outcomes (level 2) is measured by listing outputs in the five operational areas (transport, water, energy, finance and education) which are, incidentally, not identical to the five core operational areas (infrastructure, finance, education, environment and regional integration). Also, the Strategy only includes a commitment to have 80% of ADB projects in these five core operational areas by 2012, but no commitments on the contribution of ADB to IG. Thus at this stage, there does not appear to be an institutional process based on the 2020 Strategy or the Results Framework that systematically tracks progress in IG and the ADB contribution to it. As a result, the development effectiveness reports of the ADB (see ADB, 2009 and 2010) only talk about the contribution of ADB operations to IG at a very general level.

If inclusive growth is to be taken as more than an overarching concept that guides some of its work, it is clearly useful and important for ADB to develop clear indicators for IG that will allow it to monitor IG at the country level, including its contribution to it through its lending, policy, and knowledge work. The Results Framework would clearly be a useful place to incorporate such indicators.

Thus while ADB has put the concept of IG at the centre of its policy framework, it is not operational at this stage. At the same time, there are a number of research and policy research documents produced by, or on behalf of, the ADB as well as other development organisations that have examined the concept of IG in considerably more depth. These are discussed in turn. While these are all useful contributions to the debate on IG, the fact that none of them have led to a clear approach to monitor IG in an operational fashion suggest that the debate on this subject is not complete.[7]

Research and policy documents on IG

Rauniyar and Kanbur (2010): IG is growth with declining inequality

Rauniyar and Kanbur (2010) provide a literature survey of the uses of IG within the ADB, discuss conceptual issues surrounding IG, and then propose a precise definition of it. Their definition of inclusive (income) growth is growth that is accompanied by declining (income) inequality. This is nearly identical to the concept of relative pro-poor growth which is also growth accompanied by declining income inequality between the poor and the non-poor. The only (slight) difference is that relative pro-poor growth focuses on the relative growth and inequality of the poor versus the non-poor, while IG considers changes in inequality more generally. One can construct cases where growth is relatively pro-poor in the sense that income growth of the poor was faster than among the non-poor (thus reducing inequality between the two groups) while it might still be non-inclusive if the income growth of the poorer non-poor was smaller than the income growth of the rich so that overall inequality is still increasing. In practice, this is rather rare so that in virtually all cases relative pro-poor growth and IG defined in this way will yield the same results. In my view, defining IG in this way does not add much to the concept.

The extension to non-income dimensions is more interesting because this is considered more rarely. But also here, inclusive development (improvements in non-income dimensions of wellbeing accompanied by declining inequality in these dimensions) is mostly identical to declining relative pro-poor growth in non-income dimensions, an issue examined in detail by Klasen (2008) and Grosse et al (2008).

In short, defining IG as growth with declining inequality in income and non-income dimensions does not, in my view, add much beyond the existing pro-poor growth concepts.

Ali and Son (2007): IG as pro-poor improvements in social opportunities

This paper defines IG as pro-poor improvements in social opportunities. It examines to what extent social opportunities (such as access to health or education) are distributed along the income distribution and how this distribution changes over time; IG is if these improvements are tilted towards the income poor.[8] So it is entirely concerned about levels and trends in non-income dimensions of wellbeing, how they are distributed along the income distribution, and whether the improvements were pro-poor or not. This concept of IG is very closely related to the Non-Income Growth Incidence Curves proposed by Klasen (2008) and Grosse et al (2008), where growth incidence curves are drawn for improvements of non-income dimensions of wellbeing such as education or health.

This formulation of IG is quite different from other ADB IG concepts. While this paper emanates from the ADB, it seems at odds with the most other ADB documents on IG which are all concerned about the pattern of *income* growth in one way or another, an issue that does not arise at all in the Ali-Son framework. Thus, this paper is fitting into an approach examining the patterns of non-income levels of wellbeing, which is not the starting point of ADB's approach to IG (but could be an valuable extension and addition). Clearly one can have pro-poor improvements in health or education with little or no income growth (as demonstrated by the examples of Sri Lanka, Kerala or some Latin American countries in the 1970s and 1980s); much of it will depend on public policies which may take place with or without economic growth. The precise link between income growth and this form of 'inclusive' growth is not at all investigated.

Linking this concept to the growth process might be a way forward. One could examine the relationship between income growth and the opportunity curves in two ways to bring it closer to the IG debate. First, one could examine to what extent income growth is affected by social opportunity curves. For example, if social opportunities are more equally distributed, does this insure greater growth and greater participation of the poor in growth? Second, the reverse question is also relevant: To what extent does income growth promote more pro-poor expansions of social opportunities.

Ali and Zhuang (2007), Zhuang and Ali (2012): IG promotes equal opportunities and equal access to them

In two different papers, Ali and Zhuang (2007), Zhuang and Ali (2012) define 'inclusive growth' as growth that promotes equal opportunities and increases access to these opportunities: growth that allows all members of society to participate in and contribute equally to economic growth, regardless of individual circumstances. Given the role these papers played in Strategy 2020, they are quite closely related to the IG concept discussed there. But they go beyond that. Their definition of IG is quite close to two concepts. The first is the concept of pro-poor growth advocated by the Development Assistance Committee of the OECD (OECD-DAC) which calls for a pace and pattern of growth that leads to rapid poverty reduction. A pro-poor growth process must allow poor women and men to participate actively in, and benefit from economic growth. The differences are threefold:

- The Ali and Zhuang definition is concerned about the overall pattern of the growth process, while OECD-DAC focuses on how growth affects the poor (as agents and beneficiaries).
- Also, the OECD-DAC concept allows for growth to be pro-poor if the poor are important beneficiaries of growth (such as through the tax-transfer system) even if they are not active participants, which is not allowed for in the Ali and Zhuang definition; thus it is more outcome-focused while Ali and Zhuang is more process-oriented.
- Lastly, the OECD-DAC approach explicitly considers poverty to be a multidimensional phenomenon and thus the impact of growth on non-income dimensions of poverty are important (not only to the extent they affect growth but also to the extent they affect wellbeing of the poor).

The Ali and Zhuang definition is also closely related to the concept of equal opportunities of John Roemer (1998) which was taken up by the World Bank's 2006 WDR Equity in Development and a range of research papers (such as Bourguignon et al, 2007; Ferreira and Gignoux, 2008). Equality of opportunities exists if a person's wellbeing (usually measured in income terms; that is, that person's income) is only related to effort, but not to individual circumstance. Growth that promotes equality of opportunity would be IG in that definition.

To take this approach seriously would require a great deal of worthwhile conceptual and empirical work. First, one would need to examine to what inequality of opportunities exist in Asia, a demanding but worthwhile research programme that would involve rather complex micro data analysis (see Ferreira and Gignoux, 2008, for such an analysis for selected Latin American countries). In practice, one would have to consider to what extent achievements of individuals in income and non-income dimensions of wellbeing are related to circumstances beyond the control of individuals versus individual choices and efforts. After this has been established, one would then have to examine to what extent the growth process reduced this inequality of opportunities. This would involve examining whether the impact of circumstances on individual incomes has shrunk over time. Of course, ADB would then probably also want to know to what extent this reduction in inequality of opportunities was related to policies and programmes of governments and donors (such as the ADB). Clearly, taking the idea of growth with equal opportunities seriously in this context would go far beyond the scope of this current policy research programme, but it would be a very interesting, worthwhile and policy-relevant research programme to examine levels and trends in inequality of opportunities in the Asian context. It is likely that this inequality of opportunities exist in many Asian countries (often affecting ethnic minorities, remotely located people, women, migrants, among others).

Thus this concept of IG is indeed very interesting and relevant. As it appears that ADB's Strategy 2020 is closely related to this approach, a logical next step would be for ADB to start a work programme that examines the extent of inequality of opportunities and to what extent it can be overcome by different types of growth processes. How else could one conclude that growth was based on equal opportunities or expanded them?

ADB Brief on Implementing Strategy 2020: Inclusive Growth

Partly in response to this work programme on trying to define indicators for monitoring IG at the country and programme/project level, the Strategy and Policy Department of ADB produced – in May 2010 – a short draft brief on IG. The note largely restates the Strategy 2020 approach to IG and then moves on to argue to what extent the operational activities of ADB in the fields of infrastructure and human capital can be seen as furthering IG, as they either are part of an overall country-strategy promoting IG, or directly or indirectly promote participation of disadvantaged groups in growth. While it is likely that many of the discussed projects could be seen as 'inclusive' in the sense advocated here (non-discriminatory and disadvantage-reducing growth), the brief entirely sidesteps the question what exactly IG is, what income growth episodes that are not inclusive look like, and to what extent one can precisely measure a contribution to inclusive growth. The paper also does not clarify the role of IG targets (if any) for the Result Framework of Strategy 2020.

World Bank, 2009: Pace, Pattern plus Productive Employment

In many ways, the World Bank's approach to IG is quite similar to the OECD-DAC approach to pro-poor growth. It is also concerned about the pace and pattern of economic growth. The main new idea in the World Bank approach (which is also rather vague and does not clearly distinguish itself from other approaches) is to focus on *productive employment* as an important element of IG. The idea is (presumably) that increasing employment (number of jobs) and productivity of employment (earnings from jobs) is particularly important for a sustainable growth strategy that leads to poverty reduction as the poor mostly rely on labour as their most important asset. Thus the main distinction in this IG approach to a more general focus on pro-poor growth (and thus, for example, the OECD-DAC approach) is that one concentrates on the poor as participants and contributors to economic growth and explicitly rules out a focus on the poor as beneficiaries of growth (for example, through transfer programmes or explicit redistribution). In that sense, the IG approach highlighted here bears some relation to the also more process-oriented approach of Ali and Zhuang (2007), Zhuang and Ali (2012); but it does not lend itself easily to monitoring using a simple set of indicators.

UNDP approach: all of the above plus empowerment

UNDP recently renamed its International Poverty Center in Brasilia the International Policy Center on Inclusive Growth. On its website, it does not produce a very formal definition of IG, but emphasises that IG is growth with low and declining inequality, economic and political participation of the poor in the growth process, and benefit sharing from that process.[9] It is thus perhaps the broadest of the concepts discussed here, including process and outcome, income and non-income dimensions, and participation and decision making. At the same time, this concept would require a very broad set of indicators and surely then the question would arise how to weight and aggregate the many concepts that are included in this concept of IG.

OECD Inclusive Growth Framework (OECD, 2014)

The OECD emphasises in its framework for IG that not only income growth matters for improving living standards, but also income inequality, and key non-income dimensions of wellbeing such as good health and employment. It first transforms life expectancy and unemployment into equivalent income based on subjective wellbeing regressions, and then aggregate income using Atkinson's approach of applying a penalty for income inequality. Thus its concept of IG is (implicitly) one that is associated with rising life expectancy, falling unemployment and lower income inequality. While this proposal is a useful addition to the debate, particularly with its reference to employment and inequality, the OECD concept appears to be really another multidimensional wellbeing indicator. While it hints at process, it ultimately remains focused on outcomes, albeit in a multidimensional setting, and it remains wedded to the primacy of incomes by translating achievements in non-income dimensions into equivalent incomes. This latter transformation creates additional difficulties, including the reliance on a problematic subjective wellbeing indicator, as well as the difficulty of considering inequality in non-income dimensions in this approach.

World Economic Forum Inclusive Growth and Development Report (WEF, 2015, 2017)

The World Economic Forum provides a scorecard for countries using a wide array of indicators to assess the 'structural and institutional features of a modern economy that particularly matter for achieving broad-based improvement in living standards' (WEF, 2015: 18). Dozens of (often subjective) indicators are consulted in a dashboard approach, sorted into seven pillars (education, employment, assets, financial intermediation, corruption, services and fiscal transfers). Again this considers a useful set of issues and the approach covering the whole world is interesting and unique. At the same time, it mixes process with outcome issues, is quite narrowly focused on economic issues, and of course the subjective assessments are open to question. At the time of going to press, the WEF had compiled and published its composite global index, the 'Inclusive Development Index' (IDI) (WEF, 2017), measuring the accumulated level as well as the most recent five-year trends that allow governments and stakeholders to assess the effect of changes in policy and conditions within a typical political cycle.

'Inclusive growth' priority as part of Scotland's economic strategy (Scottish Government, 2015)

As an example of a policy document using IG, we examine Scotland's economic strategy which sees IG as one of its four priority areas. In this document, IG includes areas of attention: fair work (mainly concerned about living wages), inequalities in access into the labour market and in health outcomes, reduction of inequality of opportunities through interventions in early childhood and education, and reductions in regional inequality through investments in backward regions. While this document does not propose a clear definition of IG, it is focused quite strongly on processes (as well as some outcomes), and has a strong emphasis on disadvantage reduction, which will also be highlighted below.

Categorising the concepts

In Table 5.1, an attempt is made to categorise the various concepts along different dimensions to see their differences, relative merits and drawbacks. While this does not capture the complexity of the concepts, it might help organise ideas.

Table 5.1 Different approaches to inclusive growth

Concept	Key idea	Process/Outcome	Income/Non-Income?	Income growth necessary?	Ease of measurement	Innovation
Strategy 2020	Growth that creates opportunities and expands access	Largely process	Income	Yes	Rather vague and this unclear	Very close to Ali and Zhuang
Rauniyar and Kanbur	Growth with declining inequality	Outcome	Both possible	For income dimension yes	Straightforward	Nearly identical to relative PPG
Ali and Son	Pro-poor improvements in non-income dimensions	Outcome*	Non-income	No	Straightforward	Close to non-income growth incidence curves
Ali and Zhuang	Growth that is based on and expands *equal* opportunities and access	Largely process	Both	Yes	Quite difficult technically	Close to/ extension of equality of opportunity concept
World Bank	Growth that promotes productive employment	Largely process	Both	Yes	Difficult as it is vague	Some relation to Ali and Zhuang approach
UNDP	Growth with equality	Process and outcome	Both	Not necessarily	Difficult as it is very broad	Some relation to many related concepts
OECD	Growth in multidimensional wellbeing	Outcome	Both (but translated into incomes)	Yes	Straightforward but some assumptions controversial	Use of equivalent income
WEF	Inclusive economy dashboard	Outcomes and processes	Both	Not necessarily	Comprehensive but complex	Global application
Scotland	Inclusive growth priority	Mostly process	Non-income	Not necessarily	Not so clear	Role of disadvantage reduction

Note: *I categorise this approach as outcome-based as it does not consider the process of producing these opportunities. As these opportunities themselves can be used to generate human development and income outcomes, they could be seen as processes in this sense.

A proposed conceptual framework for defining and measuring IG

From this review of the literature is appears that the new and innovative aspects of the IG concept are the focus on both process and outcomes, and a concern with non-discrimination and disadvantage reduction. Maybe the first-best approach to define a concept would be to take Ali and Zhuang seriously and propose a work programme that carefully examines inequality of opportunities, its link to growth processes, and the ability to affect such inequality of opportunities through policy interventions. As I argued earlier, this is a fruitful but demanding approach to IG. Instead, a somewhat simpler approach is needed at this stage to examine IG. This is proposed below.

Taking the cue from the discussion above, we propose to define an income growth episode 'inclusive' if it

1. allows all members of society to participate in and contribute to with particular emphasis on the ability of the poor and disadvantaged to participate in growth ('the non-discriminatory' aspect of growth); and
2. is associated with declining inequality in non-income dimensions of wellbeing that are particularly important for promoting economic opportunities (education, health, nutrition, social integration); the 'disadvantage-reducing' aspect of IG.

More formally, the following conditions (at impact level) are to be met for an IG episode:

A. Per capita income growth rates are positive. This is a necessary condition for IG.
B. Growth rates of primary incomes (pre-tax earnings and self-employment incomes) for pre-defined disadvantaged groups (such as ethnic minorities, backward regions, the income poor, rural areas and women) are at least as high as growth rates of per capita incomes. If this were the case, it indicates that these pre-defined disadvantaged groups have been able to participate at least proportionately in the growth process by being able to improve their incomes at the average rate.[10]
C. Expansions of non-income dimensions of wellbeing are larger than average for pre-defined disadvantaged groups.[11] The non-income dimensions to consider are schooling achievements, improvements in survival rates (for example, inverse of under 1 and under 5

mortality rates), improvements in nutritional status, an access to transport, communications, and household services (such as clean water, electricity, refuse removal). This way one would ensure that an income growth episode was disadvantage-reducing.[12]

Please note that in this way it is perfectly possible that an income growth episode is inclusive in some ways but not in others. For example, given the three conditions above, it is perfectly possible for an income growth episode to have been inclusive in terms of leading to higher primary incomes for rural areas and women and promoting faster expansion of education and access to household services for the poor, rural areas and backward regions. That same episode would then be considered as not inclusive as growth of primary incomes of ethnic minorities was lower than average, and they also expanded their non-income dimensions of wellbeing at lower than average rates. This is not a problem at all and in fact it would be quite illuminating to emphasise to what extent the growth process of country has been inclusive and in which ways it has not.

Using this approach, one would be able to determine whether a particular growth episode was 'inclusive' in the non-discriminatory and disadvantage-reducing senses for particular disadvantaged groups. In line with the discussion on pro-poor growth, it might also be useful not only to consider the question of the *state* of IG, but also the *rate* of IG: we not only want to know whether growth was inclusive or not, but how high the rate of IG has been.[13] Here I would simply suggest to adapt the toolbox from pro-poor growth research to measurement of IG. In particular, adapting the proposals of Kakwani and Son (2008) on the 'poverty equivalent growth rate', one could define an 'inclusive growth rate' for a disadvantaged group as simply the following:

$$IG_{ij} = \frac{G_{ij}}{\bar{\bar{G}}_j} \times \bar{G}_j$$

Where i refers to a particular disadvantaged group and j refers to the indicator in question (such as income growth or expansion in education).[14] The first term, the ratio of the growth rate in a particular dimension for a particular disadvantaged group to the overall growth rate in that dimension, measures the 'inclusiveness' of growth which is then multiplied by the second term, which is the amount of growth of an indicator in question. This way the rate of IG depends on the amount of growth and its inclusiveness.

While the rate of inclusive growth is useful to track the expansion of disadvantaged groups, when comparing two growth episodes, it is not clear that a higher rate of IG is necessarily the more inclusive one of the two. The higher rate can just have come about by higher growth overall, rather than a particularly inclusive version of it.

Tracking inclusive growth

In order to track the state and rate of IG, the first task would be to define disadvantaged groups which are central to the concept of non discriminatory and disadvantage-reducing growth. We will illustrate this with the case of a developing country. In an advanced country setting, the indicators would have to be adjusted. A starting point could be a poverty profile that identifies those disproportionately affected by income and non-income poverty. Once the groups are defined, one would then compare their income growth and expansions of non-income dimensions of wellbeing over time. While this is clearly possible, it is not easily done and would usually require micro data to answer these questions.[15] But this is in principle possible and then one can assess whether a country's growth episode has been inclusive and if, with respect to which disadvantaged groups.

Of course there might also be the interest to investigate to what extent a particular intervention (a development project of programme) can be part of an IG agenda. At the sector level, projects and programmes try to affect inclusive growth at the country level but usually focus on either particular groups or particular aspects of an IG agenda. So the country level indicators would be too crude to assess the impact of projects or programmes on IG. At the same time it would be hard to generate and analyse specific micro data for each project or programme. Instead, one should focus more on measuring the contribution to inclusive growth at the project level, by assessing what projects are aiming for in terms of beneficiaries and project goals and then compare this to an IG agenda. Possible indicators could that could be helpful in this way may be the following:[16]

1. Is the project/programme aiming to reduce absolute income poverty (using, for example, the $3.10/day international poverty indicator in a developing country setting) by targeting people below US$3.10/a day as predominant direct or indirect beneficiaries?
2. Is the project/programme aimed at and likely to lead to increasing (formal sector?) employment of poor people (using the US$3.10/day indicator)?
3. Is the project/programme aimed at reducing economic and social disparities in income or non-income dimensions of wellbeing by specifically focusing on removing structural barriers and pro-active policies of inclusion of regions/groups that are disadvantaged (such as poorer regions, members from disadvantaged ethnic minorities, disadvantaged females, people with disabilities)?
4. Is the project/programme promoting the human capacities of poor people (especially in terms of health and education of poor people so that they are better able to contribute to/benefit from economic growth). Indicators would be projected improvements in health or education of poor people (those below US$3.10 a day) of a programme/project?
5. Is the project/programme likely to deliver benefits in non-income dimensions of wellbeing of poor and disadvantaged groups above and beyond improvements in human capacities (such as reductions in infant and child mortality, improved nutritional outcomes, improved social security, better social integration, improved housing, improved household infrastructure).

Conclusion

Despite several years of discussion on IG, the concept remains ill-defined and different definitions abound. Even those actors that have made IG a central pillar of their activities, such as the Government of India or the ADB, have not proposed and adopted a well-defined measure of IG. Interestingly, the debate in developing countries and associated international organisations are more advanced and have been going on for a longer time than the ones in advanced economies. Also there, the contributions have more specifically developed new approaches for IG, while the concepts promoted in advanced countries are younger and often rely more on multidimensional wellbeing approaches than on specifically new approaches to IG.

In this short contribution, I have tried to develop an approach to IG that tries to capture the spirit of these debates, distinguishes it from other approaches of assessing the 'quality' of growth, and provides a clear operationalisation. The proposal for growth to be inclusive is for income growth (before taxes and transfers) to be non-discriminating in the sense that it is at least as high for all disadvantaged groups, and for non-income improvements to reduce existing disadvantages. This way all were equally able to partake in the growth process and their non-income disadvantages for disadvantaged groups are falling, which of course ensures that the likelihood of them participating fully in the growth processes in future increases. The debate is not settled but hopefully this contribution helps to move towards a more well-defined and operational concept of IG.

Acknowledgements

I would like to thank Armin Bauer, Chris Deeming, Guanghua Wan, Juzhong Zhuang, Hyun Son, Bart Edes, Adrianus Rijk, Stein Hansen, Xianbin Yao, and participants at a workshop at the ADB for helpful comments and discussions. Funding from ADB in support of this work is gratefully acknowledged.

Notes

[1] See also Rauniyar and Kanbur, 2010) for a closely related conceptual discussion.

[2] There is a related debate about whether pro-poor contractions are a form of pro-poor growth. See Kakwani and Son (2008) for a discussion.

[3] This would also imply that any analysis determining ADB's contribution to IG has to consider ex ante impact assessment tools (in addition to reviewing the ex post impact on inclusive growth).

[4] In this sense, the overall approach to inclusive growth can be seen as quite similar to the World Bank's 1990 World Development Report on poverty where the three pillars of poverty reduction were seen as promotion of labour intensive growth (ADB does not, however, emphasise labour intensive growth but growth per se), investments in human capacities (ADB focuses only on education), and safety nets and targeted transfers to assist those not able to benefit from growth. Similar to the conceptual discussion above, it replaces the poverty focus of that WDR 1990 with a focus on non-discrimination.

[5] Note, however, that the ADB in its Results Framework to Strategy 2020 emphasises the Millennium Development Goals (outcome indicators). However, it fails to describe any mechanism on how to measure the ADB's contribution to those country outcomes, nor does it set any outcome targets on inclusive growth.

[6] Since regional integration is covered in the Results Framework and environment is partly covered in the MDGs, arguably the other two strategic pillars have clearer indicators in the Results Framework.

[7] Or perhaps one consciously wants to treat the concept of inclusive growth as a rather vague guiding principle rather than a firm commitment. India's approach to discussing inclusive growth in its policy documents seems to go in that direction (for example, Government of India, 2009).

[8] There is an interesting link to an older measure called the Bonferroni index, which is explored in Silber and Son (2010).

⁹ www.ipc-undp.org/

¹⁰ There is a complication here. High earnings growth for a disadvantaged group may
have come about either by higher earnings per worker (or per hour) or more people
working (or more hours worked). If this high earnings growth came about by more
workers and/or more hours worked, it may be seen the result of distress among a
disadvantaged group that makes up for it by expanding work effort. This may not
be seen as desirable. On the other hand, an expansion of employment and hours can
be seen as a true expansion of opportunities to participate in the growth process,
and thus be a key ingredient of inclusive growth. Empirically it is likely that high
earnings growth is rarely generated by expansion of distress employment (which
usually expands when earnings are falling) so that this complication may not be
relevant in many cases. If that is so, then the proposed indicator of disproportionate
earnings growth would be appropriate.

¹¹ Please note that the specific focus on disadvantaged groups goes beyond MDG
targets for social and environmental dimensions of poverty (MDG 2–7) as they
are often interpreted as not targeting the lower income groups.

¹² Please note that here we are suggesting to monitor absolute expansions in these
non-income dimensions (rather than proportionate expansions or growth rates).
This is due to the fact that in non-income dimensions, growth rates are rather
misleading concepts. For example, a growth rate of 100% in education for a
disadvantaged group might just mean an expansion of education from 1 to 2 years,
while a growth rate of 20% for the richest might mean an expansion from 10 to 12
years. In proportionate terms, this would generate the misleading impression that
improvements were much larger for the poor, while in absolute terms this problem
does not appear. For a discussion, see Klasen (2008) and Grosse et al (2008).

¹³ See Klasen (2008) for a discussion in the context of pro-poor growth.

¹⁴ An alternative (which is closer to the idea of Kakwani and Son) would be to take
the elasticity of the indicator $_j$ for the disadvantaged group $_i$ and multiply that with
the growth rate of indicator $_j$. For example, one would take the elasticity of rural
growth with respect to overall growth and multiply that by the growth rate.

¹⁵ See, for example, the Global Monitoring Reports by UNESCO which examine
educational expansion for disadvantaged groups (such as UNESCO, 2009).

¹⁶ The consultant team has further detailed those criteria by setting indicators for
the energy, transport, agriculture, and small and medium enterprise development
sectors and for the environmental theme. They have then proposed a weighted
rating system to score in a transparent matter ADB's contribution to inclusive
growth – at the project goal level – against those criteria. See Rijk (2010), Hansen
(2010) and Laplante (2010).

References

Ali, I. and J. Zhuang (2007) 'Inclusive Growth toward a Prosperous
Asia: Policy Implications', ERD Working Paper Series, No. 97, July,
Manila: ADB.

Ali, I. and Hyun Hwa Son (2007) 'Measuring Inclusive Growth', *Asian
Development Review* 24(1): 11–31.

Asian Development Bank (ADB) (2007) *Toward a New Asian
Development Bank in a New Asia: Report of the Eminent Persons Group*,
Manila: ADB.

ADB (2008) *Strategy 2020*, Manila: ADB.

ADB (2010) *Development Effectiveness Report 2009*, Manila: ADB.

ADB (2009) *Development Effectiveness Review 2008*, Manila: ADB.

Beatty, C., R. Crisp and T. Gore (2016) *An inclusive growth monitor for measuring the relationship between poverty and growth*, Water End: Rowntree Foundation.

Bourguignon, F., F. Ferreira and M. Menendez (2007) 'Inequality of opportunity in Brazil', *Review of Income and Wealth*, 53(4): 585–618.

Government of India (2008) *11th Five-Year Plan; Inclusive Growth*, New Delhi: Oxford University Press.

Government of India (2009) *Economic Survey of India: Microfoundations of Inclusive Growth*, New Delhi: Ministry of Finance.

Grosse, M., K. Harttgen, and S. Klasen (2008) 'Measuring pro-poor growth using non-income dimensions', *World Development* 36(6): 1021–47.

Ferreira, F. and J. Gignoux (2008) *The measurement of inequality of opportunity*, World Bank Policy Research Working Paper 4659, Washington, DC: The World Bank.

Hansen, S. (2010) *ADB's Contribution to Inclusive Growth in Energy and Transport*, mimeographed, Manila: ADB.

Kakwani, N. and H. Son. (2008) 'Poverty Equivalent Growth Rate', *Review of Income and Wealth* 54(4): 643–55.

Klasen, S. (2008) 'Economic Growth and Poverty Reduction: Measurement issues in income and non-income dimensions', *World Development* 36(3): 420–45.

Laplante, B. (2010) *A Concept for Assessing ADB's Contribution to Inclusive Growth in Projects Promoting Environmental Sustainability*, mimeographed, Manila: ADB.

McKinley, T. (2010) 'Proposing Indicators for Monitoring Inclusive Growth', Initial Notes, 4 January, CDPR, SOAS.

OECD (2014) *Report on the OECD Framework for Inclusive Growth*, Paris: OECD.

OECD (2016) *Proceedings from the Launch of the Inclusive Growth in Cities Campaign*, Paris: OECD.

Rauniyar, G. and R. Kanbur (2010) 'Inclusive Growth and Inclusive Development: A review and synthesis of Asian Development Bank literature', *Journal of the Asia Pacific Economy*, 15(4): 455–69.

Rijk, A. (2010) *ADB's Contribution to Inclusive Growth in Agriculture and SME Development Projects*, mimeographed, Manila: ADB.

Roemer, J. (1998) *Equality of Opportunity*, Cambridge, MA: Harvard University Press.

Scottish Government (2015) *Scotland's Economic Strategy*, Edinburgh.

Silber, J. and H. Son (2010) 'On the link between the Bonferroni index and the measurement of inclusive growth', *Economics Bulletin* 30(1): 421–8.

World Bank (2009) 'What Is Inclusive Growth?', PRMED Knowledge Brief, February 10, Economic Policy and Debt Department, Washington, DC: World Bank.

WEF (2015) *The inclusive growth and development report 2015*, Geneva: WEF.

WEF (2017) *The inclusive growth and development report 2017*, Geneva: WEF.

UNESCO (2009) *Global Monitoring Report: Overcoming Marginalization*. Paris: UNESCO.

UNDP (2016) 'What does inclusive economic growth actually mean in practice?', Our Perspectives, United Nations Development Programme, www.undp.org/content/undp/en/home/blog/2015/7/31/What-does-inclusive-economic-growth-actually-mean-in-practice-.html

Zhuang, J. and I. Ali (2012) 'Poverty, inequality and inclusive growth in Asia', in J. Zhuang, J. (ed.) *Poverty, Inequality, and Inclusive Growth in Asia*, Manila: Anthem Press, 1–32.

SIX

Towards an employment strategy of inclusive growth

Günther Schmid

Setting the scene

There is one thing 'developed' (high income) and developing (low and middle income) countries have in common: the lack of good jobs for a decent income to all. Whereas underdeveloped and emerging countries are struggling to create more jobs in the formal economy because only these jobs seem to ensure decent and stable income over the life course, advanced economies are struggling to build dams against the intrusion of informal and 'nonstandard' jobs to prevent increasing poverty and inequality. Is there any common ground in fighting against 'informal' for more 'formal jobs' and fighting against 'informal' for maintaining 'formal jobs', which means so-called standard employment relationships? Could it be that – at the global level – a common ground of social policy appears to become one of the most urgent requirements of ensuring more and better jobs on both sides of the world of work?

The argument in the following chapter is straightforward: a full employment strategy based on the 'standard employment contract' will fail on both sides. Social security based on the institution of full-time, open-ended and dependent wage work cannot be the paradigm of global social policy. Ultimately, people have to be protected, not jobs. Without jobs in some formalised – legally ensured *and* socially recognised – labour contract, however, protection of people remains an empty promise. A sustainable employment strategy has to acknowledge the instrumental (earning income) as well as the intrinsic value of employment, which means the identity building aspect of labour relationships. Whereas the 'developed' world can learn from the virtues of flexible and imaginative informal jobs, the 'underdeveloped' world can learn from the virtues of smartly regulated labour contracts. Flexibility through social security and social identity is the solution, and not the neoliberal credo of security through flexibility and market arbitrariness.

In the following, I intend to corroborate this argument by two provocative empirical observations, their explanation and theoretical generalisation. From the European point of view, it is the variability of employment relationships – in particular in terms of working time – which provides the clue to inclusive growth. From the point of view of less developed or emerging countries it is work related income guarantees, in particular the state as employer of last resort, that are a promising path towards smartly formalised employment relationships. At the end, these insights are drawn together into a common employment strategy based on the regulatory idea of the inclusive labour contract illustrated by good practice examples. Characterising the idea as 'regulatory', however, should make clear that its transformation into concrete law would have to be different depending on the cultural context.

Nonstandard forms of employment in Europe: a curse or a blessing?

The past several decades have witnessed the rise of nonstandard forms of employment (NSFE) in many parts of the industrialised world. The reasons for this shift are multi-faceted, including increased competition as result of globalisation, technological change that has facilitated business and work re-organisation, the increased participation of women in the labour market, and the emergence of new types of contractual arrangements, sometimes as result of legal changes, but also in response to changes in the business model. NSFE include part-time work, temporary work (fixed or project based contracts, casual labour, minijobs or even zero-hour contracts), triangular employment relationships through temporary agencies or subcontracting companies and self-employment, in particular own-account work.

In the following brief account for all member states of the European Union (EU28),[1] a simplified typology is used on the consistent database of the European Labour Force Survey (ELFS) for the period 1998 to 2014. Standard employment (SE) is considered as employment in open-ended contracts, in full-time work and in a wage/ or salary relationship. Three basis components of NSFE are distinguished: part-time work, temporary work and self-employment. All figures are calculated as a percentage of the working age population (age 15 to 64).[2] The original analysis goes beyond description by testing possible causes of this development and by demonstrating the consequences of NSFE

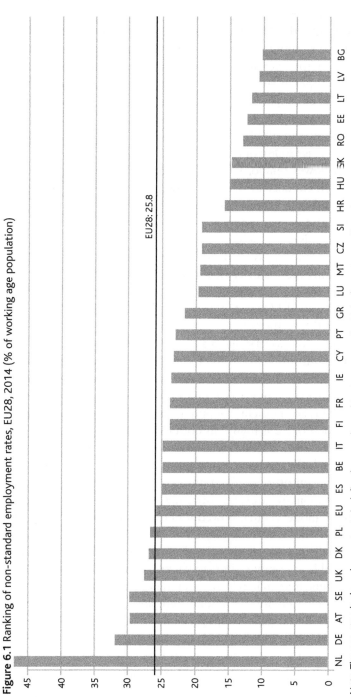

Figure 6.1 Ranking of non-standard employment rates, EU28, 2014 (% of working age population)

Note: The non-standard employment rate is defined as people working in non-standard jobs (part-time, self-employment without employees, temporary or fixed-term contracts) in percent of working age population (15–64) and controlled for overlaps (such as fixed-term part-time or part-time self-employed).

Sources: European Labour Force Survey; own calculations (Schmid and Wagner, 2017)

for economic performance and social inclusion. In the following, only the main results will be reported with a focus on one rather new and provocative observation.

In the EU28, the NSFE rate increased to a level of 25.8% (2014); in other words, about a quarter of the working age population works – controlled for overlaps – either in part-time, temporary work or in self-employment (Figure 6.1). Since the overall activity rate (SE+NSFE+Unemployed) is 72.1%, the share of NSFE is 36%; related to the total employment rate (64.5%), the share of NSFE is 40%.

The dynamics of NSFE, however, slowed down drastically after the economic crisis (2008): only part-time employment increased further, albeit at a slower tempo, whereas the share of temporary work and self-employment decreased; in the most recent period part-time work increased particularly among senior workers (55–64).

Country differences within the EU28 are huge: the NSFE rate in the Netherlands is 47.2% (share of total employment: 65%), compared to only 10.6% in Bulgaria (share of total employment: 17%). Part-time work explains the majority of this difference. The same holds true for gender: women are slightly overrepresented in total NSFE. Their NSFE rate in the EU28 is 27.9%, varying between 7.5% in Romania, and 57% in the Netherlands.

A simple causal model suggests a two-dimensional approach based on whether labour supply is contingent or career-oriented and whether labour demand is fluctuating or stable. When contingent supply and fluctuating demand come together, the likelihood of precarious NSFE is high; when career-oriented supply and stable demand come together, the likelihood of SE is high – in both cases relatively independent of labour market institutions. In the two other combinations (contingent supply + stable demand; career-oriented supply + fluctuating demand), labour market institutions play a stronger role in determining whether the employment relationship becomes 'standard' or 'nonstandard'. This simple model is quite powerful in explaining the following brief account of NSFE according to sectors, education and age.[3]

Part-time employment is – in all countries – most common in services and least common in manufacturing; within services we find most part-time roles in hotels and restaurants, health and social services, and household activities; temporary employment is common in all sectors, even in manufacturing, particularly, however, again in hotels and restaurants and in household activities.

The probability of (career-oriented) high skilled workers to be in NSFE is lower than for low skilled; the probability of (career-oriented) middle aged workers (25–54) to be in NSFE is lower than for the two 'marginal' age groups: the young and the mature aged workers.

Employment protection is one of the major institutional determinants for NSFE. It is in particular strong individual employment protection, which induces employers to utilise NSFE, in particular full-time fixed-term employment. Lax employment protection related to temporary work seems to induce high levels of (all kinds of) part-time work; employers use more and more temporary work, in particular part-time work as a screening device.

For men, the strongest reason for being in part-time is 'not finding a full-time job' (40%); another reason is combining part-time with education or training (19%). For women, the strongest reason for being in part-time is 'looking after children or incapacitated adults' (27%); 26% of women are involuntarily working part-time. Over 1998–2014, involuntary part-time work has increased slightly. On a cross-section basis, however, involuntary part-time work is lowest in countries with high shares of part-time work, such as the Netherlands, and highest in countries with low shares of part-time work, such as Bulgaria. There is no significant gender difference related to temporary work or fixed-term contracts: on average in the EU28, about two thirds prefer a permanent full-time job; almost one in five workers combines temporary work with education or training.

In the meantime, myriads of studies on the consequences of NSFE confirm that NSFE lead more or less to lower wages, higher inequality, (gender) segmented labour markets, and even (to some extent) to a 'new dangerous class' of precariat.[4] Here, I refer to only one seminal study, which reports results from the intermediary role of institutions. Women face overall not only a higher risk of being in part-time roles but also a higher risk of receiving low wages, in particular in occupations requiring only low skills; institutions do not matter much here. In occupations requiring high skills (such as teaching), however, institutions matter. It is in particular full-time equivalent childcare provision and public employment that is preventing or at least mitigating the risk of being in part-time and low-wage employment at the same time (Leschke, 2015).

The literature on the relationship between NSFE and social protection is also unanimous in demonstrating that people in NSFE are less well covered by social protection (health, pension and unemployment insurance), and underrepresented in active labour market policies. The most common difference with standard workers is the exclusion of NSFE from benefits related to unemployment and work injury.

These observations certainly contribute to the widespread opinion that NSFE are rather a curse than a blessing. The counterpart of this partially justified criticism, however, has been neglected so far. It is the fact that NSFE rates strongly correlate positively with labour force participation ('inclusion' indicator), GDP per capita ('wealth' indicator) and with GDP per hour ('productivity' indicator).

Tables 6.1 and 6.2 display the evidence for social inclusion and labour productivity. Although correlations do not allow reading them as (one-directional) causal relations (here in the sense that NSFE causes higher labour force participation, higher economic wealth or productivity), there are good reasons for generic causal links. Regarding social inclusion, it is quite evident and requires no further explanations that variability in working time makes it easier for young adults with child or elderly care obligations to participate in the labour market. Regarding the link to wealth, it suffices to remind Adam Smith's insight that, apart from skills, the level of labour market participation (as indicator for inclusion) determines the nation's prosperity.[5]

With regard to productivity, the aggregate cross-country evidence observed here is confirmed by various micro-studies.[6] They show, for instance, that excessive use of temporary work or fixed-term employment does *not* contribute to wealth or productivity; it is rather the contrary because thriving innovation and high productivity require a high quality work organisation, which again needs open-ended employment relationships that foster skill accumulation, cooperation, loyalty and high commitment to work (Appelbaum et al, 2000).

Table 6.1 Correlates of the shares of non-standard employment and labour force participation rates, EU28, 1998–2014, 452 observations

	Total	Men	Women
Part-time open-ended	**.55**	**.54**	**.32**
Part-time fixed-term	**.48**	**.43**	**.28**
Part-time solo self-employed	.03	- .15	.01
Full-time fixed- term	.10	- .03	- .08
Full-time solo self-employed	**- .43**	-.13	**- .38**
Self-employed with employees	**- .25**	.10	**- .36**

Note: Bold figures significant at 1% level.
Sources: European Labour Force Survey, Eurostat; own calculations; Schmid and Wagner (2017)

Table 6.2 Correlates of non-standard employment rates and labour productivity (GDP/H), EU27, 1998–2014, 354 observations

	Total	Men	Women
Part-time open-ended	.77	.65	.78
Part-time fixed-term	.57	.50	.60
Part-time solo self-employed	- .01	- .02	.01
Full-time fixed- term	.00	- .09	.06
Full-time solo self-employed	- .31	- .23	- .46
Self-employed with employees	.21	.23	.04
Total Non-standard employment	.68	.29	.76
Total standard employment	.28	.19	- .54

Notes: Luxembourg is not included; figures in bold significant at 1% level.
Sources: Eurostat (ELFS); own calculations; Schmid and Wagner (2016)

As Table 6.2 shows, the strong positive correlation between NSFE and productivity at the aggregate level stems only from the component of part-time work, and even more specifically – not shown in Table 6.2 – from voluntary part-time work.[7] There are, among other reasons, five plausible explanations for this astonishing result: First, part-time work allows tapping the (otherwise) underutilised resources of high qualified women (work–life balance); second, as economies move towards (often knowledge intensive) services, employers need a more flexible work organisation (24 hours economy); third, increasing the variability of employment contracts (such as through part-time work) enhances further labour division which is often related to higher productivity (remind old Adam Smith); fourth, voluntary part-time work is often combined with training and education fostering employability and productivity of all workers, not least migrant workers who need language abilities – best acquired in combination with part-time work – to prove their employability (life-long learning); and fifth, marginal individual productivity (after increasing at the beginning) decreases with the length of working time (U-shaped productivity curve).[8]

Before discussing the employment strategies that might properly respond to these trends, we turn to the case of developing or emerging countries. Most of them are confronted with the challenge of large, and in some cases even increasing, informal labour markets. Leaving aside countries with very low economic development,[9] I will concentrate on two emerging countries: Brazil and India.

The role of nonstandard forms of employment in emerging countries: Brazil

Brazil has achieved remarkable success in reducing poverty, but its inequality is still one of the highest among developed or emerging countries. In contrast to Europe, Brazil's employment dynamic was mainly driven by formal full-time employment, and informal employment fell from about 55% to 44% of total employment. Among NSFE, self-employment is the strongest part (30%); temporary and part-time work have about equal shares (15%) (Table 6.3).

Brazil's labour market is exceptional for its high labour turnover on the one hand, and for its wage premiums related to part-time work and self-employment. Trade unions play an important role, and the formalised sector is strongly regulated in terms of minimum wages and employment or social protection. In the informal sectors of the metropolitan areas (*favelas*) and particular in rural areas, poverty, however, still looms large but recently has been successfully attacked by a programme named *Bolsa Família* inspired by the concept of conditional cash transfers (CCT).

Table 6.3 Non-standard forms of employment, Brazil (% of salaried workers)

Six urban areas	2003	2013	Hourly wage gaps related to regular employment (%)
Formal wage earners	69.7	81.8	
Temporary employed	4.2	3.0	
Temporary employed informal		13.0	-7.7
Temporary employed formal		1.0	-13.3
Part-time employed total	15.3	15.5	36.5 Formal/32.7 Informal
Part-time involuntary	3.1	1.0	35.5 Formal/31.8 Informal
[Self-employed, 2008]		29.0	n.a.

Source: Schmid and Wagner (2016: Table 14)

The idea of the CCT was first implemented as an experiment in Mexico (*Progresa*), and it subsequently spread to other world regions and developing countries. The concept starts from the insight that children in extreme poor families often contribute substantially to the family's livelihood instead of going to school. The idea, therefore, is to give regular payments to poor families, in the form of cash or electronic transfers into their bank accounts, if they meet certain requirements. The requirements vary, but many countries employ those originally used by Mexico (now renamed *Oportunidades*): families must keep their children in school and go for regular medical check-ups, and the family head must attend workshops on subjects like nutrition or disease prevention. The payments almost always go to women, as they are the most likely to spend the money on their families. Extreme poverty is prevented today while breaking the cycle of poverty for tomorrow, which starts when there is no opportunity for income generation due to the absolute priority of caring for the minimum of existence.

Bolsa Família was subsequently introduced in 2003, combining and reforming existing programmes and significantly expanding coverage from 5.1 million families of a former programme to some 14 million families by 2011. In 2013, the government spent 0.44% of its GDP, covering about 58 million Brazilians, about a quarter of the country's population; it pays a monthly stipend of about $13 to poor families for each child 15 or younger who is attending school, up to three children. Families can get additional payments of $19 a month for each child of 16 or 17 still in school, up to two children. Families that live in extreme poverty get a basic benefit of about $40, with no conditions. *Bolsa* is implemented by the municipalities, which use social workers to bring additional support and diagnostics to households where children fail to meet their co-responsibilities. Compared with *Oportunidades*, its focus is more on the redistributive transfer side than on the conditional side. A robust evaluation of this programme, however, does not exist. Its different focus compared to Mexico, nevertheless, seems to be justified related to recent experiences collected with CCT.

Banerjee and Duflo (2011) report results of studies, which asked whether an *unconditional* programme could have the same effect as a conditional transfer. They refer to a World Bank study, which found, provocatively, that conditionality does not matter at all. An experimental programme in Malawi confirmed again the tremendous positive effect of cash transfers to poor families in terms of improved schooling of their children, but a control group (unconditional) did as well as the treated (conditional) group. Subsequently, another study that compared conditional and unconditional transfers in Morocco found similar results. Several factors explain this result, among others the fact that income transfers – by moving parents out of extreme poverty – may also have given the mental space to take a longer view of life. Schooling is something where the costs are paid now (you have to nag – or drag – your children into school now) and it only pays off when they are older – a reason which corroborates the principle of ex ante redistribution in social investment strategies (Schmid, 2015, 2017).

In other words, income per se matters for education decisions. In their 18 country study, Banerjee and Duflo found that the share of spending on education increases as we move up from those who live on 99 cents a day to those in the US$6–10 category. Basic income security for the extreme poor, be it conditional or not, has without any doubt a positive effect on employment – the income capacities of the very poor. What matters, too, are effective employment or social services at the decentral level to implement such programmes. Furthermore, because income differentials are reflected sooner or later in educational differentials, the entitlement to basic education should be a human right for all, which is a common good that – at the end of the day – will have to be enforced through mandatory schooling of children because financial incentives might not be sufficient; public provision of the respective infrastructure is also necessary. Moreover, service delivery through teachers having a sufficient standard of knowledge has to be enforced to prevent absenteeism of teachers, which is a chronic failure in 'developing' countries, especially in rural areas.

The message from the Brazilian case is therefore clear: Labour markets can only function properly when (potential) workers dispose of a minimum income for a decent livelihood as well as of a minimum education for understanding the tasks and communication related to a market based on labour division. Apart from the capability approach (Sen, 2009) and the modern efficiency wage theory (Akerlof and Shiller 2009), even the original concept of 'neoliberalism' was accepting this truth in its famous 1938 critic against market radicalism.[10]

The Brazil approach has been described by ILO (2015) as 'basic universalism' – the combination of social insurance and intentionally broadly targeted social assistance, framed as a citizenship right. Although estimates of the relative contribution of different programmes and policies to the decline in inequality vary considerably, one of the most widely cited studies suggests that about half of the decline of inequality in Brazil was the result of greater equality in the distribution of labour income, while the remainder was the result of social spending. In particular, investment in universal education since the 1990s has resulted in a decline in the skills premium, while the increase in the minimum wage has raised earnings for unskilled workers, both of which contribute to reduced inequality in labour income.

The role of nonstandard forms of employment in emerging countries: India

The case of India is different. For the Indian labour market, Europe's concept of NSFE fails completely (Table 6.4). The informal sector employs about 90% of the labour force. Furthermore, India's labour market is split between urban areas (comprising only about 25% of the population) and agricultural areas.

In contrast to China, India's labour market suffers in addition from the low adult literacy rate, which is only 51% for women and 75% for men; labour force participation of women is also one of the lowest in Asian countries (Drèze and Sen 2013: 293). Within the informal sector, self-employment is most common (about 50%), next comes casual work (about 30%) and a tiny layer of regular work (about 20%). Part-time work, albeit certainly existing to some extent in urban areas, is even not existent in India's (otherwise) extremely differentiated official statistics (Table 6.4).

Table 6.4 Share of employees according to status, India (% of total employment)

	Men			Women		
	Self-employed	Regular	Casual	Self-employed	Regular	Casual
Urban						
1987/88	41.7	43.7	14.6	47.1	27.5	25.4
1999/00	41.5	41.7	16.8	45.3	33.3	21.4
2011/12	41.7	43.4	14.9	42.8	42.8	14.3
Rural						
1987/88	58.6	10.0	31.4	60.8	3.7	35.5
1999/00	55.0	8.8	36.2	57.3	3.1	39.6
2011/12	54.5	10.0	35.5	59.3	5.6	35.1
Total*	50.7	20.2	29.3	54.4	16.8	28.9

Note: * Total for 2011/12; own calculation based on weighting urban by 0.3 and rural by 0.7.

Source: Schmid and Wagner (2016: Table 12)

Over 92% of all workers in India are outside the purview of labour legislation on job and social security. The Indian government undertakes steps towards a much stronger formalisation of the labour market with obvious positive results in urban labour markets, but poverty is still looming large especially in rural areas. India, however, is unique in collecting experiences with the world's largest public works programme, the National Rural Employment Guarantee Act (NREGA), introduced in 2006 and covering at its height 50 million households in rural areas. NREGA replaced a variety of similar programmes on a smaller scale. In the meantime, this programme is worldwide perceived as a successful paradigm for fighting poverty so that it makes sense to have a closer look on the overall potential of employment guarantees by the state.

NREGA guarantees up to 100 days work each year to rural Indians and is based on the revolutionary principle of self-selection and the right to work: 'anyone who joins the worksites is recognized to be in need of social support' (Drèze and Sen 2013: 200). Households can apply for work at any time of the year, and men and women are paid equally at the minimum wage. At its height in 2012/13, about 50 million rural households were covered at a cost of US$8.9 billion or about 1% of GDP; the average employment per rural household is 44 days per year. The costs of the programme are shared between the federal government (75%) and state governments (25%). At least one third of the NREGA workforce in a village is required to be female, yet in reality women's share reached almost 50%.

Many studies have followed up its impact and the majority of them came up with a positive balance. Currently, however, the programme stands under fire set by the scathing criticism of Prime Minister Narendra Modri, who condemned the programme as a 'monument to 60 years of failure'. According to his view, public employment contributes nothing to stimulate private investments and employment for which he considers deregulation and attraction of foreign investors as crucial. This view might be correct related to the infamous Indian championship of overregulated product and labour markets, but it is misplaced related to the objectives and target groups of public employment. The arguments in favour of such an employment guarantee are persuasive or at least showing in a clear way under which conditions such programmes might work in other countries.

First of all, NREGA has actually boosted agricultural productivity through development of wasteland land, the construction of post-harvest storage facilities and work sheds. It also helped create rural assets and infrastructure, ranging from *anganwadis* (local centres to combat child hunger and malnutrition), toilets for individual households, crematoria, cyclone shelters, and playgrounds for children, to drought proofing, flood protection and control, water conservation and harvesting, and rural road connectivity. NREGA works also contributed to improved ground water levels, increased water availability for irrigation, increased area irrigated by ground and surface water sources, and increased availability of drinking water for humans and livestock, and regenerating the rural ecosystem.

Second and not less important, NREGA has been a critical source of income for female-headed households, providing as much as 15% of the household income in some states, and it encouraged rural entrepreneurship, with households using the supplementary income to start a rural business. In many states, up to half of the NREGA income was spent on food, which improved health and nutrition – a critical factor in a country plagued by malnutrition. And since only the poorest sought work under this Act, it was an accurate self-targeting scheme, with a major proportion of the beneficiaries (much higher than their percentage in the general population) belonging to Scheduled Castes or Tribes and other marginalised communities. Some studies, however, find that NREGA was less successful in terms of reaching the most deprived population as claimed and expected. And although the benefits in terms of local infrastructure, water provision and land cultivation has to be acknowledged, the programme did much less well in providing health and childcare facilities for working women (Zepeda et al, 2013).

Third, NREGA has also a multiplier effect on the rural economy, with the additional purchasing power generated from it spent on items produced in the rural economy (second round effects). Furthermore, the programme effectively reduced the differences in minimum wages across the states and guaranteed to some extent an effective wage floor (Zepeda et al, 2013: 243–5). In this way, the programme may also have altered the power balance in favour of the landless poor against their employers (agricultural landlords, labour contractors). Last, but not least, by raising rural incomes, NREGA has decreased distress migration to the cities, thereby reducing the numbers of the reserve army of labour, and increasing the cost of labour.

Even mainstream and sophisticated econometric studies agree that NREGA effectively fulfils a social protection function in the absence of a universal social insurance scheme on which most Europeans can count. In particular, it serves quite well as an income safety net, especially for poor women in agricultural areas, both in terms of improving their economic *and* social power. The take up of publicly guaranteed employment follows external shocks, such as heavy rain falls or droughts, so that continuity of family income – even if small – is guaranteed.

Many evaluation studies, however, also agree that the impact of public works on sustainable and regular employment is small

(Zimmermann, 2014; Zepeda et al, 2013). Two main strategies could improve the effectiveness of such employment guarantee programmes: first, *capacity building* for better implementing, monitoring, controlling and evaluation of the programme to prevent (or at least to mitigate) various forms of corruption. Many studies found that local ruling parties were channelling funds to its base in swing constituencies; local functionaries still seem to have the potential to act as 'valves' to direct funds to certain constituencies. Drèze and Sen (2013: 203), while acknowledging a great deal of embezzlement, correctly turn the corruption critic on its head.

> NREGA is in fact a potential weapon against corruption … it has also been a lively laboratory for anti-corruption efforts, involving a whole series of innovations … the use of Internet to place all essential records … in the public domain, the payment of wages through bank accounts, and the practice of regular social audits.

This capacity building should be addressed in particular to three accountability provisions of NREGA that are still largely unused and dormant: the duty of the state government to pay unemployment allowances when work is not provided, a right to compensation when wages are not paid on time, and a penalty clause whereby any officer who fails to do his or her duty under the law is liable to a fine (Drèze and Sen, 2013: 201).

Because implementation deficits often cause supply constraints of public works, the second strategy for improvement should ensure a *stronger demand orientation* that guides the content of public works programmes more towards an infrastructure that has immediate effects on skilled labour supply (such as better schools, hospitals, day care centres) and sustainable job creation (risk capital for start-ups, intermediary wage-cost and training subsidies for small firms that increase employment, public transport systems, and public investments in education, health and care infrastructure).

Summing up: from the European point of view, efficient – which means productivity enhancing – employment growth is closely linked to increasing variability of employment relationships, in particular voluntary part-time work. It is this observation that provides the clue to inclusive growth because this employment dynamic favours both the employment chances of young adults with child or elderly care obligations, as well as for mature aged workers whose working capacities become restricted. Last but not least, adult workers, in particular migrants, who want to combine work with continuous training and education also profit from contract variability. From the point of view of 'underdeveloped' or emerging countries, it is basic income security through (conditional or not) cash transfers, and in particular public employment guarantees that support the transformation from insecure informal labour markets towards more and smartly formalised employment relationships. What conclusions can be drawn towards an employment strategy for inclusive growth?

The inclusive labour contract as key element of global social policy

In view of the complexity of the world of work, the overall conclusion has to be rather more general than specific. The main message of this chapter is that both – informal work as well as nonstandard forms of employment – should be embraced rather as an opportunity than as a danger. For Europe, NSFE are to some extent the tribute to external challenges of the traditional welfare state through globalisation as well as to internal challenges stemming from rising demands of social inclusion through gender equality and human capability equality, especially related to ageing populations, the increase in chronic health conditions, high and growing disability prevalence and the increasing streams of migrants. So far, the *dangerous elements* of risks related to NSFE have been emphasised: precarious and dead end jobs, rising inequality and segmentation. This view is certainly justified by the facts, but I hope to have added and justified a more optimistic view by pointing to the *opportunity elements* of risks related to NSFE – enhancing productivity through increasing the variability of employment relationships and greater sovereignty of workers for choosing the most suitable form of employment relationship over the changing needs and preferences of the life course.

On the other hand, informal work as experienced in less developed and emerging industrialising countries (like India or Brazil) is for the majority of people still the only realistic basis for generating income, in particular in form of self-employment. A development strategy concentrating only on forms of standard employment as we know in Europe would soon turn out to be a complete failure. There must be some intermediary forms of decent employment and social protections measures independent of the labour market status.

A new labour standard based on the idea of a right to a decent income beyond formal employment might be the solution. Expanding the range of the labour contract to all forms of work, including even unpaid but socially highly valued work as proposed for instance by the Supiot Report (Supiot, 2001), seems to be the most radical and promising route towards a new standard. The main aim is the move from protecting jobs to protecting the employability of people, or from job security to labour market security (Auer, 2007). Social security linked to traditional employment relationships would be extended in the new standard to include income and employment risks related to transitions between various employment and labour market statuses (Schmid, 2008, 2015).

Before we move to outline the elements of a new labour standard, a reminder of the productive function of social protection seems appropriate. Neoliberal and many mainstream economists often neglect or even deny this function by concentrating solely on the possible negative behavioural impact of any kind of social protection or insurance, namely 'moral hazard'. They disregard or omit the positive counterpart of 'moral hazard', namely 'moral ensurance' related to other or social centred behaviour as Table 6.5 shows. As the illuminating book by Peter Bernstein (1996) emphasises, risk has always two aspects: the potential loss in case of misfortune, which reflects the dangerous element of risk; but also the potential (and often greater) gain in case of fortune, which reflects the chance or opportunity element of risk. Moreover, people can respond to these two aspects in two different ways: If ego centred behaviour dominates, 'moral hazard' occurs in two forms: misuse of protection and careless or exploitative use of protection. If other or social centred behaviour dominates, 'moral ensurance' leads to legitimate use of protection in case of involuntary lack or loss of income, health or employment which contributes to social cohesion and trust; it may, however, also lead to calculated or even innovative use of protection in case of potential large gains. If, in other words, workers can rely on social protection in case of misfortune, they will overcome their innate risk aversion and be encouraged to calculated risk taking, for example, to moving jobs, investing in continuous vocational training thereby contributing to mobility, innovation and structural change. Moreover, they will be inclined towards more cooperation with colleagues and loyalty to employers because they would trust in fair redistribution in case of misfortune. Both aspects of 'moral ensurance' enhance productivity and economic prosperity if the other possible behavioural response to social protection ('moral hazard') is effectively controlled.

Table 6.5 Two possible behavioural responses to social protection or social insurance

	Risk aspect I	Risk aspect II	Policies
	Loss (danger)	Gain (chance)	
Ego centred behaviour	Moral hazard I Misuse of protection	Moral hazard II Careless or exploitative use of protection	Avoid or reduce
Other (social) centred behaviour	Moral ensurance I Legitimate use of protection	Moral ensurance II Calculated or innovative use of protection	Encourage or increase

The core is the establishment of new social rights *and* new social obligations on both sides of the labour market. The *new social rights* would be new in that they cover subjects unfamiliar to industrial wage-earners on which the traditional standard employment relationship builds: rights to education and training, to appropriate working hours including the right to request shorter working hours (Coote, 2013: XXI), to a family life, to occupational redeployment, retraining or vocational rehabilitation, and – last but not least – to a flexible employment guarantee through the state (Atkinson, 2015: 140–7).

In contrast to earlier job guarantees, this guarantee would be flexible in three respects: First, individuals are free to choose an offer by the state; second, individuals can combine this right with various 'nonstandard' forms of employment, such as involuntary part-time; third, the guarantee can also take the form of subsidised private employment. This right is also an immediate conclusion from the insight that employment has not only instrumental but also intrinsic features. Providing job opportunities can for instance take youth out of their 'natural' neighbourhood and eliminate, at least for a time, the often negative effects of peer groups in disadvantaged environments (Akerlof and Kranton, 2010).

The *scope of new social rights* would also be new since they would cover not only 'standard' wage-earners but also the 'nonstandard' part-time workers, the self-employed or semi-self-employed, the temp agency and marginal workers and even zero-hours contract workers (Schmid and Wagner 2017). One example would be including the risk of reduced earnings capacity in a way analogue to short-time work (of full-time workers) covered by unemployment insurance: The income loss induced by reduced working time (due to, for example, unpaid care obligations) could be compensated by part-time unemployment benefits or – as in the German case – a wage related parental leave allowance. Such an insurance benefit would also be helpful related to the increasing demand of care for frail elderly which, for example in Germany, in its majority (three quarters) is still provided within families and again predominantly by women (Schmid, 2017).

The new social rights are *new in nature* because they often take the form of vouchers, social drawing rights or personnel accounts, which provide transition securities from one labour contract to another and allow workers to rely on solidarity within defined and perhaps collectively bargained limits when exercising their new freedom to act (Korver and Schmid, 2012). A good practice example for such coordinated flexibility is the German collective agreement in the chemical industry in April 2008 setting up so-called demography funds. This overall framework agreement requires all employers to contribute €300 yearly for each employee into a fund, which can be utilised after corresponding negotiations and deliberations at the firm level for various aims, among others for training or retraining, for buying occupational disability insurance or for early retirement; however, under the condition of building a bridge for young workers entering employment.

To the extent that these new rights enhance the range of individual choices, a corresponding new field of individual responsibilities opens up. This dimension, strange enough, is not covered in the Supiot Report. Amartya Sen, however, is quite outspoken in this respect:

> Freedom to choose gives us the opportunity to decide what we should do, but with the opportunity comes the responsibility for what we do – to the extent that they are chosen actions. Since a capability is the power to do something, the accountability that emanates from that ability – that power – is a part of the capability perspective, and this can make room for demands of duty – what can be broadly called deontological demands. (Sen, 2009: 19)

The *new social obligations* arising from the extended room of individual freedom to act would be new in that they cover subjects unfamiliar in the traditional employment relationship: obligations to training and retraining both for employees as well as for employers to maintain employability, to actively searching a new job or accepting a less well paid job under fair compensating rules, to healthy lifestyles and occupational rehabilitation, to reasonable workplace adjustments according to the capabilities of workers (Deakin, 2009) or to changing working times according to the needs either related to the individual life course or to volatile market demands of goods and services. A good example in this direction was the modification of the German law for severely disabled people in 2010, which stipulates the right of disabled workers to an employment that enables them to utilise and to develop further their abilities and knowledge, the right to privileged access to firm-specific training, the rights to facilitation for participation in external training, the right to a disability-adapted work environment, and the right to a workplace with the required technical facilities. It is evident that these kinds of duties require support through collective agreements or social pacts between firms and other key actors at the local or regional labour market.

The *scope of new social obligations* would also be new since they would cover not only certain categories of workers or employers but also the core workers in open-ended contracts and all firms independent of size and function. The exemption of civil servants or self-employed from contributing to social security (especially pensions and unemployment insurance), as for instance in Germany, would not be justified under the regulatory idea of an inclusive labour contract. A good practice example is the obligation to offer work-sharing in case of cyclical troughs of demand if workers' representatives (*Betriebsrat*) request this from the employer where the law entitles workers to ask employers for work-sharing as a way to maintain the employment relationship. The German scheme of short-time work (*Kurzarbeit*) demonstrates the usefulness of such a device for internal flexibility (Möller, 2010; Schmid, 2015: 84–6).

The new social obligations would be *new in nature* since they often take the form of 'voice': being ready to negotiate at individual, firm, regional and branch level in order to reach mutual agreements and to accept compromises in case of different interests, so-called negotiated flexicurity (Schmid, 2008: 317–22). Voice as adjustment mechanism to structural change involving high uncertainty is known in the literature on industrial relations as legally acknowledged *learning communities*. A good practice case is *covenants* which, for instance, are widely used as a governance instrument in the Netherlands. A covenant is an undersigned written agreement, or a system of agreements, between two or more parties, at least one that is or represents a public authority, meant to effectuate governmental policy. There is not one format for covenants, but they share common features: enough overlapping interests of participants, mechanisms bringing about both definition and the machinery of achievements, the parties cooperate, and formal sanctions are absent, yet parties have the opportunity to go to court in case of another party's default. Covenants could also be understood as a 'pressure' or 'incentive' mechanism for coordination to economise on the most scarce and strategic resource: the ability to take adequate decisions and to avoid decision traps in uncertain environments (Korver and Schmid, 2012: 39–41).

To sum up: new social rights *and* obligations under the regulatory idea of the *inclusive labour contract* would increase internal flexibility of 'standard' employment as functional equivalent to external flexibility which often ends up in precarious NSFE. The establishment of new social rights and new social obligations into an inclusive labour contract would also ensure the development of capabilities that not only make workers fit to the market, but that also make the market fit to the workers (Gazier, 2007; Schmid, 2008). An employment strategy of inclusive growth should be based on the regulatory idea of a new labour standard, which goes beyond employment and includes all kinds of work that are socially valued or even obligatory. The inclusive labour contract brings together the supply strategy of investments into human capabilities over the whole life course, and the demand strategy of inclusive growth through job creation by proper fiscal and monetary policies enhanced by protected variability of labour contracts. This would be an essential element of a global social policy that aims to prevent a vicious cycle or cut-throat global competition, which Ferdinand Lassalle originally described as the iron law of falling real net wages towards an existence minimum (Supiot, 2016: XXXVIII). Our aim should be to turn this threatening vicious circle into a virtuous circle through a strategy for inclusive growth that globally guarantees a minimum income or employment with decent wages for all.

Notes

[1]   This account is based on Schmid and Wagner (2017).

[2]   A rich Appendix in Schmid and Wagner (2016) provides further differentiation by age groups (15–24, 25–54, 55–64) and by education level (low, medium and high skill) for all EU member states, and aggregated for EU28 and EU19 (Eurozone).

[3]   For an extended explanation supported by figures, see Schmid and Wagner (2016).

[4]   To mention only a few: Eichhorst and Marx (2015); OECD (2015); ILO (2015); Standing (2011).

[5]   'The wealth per capita must in every nation be regulated by two different circumstances; first, by the skill, dexterity, and judgement with which its labour is generally applied; and second, by the proportion between the number of those who are employed in useful labour, and that of those who are not so employed' (Smith, 1776/1937, vol. 1, p. VII).

[6]   See, among others, Kleinknecht et al (2014), Lisi (2013), and Martin and Scarpetta (2011).

[7]   The correlation between involuntary part-time and GDP/H (productivity) is significantly negative (-.33).

8   For a further discussion of these provoking results, see Schmid and Wagner (2016: 33–5).

9   For Uganda and Kenya, see Schmid and Wagner (2016).

10 The modern identification of 'neoliberalism' with libertarian or radical market ideas was channelled through the Pinochet reforms in Chile, which relied heavily on the radical market philosophy of Milton Friedman and other scholars from the 'Chicago School'. The original 'neoliberal' concept, striving towards a 'Social Market Economy', was consciously developed as a 'third way' between market and socialist economy, but has now turned almost into a perverse form.

References

Akerlof, G.A. and R.E. Kranton (2010) *Identity Economics – How Our Identities Shape our Work, Wages, and Wellbeing*, Princeton: Princeton University Press.

Akerlof, G.A. and R.J. Shiller (2009) *Animal Spirits – How human Psychology Dives the Economy and Why it Matters for Global Capitalism*, Princeton: Princeton University Press.

Appelbaum E., T. Bailey, P. Berg and A. Kalleberg (2000) *Manufacturing Advantage: Why High Performance Work Systems Pay Off*, Ithaca, NY, and London: ILR Press.

Atkinson, A.B. (2015) *Inequality – What Can Be Done?*, Cambridge, MA and London: Harvard University Press.

Auer, P. (2007) 'In Search of Optimal Labour Market Institutions', in H. Jørgensen and P.K. Madsen (eds), *Flexicurity and Beyond – Finding a New Agenda for the European Social Model*, Copenhagen: DJØF Publishing, 67–98.

Banerjee, A.V. and E. Duflo (2011) *Poor Economics: A Radical Rethinking of the Way to Fight Poverty*, New York, Perseus Books.

Bernstein, P.L. (1996) *Against the Gods – The Remarkable Story of Risk*, New York: John Wiley & Sons.

Coote, A. (2013) 'Introduction: A New Economics of Work and Time', in A. Coote and J. Franklin (eds), *Time on Our Side*, London: nef.

Deakin, S. (2009) 'Capacitas: Contract Law, Capabilities and the Legal Foundations', in S. Deakin and A. Supiot (eds), *Capacitas – Contract Law and the Institutional Preconditions of a Market Economy*, Oxford and Portland: Hart Publishing, 1–29.

Drèze, J. and A. Sen (2013) *An Uncertain Glory: India and its Contradictions*, London: Allen Lane.

Eichhorst, W. and P. Marx (eds) (2015) *Non-standard Employment in Post-industrial Labour Markets: An Occupational Perspective*, Cheltenham: Edward Elgar.

Gazier, B. (2007) 'Making Transitions Pay: The 'Transitional Labour Markets' Approach to 'Flexicurity'', in H. Jørgensen and P.K. Madsen (eds), *Flexicurity and Beyond – Finding a New Agenda for the European Social Model*, Copenhagen, DJØF Publishing, 99–130.

ILO (2015) 'Non-standard Forms of Employment', Report for discussion at the Meeting of Expert on Non-Standard Forms of Employment, Geneva, 16–19 February, mimeo, Geneva: International Labour Office.

Kleinknecht, A., F.N. van Schaik and H. Zhou (2014) 'Is flexible labour good for innovation? Evidence from firm-level data', *Cambridge Journal of Economics* 38(5): 1207–19.

Korver, T. and G. Schmid (2012) 'Enhancing Transition Capacities and Sustainable Transitions', in J. de Munck, C. Didry, I. Ferreras and A. Jobert (eds), *Renewing Democratic Deliberation in Europe: The Challenge of Social and Civil Dialogue*, Brussels: Peter Lang, 23–55.

Leschke, J. (2015) 'Non-standard employment of women in service sector occupations: a comparison of European countries', in W. Eichhorst and P. Marx (eds), *Non-standard Employment in Post-industrial Labour Markets: An Occupational Perspective*, Cheltenham: Edward Elgar, 324–52.

Lisi, D. (2013) 'The Impact of Temporary Employment and Employment Protection on Labour Productivity: Evidence from an Industry-Level Panel', *Journal of Labour Market Research* 46(2): 119–44.

Martin, J.P. and S. Scarpetta (2011) 'Setting It Right: Employment Protection, Labour Reallocation and Productivity', IZA Policy Paper No. 25, Bonn: IZA.

Möller, J. (2010) 'The German Labor Market Response in the World Recession – De-mystifying a Miracle', *Journal for Labour Market Research* 42(4): 325–36.

OECD (2015) 'Non-standard Work, Job Polarisation and Inequality', in OECD, *In It Together: Why Less Inequality Benefits All*, Paris: OECD Publishing.

Schmid, G. (2008) *Full Employment in Europe – Managing Labour Market Transitions and Risks,* Cheltenham: Edward Elgar.

Schmid, G. (2015) 'Sharing Risks of Labour Market Transitions: Towards a System of Employment Insurance', *British Journal of Industrial Relations* 53(1): 70–93.

Schmid, G. (2017) 'Towards Employment Insurance?', in A. Hemerijck (ed.), *The Uses of Social Investment*, Oxford: Oxford University Press, 108–17.

Schmid, G. and J. Wagner (2016) 'Managing Social Risks of Non-standard Employment: Europe Compared to Countries in Asia, Latin America and Africa,' Berlin, mimeo, www.guentherschmid.eu/pdf/discussion/Managing_Social_Risks.pdf (accessed 14 June 2017).

Schmid, G. and J. Wagner (2017) 'Managing Social Risks of Non-standard Employment in Europe,' Working Paper Conditions of Work and Employment Series No. 91, Geneva: ILO.

Sen, A. (2009) *The Idea of Justice*, London: Allan Lane.

Smith, A. (1937) [1776], *The Wealth of Nations*, New York, Random House.

Standing, G. (2011) *The Precariat: The New Dangerous Class*, London and New York: Bloomsbury Academic.

Supiot, A. (2001) *Beyond Employment: Changes in Work and the Future of Labour Law in Europe*, Oxford: Oxford University Press; (2016) second edition with a new preface in French by Alain Supiot.

Zepeda, E., D. Alarcon, S. McDonald, C. Sapkota, M. Panda and G. Kumar (2013) 'Guaranteeing Jobs for the Rural Poor: An Assessment of India's MGNREGA Public Works Programme', in UNDP, *Social Protection, Growth and Employment*, New York: UNDP, 235–56.

Zimmermann, L. (2014) 'Public Works Programs in Developing Countries Have the Potential to Reduce Poverty', IZA World of Labor: 25, Bonn: IZA.

SEVEN

Active labour market policies for an inclusive growth

Giuliano Bonoli

Introduction

At first sight, active labour market policies (ALMPs) are an ideal instrument to promote an inclusive growth strategy. They promote labour market participation and, as a result, access to incomes for disadvantaged people. In this way they allow them to make the most of their potential, to participate to economic growth. ALMPs consist of a broad range of tools, including training, work experience programmes, wage subsidies, job search assistance, and so forth (European Commission, 2016). If used appropriately, and if of sufficient quality, they can help jobless individuals to re-enter the labour market. It is a typical example of a productive or investment oriented social policy, which entails helping disadvantaged people not by redistribution but by investing in their human capital and by facilitating their participation in productive processes.

ALMPs, however, do not exist in a vacuum. They operate within specific labour markets, and their overall impact on social stratification will depend on the characteristics of the labour market in which they operate. More precisely, if ALMPs operate in balanced labour markets, where structural unemployment is low, then it is likely that they will serve well the objectives of an inclusive growth strategy. The few excluded individuals can be effectively helped to get a place in productive processes and, as a result, improve their living conditions and contribute to wealth creation.

In contrast, if ALMPs operate in unbalanced labour markets, where labour supply vastly exceeds demand and where structural unemployment is high, then the outcome may be different. Unbalanced labour markets produce low quality employment, with wages that may be insufficient to afford above poverty living conditions to even small households. Even when successful in putting jobless people back into the labour market, ALMPs may well be powerless in helping them out of poverty. In addition, the low quality employment produced by unbalanced labour markets tends to be unstable, and many individual trajectories are characterised by frequent moves between social benefits and precarious employment. ALMPs, in such a context, can at best help manage labour market exclusion. Whether they contribute to an inclusive growth strategy, however, remains doubtful.

In this chapter I argue that the conditions described here prevail in the low skill segment of the labour market in a majority of OECD countries. Globalisation, technological progress and mass migration have concurred in creating this situation. The result is that, today, low skilled individuals face formidable hurdles in accessing good quality employment. This observation is highly relevant to the assessment of ALMPs. In fact, this type of policy intervention concerns mostly low skilled individuals, at least since the 'activation turn' that took place in the 1990s in a majority of OECD countries (Bonoli, 2010, 2013).

The low skilled – the victims of structural transformation

It is well known among labour market specialists that being low skilled represents a major source of disadvantage in today's economies. Generally this outcome is explained with reference to the notion of skilled biased technological change (SBTC), which refers to the fact that in advanced post-industrial economies, labour demand tends to shift upwards in the skill distribution, leaving unskilled persons competing for a smaller pool of jobs. According to many observers, SBTC is the main culprit for the plight experienced by low skilled people. However, it produces different problems in different institutional contexts. In the flexible US labour market SBTC results in lower wages for low skill people and as a result higher levels of inequality (see, for example, Blau and Kahn, 1996). In Europe, higher minimum wages and social benefits prevent the downward adjustment of wages so that SBTC creates low skill unemployment (Blau and Kahn, 2002). True, the theory of SBTC has been subjected to criticism. However, most of it has been directed against its use as an explanation of rising inequality in the US and unemployment in Europe (DiPrete, 2005; Ebbinghaus and Kittel, 2005).

In general, few dispute the fact that skill biased technological change is taking place, though some have identified a trend towards polarisation in labour demand, at least in some countries (Oesch and Rodriguez Menes, 2011). According to this view, technological change reduces labour demand for occupations requiring intermediate skills, such as clerical jobs. In the low skill segment of the labour market, where many activities cannot be easily substituted by machines, employment continues to expand. Empirical analysis shows that while the expansion of high skill employment is pervasive, only some countries are also creating jobs in the low skill segment. This is the case in particular of countries with more flexible wage setting institutions (such as the USA and UK; Kenworthy, 2004; Oesch and Rodriguez Menes, 2011).

Polarisation is a mixed blessing for the low skilled. On the one hand, more low skill jobs are created. On the other, however, job losses in the middle of the skill distribution lead to the displacement of workers with intermediate skills in the low skilled segment, pushing out low skilled individuals from the labour market (Gesthuizen et al, 2011). Whether because of SBTC or polarisation, low skilled individuals are clearly penalised by recent and current structural developments.

Excess supply of low skilled labour is further reinforced by immigration. In fact, in spite of many attempts by rich countries to be more selective and encourage the immigration of highly skill foreign born professionals, for various reasons, unskilled migration remains sizeable throughout the OECD world. The unskilled tend to enter rich countries through a variety of channels, often unrelated to formal labour recruitment, such as asylum applications, family reunion or undeclared work. Governments have little control over these forms of migration (OECD, 2008).

These developments translate in a major imbalance in the low skill segment that is visible in various statistics. First, low educated persons are considerably less likely to be in employment than are higher skilled individuals (Table 7.1). This effect is generalised across OECD countries and it is fairly stable across time.

What is more, when jobs can be created, these tend to be poorly paid (in relative terms) and/or based on insecure labour contracts. One of the consequences of this situation is that in Europe, low skilled people are overrepresented among the recipients of working age benefits. Given the different institutional structures that are found across Europe, it is difficult to provide fully comparable data. The information we can obtain from some individual countries, however, confirms that this is the case. In Germany, for instance, people without vocational training make up 53% of the beneficiaries of Unemployment benefit II (commonly known as Hartz IV); they constitute only 14% of the adult population (BA, 2010). In France some 67% of unemployed beneficiaries of the RSA (the last resort safety net) have an education level lower than the *Baccalauréat* (Pôle Emploi, 2012). In the general population, this proportion is 45%.[1] In the UK, some 34% of recipients

Table 7.1 Employment rates by educational attainment (ages 25–64), selected OECD countries, 2005–14 (%)

	(1) Below upper secondary		(2) Upper secondary		(3) Tertiary		Gap (1–3)	
	2005	2014	2005	2014	2005	2014	2005	2014
Germany	52	58	71	80	83	88	-31	-30
France	59	54	76	73	83	84	-24	-30
Italy	52	50	74	70	80	78	-28	-28
US	57	55	73	68	82	80	-25	-25
UK	65	60	82	80	88	85	-23	-25
Denmark	62	62	80	79	86	86	-24	-24
Sweden	66	66	81	85	87	89	-21	-23

Source: OECD (2015)

of incapacity benefit have no qualifications, against 14% in the general population (Kemp and Davidson, 2007). In Switzerland 57% of those on social assistance aged 18 or over have no professional qualification, against 30% in the general population (OFS, 2011).

In addition, it should also be noted that these figures underestimate the importance of skills as a determinant of benefit dependency. In fact, it is very likely that among the recipients who have more advanced levels of formal education, many possess obsolete or non-well maintained skills, putting them de facto on a par with those who have no qualification. The true number of people with little marketable skills who have to rely on benefits is likely to be considerably bigger than suggested by the figures reported above.

ALMPs in an unbalanced labour market

Since the 1990s, active labour market policy has been the main response to labour market problems. Alternatives, such as a voluntaristic industrial policy geared towards preserving or developing low skill employment, have often been advocated but never seriously pursued. In this section, on the basis of the evaluation literature, I try to provide a picture of the potential of ALMPs as a response to the labour market problem highlighted above.

Under the rubric of ALMPs, several different types of interventions have been developed. Elsewhere, I have developed a typology that tries to arrange the various types of interventions that are found in OECD countries across two dimensions: the extent to which they invest in human capital, and the extent to which they promote entry in market employment. In this chapter, I will follow the same distinction among four types of ALMPs, presented in Table 7.2 (although I use somewhat different labels). Of course this is not the only possible way to categorise ALMPs. Here it is used as a convenient tool to organise the discussion of the evaluation literature.

Table 7.2 Four types of active labour market policy

		Investment in human capital		
		None	**Weak**	**Strong**
Pro-market employment orientation	Weak	(passive benefits)	**Preservation of human capital** job creation schemes in the public sector non employment-related training programmes	(basic education)
	Strong	**Putting pressure** Time limits on recipiency Benefit reductions Benefit conditionality	**Improve matching** Placement services Job subsidies in the private sector Counselling Job search programmes	**Upskilling** Job related vocational training

Source: Adapted from Bonoli (2010)

Upskilling

Given the characterisation of the current employment problem presented above, and given what we know about the power of human capital as a protection against disadvantage, the obvious policy response to the post-industrial employment problem is a massive qualification offensive for the unskilled population. This solution, however, is regarded as problematic by many of those who have studied the impact of training programmes for unemployed people. Evaluations of training programmes have come to the conclusion that training based forms of active labour market policy have few positive effects on the probability of re-entering the labour market and/or on the earnings of those who participate (see, for example, Heckman et al, 1999; Martin and Grubb, 2001; Kluve, 2010).

Why is labour market related training largely ineffective, while investments in human capital in general produce impressive returns? Heckman and colleagues argue that learning successfully requires a set of cognitive and non-cognitive skills that can only be acquired during childhood and early adolescence. What is more, these need to be maintained during adulthood. Most of those who participate in labour market related programme are unskilled people who tend not to possess these essential skills. As a result, training programmes targeted on disadvantaged adults are bound to be ineffective. Much more promising are investments in childhood and interventions allowing people to maintain their human capital such as lifelong learning (Heckman, 2000; Heckman and Jacobs, 2009).

Studies of the impact of more ambitious training programmes help shed some light on this issue, though they are not numerous. Winter-Ebmer (2006), for instance, studied the impact of providing full vocational training to workers who had been dismissed during the restructuring of the Austrian steel industry in the late 1980s. He found that those who had participated in such training had better earnings (5–7% higher than non-participants) and were more likely to be in employment over a five-year period (Winter-Ebmer, 2006). A similar result was found by Lechner and colleagues who examined the impact of long-term training in Germany over a period of eight years (Lechner et al, 2004). They analysed the impact of various types of training programmes and found that most of them were effective in increasing the employment rate by around 10 percentage points sustained over the eight-year period of observation. They found that the more intensive training programme, a two-year full time re-training in a new profession, was the most effective after eight years, with employment gains close to 19 percentage points relative to non-participants.

In sum, the few studies that have looked at the long-term impact of more ambitious training programmes seem to provide a less pessimistic picture than short-term evaluations of more modest programmes. However, the effects obtained remain modest, with employment gains mostly in the region of 10–15 percentage points.

These studies, however, also suggest that not everyone is likely to benefit from these training programmes. In the Austrian programme, only 12% of eligible workers chose to undertake training, in spite of it being of very high quality. In that case, as well as in the aggregate in German programmes, participants tended to be better educated than non-participants. Labour market related training suffers from the same paradox that one finds in all forms of adult training: the more educated have better access to it, in a way vindicating Heckman's claim that a given level of cognitive and non-cognitive skills is essential in order to succeed in adult training.

It is clear that better educated unemployed people are overrepresented among participants in the more ambitious training programmes. This bias is thought to be controlled for in the impact studies reviewed above, but it may be the case that training is effective for individuals who have more than just basic education and who possess the non-cognitive skills that are needed to succeed in the classroom. This impression is confirmed also by a Swedish study that found that people with only primary education obtain no payoff from participation in training programmes (Andrén and Gustafsson, 2002)

Interestingly, in econometric studies, a variable that is strongly associated with the success of participation in training is the unemployment rate at the time of entry into the programme: the higher the unemployment rate, the bigger the positive impact of training (Lechner and Wunsch, 2009; Kluve, 2010). The most convincing explanation of this apparently counterintuitive observation is that at times of high unemployment, people with better cognitive and non-cognitive skills are more likely to enter training than when jobs are plentiful, and they are the ones who are more likely to profit from it.

Evaluations of German short-term training programmes (*Trainingmassnhamen*) have generally found positive outcomes (Fitzenberger et al, 2008), with sometimes stronger effects than those found for long-term training. A few months after programme completion, participants have employment rates between 10 and 17 percentage points higher than non-participants. The effect is sustained over the 30-month period of observation, and is strongest for those who enter short term training between the 7th and the 12th month of unemployment. However, these programmes are more akin to job search assistance, since the content of training is very much related to improving participants' job search skills. Only a minority of participants receive pure training, consisting mostly of computing or language courses (about 11% according to a survey). The majority of participants are trained in job search only[2] or receive a combination of skills (Kurtz, 2003).

Fouarge et al have studied the reasons behind the fact that low educated people are less likely to undergo training. They conclude that the lower willingness of the low educated to enrol in such programmes is essentially explained by lack of non-cognitive skills, for example, feeling in control of one's situation, exam anxiety and openness to experience (Fouarge et al, 2010).

Evaluations of training programmes for unemployed people suggest that a qualification offensive is unlikely to solve the employment problem presented above. The effects, though non-negligible, are limited to small minorities of participants. Clearly, training should not simply be dismissed as irrelevant. On the contrary, the studies reviewed here suggest that at least a minority of low skilled jobless people may truly benefit from long-term training. More research is needed on the factors that are associated with success in training but also on how these can be promoted. At the same time, policies designed to help low skilled people who cannot profit from training should be developed. These can aim at improving the process of labour market matching.

Improving labour market matching

The labour market is a very imperfect market, in the sense that information does not circulate well in it. Two types of information are particularly crucial and difficult to obtain for labour market participants: for jobseekers, information with regard to vacancies; and for employers, information about applicants' true productivity and personal qualities.

These labour market information problems are both likely to be conducive to durable labour market exclusion for some low skilled people. First, information about job vacancies is particularly opaque in the low skilled segment of all labour markets. Figure 7.1 shows the proportion of employees who have found their current (or last) job through an informal channel (personal contact or unsolicited application) in a sample of selected countries. In all these countries, substantial proportions of low skilled people have made use of an informal channel to find their current or last job. Everywhere (including in other countries not included in the figure, but for which data is available), the low skilled depend much more on these informal channels than higher educated workers. In some countries (southern Europe) the low skilled segment of the labour market is essentially based on informal matching (over 80%).

This result is confirmed by studies focusing on employers, who find that when recruiting low skilled personnel, the preferred recruitment channel is often an informal one. When surveyed, employers frequently mention the reliance on recommendations by their own employees for filling unskilled vacancies (Bonoli and Hinrichs, 2012; Marsden and Campbell, 1990; Rebien, 2010). Taken together these results suggest that, contrary to what one may expect, finding jobs in the low skilled segment requires good connections and job search skills. Getting access to information about vacancies depends on networks and on the ability to directly approach potential employers. Low skilled people looking for jobs only through traditional formal channels are unlikely to get far.

The second information problem, employers' difficulty in obtaining reliable information concerning applicants' true qualities, provides an additional barrier to the labour market for disadvantaged low educated people. A vast literature has persuasively demonstrated that a key strategy used by recruiters to get around this information problem is to rely on

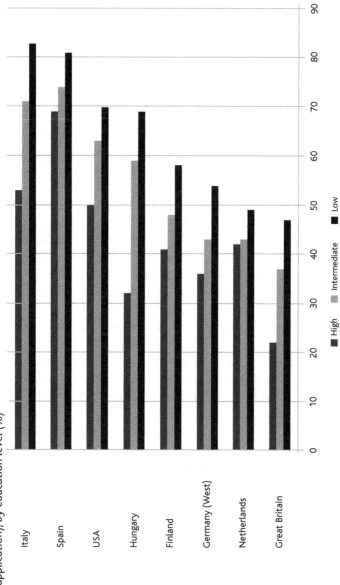

Figure 7.1 Employed (and formerly employed) persons having first heard about their job through an informal channel (personal contact or unsolicited application), by education level (%)

Note: Countries are ranked according to level for the low educated. Other possible sources of information were: public employment agency, private employment agency, school or university office, advertisement, contact by employer. The options 'Don't know', 'Never worked' and 'Refused' are excluded. Data not weighted.

Source: ISSP Research Group (2003)

easily observable features of applicants that are believed to be related to their productivity and personal qualities. This practice, known in the literature as 'statistical discrimination' entails excluding applicants that belong to certain groups considered to be more problematic (see, for example, Akerlof, 1970). These may include people with a given ethnic background, older people and ex-offenders. Inclusive growth and social investment policies investing in human capital pose a range of issues and challenges in ageing OECD societies for example (Deeming and Smyth, 2016). Some studies have also suggested that low skilled status may be used as a negative signal by employers, even when recruiting for jobs for which no particular skills are required. In fact, a higher level of education is simply regarded as an indication of better ability in general (Solga, 2002). This stigmatisation of low skilled status when competing for low skilled jobs may become particularly problematic when jobs requiring intermediate skills disappear, and medium skilled people compete in the low skilled segment, a phenomenon known as displacement (Gesthuizen et al, 2011). There is also evidence that long-term unemployed status is regarded by many employers as a negative signal (Bonoli, 2014; Atkinson et al, 1996; Oberholzer-Gee, 2008). To the extent that low skilled people are more likely to be unemployed than other groups, reasoning based on statistical discrimination is likely to add further to their disadvantage. In addition, many of the correlates of low skilled status, such as immigrant origin or older age, are also likely to carry some stigma in recruitment procedures.

To sum up, low skilled people looking for jobs face a number of formidable obstacles. First, information about vacancies is difficult to obtain, and circulates mostly through informal channels. Second, education level may be used by employers as a signal for ability, and lead to the exclusion of some of them from recruitment procedures, even when the position to be filled does not require any particular skills. Finally, many of the correlates of low skilled status – unemployment, long-term unemployment, immigrant origin, old age – are also likely to be used as negative signals in recruitment procedures.

Against this background, it is perhaps not surprising that some of the most effective labour market interventions are precisely those that assist and support job seekers in search efforts. Two types of interventions come up as particularly effective in most evaluation studies: job search assistance programmes and time limited recruitment subsidies to private employers (Kluve, 2010; Martin and Grubb, 2001; OECD, 2006). These two types of measure impact precisely on the job matching process, by making search more effective. Employment subsidies can compensate for the negative signals associated with low skilled status and some of its correlates.

What sort of employment gains are these programmes capable of producing? As seen above, much of what Germany classifies under 'short-term training' belongs in fact to the category of job search assistance. In this case, employment gains are in the region of 10 percentage points with slightly higher values for some groups (Fitzenberger et al, 2008). A French programme of intensive coaching produced employment gains of approximately 10% sustained over the 12-month period of observation (Behaghel et al, 2009). Other German job search assistance programmes obtained effects of up to a 10 percentage point increase in the probability of being in employment after 22 months (BA, 2004).

Effects are somewhat larger with employment subsidies. These are generally targeted on unemployed people who are particularly disadvantaged (older people, long-term unemployed), who, in the absence of the subsidies, have a rather low probability of finding a job. In addition, the evaluation of this type of intervention is problematic, because the subsidy is paid once the participant has found a job. This makes it difficult to construct an appropriate control group. A German study of employment subsidies for long-term unemployed people found a strong positive effect, with beneficiaries having employment rates up to 40 percentage points higher than non-participants some 20 months after the beginning of the programme. Of course, the comparison is difficult, since one group (beneficiaries) has by definition obtained a job at the beginning of the evaluation. However, employment outcomes are observed long after the expiration of the subsidy (in most cases between three and six months) and the subsequent no-layoff period of the same duration of the subsidy (Bernhard et al 2008). In a Swedish study of a six-month employment subsidy, after five years participants were still more likely to be in employment than a matched control group, the difference being around 15 percentage points (Forslund et al, 2004).

Job search assistance programmes may include a very wide variety of different interventions. Several programmes are simply based on intensive coaching by a personal advisor who usually has to care for a reduced number of jobseekers. Other examples include job clubs, where jobseekers share office space and are mutually supportive of each other search efforts. Job clubs may produce positive group dynamics and contribute to create a useful network for job seekers (Brown, 1997). Network creation and how to gain knowledge of non-advertised vacancies is also central to many such programmes. Overall, the notion of job search assistance programmes encompasses a rather broad variety of interventions.

Interventions that aim to improve labour market matching are considered among the most effective in the evaluation literature. They also tend to be less costly than training, especially long duration training. For this reason, they have seen a rapid expansion over the last few years in most European countries. Their potential, however, is also rather limited, with employment gains in the region of 10 percentage points. Employment subsidies may produce larger employment gains, but their very nature makes unbiased evaluation difficult to achieve. In addition, employment subsidies are likely to lead to deadweight losses and substitution effects.

Putting pressure

Much of the recent reorientation of social policies towards activation has involved increasing the pressure on non-working individuals to accept paid employment. However, it is rather difficult to measure or to document the extent to which jobseekers are put under pressure to accept a new job. There have been some attempts at collecting institutional data on this aspect of active labour market policy, focusing on dimensions such as the intensity of job search requirement and verification or the systematic and compulsory character of activation (Hasselpflug, 2005; OECD, 2007). In general, however, these institutional databases fail to convey a convincing image of the degree to which benefit recipients are put under pressure to accept a job.

In part, this is due to the fact that employment services can use various tools in order to increase pressure on benefit recipients to accept a job. For instance, it has been shown that the probability to exit unemployment tends to increase just before the planned entry into a labour market programme such as job creation or training. This effect, known as 'motivation' or 'deterrence' in the literature, is widely known and exploited by case workers in many countries (OECD, 2005).

Arguably, however, a better indication of the degree of pressure put on jobseekers is the use of sanctions. Sanctions tend to be considered as an intervention in evaluations of ALMPs. In general, econometric studies have highlighted a positive impact of sanctions on employment probability. Studies of the impact of sanctions exist at the aggregate level, comparing for example different programmes or employment agencies with different sanction rates, and the individual level, comparing individuals who are sanctioned to those who are not.

Studies of the former type tend to find clear positive effects of sanctioning. This was a clear result of the US multi-site evaluation of welfare to work schemes (Hamilton et al, 2001). In Switzerland, a comparison of sanction rates among employment offices and among personal advisors produced similar results (Frölich et al, 2007).

A similar result is found in studies at the individual level, which show that after being sanctioned, the probability of finding a job tends to increase (see, for example, Hofmann, 2008, for Germany; Lalive et al, 2005, for Switzerland). Here too, however, the size of the effect is rather limited. For Germany, Hofmann finds a 5–10 percentage points increase in the probability of being in employment during a two-month period following a sanction. The size of the effect varies across sub-groups and is stronger for young unemployed (Hofmann, 2008). Little is known about the longer-term impact of putting pressure on jobseekers. It can be hypothesised that the stronger the pressure, the more jobseekers will accept jobs that do not reflect their initial aspirations. A more recent study by Arni et al (2009) suggests that sanctions have a substantial impact on the type of employment found. Jobseekers who receive a sanction and subsequently enter employment have a 15% higher probability of becoming unemployed again, relative to those who have not been sanctioned. The impact on earnings is also strong, with those who are sanctioned accepting a larger drop in earnings relative to their previous job (on average, by some 10 percentage points larger than those who were not sanctioned). The study also shows that those who are sanctioned are more likely to exit to non-employment but then re-enter the labour market, suggesting that in order to find a job they deem suitable, they are prepared to renounce unemployment benefit (Arni et al, 2009).

The impression that one gets from the study quoted above is quite different from the popular image of sanctions being an effective tool to police the workshy. Instead, those who are sanctioned seem to aspire to a job that pays nearly as much as their previous one, but are unable to find it. The effectiveness of sanctions seems to be limited to a lowering of the reservation wage.

Preserving human capital

The fourth group of ALMPs identified above aims at slowing down the process of human capital depletion that occurs with an unemployment spell. It mostly involves job creation programmes in the public or non-profit sector. Beneficiaries perform some work over a limited period of time, and have the opportunity to practise and develop their work-related skills. Often, the main function of these programmes is to allow participants to maintain or develop soft skills – general personal competencies that are required in the labour market (be on time, how to relate to management and colleagues, and so on).

The evaluations of job creation programmes are generally negative. This conclusion is reached in the meta-analyses (Martin and Grubb, 2001; Kluve, 2010) and in several single programme evaluations. Out of 23 evaluation studies of public employment schemes reviewed by Kluve, only five report positive results. The rest were found to have either no impact or even a negative impact. In general, the negative impact is explained by a strong lock in effect that occurs with this type of programmes. When employed in a temporary public job, jobseekers reduce their search efforts, and the gain in terms of preservation of human capital and social skills seems to be insufficient most of the time to compensate for this. Even more than the other categories of ALMPs discussed in this chapter, job creation schemes are considered as being of little help.

ALMPs in developing countries are generally much less developed than in the OECD world. Some countries, especially in the Latin America/Caribbean region, have experimented with training programmes for disadvantaged groups, often the young. Evaluation studies are rare and, like those carried out in OECD countries, provide some mixed evidence with regard to the effectiveness of these interventions (Sanchez Puerta, 2010).

The impact of ALMPs on low skilled employment

The literature reviewed above suggests that ALMPs have produced at best modest results. The best results are obtained by programmes that manage to increase employment rates by 10–15 percentage points relative to non-participants. This impact is not negligible, and probably worthwhile on the basis of a cost-benefit analysis (see Hamilton et al, 2001). However, the contribution of ALMPs to solving the macro-level employment problem is limited. The extent to which countries have managed to expand low skilled employment between 1997–99 and 2007–09 seems to be completely unrelated to the effort they have made in ALMPs over the same period. Increases in inequality and possibly labour market deregulation in some countries have probably played a bigger role in accounting for the expansion in low skilled employment in the late 1990s and into the 2000s.

ALMPs in developing countries are generally much less developed than in the OECD world. Some countries, especially in the Latin

America/Caribbean region, have experimented with training programmes for disadvantaged groups, often the young. Evaluation studies are rare and, like those carried out in OECD countries, provide some mixed evidence with regard to the effectiveness of these interventions (Sanchez Puerta, 2010).

Conclusion: bringing redistribution back

ALMPs are a useful tool that can be of help to many disadvantaged unemployed people. They are, however, insufficient to redress the fundamental imbalances that plague today's labour markets in OECD countries. Skill biased technological change produces a distribution of resources that is strongly skewed in favour of those who possess marketable skills. The result is that those who do not are bound to experience severe disadvantage, whether they manage to access employment or not. For this reason, ALMPs alone are unlikely to promote an inclusive growth strategy in today's labour market context.

In these concluding remarks, I argue that an inclusive growth strategy should combine ALMPs with intelligent redistribution. By 'intelligent redistribution' I mean income transfers that do not undermine work incentives in the current context, and reward participation in productive processes. Examples of such income transfers are tax credits paid to low income working individuals and families in countries such as the USA and the UK. These programmes have become part of the standard social policy kit in a post-industrial economy, and try to redress some of the problems created by rising levels of inequality.

Redistribution could also take other forms that need to be adapted to the volatile nature of low skilled employment in the post-industrial age. Typically, tax credits are complex to administer and deliver amounts that are known only at the end of a taxation year, and in this respect are unsuited to the rapidly changing employment situation of many low educated individuals in today's labour markets. Alternatives worth exploring include forms of progressive VAT or institutionalised discriminatory pricing. High levels of inequality mean that mid to high income individuals are probably prepared to pay considerably more than low income persons for the same service. Forms of discriminatory pricing could be institutionalised, for example by means of social cards[3] that allow certain categories of consumers to pay less for some goods and services.

Notes

[1] In the population aged between 25 and 50: see www.insee.fr/fr/themes/tableau. asp?reg_id=0&ref_id=NATTEF07232 (accessed 14 June 2017).

[2] Under this rubric one finds a range of different interventions, including an assessment of the suitability for different jobs (33% of participants, according to a survey) support to job search (13%) and tests of availability for work (5%); see Kurtz (2003: 15).

[3] In Italy, a Social Card is provided to some low income individuals and households. It allows them to buy goods and services at a discount in 10,000 shops that participate in the scheme. For more details, see www.mef.gov.it/focus/carta_acquisti/documenti/carta_acquisti_aggiornamento.pdf (accessed 14 June 2017).

References

Akerlof, G.A. (1970) 'Market for lemons – quality uncertainty and market mechanism', *Quarterly Journal of Economics* 84: 488–500.

Andrén, T. and B. Gustafsson (2002) *Income Effects from Labor Market Training Programs in Sweden During the 80s and 90s*, DP No. 603, Bonn: IZA.

Arni, P., R. Lalive and J.C. van Ours (2009) *How Effective Are Unemployment Benefit Sanctions? Looking Beyond Unemployment Exit*, DP No. 4509, Bonn: IZA.

Atkinson, J., G. Lesley and N. Meager (1996) *Employers, recruitment and the unemployed*, London, Institute for Employment Studies.

BA (2004) *Evaluation des hessischen Modells – Kurzbericht*, Frankfurt: BA (Bundesagentur für Arbeit) Regionaldirektion Hessen.

BA (2010) *Jarhesbericht SGBII*, Nürnberg: BA (Bundesagentur für Arbeit).

Behaghel, L., B. Crépon and M. Gurgand (2009) *Evaluation des expérimentations d'accompagnement renforcé des chômeurs de longue durée*, Paris: Paris School of Economics.

Bernhard, S., H. Gartner and G. Stephan (2008) *Wage subsidies for needy job-seekers and their effect on individual labour market outcomes after the German reforms*, IAB Discussion Paper(No. 21), Nürenberg: IAB.

Blau, F.D. and L.M. Kahn (1996) 'International differences in male wage inequality: Institutions versus market forces', *Journal of Political Economy* 104: 791–837.

Blau, F.D. and L.M. Kahn (2002) *At home and abroad: U.S. labor market performance in international perspective*, New York: Russell Sage.

Bonoli, G. (2010) 'The political economy of active labour market policies', *Politics & Society* 38: 435–57.

Bonoli, G. (2013) *The Origins of Active Social Policy. Active labour market and childcare polcies in a comparative perspective*, Oxford, Oxford University Press.

Bonoli, G. (2014) 'Employers' attitudes toward long-term unemployed people and the role of activation in Switzerland', *International Journal of Social Welfare* 23: 421–30.

Bonoli, G. and K. Hinrichs (2012) 'Statistical discrimination and employers' recruitment practices for low skilled workers', *European Societies* 14(3): 338–61.

Brown, A. (1997) *Work First. How to Implement an Employment-Focused Approach to Welfare Reform*, Washington, DC: MDRC.

Deeming, C. and P. Smyth (2016) 'Reassessing the 'Social Investment Perspective' for 'Inclusive Growth': Where do older workers fit?', *Social Policy and Society* 15(4): 659–74.

DiPrete, T.A. (2005) 'Labor Markets, Inequality, and Change: A European Perspective', *Work and Occupations* 32: 119–39.

Ebbinghaus, B. and B. Kittel (2005) 'European rigidity versus American flexibility? The institutional adaptability of collective bargaining', *Work and Occupations* 32: 163–95.

Escudero, V. (2015) *Are active labour market policies effective in activating and integrating low-skilled individuals? An international comparison*, Working paper No. 3, Geneva: ILO.

European Commission (2016) *Active Labour Market Policies, European Semester Thematic Fiche*, http://ec.europa.eu/europe2020/pdf/themes/2016/active_labour_market_policies_201605.pdf (accessed 14 June 2017).

Fitzenberger, B., O. Orlyanskaya, A. Osikominu and M. Waller (2008) *Déjà Vu? Short-Term Training in Germany 1980–1992 and 2000–2003*, IAB DIscussion paper 27/2008, Nürnberg: IAB.

Forslund, A., P. Johansson and L. Lindqvist (2004) *Employment Subsidies – a Fast Lane from Unemployment to Work?*, IFAU Working Paper 2004:18, Uppsala: IFAU.

Fouarge, D., T. Schils and A. de Grip (2010) *Why Do Low-Educated Workers Invest Less in Further Training?*, IZA DP No. 5180, Bonn: IZA.

Frölich, M., M. Lechner, S. Behncke, S. Hammer, N. Schmidt, S. Menegale, A. Lehmann and R. Iten (2007) *Influence des ORP sur la reinsertion des demandeurs d'emploi*, Arbeitsmarktpolitik No 20, Bern: SECO Publikation.

Gesthuizen, M., H. Solga and R. Kunster (2011) 'Context Matters: Economic Marginalization of Low-Educated Workers in Cross-National Perspective', *European Sociological Review* 27: 264–80.

Hamilton, G., S. Freedman, L. Gennetian, C. Michalopoulos, J. Walter, D. Adams-Ciardullo and A. Gassman-Pines (2001) *National evaluation of welfare-to-work strategies*, Washington, DC: Manpower Demonstration Research Corporation.

Hasselpflug, S. (2005) *Availability criteria in 25 countries*, working paper No 12, Copenhagen: Ministry of Finance.

Heckman, J. (2000) 'Policies to foster human capital', *Research in Economics* 54: 3–56.

Heckman, J., R. Lalonde and J. Smith (1999) 'The economics and econometrics of active labour market programs', in A. Ashenfelter and D. Card (eds) *Handbook of Labor Economics, Volume 3*, Amsterdam: Elsevier, 1865–2097.

Heckman, J.J. and B. Jacobs (2009) *Policies to Create and Destroy Human Capital in Europe*, IZA DP No. 4680, Bonn: IZA.

Hofmann, B. (2008) *Work Incentives? Ex-Post Effects of Unemployment Insurance Sanctions - Evidence from West Germany*, IAB Discussion Paper 43, Nürenberg: IAB.

ISSP Research Group (2003) *International Social Survey Programme: Social Relations and Support Systems / Social Networks II – ISSP 2001*, GESIS Data Archive, Cologne. ZA3680 Data file Version 1.0.0, doi:10.4232/1.3680.

Kemp, P.A. and Davidson, J. (2007) *Routes onto Incapacity Benefit: Findings from a survey of recent claimants*, Research Report No 469, London: Department for Work and Pensions.

Kenworthy, L. (2004) *Egalitarian Capitalism. Jobs, Incomes and Growth in Affluent Countries*, New York: Russell Sage Foundation.

Kluve, J. (2010) 'The effectiveness of European active labor market programs', *Labour Economics* 17: 904–18.

Kurtz, B. (2003) *Trainingsmaßnahmen – Was verbirgt sich dahinter?*, IAB Werkstattbericht No. 8, Nürnberg: IAB.

Lalive, R., J. Zweimuller and J.C. van Ours (2005) 'The effect of benefit sanctions on the duration of unemployment', *Journal of the European Economic Association* 3: 1386–417.

Lechner, M., R. Miquel and C. Wunsch (2004) *Long-run Effects of Public Sector Sponsored Training in West Germany*, St. Gallen: University of St. Gallen, Department of Economics.

Lechner, M. and C. Wunsch (2009) 'Are Training Programs More Effective When Unemployment Is High?', *Journal of Labor Economics* 27: 653–92.

Marsden, P. and C. Campbell (1990) 'Recruitment and selection processes: the organisational side of job searches', in R. Breiger (ed.) *Social mobility and social structure*, Cambridge: Cambridge University Press, 59–79.

Martin, J. and D. Grubb (2001) 'What works and for whom: A review of OECD countries' experiences with active labour market policies', *Swedish Economic Policy Review* 8: 9–56.

Oberholzer-Gee, F. (2008) 'Nonemployment stigma as rational herding: A field experiment', *Journal of Economic Behavior & Organization* 65: 30–40.

OECD (2005) 'Labour Market Programmes and Activation Strategies: Evaluating the Impacts', *OECD Employment Outlook 2005*, 173–208.

OECD (2006) 'General Policies to Improve Employment Opportunities for All', *Employment Outlook 2006*, 47–126.

OECD (2007) 'Activating the unemployed: what countries do', *OECD Employment Outlook*, 207–41.

OECD (2008) 'Management of low skill migration', *OECD Migration Outlook 2008*, 125–59.

OECD (2015) *Education at a glance*, Paris: OECD.

Oesch, D. and J. Rodriguez Menes (2011) 'Upgrading or polarization? Occupational change in Britain, Germany, Spain and Switzerland, 1990–2008', *Socio-Economic Review* 9: 503–31.

OFS (2011) *Statistique de l'aide sociale. Résultats nationaux*, Neuchâtel: OFS.

Pôle Emploi (2012) *Les demandeurs d'emploi* bénéficiaires du RSA en décembre 2011, www.pole-emploi.org/file/galleryelement/pj/f1/9a/68/43/rsa3370177883412899103.pdf (accessed 14 June 2017).

Rebien, M. (2010) *The use of social networks in recruiting processes from a firms perspective*, IAB Discussion Paper 5/2010, Nürnberg: IAB.

Sanchez Puerta, L. (2010) *Labor Market Policy Research for Developing Countries: Recent Examples from the Literature. What do we know and what should we know?*, Social Protection Discussion Paper 1001, Washington, DC: The World Bank.

Solga, H. (2002) 'Stigmatization by negative selection. Explaining less educated people's decreasing employment opportunities', *European Sociological Review* 18: 159–78.

Winter-Ebmer, R. (2006) 'Coping with a structural crisis: evaluating an innovative redundancy-retraining project', *International Journal of Manpower* 27: 700–21.

EIGHT

Education and skills for inclusive growth

Marius R. Busemeyer

Introduction and motivation

Policies about education and skill formation occupy a central place in the social investment paradigm (Morel et al, 2012: 2). Policymakers and scholars alike emphasise the potential of education to contribute to a more egalitarian society by supporting the labour market integration of young people as well as to boost the productive potential of the labour force in service-oriented knowledge economies (see, for example, Bonoli, 2013; Hemerijck, 2013; Morel et al, 2012; Vandenbroucke and Vleminckx, 2011). In many ways, the social investment model of the welfare state can be regarded as the renewal of the old social democratic promise of wedding the economic power of free market capitalism with some form of redistribution via the welfare state. However, as has been extensively described elsewhere (Hemerijck, 2012; Morel et al, 2012), the social investment model is also different from the traditional Keynesian paradigm in emphasising the *productive contribution* of social policies rather than their redistributive aspects. In other words, the primary goal of social investment policies is to expand the size of the (economic) pie rather than focusing on redistribution between different constituency groups.

The latter point is reinforced by arguments about the potential of different social policies to promote economic growth. Even though the often-assumed trade-off between equality and efficiency has, by and large, not materialised (Lindert, 2004), there are still lingering concerns about the economic implications of social policy in public and academic debates – with important political implications. A common concern is that a large (and redistributive) welfare state might blunt incentives to invest in economic activities and participate in the labour market. Furthermore, in times of economic globalisation, a generous welfare state might increasingly turn into a liability for governments keen on attracting mobile capital. Larger welfare states imply higher levels of taxation, which are hard to maintain in a competitive environment (Busemeyer, 2009).

The social investment literature cited above as well as the debate on Varieties of Capitalism (VoC; Hall and Soskice, 2001; Iversen and Soskice, 2001; Iversen, 2005; Hall and Gingerich, 2009) have developed a powerful counter argument to this line of reasoning by providing a rich and compelling explanation for the conditions under which social policies can become an *asset* rather than a liability both for economic growth as well as social inclusion. VoC scholars, for instance, argue that the welfare state serves as an insurance for workers with a particular skill set ('specific skills'), which in turn allows firms in the coordinated market economies of Continental and Northern Europe to develop a competitive edge in high quality manufacturing and similar industries (Hall and Soskice, 2001; Iversen and Soskice, 2001). The social investment perspective, in turn, puts more emphasis on the role of early childhood education, active labour market policies and lifelong learning in boosting the employability and human capital of individuals (Bonoli, 2013). This argument is also developed in new theories of endogenous economic growth (for example, Romer, 1986). This and related literatures in economics have repeatedly shown that investments in education have significant positive effects on economic growth (Krueger and Lindahl, 2001; Hawkes and Ugur, 2012; Hanushek and Woessmann, 2012), because educational investments – despite significant variation across countries as well as educational levels – have positive private and public returns on average.

Thus, both from the perspective of (inclusive) growth theories and social investment debates, investing in education seems to be the obvious answer to many of the current challenges facing post-industrial economies. Furthermore, from a more political perspective, many have argued that investing in education, and boosting social investment more generally, is hugely popular with voters. For instance, as Ansell (2010: 136) writes: 'Promising to support education is an archetypical crowd-pleaser.' This hunch is generally confirmed in surveys of public opinion. In many OECD countries, for instance in Spain, Ireland, the US and Germany, the share of the population demanding more or even much more spending on education is more than 80% (Busemeyer, 2012: 225). With regard to social investment more specifically, Bonoli has argued that it is politically attractive as it allows for 'affordable credit-claiming' (Bonoli, 2013: 8): Expanding opportunities in early childhood education and care or helping the disadvantaged to find a new job are popular policies and, relative to the core pillars of the welfare state in healthcare or pensions, these policies are rather inexpensive.

The purpose of this chapter is to re-visit some of these claims and to provide a critical re-assessment. In the following sections, I discuss the potential (and limitations) of social investment policies to contribute to lowering inequalities and inclusive growth with a particular focus on education and skill formation. I pay particular attention to two factors: the importance of post-secondary vocational education and training relative to academic higher education; and the division of labour between public and private sources of funding. Empirically, I focus on Western OECD countries, though some of the theses put forward in this chapter are also relevant for non-OECD countries.

Education and inequality

As is mentioned in the introduction to this volume, the integration of the social investment agenda with new perspective on 'inclusive growth' holds enormous potential. In this integrated framework, the social investment perspective is primarily concerned with the supply side of the labour market, whereas inclusive growth strategies are more aimed at ensuring a fair distribution of the gains of economic growth. In a certain way, education serves a bridging function between the supply and the demand side of the labour market, because it influences the distribution of skills, but also can become a significant source of public employment opportunities itself.

Primarily, the institutional set-up of the education and training system influences the supply (and distribution) of skills in a given economy (Busemeyer and Iversen, 2012; Goldin and Katz, 2008). In doing this, it has significant potential to mitigate but also exacerbate existing inequalities. Most famously, Goldin and Katz (2008) have argued that skill-biased technological change explains why inequality has increased significantly in the recent period, in particular in the US. According to this perspective, technological change – the spread of new information and communication technologies – has increased the (private) economic returns of investments in higher education, since high skilled individuals are more demanded on the labour market. Of course, this is by itself not a new phenomenon, but what has changed in the recent period is that the number of high skilled graduates has reached a natural saturation point, at least in many OECD countries, where levels of tertiary enrolment are approaching the 50% mark. As a consequence, since the supply of highly skilled individuals can no longer keep up with increasing demand fuelled by technological change, inequality rises, as posited by Goldin and Katz (2008).

Even though the basic logic of this argument is compelling, there are some major flaws in it. First of all, and most obviously, there is a significant cross-national variation in the degree of inequality across countries at a similar level of economic development (and that may even have similar levels of overall educational attainment). For instance, according to the most recent figures provided by the OECD, the US and Sweden are very similar with regard to the share of the population between 25 and 34 years of age who have attained tertiary education: 45.7% in the US (2014) compared to 46.0% in Sweden (OECD, 2016a). However, as is also well-known, these two countries (still) differ enormously with regard to income inequality: the Gini coefficient for the distribution of disposable income (post taxes and transfers) is 0.39 for the US, compared to 0.27 for Sweden (OECD, 2016b).

The obvious conclusion from this brief example is that the absolute level of educational attainment as such does not necessarily determine levels of socioeconomic inequality. Of course, as is well-known from scholarship on the determinants of inequality in comparative political economy (for example, Bradley et al, 2003; Pontusson et al, 2002; Iversen and Soskice, 2009; Lupu and Pontusson, 2011; Huber and Stephens, 2014), labour market institutions such as collective wage bargaining institutions as well as the power of labour unions or left parties in government shape both the primary distribution of incomes on the labour market as well as the degree of redistribution in the welfare state. In other words, these factors influence the extent to which the primary distribution of skills (produced by the education system) is mirrored in labour market inequalities. Thus, labour market institutions in terms of wage-setting mechanisms and public policies can have significant consequences for the distribution of post-tax and transfer income.

In spite of these considerations, the institutional set-up of the education and training system also has implications for the primary distribution of skills: the 'supply side' of the labour market. If class-related biases in access to higher education persist (as they do in many countries, see Breen and Jonsson, 2005; Breen et al, 2009), then subsequent efforts to redistribute via social policies or taxation schemes might fail, be ineffective and/or have negative consequences for economic growth. Hence, it seems that a broad provision of education, in particular higher education, would be an important necessary (though not sufficient) precondition for education to promote both economic growth and social inclusion. And this is exactly the reason why actors such as the OECD and the EU focus on expanding tertiary enrolment: The EU's Strategic Framework 'Education and Training 2020' aims at increasing the share of people aged 30–34 with a tertiary education degree (or similar) to 40% by 2020 across the EU (European Commission, 2015). And even though class biases in access to higher education are difficult to abolish in the short term, the ongoing expansion of tertiary enrolment should in the long term at least diminish these inequalities (Breen et al, 2009).

However, as I will argue in the following, the story is more complex. Providing (higher) education for all is not a panacea, since its contribution to lowering inequality depends critically on the way higher education is financed. Furthermore, the potential impact of other types of upper and post-secondary education – vocational education and training – is often underestimated in public and academic debates. When examining the potential of different types of post-secondary education to contribute to inclusive growth, a differentiated picture emerges.

I start my line of reasoning with a precautionary note. As can be seen from Figure 8.1, the overall association between educational and socioeconomic inequality is rather loose as documented by the flat slope of the regression line (see Busemeyer, 2015: Chapter 4; Solga 2014). If anything, the tendency is slightly negative, which runs counter to expectations (that countries with higher levels of educational inequality have a lower degree of socioeconomic inequality). The figure represents average values for the period from the late 1990s until the onset of the economic and fiscal crisis in 2008. I limit the period of observation to this timeframe, because the effects of the economic and fiscal crisis could bias the results. The x axis depicts a measure of educational inequality, which is derived from the OECD PISA studies (OECD, 2010: 34). It captures the impact of parental background on the educational attainment of 15-year-old students in reading. Higher values indicate that parental background has a stronger effect in the respective country and vice versa. The y axis is the Gini coefficient of the distribution of incomes after taxes and transfers (average values calculated with data from Solt, 2009). Figure 8.1 shows that countries scatter across the whole range of values in these two dimensions, suggesting that simply reducing existing levels of educational inequality – though an important policy goal by itself – might not directly spill over into lower levels of socioeconomic inequality.

A couple of illustrative examples reinforce this point. For instance, Germany is usually regarded as a country with a high degree of educational inequality, because of its segmented secondary school

Figure 8.1 The (non-) association between educational and socioeconomic inequality, OECD countries

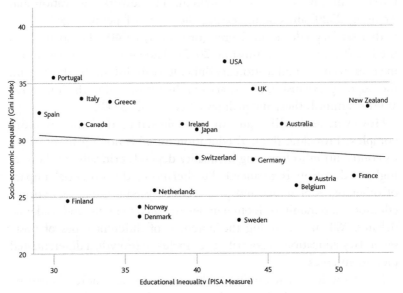

Sources: Solt (2009); OECD (2010: 34)

system with early tracking and a strict separation between vocational education and higher education, stifling educational (and, by implication, social) mobility (Pfeffer, 2008). In terms of socioeconomic inequality, however, Germany performs much better compared to other countries. In contrast, the US is a case in which the existence of comprehensive schools in combination with a diversified and open higher education sector and above average levels of tertiary enrolment should contribute to lowering educational inequalities, even though socioeconomic inequalities in terms of income and wealth are exceptionally high. Scandinavian countries, finally, such as Finland manage to combine low levels of educational inequality with low levels of socioeconomic inequality. This might be because these countries, besides having a generally more open higher education system, have also established vocational education tracks as a viable alternative to academic higher and upper secondary education.

Of course, there are many different ways of how to measure educational inequality and depending on which measure is used, the association to socioeconomic inequality might be stronger or weaker (see Solga, 2014, for a comprehensive analysis). Furthermore, measuring educational inequality is not merely a methodological problem, since there are significant differences in the underlying concepts. Educational inequality could be related to the link between parental background and attainment (as in the measure used above), to differences in students' expectations on completing higher education, to class-related differences in access to particular sectors of the education system or simply to the distribution of educational certificates in the population. Many of these indicators do not sufficiently take into account more implicit forms of stratification, since these are difficult to measure. For instance, in some countries such as the US and the UK (Gingrich and Ansell, 2014), educational choices and opportunities are very much linked to residential patterns. Hence, even though formally speaking, secondary education takes place in comprehensive schools, access to these schools de facto correlates with socioeconomic background as the latter also affects residential choices.

Vocational education as social investment?

Summing up, it seems, that the potential of education to mitigate inequality is limited through various filters. However, this does not necessarily mean that it does not have any effect at all. The existing social investment literature primarily emphasises the importance of early childhood education and care in preventing the emergence of inequalities in later stages of the life course (see in particular Esping-Andersen, 2002; Bonoli, 2013; Bonoli and Reber, 2010; Naumann, 2012; Van Lancker, 2013). Building largely on the work of Heckman (2006), the argument is that early intervention in children's intellectual development is particularly effective in levelling innate differences. From this perspective, this is both more efficient and fairer than trying to mitigate differences in later stages of educational careers. Besides early childhood education and care, the social investment strategy focuses mostly on active labour market policies, lifelong learning and innovation 'in the knowledge-based service economy' (see Chapter One by Deeming and Smyth in this volume) – higher education rather than vocational education and training (VET).

Thus, in general, the potential of VET as a social investment tool to promote inclusive growth is somewhat underestimated in the existing literature. This is likely the case for two reasons: first, there is a widespread believe that investing in VET is less effective in supporting the structural transformation towards the service-based knowledge economy compared to tertiary education (Wren, 2013). Furthermore, if anything, school-based variants of VET are expected to be superior to firm-based apprenticeship training (Anderson and

Hassel, 2013), since the former usually contain more theoretical training and offer better opportunities to proceed from VET to higher education. Second, on the background of a pervasive trend towards higher education ('academic drift'), the continued existence of VET in some countries is often associated with a higher degree of educational stratification and inequality. From that perspective, VET could serve as a 'diversion' of students from weaker socioeconomic backgrounds who might otherwise pursue academic higher education (Shavit and Müller 2000). Because of this diversion effect, one might assume, VET should not necessarily have a positive effect on social inclusion and educational mobility.

In the following, I will tackle each of these arguments in turn. First of all, Figures 8.2 and 8.3 depict the bivariate association between the prevalence of VET and higher education, respectively, on the one hand and socioeconomic inequality on the other. Figure 8.2 documents a clearly negative association between the share of upper secondary students in VET tracks and socioeconomic inequality (see also Estévez-Abe et al, 2001, for a similar finding for an earlier period).[1] Hence, levels of socioeconomic inequality are significantly lower in countries with extensive provision of VET. This measure of the extensiveness of VET includes both school-based as well as workplace-based (apprenticeship)

Figure 8.2 The association between extensiveness of VET and socioeconomic inequality, OECD countries

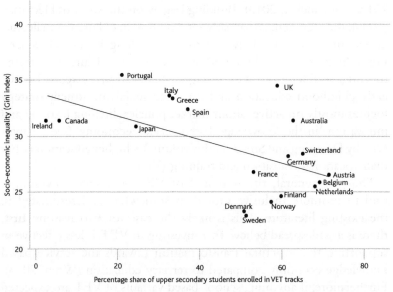

Source: Busemeyer (2015: 191) (Reproduced with permission of the copyright owner)

types of VET, which is why countries such as Belgium and Norway with extensive school-based VET are on a level similar to Germany, Austria and Switzerland.

How to explain this negative association? Even though VET can be regarded as a 'diversion' from higher education, it also serves the purpose of a 'safety net' (Shavit and Müller, 2000). Well-developed VET systems open up educational alternatives and opportunities for those in the lower half of the innate distribution of academic skills, which often connect to relatively secure and well-paid employment in the labour market in those countries, where VET is an established alternative and therefore recognised by employers. As is well-known by now, transitions from education and training to employment are much smoother and levels of youth unemployment significantly lower in countries with extensive provision of VET, in particular firm-based apprenticeships (Breen, 2005; Gangl, 2003; Wolbers, 2007; Busemeyer, 2015: Chapter 4). In contrast, the strict demarcation between higher (university or college) education on the one hand and (lower) secondary education on the other as it is often found in liberal Anglo-Saxon countries without well-established VET tracks can promote the polarisation of skills and therefore labour market opportunities.

Higher education

In Figure 8.3, I display the (bivariate) association between tertiary enrolment and socioeconomic inequality.[2] As can be seen, the link between these two measures is much less tight than in the previous case (even though there is a slight negative tendency). This is likely to be related to two factors: first, educational investments always create public and private returns, and in the case of higher education, private returns are higher than in the case of VET. Educational investments create private returns in the sense that those with higher levels of education earn higher wages on the labour market. Across all OECD countries, private returns ('earnings advantages') are always higher for individuals with a tertiary education compared to those with secondary education only, even though there is of course a large cross-national variation (OECD, 2015: 116).

Hence, the expansion of opportunities in tertiary education first of all benefits those who have a decent chance of obtaining a tertiary degree, usually those in the upper half of the academic distribution of skills. Even though an expansion of the number of high skilled individuals should lower their wage premiums because of intensified wage competition, the relative position of those in the lower half of

Figure 8.3 The association between tertiary enrolment and socioeconomic inequality, OECD countries

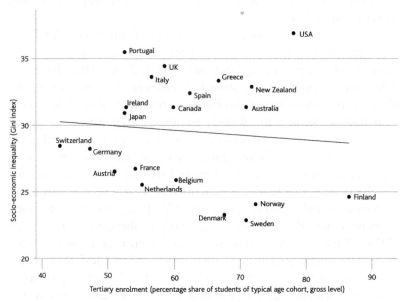

Source: Busemeyer (2015: 194) (Reproduced with permission of the copyright owner)

the skills distribution is not directly affected by this. Therefore, the potential contribution of an expansion of tertiary enrolment towards lowering inequality is hampered by the fact that it first benefits those who are already better off in the first place.

This is partly related to the second factor: the division of labour between public and private sources of funding in (higher) education. As can be seen in Figure 8.3, there are a number of country cases (Norway, Denmark, Sweden and Finland) with high levels of tertiary enrolment and low levels of socioeconomic inequality. In contrast, another cluster of countries above the regression line (mostly Anglo-Saxon countries, but also some Southern European states) exhibits much higher levels of socioeconomic inequality despite having similar levels of tertiary enrolment. A crucial variable separating these two country clusters is the division between public and private sources of education funding. This is primarily important for the case of higher education, where the bulk of private spending on education stems from tuition fees (although the OECD data also include contributions from other private entities such as businesses and foundations; see Wolf, 2009: 51).

Figure 8.4 is a further corroboration of the hunch that the level of socioeconomic inequality is higher in countries with a higher share of private spending: it displays a clearly positive association between these two measures.[3] Countries with extensive private spending on education also exhibit higher levels of socioeconomic inequality, whereas public funding of higher education is associated with lower levels of inequality. The causal mechanisms underlying this associations might be rather complex. A first obvious explanation is that high levels of private spending (such as tuition fees) might deter children from poorer social backgrounds from participating in higher education, because they cannot afford it. There might be some truth to this claim, in particular when tuition fees reach very high levels, fuelling student-related debts, as is happening in the US (Mettler 2014). However, high tuition fees often go hand in hand with high levels of tertiary enrolment, because tuition fees are partly compensated for with generous student subsidy programmes (Garritzmann, 2015, 2016).

Hence, a second explanation for the association between private education spending and wage inequality focuses on the implications of private spending for welfare state politics. As is shown in Busemeyer (2013), individuals living in countries with higher levels of private education spending tend to be more reluctant in supporting redistribution and an expansion of the welfare state. This might be related to cultural or ideological predispositions towards the welfare

Figure 8.4 The association between share of private spending in tertiary education and socioeconomic inequality, OECD countries

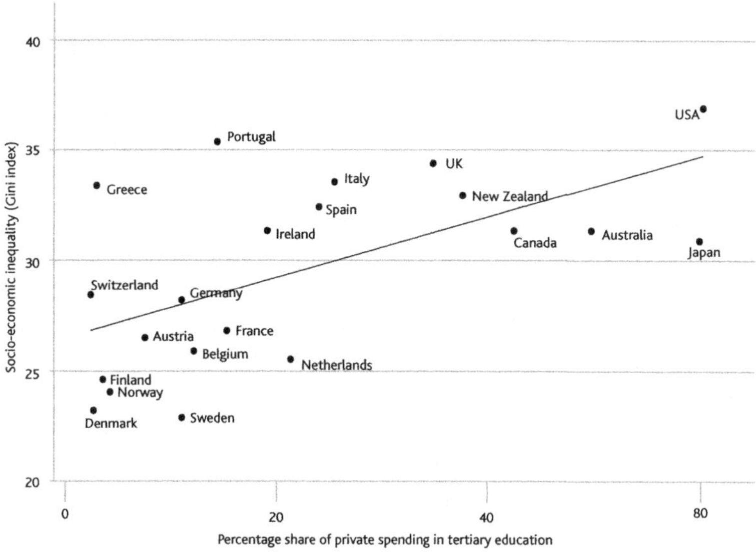

Source: Busemeyer (2015: 194) (Reproduced with permission of the copyright owner)

state; a culture of individualism and meritocracy might be associated with a greater tolerance for private contributions to both education and social policy. It might also be a consequence of the simple fact that individuals who have incurred significant private investments in their skill formation would like to recoup these investments in the form of higher wage premiums on the labour market and therefore oppose government intervention and redistribution.

At this point, it is also interesting to note that the Scandinavian countries, which are characterised by high levels of tertiary enrolment, low levels of private spending on education as well as lower levels of socioeconomic inequality, are incidentally also characterised by above average levels of enrolment in VET tracks at the upper secondary education level (see Figure 8.2). This is not a coincidence; it simply shows that in these countries pursuing VET instead of general academic education at the secondary level does not represent an educational dead-end, because VET is fully integrated into the general secondary education system and also opens up the possibility to move on to tertiary education afterwards. However, the case of Sweden, which suffers from above average levels of youth unemployment, also shows the negative side effects of a purely school-based VET system, which is not connected as well to the labour market as the Danish or the Norwegian system, where firm-based training plays a stronger role.

Education and economic growth

So far, we have mostly focused on the potential contribution of different types of education to social inclusion – the inclusive aspect of 'inclusive growth'. What about the connection between education and economic growth? As mentioned above, a large literature in economics has shown that, by and large, education has a positive effect on economic growth, in particular in the developing countries (Hawkes and Ugur, 2012). Above, I also briefly mentioned the argument that higher education is expected to have a much bigger positive impact on economic growth compared to VET, because it more effectively promotes the transformation towards service-based knowledge economies (Wren, 2013).

Figures 8.5 and 8.6 partly confirm this expectation. Again, the data used are average values for the time period from the late 1990s until 2008. In that period, Ireland was a significant outlier in terms of economic growth. Therefore, I display fitted regression lines both with and without the case of Ireland. Figure 8.5 reveals a clearly positive association between the level of tertiary enrolment and average levels of growth across OECD countries. When excluding the outlier case of Ireland (dashed line), the association is even more pronounced. Hence, there is certainly some truth to the claim that the expansion of tertiary education also promotes economic dynamism and growth. However, taking a closer look also reveals some puzzling findings. For instance, some Southern European countries such as Greece and Spain are characterised by high levels of tertiary enrolment and above average levels of economic growth during the period of observation, but this growth later turned out to be fuelled more by public and private debt rather than the economic contributions of high skilled labour. Furthermore, countries like Germany and Switzerland are characterised by very low levels of tertiary enrolment because of the importance of alternatives in VET in these countries. These countries also did not excel with above average levels of growth in the first half of the 2000s, but they weathered the subsequent crisis relatively well.

Figure 8.6 shows that the association between enrolment in VET and economic growth is much less clear-cut than in the case of tertiary education. Excluding the outlier case of Ireland, there is basically no association between these two measures. Thus, having a well-developed VET system does not necessarily promote economic growth, but it

Figure 8.5 The association between tertiary enrolment and average GDP growth before the crisis, OECD countries, 1996–2008

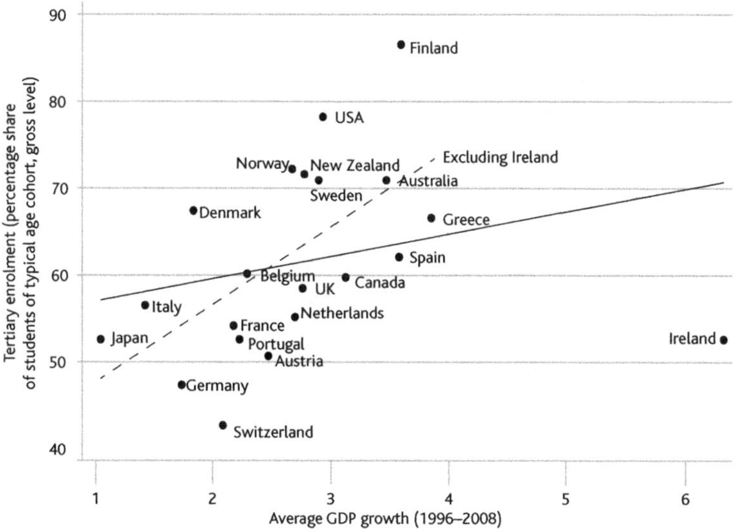

Sources: UNESCO Education Statistics Database; Armingeon et al (2011)

also does not hurt it. Following up on the argument by Anderson and Hassel (2013) that countries with school-based rather than firm-based VET systems are better placed to reap the benefits of the service-based knowledge economy, Figure 8.6 reveals some tentative evidence in support of this claim: countries with extensive school-based VET (such as Finland, the Netherlands, Norway and Sweden) fare slightly better in terms of growth than countries with a strong apprenticeship training system (Germany, Switzerland, Denmark and Austria). However, it needs to be emphasised (again) that these are all simply bivariate associations and there are many factors influencing economic growth besides education and training institutions. Furthermore, the data on VET enrolment provided by the OECD raise some questions with regard to measurement and data quality. Judging from this data, the UK and Australia seem to have similar levels of VET enrolment as Germany and Switzerland have, even though the case-study evidence from these countries clearly finds that there are huge differences in the institutional set-up of vocational training between these countries and that the commitment of employers and the state to VET is significantly higher in the German-speaking countries compared to the liberal market economies of the Anglo-Saxon world (Fuller and Unwin, 2009, 2011; Keep, 2006).

Figure 8.6 The association between extensiveness of VET and average GDP growth before the crisis, OECD countries, 1996–2008

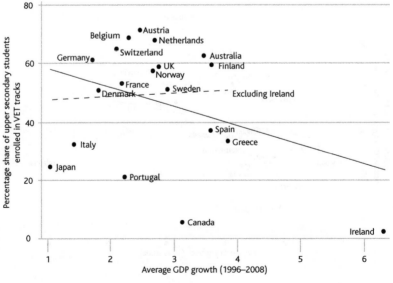

Sources: UNESCO Education Statistics Database; Armingeon et al (2011)

So far, I have talked about the links between educational institutions and growth, but how about inclusiveness on the labour market? Figure 8.7 suggests that a well-established VET system can act as a kind of insurance against increases in unemployment during economic crises. In countries with extensive firm-based training, such as Germany and Austria, labour markets have remained relatively robust in crisis times, although Denmark is different from these because of its rather flexible employment protection legislation. The Southern European cases of Spain and Greece demonstrate that above average levels of tertiary enrolment can go along with a significant increase in general as well as youth unemployment, which has reached astronomical levels in these countries in the crisis years. However, there are of course also country cases with above average levels of tertiary enrolment, which have weathered the crisis relatively well in terms of unemployment, such as Canada or Australia (although these countries have also been less affected because of other factors).

Why should countries with extensive provision of VET be more protected against unemployment increases? This is because employers are more involved in and committed to vocational training, in particular in countries with dual apprenticeship training, the so-called collective

Figure 8.7 The association between extensiveness of VET and unemployment during the crisis years, 2008–11

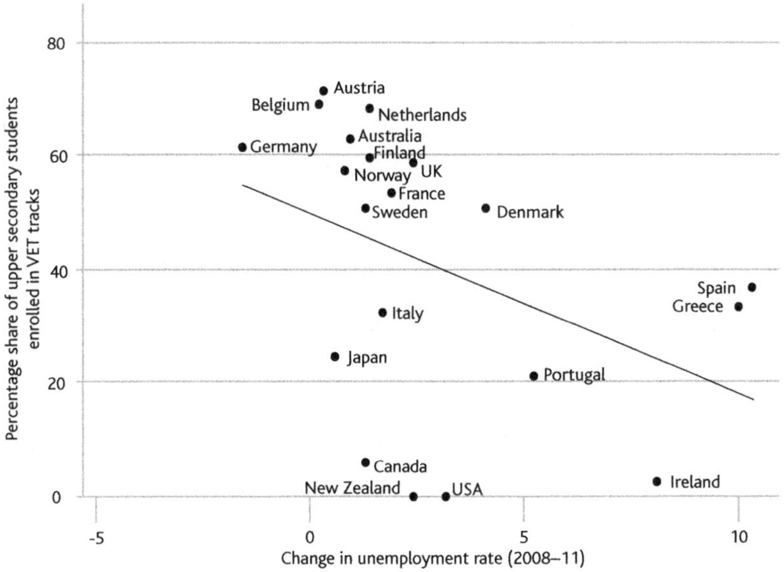

Sources: UNESCO Education Statistics Database; Armingeon et al (2011)

skill formation regimes (Busemeyer and Trampusch, 2012; Thelen, 2004). This kind of cross-class cooperation between employers' associations and labour unions in the governance and financing of vocational training encourages joint investments in 'co-specific assets' (Cusack et al, 2007: 377). Human capital, for instance, is one such asset, where employers invest in skill formation and training, which goes beyond the concrete short-term training needs of a specific firm. This then sets in motion a beneficial feedback effect when, in exchange, employees commit to staying with the training firm after completing their training, which in turn enhances the willingness of firms to make this investment in the first place. Of course, these arrangements of 'coordinated' capitalism (Hall and Soskice, 2001) are stabilised by various institutions such as collective wage bargaining, labour market regulation (employment protection, in particular) and social policies (Streeck, 1989; Estévez-Abe et al, 2001). These regimes have been economically and politically viable in the long term, because skill formation institutions encourage firms to specialise and develop a competitive edge in certain product markets such as high quality manufacturing. They remain vulnerable, however, to the possibility that demand for such goods on global markets might decline significantly due the forces of technological change and globalisation.

In times of economic crisis, employers in these coordinated market economies then have a strong incentive to keep their workforce employed, because they have invested a lot in the formation of their skills. This is one of the reasons why unemployment has remained rather low during the crisis years in Germany, even though precarious employment continued to expand in the periphery of the labour market (Eichhorst, 2015). In countries with deregulated labour markets, unemployment may increase more in the short term. This in turn encourages workers and young people to invest in academic higher education rather than vocational education, because the risk that skills may become obsolete is greater in the case of the latter compared to the former. Hence, liberal market economies such as the US typically combine flexible and dynamic labour markets with a focus on general academic higher education, setting incentives for firms to engage in radical product innovation strategies rather than the more incremental pace of innovation to be found in many Continental European countries (Hall and Soskice, 2001).

The potential and limitations of education and skill formation in promoting inclusive growth

How can these diverse findings be integrated and interpreted? As mentioned earlier, I presented suggestive evidence in terms of correlations and associations rather than hard causal statements, but sifting through this data reveals a rather coherent message: education and skill formations matter for both growth and social cohesion. The institutional set-up of education and training systems influences the distribution of skills on the labour market, the degree of educational inequality and stratification as well as the linkages between education and the world of work. Early childhood education and care certainly plays a crucial role, as the canonical texts in the social investment literature suggest (Esping-Andersen, 2002; Bonoli, 2013; Hemerijck, 2013; Morel et al, 2012), but in this chapter, I wanted to raise the awareness that differences in the design of post-secondary education – in particular the relationship between VET and academic higher education and the division of labour between public and private sources of funding – have consequences as well in terms of socioeconomic inequality.

The empirical data also hints at the existence of various trade-offs and dilemmas that policymakers face. Expanding access to tertiary education might be associated with positive economic benefits as suggested above but, in many countries of the OECD world, increasing public spending on education is an uphill political battle. Even though education may be very popular with voters (Ansell, 2010; Bonoli, 2013), it is difficult to increase public investments in times of hard budget constraints since other parts of the welfare state would have to be cut. However, as seen above, expanding the private share of spending on education might in the long term contribute to significant inequities in access to education as well as on the labour market.

This hunch is confirmed in a recent survey of public opinion in eight Western European countries[4] in the context of the INVEDUC ('Investing in Education in Europe: Attitudes, Politics and Policies') project (see Busemeyer et al, 2017; Busemeyer, 2017).[5] Employing an experimental set-up, where respondents are randomly assigned to different 'treatment' groups, this data shows the following: when asked about their preferences for education spending without mentioning any constraints, about 71% of respondents demand more or even much more spending on education. Support for additional spending decreases significantly, however, when respondents are confronted with different kinds of constraints: it drops to 48% when respondents are confronted with paying higher taxes for additional spending, to 41% when it would result in higher levels of public debt and to a mere 26% if other parts of the welfare state (specifically pensions) would have to be cut back. This data suggests that increasing public investments on education is not impossible, but it also carries political risks, in particular if it would result in cutbacks of other parts of the welfare state.

More broadly speaking, this also lends support to those voices which argue that the expansion of the social investment pillar should not be accompanied with extensive retrenchment in the social insurance pillar (see for example Hemerijck, 2013; Solga, 2014; Vandenbroucke and Vleminckx, 2011; Busemeyer, 2017). Attempts to increase social investment spending while also cutting back more traditional types of social insurance and transfer spending will most likely meet considerable political resistance. Our public opinion data suggests that, when forced to choose, citizens would rather accept higher levels of taxes than cutbacks in cherished welfare state benefits. Given that some forms of social investment tend to be less progressive than many types of social transfers, combining social investment with classical forms of social insurance and redistribution also seems adequate from the perspective of social justice.

Furthermore, education policies that are only concerned with expanding higher education while neglecting other parts of the education system, in particular vocational education, run the risk of subsuming the aspect of social inclusion under concerns for economic growth. Expanding opportunities in tertiary education certainly has positive consequences with regard to the transformation towards service-based knowledge economies, but not everybody can be a knowledge worker. Thus, the transformation towards the knowledge economy needs to be complemented with policies that ensure a fair distribution of the benefits of this transformation by paying more attention to basic skills of young adults and lifelong learning. These concerns are already addressed in the strategic goals of the EU's 'Education and Training 2020' framework.[6] What remains underestimated, however, is the role of vocational education and training.

VET can make important contributions to the promotion of inclusive growth. By opening up educational opportunities and pathways to skilled employment for those in the lower half of the academic distribution of skills, a well-developed VET system can contribute to a more balanced distribution of skills, income and life chances. The focus of this chapter was on the OECD countries, but the argument about the central role of VET is probably even more fitting in the context of developing countries. In these cases, there are more labour market opportunities at the intermediate skill level, and the promotion of VET opportunities would thus further both the social inclusion of individuals without access to higher education and economic development. Simply focusing on the expansion of access to higher education would be less effective if there are relatively few labour market opportunities for university graduates (for example, because of the existence of a large informal economy) and if there are many who lack foundational skills.

When VET is not detached from the world of work, but when employers and unions are involved in the governance and financing of VET schemes, a close linkage between the skill demands of firms and the supply produced by the education and training system can be achieved. Cross-class cooperation between unions and employers is key in order to ensure that skill portfolios are not too firm-specific and take the interests of both sides into account. The close connection between training and employment also ensures that VET remains a viable alternative in the service-based knowledge economy, since training opportunities at the intermediate skill level also exist in this new economic environment. For instance, in Germany, the majority of apprenticeships are now in service sector occupations rather than in manufacturing.

However, VET must not become an educational dead-end. Hence, it is crucial to ensure that transitions from VET to higher education are possible and supported by policies and institutions. The data presented above suggest that countries that manage to combine extensive provision of VET with high levels of enrolment in tertiary education perform particularly well. Also, there is not a single 'best practice' model, but different combinations in 'hybrid' models are possible. Australia is a country that combines high levels of enrolment in VET tracks with a well-developed higher education sector in a 'liberal' setting, whereas Denmark would be an example of a hybrid between the Scandinavian comprehensive model of secondary schooling and the German collective model of apprenticeship training.

Notes

[1] As is the case for all figures in this chapter, the data used to construct this figure are average values for the time period from the late 1990s until the onset of the economic crisis in 2008. Furthermore, all bivariate associations are tested for robustness in multivariate regression settings, which includes a multitude of control variables, such as unemployment, GDP growth, balance of power between capital and labour, and labour market institutions, among others. Also, I discuss findings in terms of correlations rather than causal statements. Finally, it needs to be emphasised that there is, of course, a certain time lag involved: the measures related to education capture the state of the education system in the 2000s, but

data on inequality refers to the adult population in the same period, who have acquired their education in an earlier time period. Because of data limitations for data on education policies, it is not possible to go back much further in time, but the institutional structures of education systems change very slowly so that the identified associations should remain quite robust over time.

[2] I use gross levels of enrolment in tertiary education, which is a relative rough measure, because it does not take into account things like graduation/completion rates and the share of foreign students. The advantage is that is easily available and comparable across countries.

[3] Again, this bivariate finding holds up in more sophisticated multivariate regression analyses (see Note 1).

[4] These countries are Denmark, Sweden, the UK, Ireland, Germany, France, Spain and Italy.

[5] The project is funded by a Starting Grant from the European Research Council (ERC) (Grant No. 311769) and located at the University of Konstanz, Germany.

[6] For instance, the framework aims to reduce the rate of early school leavers to below 10%, increasing the share of adults participating in lifelong learning to at least 15% and decreasing the share of 15 year olds with basic skills to less than 15%.

References

Anderson, K.M. and A. Hassel (2013) 'Pathways of Change in CMEs: Training Regimes in Germany and the Netherlands', in A. Wren (ed.), In *The Political Economy of the Service Transition*, Oxford, New York: Oxford University Press, 171–94.

Ansell, B.W. (2010) *From the Ballot to the Blackboard: The Redistributive Political Economy of Education*, Cambridge: Cambridge University Press.

Armingeon, K., S. Engler, P. Potolidis, M. Gerber, and P. Leimgruber (2011) *Comparative Political Dataset 1960-2008. Institute of Political Science*, University of Berne, www.cpds-data.org.

Bonoli, G. (2013) *The Origins of Active Social Policy: Labour Market and Childcare Policies in a Comparative Perspective*, Oxford, New York: Oxford University Press.

Bonoli, G. and F. Reber (2010) 'The Political Economy of Childcare in OECD Countries: Explaining Cross-National Variation in Spending and Coverage Rates', *European Journal of Political Research* 49: 97–118.

Bradley, D., E. Huber, S. Moller, F. Nielsen and J.D. Stephens. (2003) 'Distribution and Redistribution in Postindustrial Democracies', *World Politics* 55: 193–228.

Breen, R. (2005) 'Explaining Cross-National Variation in Youth Unemployment', *European Sociological Review* 21: 125–34.

Breen, R. and J.O. Jonsson (2005) 'Inequality of Opportunity in Comparative Perspective: Recent Research on Educational Attainment and Social Mobility', *Annual Review of Sociology* 31: 223–43.

Breen, R., R. Luijkx, W. Müller and R. Pollak (2009) 'Nonpersistent Inequality in Educational Attainment: Evidence from Eight European Countries', *American Journal of Sociology* 114: 1475–521.

Busemeyer, M.R. (2009) 'From Myth to Reality: Globalization and Public Spending in OECD Countries Revisited', *European Journal of Political Research* 48: 455–82.

Busemeyer, M.R. (2012) 'Inequality and the Political Economy of Education: An Analysis of Individual Preferences in OECD Countries', *Journal of European Social Policy* 22: 219–40.

Busemeyer, M.R. (2013) 'Education Funding and Individual Preferences for Redistribution', *European Sociological Review* 29: 707–19.

Busemeyer, M.R. (2015) *Skills and Inequality: The Political Economy of Education and Training Reforms in Western Welfare States*, Cambridge, New York: Cambridge University Press, 358–67.

Busemeyer, M.R. (2017) 'Public Opinion and the Politics of Social Investment,' in A.C. Hemerijck (ed.) *Social Investment and Its Critics*, Oxford, New York: Oxford University Press.

Busemeyer, M.R. and T. Iversen (2012) 'Collective Skill Systems, Wage Bargaining, and Labor Market Stratification', in M.R. Busemeyer and C. Trampusch (eds), *The Political Economy of Collective Skill Formation*, Oxford, New York: Oxford University Press, 205–33.

Busemeyer, M.R. and C. Trampusch (2012) 'Introduction: The Comparative Political Economy of Collective Skill Formation' in M.R. Busemeyer and C. Trampusch (eds), *The Political Economy of Collective Skill Formation*, Oxford, New York: Oxford University Press, 3–38.

Busemeyer, M.R., J.L. Garritzmann, E. Neimanns and R. Nezi (2017) 'Investing in Education in Europe: Evidence from a Survey of Public Opinion', *Journal of European Social Policy*, DOI: 10.1177/0958928717700562

Cusack, T.R., T. Iversen and D. Soskice (2007) 'Economic Interests and the Origins of Electoral Systems', *American Political Science Review* 101: 373–91.

Eichhorst, W. (2015) 'The Unexpected Appearance of a New German Model', *British Journal of Industrial Relations* 53: 49–69.

Esping-Andersen, G. (2002) 'A Child-Centred Social Investment Strategy', in G. Esping-Andersen (ed.), *Why We Need a New Welfare State*, Oxford, New York: Oxford University Press, 26–67.

Estévez-Abe, M., T. Iversen, and D. Soskice (2001) 'Social Protection and the Formation of Skills: A Reinterpretation of the Welfare State', in P.A. Hall and D. Soskice (eds), *Varieties of Capitalism: The Institutional Foundations of Comparative Advantage*, Oxford, New York: Oxford University Press, 145–83.

European Commission (2015) 'Strategic Framework – Education and Training 2020', http://ec.europa.eu/education/policy/strategic-framework/index_en.htm

Fuller, A. and L. Unwin (2009) 'Change and Continuity in Apprenticeship: The Resilience of a Model of Learning,' *Journal of Education and Work* 22: 405–16.

Fuller, A. and L. Unwin (2011) 'Vocational Education and Training in the Spotlight: Back to the Future for the UK's Coalition Government?', *London Review of Education* 9: 191–204.

Gangl, M. (2003) 'The Structure of Labour Market Entry in Europe: A Typological Analysis', in W. Müller and M. Gangl (eds), *Transitions from Education to Work in Europe: The Integration of Youth into EU Labour Markets*, Oxford: Oxford University Press, 107–28.

Garritzmann, J.L. (2015) 'Attitudes Towards Student Support: How Positive Feedback Effects Prevent Change in the Four World of Student Finance', *Journal of European Social Policy* 25: 139–58.

Garritzmann, J.L. (2016) *The Political Economy of Higher Education Finance: The Politics of Tuition Fees and Subsidies in OECD Countries, 1945–2015*, Basingstoke: Palgrave Macmillan.

Gingrich, J. and B.W. Ansell (2014) 'Sorting for Schools: Housing, Education and Inequality', *Socio-Economic Review* 12: 329–51.

Goldin, C. and L.F. Katz. (2008) *The Race between Education and Technology*, Cambridge, MA: Belknap Press.

Hall, P.A. and D.W. Gingerich (2009) 'Varieties of Capitalism and Institutional Complementarities in the Political Economy: An Empirical Analysis', *British Journal of Political Science* 39: 449–82.

Hall, P.A., and D. Soskice (2001) 'An Introduction to Varieties of Capitalism', in P.A. Hall and D. Soskice (eds), *Varieties of Capitalism: The Institutional Foundations of Comparative Advantage*, Oxford, New York: Oxford University Press, 1–68.

Hanushek, E.A. and L. Woessmann (2012) 'Do Better Schools Lead to More Growth? Cognitive Skills, Economic Outcomes, and Causation', *Journal of Economic Growth* 17: 267–321.

Hawkes, D. and M. Ugur (2012) *Evidence on the Relationship between Education, Skills and Economic Growth in Low-Income Countries: A Systematic Review*, London: EEPI-Centre, Social Science Research Unit, Institute of Education, University of London.

Heckman, J.J. (2006) 'Skill Formation and the Economics of Investing in Disadvantaged Children', *Science* 312: 1900–02.

Hemerijck, A. (2012) 'Two or Three Waves of Welfare State Transformation?', in N. Morel, B. Palier and J. Palme (eds), *Towards a Social Investment Welfare State? Ideas, Policies and Challenges*, Bristol, UK, Chicago, IL: Policy Press, 33–60.

Hemerijck, A. (2013) *Changing Welfare States*, Oxford, New York: Oxford University Press.

Huber, E. and J.D. Stephens (2014) 'Income Inequality and Redistribution in Post-Industrial Democracies: Demographic, Economic and Political Determinants', *Socio-Economic Review* 12: 245–67.

Iversen, T. (2005) *Capitalism, Democracy, and Welfare*, Cambridge: Cambridge University Press.

Iversen, T. and D. Soskice (2001) 'An Asset Theory of Social Policy Preferences', *American Political Science Review* 95: 875–93.

Iversen, T. and D. Soskice (2009) 'Distribution and Redistribution: The Shadow of the Nineteenth Century', *World Politics* 61: 438–86.

Keep, E. (2006) 'State Control of the English Education and Training System – Playing with the Biggest Train Set in the World', *Journal of Vocational Education and Training* 58: 47–64.

Krueger, A.B., and M. Lindahl (2001) 'Education for Growth: Why and for Whom?', *Journal of Economic Literature* XXXIX: 1101–36.

Lindert, P.H. (2004) *Growing Public: Social Spending and Economic Growth since the Eighteenth Century, Volume I*, Cambridge: Cambridge University Press.

Lupu, N. and J. Pontusson (2011) 'The Structure of Inequality and the Politics of Redistribution', *American Political Science Review* 105: 316–36.

Mettler, S. (2014) *Degrees of Inequality: How the Politics of Higher Education Sabotaged the American Dream*, New York: Basic Books.

Morel, N., B. Palier, and J. Palme (2012) 'Beyond the Welfare State as We Knew It?', in N. Morel, B. Palier and J. Palme (eds), *Towards a Social Investment Welfare State? Ideas, policies and challenges*, Bristol: Policy Press, 1–30.

Naumann, I. (2012) 'Childcare Politics in the 'New' Welfare State: Class, Religion, and Gender in the Shaping of Political Agendas', in G. Bonoli and D. Natali (eds), *The Politics of the New Welfare State*, Oxford: Oxford University Press, 158–81.

OECD (2010) *Pisa 2009 Results: Overcoming Social Background: Equity in Learning Opportunities and Outcomes, Volume II*. Paris: Organisation for Economic Co-Operation and Development.

OECD (2015) *Education at a glance: OECD Indicators*, Paris: OECD.

OECD (2016a) 'Educational attainment', *OECD World Factbook 2015*, www.oecd-ilibrary.org/sites/factbook-2015-en/table-150.html?cont entType=&itemId=%2fcontent%2ftable%2ffactbook-2015-table150-en&mimeType=text%2fhtml&containerItemId=%2fcontent%2fboo k%2ffactbook-2015-en&accessItemIds=

OECD (2016b) 'Income inequality', *OECD World Factbook 2015*, www.oecd-ilibrary.org/sites/factbook-2015-en/table-43.html?conte ntType=&itemId=%2fcontent%2ftable%2ffactbook-2015-table43-en &mimeType=text%2fhtml&containerItemId=%2fcontent%2fbook% 2ffactbook-2015-en&accessItemIds=

Pfeffer, F.T. (2008) 'Persistent Inequality in Educational Attainment and Its Institutional Context', *European Sociological Review* 24: 543–65.

Pontusson, J., D. Rueda and C.R. Way (2002) 'Comparative Political Economy of Wage Distribution: The Role of Partisanship and Labour Market Institutions', *British Journal of Political Science* 32: 281–308.

Romer, P.M. (1986) 'Increasing Returns and Long-Run Growth', *Journal of Political Economy* 94: 1002–37.

Shavit, Y. and W. Müller (2000) 'Vocational Secondary Education: Where Diversion and Where Safety Net?', *European Societies* 2: 29–50.

Solga, H. (2014) 'Education, Economic Inequality and the Promises of the Social Investment State', *Socio-Economic Review* 12: 269–97.

Solt, F. (2009) 'Standardizing the World Income Inequality Database', *Social Science Quarterly* 90: 231–42.

Streeck, W. (1989) 'Skills and the Limits of Neo-Liberalism: The Enterprise of the Future as a Place of Learning', *Work, Employment & Society* 3: 89–104.

Thelen, K. (2004) *How Institutions Evolve: The Political Economy of Skills in Germany, Britain, the United States and Japan*, Cambridge: Cambridge University Press.

Van Lancker, W. (2013) 'Putting the Child-Centred Investment Strategy to the Test: Evidence for the EU27', *European Journal of Social Security* 15: 4–27.

Vandenbroucke, F. and K. Vleminckx (2011) 'Disappointing Poverty Trends: Is the Social Investment State to Blame?', *Journal of European Social Policy* 21: 450–71.

Wolbers, M.H.J. (2007) 'Patterns of Labour Market Entry: A Comparative Perspective on School-to-Work Transitions in 11 European Countries', *Acta Sociologica* 50: 189–210.

Wolf, F. (2009) 'The Division of Labour in Education Funding: A Cross-National Comparison of Public and Private Education Expenditure in 28 OECD Countries', *Acta Politica* 44: 50–73.

Wren, A. (2013) 'Introduction: The Political Economy of Post-Industrial Societies,' in A. Wren (ed.), *The Political Economy of the Service Transition*, Oxford: Oxford University Press, 1–70.

NINE

Inclusive growth and social investments over the life course

Jon Kvist

Introduction

Marrying the goals of inclusive growth with the means of social investments over the life course may become one of the most promising innovations in global social policy thinking in the 21st century.

Inclusive growth was one of three flagship objectives of the EU's Europe 2020 strategy. Launched in 2010 this strategy aimed at inclusive growth by creating more and better jobs, especially for women, young people and older workers, helping people of all ages anticipate and manage change through investments in skills and training, by modernising labour markets and welfare systems and by ensuring the benefits of growth reach all parts of the EU.

Since 2010, however, a lot has happened both in the way we think about social policies and in the initiatives of the EU in social policy. And the thinking and the policies are starting to align, at least at the EU level. Most prominently the European Commission launched the Social Investment Package in 2013, which brought together many policies hitherto with separate strategies like education, employment, and health and social policy. Social investments, according to the European Commission and other international agencies, are potential 'win–win' reforms (European Commission, 2013a, 2013b; European Parliament, 2012).

Social investments are those policies that are designed to strengthen people's skills and capacities in order to enable them to participate fully in education, employment and social life. Such policies aim not only to improve the life of individuals but also the economic prospects of countries through more tax revenues from work and lower social and health expenditures.

Although the aim and policies constitute a new approach to social policy the terminology used in the Social Investment Package was still reminiscent of conventional social policy thinking in its lifecycle perspective by using such terms as 'from cradle to grave' and 'life cycle stages' (European Commission, 2013a). The life cycle perspective on social policy dates back to Seebohm Rowntree more than a century ago. In the meantime, not least social policy scholars have contributed to a new agenda on global social policy, that of social investments (Jenson, 2010; Deeming and Smyth, 2015).

At the macro level sociologists like Gøsta Esping-Andersen (2002) argue that social and economic change has created a set of new social risks that calls for new social policies: social investment policies. In particular, the surges in female education and employment create a need for policies that enable a better reconciliation of work and family life. Reconciliation policies aim to ensure that increased work does not adversely affect fertility and, vice versa, that care of children does not prevent women and society from harvesting the fruits of higher human capital. Childcare has been central to social investment scholars as it serves the dual purpose of reconciling family and work and of investing early in children, which has been proven to yield positive effects on a wide range of economic, social and health outcomes (Heckman, 2000).

To realise the full potential of social investments calls for a conceptual framework and empirical studies on social investment and their returns. Unfortunately, many of the exponentially growing number of social investment studies by social policy scholars have difficulties showing the way towards social investments because their analytical designs suffer from three limitations: too few policies and returns; inadequate explanations of the causal links between policies and returns; and invalid operationalisation of social investments policies and returns. Hence, studies focus almost exclusively on childcare and active labour market policies and rarely on health, education and social services and how these interact; studies rarely examine returns and outcomes beyond labour market participation of women and poverty rates. Studies do not explain how policies result in returns in terms of causal mechanisms but remain satisfied with policies being correlated with returns. Studies overwhelmingly use social expenditure on certain policy programmes, mostly childcare and active labour market policy, as a proxy for social investments. This is problematic for a number of reasons. Social spending says little about the quality and coordination of policies. Spending reflects economic, social, and demographic aspects besides policy design. Spending captures both inputs (money spent on social investment policies) and outcomes (money spent because of ineffective policies).

In these ways it is paradoxical how social policy scholars, on the one hand, have informed the reform agenda on why we need social investments but, on the other hand, have provided less knowledge about which policies work in what ways for which socioeconomic groups. As a first step to improve this situation and to unleash the potential of social investment for inclusive growth there are calls for contributions of both an empirical and a theoretical nature. Empirically there is a need for implementation of policies in different contexts and for different groups that can be studied to inform policymaking.

Theoretically, and this is where this chapter fits in, there is a need for a conceptual framework that is accordance with the new way of thinking within social policy and which can embrace the increased diversity of people's walks through life in view of social and economic change, and which can set out what policies are of potential use in what life stages. First the chapter introduces social investments in a life course perspective and how it relates to inclusive growth. The next section of the chapter describes how social investment improves people's functional capacities. The following section describes various types of social investment policies and returns. Then the intergenerational aspects are discussed before a discussion takes up the limits of the approach in a European context followed by some concluding remarks.

The life course perspective on social investments and inclusive growth

Social policy has since the famous poverty studies of Seebohm Rowntree were published in 1902 acknowledged the different needs and resources people have over the life cycle. Rowntree found that workers were 'poor and therefore underfed – (a) In childhood – when his constitution is being built up. (b) In early midlife – when he should be in his prime. (c) In old age' (Rowntree, 1901: 72). Social protection has to varying degrees across countries addressed these situations with lack of income and child families extra need for resources. Social insurance compensates lack of income when people get unemployed, sick or disabled and old. Child family allowances compensate part of the costs generated by the extra need for resources in families with children. Finally, social assistance provides an economic safety net for all.

However, the lifecycle perspective on social policy has its limitations in a modern post-industrialist world. Most importantly, social and economic change jeopardise its assumptions about uniform and unilinear life trajectories, from childhood through middle age to old age. Social change involves family diversification caused by higher rates of family break-up, (repeated) family formations, changing gender roles and lower fertility. These developments render the classical male breadwinner model lasting from marriage until death a model of the past. Single earner and dual earner couples are now the norm and often a government goal in many countries.

Globalisation and technological developments lead to important changes in the labour market with regard to skill demand and employment contracts. Lifelong employment in the same job and perhaps even for the same employer is no longer the norm. Continuous upskilling and higher labour market mobility is today the name of the game due to increased competition and demand for new skills.

Childcare has been the chief social investment policy investigated and advocated so far. This may come as no surprise for two reasons. First, investments in children have a long time to give returns thus having a big potential vis-à-vis policies at later life stages. Also James Heckman and colleagues have shown how learning begets learning. Childcare is pivotal for learning the cognitive skills that people need later in life. Second, childcare enable traditional caregivers, notably women, to participate in the labour market using their acquired skills thereby harvesting the return on earlier investments in them. However, as we shall demonstrate later, there are many other social investment policies with many other returns.

Adopting a life course perspective on social investment does more than describing how family policies of today are the pension policy of tomorrow (as argued by Esping-Andersen, 2002). The life course perspective also gives us new understandings of the nature of old risks and their possible policy solutions. Moreover, the domains offering themselves to social investments extend beyond family policies and labour markets.

In health, for example, Sir Michael Marmot (2012) has advocated the importance of addressing 'the causes of causes of health inequalities'. By this he refers to the social and economic inequalities that are behind the situation and behaviour that in turn lead to inequalities in health. Addressing socioeconomic inequalities is necessary to decrease health inequities (Marmot et al, 2012).

Numerous health studies have demonstrated how such inequalities in early life have profound effects on health in later life stages (for example, Graham and Power, 2004).

Numerous social science studies have demonstrated how social inequalities tend to pass from one generation to the next. In particular studies have shown that being raised in poverty has life lasting adverse impacts.

Absolute poverty is a problem in many regions and countries. However, in most European, East Asian and North American countries it is relative poverty and social mobility that are the major problems. If poverty was only a matter of economy we could stay within Rowntree's framework and simply raise the level of social assistance and child family allowances. But it is the social and economic situations of people relative to those of others that matter: 'inequalities matter'. And it is not only a question of monetary consumption but the much broader range of wellbeing indicators, for example, those on participation in the social and economic spheres (Stiglitz et al, 2009). This broader range fits with the multiple dimensions used by EUROSTAT's Beyond GDP and monitoring of social progress, the OECD's Better Lives (OECD, 2015a) and the UN's Sustainable Development Goals; see Chapter One in this volume for a rundown of international agencies' inclusive growth measures.

Social investments in these ways aim to enable individuals to address the old and new social risks we encounter in life. In life course terminology, risks are often called events whether they are pleasant or not. Those events that have long-lasting fundamental effects are called turning points. Social investments thus aim to help keep people on track and get those that are off track back on their feet.

Figure 9.1 shows some of the life events we may meet in our health, education, work and family trajectories over the life course. In our health trajectory we are particularly vulnerable to adverse events at both end points of the life course. Getting into nurseries, childcare, schools, and further education and training are important events in our educational trajectories. Getting siblings, partners and becoming parents and grandparents are important events in our family trajectory as is losing a partner or relatives. Getting and losing jobs and promotion may be significant work trajectory events.

Figure 9.1 Life events in different life trajectories

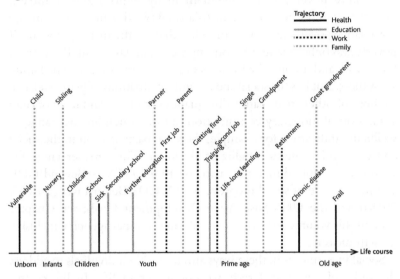

Social investments thus aim to enable people to better meet and manage life events in the many dimensions of health, education, work and family. Social investment and inclusive growth thinking aligns with the life course perspective on personal development in family, education, work and health as a lifelong process where one life stage is understood in relation to other life stages. Life trajectories refer to long-term patterns of stability and change in family, education, work or health. These trajectories have become less standardised and more interlinked due to social and economic change and to individual agency. How the social investments aim to enable people to better cope with life events is set out in the next section.

Social investments to increase an individual's skills and functional capacities

Social investment policies aim to increase people's skills and capacities to prevent them from entering situations resulting in social, economic or health problems. If people are already in such problems the aim of social investment policies is to enable people to solve these problems to the extent possible. But exactly what are the functions that social investment policies must develop, strengthen, retain and rehabilitate? Adopting the life course perspective allow us to identify what these aims are and to show how they change over the life course.

Initially the goal of social investment type policies was very much to invest in human capital as inspired by Alva and Gunnar Myrdal's work on the population question from the 1930s and Gary Beckers's and colleagues work on investment in human capital in the 1960s (see, respectively, Myrdal and Myrdal, 1934; Becker, 1964). Esping-Andersen (2002) focused on cognitive functions when he advocated greater investment in children. Heckman similarly emphasises cognitive skills, but also finds that other personal skills like perseverance can be cultivated and can have positive influences on health and economic outcomes (Heckman, 2000, 2008). Most recently, the OECD (2015b) found a positive link between, on one side, individuals' social and emotional skills and, on the other side, education, work and good health. This calls for policies that can also support personal development in psychological terms.

There are many different conceptualisations of our functionalities and these, in turn, are influenced by the environment we are in. Most often there is a gap between what we can do ideally, our capacity, and what we do in reality – our performance. The distinction between capacity and performance is integrated in perhaps the most comprehensive and well-established framework of functioning that is offered by the World Health Organisation. Its International Classification of Functioning, Disability and Health (ICF) is useful as it explicitly captures functioning over the whole life course on six dimensions: cognition (understanding and communicating); mobility (moving and getting around); self-care (hygiene, dressing, eating and staying alone); getting along (interacting with other people); life activities (domestic responsibilities, leisure, work and school); and participation (joining in community services) (WHO, 2002). The ICF has the further advantage that it can be used by practitioners and scholars alike.

The goal of social investment policies is thus to underpin and strengthen our ability to understand and communicate, move and get around, take care of ourselves, interact with other people, and participate in communities, education, work and families. The goals of social investment policies also vary over the life course as the nature and level of functioning develops throughout our lives. Individuals' functional capacities partly determine how much they can achieve on their own. In this sense, there is a disability threshold under which people need help in order to manage their lives (the dotted line in Figure 9.2).

Figure 9.2 shows how social investments over the life course aim to increase functionalities in three respects. First, the level of functionality increases exponentially in early life from pre-birth until young adult

Figure 9.2 Social investments over the life course aim to increase functional capacities

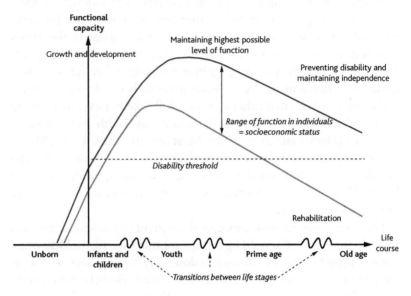

Sources: Adapted from WHO (2000) and Kvist (2015a)

life and then declines gradually as people enter into old age. Policies towards the unborn, infants and children are directed towards ensuring the best possible growth and development. In youth and prime age the goal also becomes to maintain the highest possible level of function. And in old age the prime aim is to prevent disability and maintain independence.

Second, there are large differences between those with the highest and lowest levels of functionality: those at the highest levels keep above the 'disability threshold' during most of their life whereas those at the lowest level have several and/or longer periods below that threshold. To some extent the gap measures the socioeconomic inequalities of a society. Social investment policies are directed at improving the situation especially for those individuals who come from a disadvantaged socioeconomic situation.

Third, the transitions between various stages in the life course are flexible, meaning that people do them at different biological ages. The goal of social investment policies is to increase those functional capacities that are important for making the transition from one stage to another. In sum social investment policies as well as their goals and returns vary over the life course.

Social investment policies and returns over the life course

To achieve these goals the social investment strategy contains a broad range of policies and returns from the start to the end of life. The strategy encompasses health, social, labour market and long-term care policies, to mention only a few. Returns likewise vary over the life course and occur in many different dimensions. They are likely to materialise in different dimensions and much later than the policy intervention itself.

Figure 9.3 shows how social investment policies and return vary over the life course. Because life starts in the womb there are interventions like prenatal care and health campaigns for pregnant women, especially those in disadvantaged situations. Proper nutrition at this stage is critical for brain development (Hannon, 2003). Parental support and early childhood education and care help child families perform better and increase the cognitive, language and social skills of the infant and toddler. Accessible high quality education and vocational training support personal development, and basic and occupational skills (Burger, 2010). Both medical and social research finds that early intervention has a lasting impact on people's lives in both health, social

Figure 9.3 Social investments over the life course

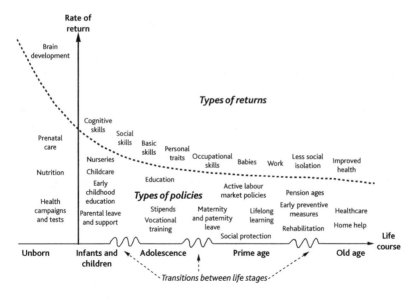

Source: Kvist (2015a)

and economic matters (Marmot et al, 2012; Heckman, 2008; Havnes and Mogstad, 2011).

In prime age social protection helps individuals undertake positive risk behaviour like taking education and changing jobs (Kvist, 2015b). ALMP and lifelong learning develop and maintain skills to keep people in work (Morel et al, 2012). Prime age is also the last stage for prophylactic health services and social services that can contribute to preventing bad health later in life, and increase the autonomy of future elderly people.

Many returns enter virtuous circles. For example, better health and cognitive skills foster better educational attainment and work, which in turn foster better health and living standards. Hence, one of the reasons that Scandinavians, who probably have the most social investment policies in Europe at the moment, can be taxed so much vis-à-vis other countries is that many policies subsidise goods that are complimentary to working and thereby ensure a high level of labour market participation (see Kleven, 2014).

Figure 9.3 also shows how social investments are directed at transitions over the life course. Transitions are movements across different dimensions of life. Transitions in family life include births, marriages or partner formation, divorce or partnership dissolution, re-partnering and deaths. Transitions often involve entries and exits in different dimensions. Transitions in work and education, for example, include entries and exits in and out of the labour market or the educational system. Transitions in health concern the occurrence of bad health or cure and rehabilitation. Social investments thus aim to enable individuals to make these transitions as successfully as possible. For young people the prime aim of social investments is to enable the shift from education to work. For the elderly the prime aim is to prevent the movement into bad health or advance the movement out of bad health.

Social investments and the intergenerational contract

Redistribution is a core business of social policies. Often we associate social policy with taking from the rich and giving to the poor. This form of redistribution resembles that of Robin Hood and is called vertical redistribution. Many social policies undertake vertical redistribution. Besides redistribution from the well-off to the less well-off, the best examples are from those in work to those out of work and from those who are in good health to those in bad health.

However, in the life course perspective on social investments the main type of redistribution is not vertical, but horizontal. At any one point in time people of working age, who are in work, finance the policies, including social investment policies that service children, youths and the elderly. In due course they will retire and their children will have become adults and take over as the generation supporting the others. In other words, redistribution takes the form of an account. To a start individuals draw on this account when they receive childcare, education, and other benefits as described in the previous section. Later they pay back what they received and also forward to what they are to receive later on in life as old age people. Redistribution is thus from myself to myself at different points in time.

For the horizontal redistribution mechanism to work smoothly two conditions must be fulfilled, namely that the generations of working and fertile age actually work and reproduce. To the extent that a generation does not work, the need for vertical redistribution increases. In other words more needs to be spent by the state, companies or families on supporting those of working age that are not in work. And vice versa: if generations through good social investment policies in earlier life stages become more able to participate and be productive in the labour market the need for vertical redistribution diminishes.

To the extent that generations do not reproduce themselves imbalances will occur. Currently the '68 generation is retiring in larger numbers than the new generation entering the labour market exactly because the '68 generation committed the sin of omission. The '68 generation did not follow their motto 'make babies, not war' and thus

Figure 9.4 The intergenerational contract: horizontal distribution over the life course

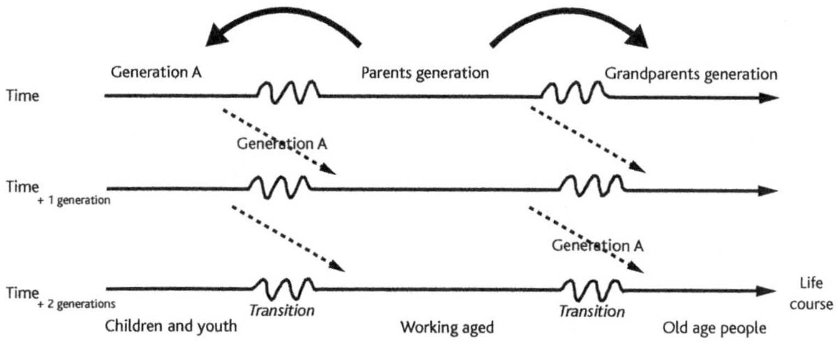

Source: Kvist (2015a)

our population is ageing and posing some of the biggest challenges to our societies.

Again social investment may have a pivotal role to play. When policies enable a population to balance work and family life there will be more people to lift the costs of vertical and horizontal redistribution. In the short term, policies can boost the labour supply of traditional carers, most often women. In the long term, they will result in higher labour supply of future workers.

Social investments and inclusive growth

Many policies and returns enter virtuous circles. This is not least the case at the individual level. For example, better health and cognitive skills foster better educational attainment and work, which in turn foster better health and living standards. It is well-established that the advantages and disadvantages of these circles tend to accumulate over time (Merton, 1968).

As described earlier social investment policies – like health services, family policies, care and education, social services and employment policies – develop, strengthen and maintain individuals' functional capacities in a range of areas. In particular social investment policies raise individuals' cognition, mobility, self-care, getting along, life activities and participation in society.

However, there are also virtuous circles between social investments and inclusive growth on the societal level. Social investment policies contribute to inclusive growth by improving individuals' functional capacities and thus better life trajectories in health, education, employment and family life.

In turn better life trajectories translate into returns on the societal level that relate to inclusive growth. In particular this concerns the six domains of health, families, education, jobs, work–life balance and community.

The virtuous circle between social investments and inclusive growth occur when the returns on both the individual and societal level improve public finances. The improvement concerns lower expenditures and higher revenues. Improved individual functional capacities and society's six domains reduce the need for certain public policies. In one word, autonomy increases. Autonomy means that people become less dependent on physical, economic and practical help in their life. Particularly large gains are likely to be realised in the areas of health, employment and crime.

Figure 9.5 The virtuous circles between social investments and inclusive growth

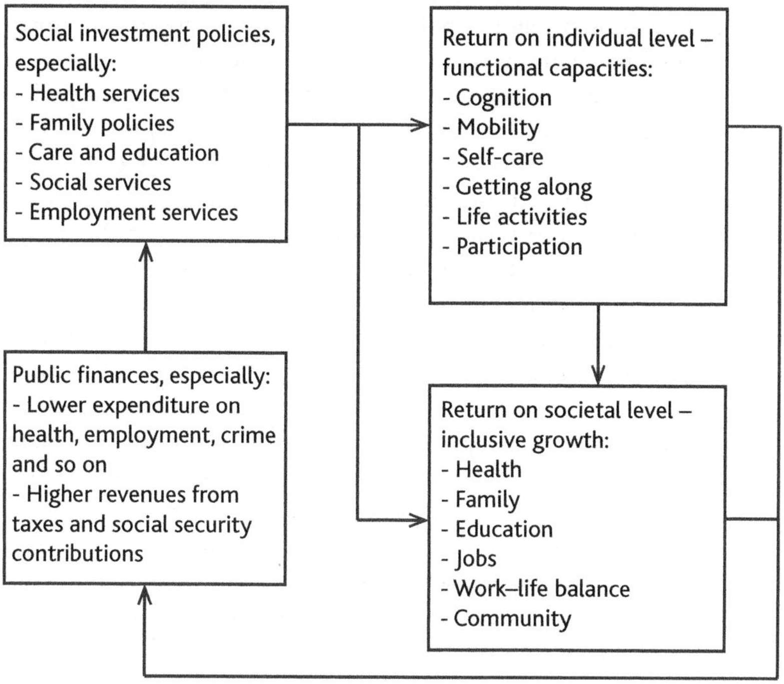

The higher revenues are also a function of the returns on the individual and societal level. Increasing individuals' functional capacities improves their performance in the labour market and in families as well as making them autonomous to a larger extent than if they had not benefitted from social investment policies.

Discussion: barriers to social investments

There are potential barriers to social investments. The immediate challenge is to establish evidence that social investments can address both economic and social goals. Here there is both good and bad news. The bad news is that it is complicated to evaluate the effects of policies due to their multidimensional and dynamic character. The challenge is to establish that a policy made at one dimension and point in time has effects in other dimensions, later in time or both. The good news is that evidence from a broad range of scientific disciplines can inform social investment policymaking (Kvist, 2016). The life course perspective offers a multi-disciplinary framework that covers scientific disciplines as diverse as medicine, sociology, economics and anthropology. Evidence from within these disciplines provides good leads on how to invest in various socioeconomic groups. Adopting the life course perspective on social investments allows policy to be informed about the causes of and causal mechanisms that foster inclusive growth.

Economically, it costs money to put in place institutions in the policy areas that are necessary for delivering social investment policies. The five most important are services to and for families, health, education, employment and social issues (Kvist, 2016). Countries with extensive coverage of these institutions are more likely to undertake social investment reforms than countries that first have to build or expand these institutions considerably.

Furthermore, as the challenge is not least to raise the skills and capacities and performance of the least advantaged, policies must be accessible to all, delivered by professionals and informed by evidence. Countries where policies are not universal or run by welfare professionals and following best practice have particularly big problems. A recent study by the European Commissions' European Social Policy Network found large cross-national differences in the extent to which EU countries have put in place social investment policies with the Nordic countries having the most and the South and certain Eastern European countries the least (Bouget et al, 2015). Tragically, this means that those countries in the South and East of Europe that are probably most in need of social investment reforms may also be the countries least likely to undertake them. Hence, the social investment approach has limits and boundaries even in a European context.

Concluding remarks

Probably the best way to achieve a more inclusive growth is through social investments over the life course. The ambition of inclusive growth of including more people in all realms of life, not only the economic dimension, demands more than redistribution through taxation and benefits in cash that characterise conventional social policies. In contrast the social investment strategy's emphasis is on raising people's functional capacities to learn, be mobile, self-care, get along, undertake life activities and to participate in work and local communities. This not only increases the inclusion and wellbeing of the individuals concerned but also improves the main domains of inclusive growth at the societal level: health, family, education, jobs, work–life balance and communities.

References

Becker, G. (2009 [1964]) *Human Capital: A theoretical and empirical analysis, with special reference to education*, Chicago, IL: University of Chicago Press.

Bouget, D., H. Frazer, E. Marlier, S. Sabato and B. Vanhercke (2015) *Social investment in Europe. A study of national policies*, Brussels: DG Employment, Social Affairs and Inclusion.

Burger, K. (2010) 'How Does Early Childhood Care and Education Affect Cognitive Development? An international review of the effects of early interventions for children from different social backgrounds', *Early Childhood Research Quarterly* 25: 140-65.

Deeming, C. and P. Smyth (2015) 'Social Investment after Neoliberalism: Policy Paradigms and Political Platforms', *Journal of Social Policy* 44(2): 297–318.

European Commission (2013a) *Towards Social Investment for Growth and Cohesion. Commission Communication*, COM(2013) 83 final, 20 February.

European Commission (2013b) *Investing in Children: breaking the cycle of disadvantage, Commission recommendation*, C(2013) 778 final, 20 February.

European Parliament (2012) 'Social Investment Pact, European Parliament resolution of 20 November 2012 on Social Investment Pact – as a response to the crisis' (2012/2003(INI)).

Esping-Andersen, G. (2002) 'A child-centred social investment strategy', in G. Esping-Andersen, D. Gallie, A. Hemerijk, and J. Myles (eds), *Why we need a new welfare state*, Oxford: Oxford University Press, 26–67.

Graham, H. and C. Power (2004) 'Childhood disadvantages and health inequalities: a framework for policy based on lifecourse research', *Child: Care, Health & Development* 30(6): 671–78.

Hannon, P. (2003) 'Developmental Neuroscience: Implications for early childhood education', *Current Pediatrics* 13: 58–63.

Havnes, T. and Mogstad, M. (2011) 'No Child Left Behind: Subsidized child care and childrens's long-run outcomes', *American Economic Journal: Economic Policy* 3(2): 97–129.

Heckman, J.J. (2000) 'Policies to foster human capital', *Research in Economics* 54(1): 3–56.

Heckman, J.J. (2008) 'Schools, Skills, and Synapses', *Economic Inquiry* 46(3): 289–324.

Jenson, J. (2010) 'Diffusing ideas for after-neoliberalism: The social investment perspective in Europe and Latin America', *Global Social Policy* 10(1): 59–84.

Kleven, H.J. (2014) 'How can Scandinavians Tax So Much', *The Journal of Economic Perspective* 38(4): 77–98.

Kvist, J. (2015a) 'A framework for social investment strategies: Integrating generational, life course and gender perspectives in the EU social investment strategy', *Comparative European Politics* 13(1): 131–49.

Kvist, J. (2015b) 'Social investment as risk management', in T. Bengtsson, M. Frederiksen and J.E. Larsen (eds), *The Danish Welfare State: a sociological investigation*, London: Palgrave, 41–56.

Kvist, J. (2016) *Fighting Poverty and Social Exclusion through Social Investment*, Brussels: European Commission.

Marmot, M., Allen, J., Bell, R., Bloomer, E., and Goldbladt, P. (2012) 'WHO European Review of Social Determinants of Health and the Health Divide', *The Lancet* 380: 1011-29.

Merton, R.K. (1968) 'The Matthew Effect in Science', *Science*, 159(2810): 56–63.

Morel, N., B. Palier and J. Palme (eds) (2012) *Towards a social investment state?* Bristol: Policy Press.

Myrdal, A. and G. Myrdal (1934) *Kris i befolkningsfrågan*, [*Population crisis*], Stockholm: Bonniers.

OECD (2015a) *Better life initiative: Measuring well-being and progress*, Paris: OECD.

OECD (2015b) *Skills for social progress: The power of social and emotional skills*, Paris: OECD.

Rowntree, S. (1901) *Poverty. A Study of Town Life*, London: Macmillan.

Stiglitz, J., A. Sen, and J.P. Fitoussi (2009) *Report by the Commission on the Measurement of Economic Performance and Social Progress*, www.insee.fr

WHO (2000) *A life course perspective of maintaining independence in older age*, Geneva: World Health Organization.

WHO (2002) *Towards a common language for functioning, disability and health – ICF*, Geneva: World Health Organization.

TEN

Inclusive economic growth for health equity: in search of the elusive evidence

Guillem López-Casasnovas and Laia Maynou

Introduction

It has to be true. Inclusive growth, less unequal wealth creation, better-distributed incomes 'must' lead to more health and health equity (certainly the growing evidence is persuasive; see Wilkinson and Pickett, 2009). But as we will see in this chapter, to test this affirmative sequence, with all the assumed linkages, proves to be very difficult. This has to do with, on one hand, the issue of reverse causality (in identifying what is causing what) and, on the other, the heterogeneity of the observed sample and country diversity. In setting the details of the empirical framework of the analysis we try to show how complex this task is. By exploring some initial results, we hope to convince our readers and further researchers in this field that, despite all those caveats, 'something' is there waiting to be found under multiple data limitations.

The literature on health and economic growth is large and extensive. The socioeconomic determinants of health provide the hidden link for the studies (Marmot, 2013). However, the analysis of the impact of economic growth on health, and the impact of health on economic growth is still a very challenging issue in the health economics research portfolio (see López-Casasnovas et al, 2005). Many contributions attempt to model the effects of health on economic growth (Bhargava et al, 2001), while others focus on the reverse: how health changes as a result of economic growth (see López-Casasnovas and Soley-Bori, 2014). Although there exists some endogeneity problems in both approaches—particularly in the variable of economic growth, since this may be explained by, among other things, the level of a population's health—we pursue here a step further in the analysis of the effects of growth on health and particularly on health inequality, and vice versa.

In general, these relevant links may be tested at the macro level through the dynamics of health and income, in a cross-section study (for a specific country) or at the micro level by testing whether the poorest today, in a place of high income and inequality, is in better health than in the past. In addition, the relationship between income and health is likely to be non-lineal and may be differentially affected by short-run impacts. Moreover, the standard view is that health inequalities seem to relate mainly to poverty and not so much to income inequality (Leigh et al, 2009). Therefore, given the dynastic patterns of health and poverty, more attention needs to be devoted to the dynamics of health over individuals' lifecycles and on the transmission mechanisms between generations, and not so much to the differences of very diverse countries' experiences.

In real life, health inequalities exist between and within countries. The Commission on Macroeconomics and Health pointed out that there might be a considerable cost in terms of foregone economic growth as a result of some countries having a much lower level of overall health than other countries. Some research has already documented significant economic benefits in the form of faster economic growth from reducing health inequalities among countries. The evidence (see Suhrcke and Cookson, 2012; Marmot, 2013) comes from both high income countries in the OECD as well as from the Eastern European and Central Asian countries. However, there continues to be a scientific debate about the extent to which the health and growth nexus truly reflects a causal relationship.

As evidenced by extensive research, the adverse economic effect of ill health is better analysed than health inequality, and both are much less controversial at the individual level. Within countries lower socioeconomic groups suffer worse health and should thus incur greater economic losses (in the form of earnings loss and labour supply), this is one basis for arguing that health inequalities likely impose a substantial economic burden to society. The true economic burden of health inequalities does, however, lie in the value people attribute to the lives lost as a result of socioeconomic differences. That value is hard to measure, but it certainly by far exceeds any narrow (and possibly non-existent) economic gains in the form of additional earnings or healthcare cost savings (reliable estimation is unlikely to be feasible).

The chapter continues as following. In the first section, we present the empirical exercise. The results are explained in section two. In the final section, we express recommendations for future research and make some policy recommendations based on our findings.

The empirical exercise

The objective of our analysis is to determine the relationship between economic performance and health at an aggregate level. In other words, the aim is to show the empirical effect of health on the economic performance of countries, once grouped by types. The main hypothesis is that countries classified within the lower quintiles of the income distribution show a higher effect on their economic performance when health increases (accounting for inequalities).

In our approach the economic performance is measured by gross domestic product (GDP) per capita (purchasing power parity, PPP) and health is proxied through the Health Human Development Index (HHDI) from 2005 to 2013. This last indicator is taken from the health component of the United Nations Human Development Index (HDI). Moreover, one of the analyses will make use of another United Nations indicator, which weights the HHDI by observed inequality. The inequality-adjusted HHDI captures the welfare derived from health using a geometric mean. The main point is that welfare from health is not just related to the size of the index, but also to its distribution. Unfortunately, this last measure is only publicly available for the year 2014.

Countries of the study

The study involves worldwide countries for which those data are available. In particular, our sample consists of 187 countries: Afghanistan, Albania, Algeria, Andorra, Angola, Antigua and Barbuda, Argentina, Armenia, Australia, Austria, Azerbaijan, Bahamas, Bahrain, Bangladesh, Barbados, Belarus, Belgium, Belize, Benin, Bhutan, Bolivia (Plurinational State of), Bosnia and Herzegovina, Botswana, Brazil, Brunei Darussalam, Bulgaria, Burkina Faso, Burundi, Cabo Verde, Cambodia, Cameroon, Canada, Central African Republic, Chad, Chile, China, Colombia, Comoros, Congo, Congo (Democratic Republic of the), Costa Rica, Croatia, Cuba, Cyprus, Czech Republic, Côte d'Ivoire, Denmark, Djibouti, Dominica, Dominican Republic, Ecuador, Egypt, El Salvador, Equatorial Guinea, Eritrea, Estonia, Ethiopia, Fiji, Finland, France, Gabon, Gambia, Georgia, Germany, Ghana, Greece, Grenada, Guatemala, Guinea, Guinea-Bissau, Guyana, Haiti, Honduras, Hong Kong, China (SAR), Hungary, Iceland, India, Indonesia, Iran (Islamic Republic of), Iraq, Ireland, Israel, Italy, Jamaica, Japan, Jordan, Kazakhstan, Kenya, Kiribati, Korea (Republic of), Kuwait, Kyrgyzstan, Lao People's Democratic Republic, Latvia, Lebanon, Lesotho, Liberia, Libya, Liechtenstein, Lithuania, Luxembourg, Madagascar, Malawi, Malaysia, Maldives, Mali, Malta, Mauritania, Mauritius, Mexico, Micronesia (Federated States of), Moldova (Republic of), Mongolia, Montenegro, Morocco,

Mozambique, Myanmar, Namibia, Nepal, Netherlands, New Zealand, Nicaragua, Niger, Nigeria, Norway, Oman, Pakistan, Palau, Panama, Papua New Guinea, Paraguay, Peru, Philippines, Poland, Portugal, Qatar, Romania, Russian Federation, Rwanda, Saint Kitts and Nevis, Saint Lucia, Saint Vincent and the Grenadines, Samoa, Sao Tome and Principe, Saudi Arabia, Senegal, Serbia, Seychelles, Sierra Leone, Singapore, Slovakia, Slovenia, Solomon Islands, South Africa, South Sudan, Spain, Sri Lanka, Sudan, Suriname, Swaziland, Sweden, Switzerland, Syrian Arab Republic, Tajikistan, Tanzania (United Republic of), Thailand, The former Yugoslav Republic of Macedonia, Timor-Leste, Togo, Tonga, Trinidad and Tobago, Tunisia, Turkey, Turkmenistan, Uganda, Ukraine, United Arab Emirates, United Kingdom, United States, Uruguay, Uzbekistan, Vanuatu, Venezuela (Bolivarian Republic of), Viet Nam, Yemen, Zambia, Zimbabwe.

The HDI is a summary measure of average achievement in key dimensions of human development: a long and healthy life, being knowledgeable and have a decent standard of living (see United Nations Development Programme, 2016). In this study, we will be using the health component of the HDI, which is assessed by the life expectancy at birth. The health dimension is defined as the difference between the actual (observed) and the minimum value of life expectancy, divided by the difference between the observed maximum value (established at 85 years) and the minimum (established at 20 years) (United Nations Development Programme, 2016). This component ranges from 0 to 1, where 1 represents a higher level of health.

Reaching our goal through this empirical analysis is not easy due to the lack of data availability and econometric limitations. The main limitation is that we only have the inequality-adjusted HHDI for one year (2014), while we have the general HHDI from 2005 to 2013. So we will not be able to account for inequalities within the HHDI in all periods. Moreover, for some other specific explanatory/control variables there are a lot of missing observations, which incorporate some issues in the estimation. Apart from that, we are aware that the econometric specification might still encounter some endogeneity issues (mainly from reverse causality as commented earlier on). Consequently we are not claiming causality in this study, but we try to show some relationships across these measures.

Another limitation has to do with the health indicator we have chosen. As López-Casasnovas and Soley-Bori (2014) state, there are controversies in defining the health indicator, mainly when dealing with inequalities. However, we follow their reasoning in order to rely on life expectancy data (HHDI) to assess health, mainly because it is a measure available in all the study countries.

Even being aware of all these difficulties, we present in the following section the results of our empirical analysis. We estimate the links between health and economic performance, using as the dependent variable the logarithm of the GDP per capita (PPP) and as an explanatory variable of interest the HHDI and the inequality–adjusted HHDI. Table 10.1 defines the variables included into our models. These variables were selected in order to control for any external source of variability of the GDP per capita. In other words, relevant variables that can explain the GDP per capita in these countries and that have been used in previous literature (for example, López–Casasnovas and Soley–Bori, 2014; Deaton, 2013; López–Casasnovas, 2010). All the data are obtained from publicly available data sources including the United Nations Development Program and World Bank websites, the WIID database from the UNU–WIDER (World Institute for Development Economic Research, United Nations) and the UCDP (Uppsala Conflict Data Program)/PRIO (International Peace Research Institute) Armed Conflict Dataset.

Some of the explanatory variables, such as external debt, Gini index and education (primary and secondary), incorporate missing observations for some countries (mainly the less developed). So, including them into the model will consistently drop the number of observations. Moreover, some variables, like HHDI and life expectancy, are correlated, which is taken into account in the specification. It is important to state that the panel database does not get to 2014 because the HHDI data is only available until 2013.[1]

Table 10.1 Variables of the study

Variables	Definition
GDP capita (PPP)	Gross domestic product (GDP) per capita based on purchasing power parity (PPP). Data are in constant 2011 international dollars. Period: 2005–14. *Source: World Bank*
Health Human Development Index (HHDI)	Health component of the HDI, assessed by the life expectancy at birth (ranges for 0 to 1). Period: 2005–13. *Source:* Human Development Report Office
Inequality-adjusted HHDI	HHDI weighted by observed inequalities through a geometric mean. Period: 2014. *Source:* Human Development Report Office
Trade (% of GDP)	Trade is the sum of exports and imports of goods and services measured as a share of Gross Domestic Product. Period: 2005–14. *Source:* World Bank
Fertility rate, total (births per woman)	Represents the number of children that would be born to a woman if she were to live to the end of her childbearing years and bear children in accordance with age-specific fertility rates of the specified year. Period: 2005–14. *Source:* World Bank
Population, total	Total population is based on the de facto definition of population, which counts all residents regardless of legal status or citizenship. The values shown are midyear estimates. Period: 2005–14. *Source:* World Bank
Life expectancy at birth	Indicates the number of years a newborn infant would live if prevailing patterns of mortality at the time of its birth were to stay the same throughout its life. Period: 2005–14. *Source:* World Bank
Health expenditure total (% GDP)	Sum of public and private health expenditure. It covers the provision of health services (preventive and curative), family planning activities, nutrition activities, and emergency aid designated for health but does not include provision of water and sanitation. Period: 2005–14. *Source:* World Bank
Health expenditure per capita (PPP)	Sum of public and private health expenditures as a ratio of total population. It covers the provision of health services (preventive and curative), family planning activities, nutrition activities, and emergency aid designated for health but does not include provision of water and sanitation. Data are in constant 2011 international dollars. Period: 2005–14. *Source:* World Bank

Variables	Definition
External debt stocks (% of GNI)	Total external debt stocks to gross national income. Sum of public, publicly guaranteed, and private nonguaranteed long-term debt, use of IMF credit, and short-term debt. GNI (formerly GNP) is the sum of value added by all resident producers plus any product taxes (less subsidies) not included in the valuation of output plus net receipts of primary income (compensation of employees and property income) from abroad. Period: 2005–14. *Source:* World Bank
War conflicts	The intensity level of the conflict per calendar year. Three different intensity levels are coded: No conflict (when the year/country is not recorded in the database) Minor: between 25 and 999 battle-related deaths in a given year. War: at least 1,000 battle-related deaths in a given year. Period: 2005–14. *Sources:* UCDP/PRIO Armed Conflict Dataset; authors' own construction
Enrolment primary education (% of population)	Total number of pupils enrolled at primary level in public and private schools divided by population. Period: 200–14. *Sources:* World Bank; authors' own construction
Enrolment secondary education (% of population)	Total number of pupils enrolled at secondary level in public and private schools. Period: 2005–14. *Sources:* World Bank; authors' own construction
GINI index	It measures the extent to which the distribution of income (or, in some cases, consumption expenditure) among individuals or households within an economy deviates from a perfectly equal distribution. Thus a Gini index of 0 represents perfect equality, while an index of 100 implies perfect inequality. Period: 2005–13. *Sources:* World Bank; WIID database

The study involves the specification of two main econometric models.

A. Panel data fixed effects model for the 187 countries from 2005 to 2013. The aim of this particular specification of the panel model is to control for the unobserved variables that are constant over time. Using a frequentist approach (instead of Bayesian), a random-effects specification would not be reliable because there exists correlation among the explanatory variables and the unobserved characteristics, as the Hausman test shows. The model that we specify is the following:

$$\log(GDPcapita_{it})$$
$$= \alpha + \beta_1 HHDI_{it} + \beta_2 TradeGDP_{it} + \beta_3 \log(Population_{it}) + \beta_4 Fertilityrate_{it}$$
$$+ \beta_5 \log(Health\exp capita_{it}) + \beta_6 enrolpripop_{it} + \beta_7 enrol\sec onpop_{it}$$
$$+ \beta_8 War\operatorname{int}esity_{it} + \beta_9 extdebtGDP_{it} + \beta_{10} GINI_{it} + S_i + \tau_t + u_{it}$$

The subscript $_i$ denotes country $(i=1,...,187)$; and $_t$ year $(t=2005,...,2013)$; α and β denote unknown parameters; S_i denotes country fixed effects; τ_t denotes year dummies and u normally distributed disturbance term.

B. Cross-section model for the year 2014 for 187 countries, in order to incorporate the information of the inequality-adjusted HHDI. The econometric specification is a linear regression model with robust standard errors.

$$\log(GDPcapita_i)$$
$$= \alpha + \beta_1 ineqadjHHDI_i + \beta_2 TradeGDP_i + \beta_3 \log(Population_i)$$
$$+ \beta_4 Fertilityrate_i + \beta_5 \log(Health\exp capita_i) + \beta_6 enrolpripop_i$$
$$+ \beta_7 enrol\sec onpop_i + \beta_8 War\operatorname{int}esity_i + \beta_9 extdebtGDP_i + \beta_{10} GINI_i + u_i$$

Our study is not just relating the HHDI with the GDP capita for all countries. The main point is to classify the countries to observe any difference on the effect. As a result, four classifications are investigated:

1. By the mean of the GDP per capita. We create a dummy variable that equals 1 when the countries are below the mean (named 'poor countries') and 0 if the countries are above the mean. For the panel data, the mean of the GDP per capita is international \$16,700 and there are 122 countries below it. For the cross-section, the mean of the GDP per capita is international \$17,500 and there are 118 countries below it.[2]

2. By quintiles of the mean of the GDP per capita. The variable has five categories (1-low GDP capita mean to 5-high GDP capita mean).
3. For the panel data, there are 37 countries at the first quintile, 36 countries at the second quintile, 37 countries at the third quintile, 36 countries at the fourth quintile and 36 countries at the fifth quintile. For the cross-section, there are 36 countries at the first quintile, 36 countries at the second quintile, 35 countries at the third quintile, 36 countries at the fourth quintile and 35 countries at the fifth quintile.[3]
4. By member of OECD. There are 35 countries that are members of the OECD. The variable is constructed as follows: 1- if the county is not a member of the OECD and 0- if the country is a member.
5. By the 2014 classification of the HDI. The HDI classifies the countries in four groups according to the HDI value: very high HDI, high HDI, medium HDI and low HDI.

Results

The descriptive analysis[4] showed that the HHDI mean goes down when it is adjusted by observed inequalities (inequality-adjusted HHDI). Moreover, it states that there is substantial variability across countries and years for these variables.

Panel models results

Regarding the results of the econometric models, as explained above, the main aim is to see the relationship between the economic performance (GDP per capita) and health (HHDI) for different types of countries. The starting point is the panel dataset.

Table 10.2 presents different models that examine this relationship taking into account all the countries, without making any classification. The difference between Model 1 to 5 is the number of explanatory variables that are included. Due to the missing observations of some variables, the number of the observations of the models drops. Model 1 to 4 has HHDI as the variable of interest. The result is statistically significant (except for Model 4) and can be interpreted as a higher HHDI is related with a higher GDP per capita. However, Model 4 incorporates as explanatory variables the Gini index and its influence seems to get rid of the significant effect of HHDI.

Model 5 drops HHDI and it includes as variable of interest the Gini index, which is positive and statistically significant. This is not a surprise since income growth usually goes hand in hand with income

Table 10.2 Panel model results, 2005–13, 187 countries. Log (GDP per capita) dependent variable

	Model 1	Model 2	Model 3	Model 4	Model 5
HHDI	0.477***[1]	0.369***	0.387**	0.225	
	(0.17)[2]	(0.13)	(0.20)	(0.26)	
Trade (% of GDP)		-0.001***	-0.001***	-0.000	-0.000
		(0.00)	(0.00)	(0.00)	(0.00)
log(Population)		-0.244***	-0.137	0.062	0.075
		(0.04)	(0.09)	(0.14)	(0.14)
Fertilityrate		-0.078***	-0.023	0.002	-0.005
		(0.01)	(0.02)	(0.03)	(0.03)
HealtexptotalGDP		-0.079***	-0.067***	-0.079***	-0.079***
		(0.00)	(0.00)	(0.01)	(0.01)
log(Healtexpcapita)		0.435***	0.420***	0.512***	0.516***
		(0.02)	(0.03)	(0.04)	(0.04)
enrolpripop			0.002	-0.004	-0.003
			(0.00)	(0.00)	(0.00)
enrolseconpop			0.005	-0.000	0.000
			(0.00)	(0.00)	(0.00)
1.Warintensity			0.008	-0.015	-0.013
			(0.01)	(0.01)	(0.01)
2.Warintensity			-0.002	-0.017	-0.021
			(0.02)	(0.03)	(0.03)
extdebtGDP			-0.0003*	-0.000	-0.000
			(0.0002)	(0.00)	(0.00)
GINI index				0.003**	0.002**
				(0.00)	(0.00)
_cons	8.622***	10.724***	8.543***	5.029**	4.980**
	(0.12)	(0.66)	(1.37)	(2.31)	(2.31)
country fixed effects	X	X	X	X	X
year dummies	X	X	X	X	X
N	1633	1541	716	314	314
within R^2	0.314	0.617	0.747	0.870	0.870
between R^2	0.622	0.673	0.760	0.936	0.915
overall R^2	0.427	0.676	0.763	0.926	0.903

Notes: [1]Coefficient, [2]Standard errors in parentheses. Significance levels: *$p<0.10$, **$p<0.05$, ***$p<0.01$

inequality. Here our variable of interest is health and health inequality. Regarding the other explanatory variables, population, fertility rate and external debt have the expected signs. Health expenditure (% of GDP) has a negative and statistical significant effect on the GDP per capita. The 'odd' effect of health expenditure is 'corrected' if we take the health expenditure per capita since this is related with a higher GDP per capita.

Once we have analysed the relationship accounting for all countries, the next step is to look at this relationship by classifying the countries into different categories in order to observe differential adjustment and structural forms within our whole sample as commented earlier on.

The following tables present the best models out of the variables that we are examining. For instance, war intensity is not appearing in these models because it was creating problems in the estimation. Table 10.3 collects the results of the models for the first two classifications, related to the mean of the GDP per capita. In these models, we have created an interaction between the dummy variable (showing the classification) and the HHDI. As we are working with a fixed effects specification, the dummy for the classification drops off the model because they are considered time invariant. In order to interpret the interaction, we need to sum the coefficient of the HHDI and the interaction of the HHDI*classification dummy. The sum of both coefficients will give us the effect for each classification.

Models 5 to 7 present the results for the first classification and they account for different explanatory variables and observations. The main result is that being a country with a GDP per capita below the mean (122 countries of the sample) implies that an increase of the HHDI is related with a higher GDP per capita compared to a country which is above the mean. So, the pursued effect is higher for the group classified as poor as expected. This goes in line with Models 8 to 10 which have classified the mean of the GDP per capita in 5 groups. The main result is that for the countries in the quintile 1, 2 and 3 (poorer countries) an increase of the HHDI increases the GDP per capita compared to quintile 5 (richer countries). When introducing explanatory variables, we can see, however, that the effect of quintile 4 gets negative and non-significant (sum of both coefficients). So, again, it seems that being a poorer country has a higher effect on the GDP per capita than being a richer country if the HHDI increases.

Table 10.4 presents the results for the last two classifications: being a non-OECD country and by the ranking in the HDI in 2014. Classification 3 can be interpreted as follows: being a country non-member of the OECD is associated with a positive and significant effect (sum of both coefficients) on the GDP per capita when the HHDI increases compare to an OECD country. Regarding the fourth classification, adding the two coefficients, we can see that when the country is ranked in a low to medium HDI, instead of very high HDI, the effect of an increase of the HHDI on the GDP per capita is positive and significant. However, as soon as we get to a country with a high HDI compared to a very high HDI, the effect turns to a negative and significant sign. So, the higher effect can be seen on the countries which are in the lower part of the HDI rank.

Both Table 10.3 and Table 10.4 show some significant coefficients for some explanatory variables. In most of the models, the health expenditure (% of GDP), trade (% of GDP) and enrolment primary education (over population) have a negative and significant effect on the GDP per capita. However, the health expenditure per capita, the enrolment secondary education (over population) and the Gini index have a positive and significant effect (in this last case as found in former models).

Cross-section results (2014)

The last analysis that we present is the cross-section study for 2014. In this case, the objective is to use the inequality-adjusted HHDI instead of the general HHDI, to incorporate the effect of the welfare from health. Table 10.5 collects the results of the best models that have been specified with the variables available (for example, the education variables and external debt were removed because they drop substantially the number of observations). First of all, Models 17 and 18 do not take into account any classification. Model 17 only includes our variable of interest and the effect is positive and significant, but as soon as we incorporate explanatory/control variables the effect turns insignificant.

Models 19 to 22 incorporate the previous classifications. In this case, as we are not using a fixed effects approximatio, for the interaction, we have to include also the dummy for classification, so the interpretation will be the sum of the three coefficients (HHDI + classification dummy + HHDI*classification dummy). The only classification that shows significant effect is the second, by quintiles. When summing the three coefficients we can observe that for the four quintiles the total effect is negative and significant compared to the fifth quintile. This means that when adjusting the HHDI by inequalities, we find reverse results. In this case, increasing the inequality-adjusted HHDI reduces the GDP per capita compared to the fifth quintile. Despite

Table 10.3 Panel model results classification 1 and 2, 2005–13, 187 countries. Log (GDP per capita) dependent variable

	Classification 1: < mean GDP capita			Classification 2: quintiles mean GDP capita		
	Model 5	Model 6	Model 7	Model 8	Model 9	Model 10
HHDI	-2.129***	-3.788**	-6.891***	-1.920***	-0.799***	-4.952***
	(0.30)	(1.65)	(1.70)	(0.31)	(0.21)	(0.65)
HHDI*poor	3.050***	4.189**	7.102***			
	(0.29)	(1.64)	(1.69)			
HHDI*quintile1				2.752***	1.777***	5.348***
				(0.33)	(0.30)	(0.66)
HHDI*quintile2				3.256***	2.634***	5.420***
				(0.39)	(0.32)	(0.66)
HHDI*quintile3				2.627***	1.021***	4.216***
				(0.41)	(0.31)	(0.62)
HHDI*quintile4				1.987***	-0.072	1.080*
				(0.62)	(0.46)	(0.58)
Trade (% of GDP)		-0.001***	-0.001*		-0.001***	-0.000
		(0.00)	(0.00)		(0.00)	(0.00)
log(Population)		-0.134	-0.004		-0.118***	0.249***
		(0.08)	(0.13)		(0.04)	(0.06)
Fertilityrate		-0.016	0.019		-0.014	0.035
		(0.02)	(0.03)		(0.02)	(0.02)
HealtexptotalGDP		-0.069***	-0.084***		-0.081***	-0.080***
		(0.00)	(0.01)		(0.00)	(0.00)
log(Healtexpcapita)		0.433***	0.552***		0.511***	0.565***
		(0.03)	(0.04)		(0.02)	(0.03)
enrolpripop		0.002	-0.001		-0.000	-0.009**
		(0.00)	(0.00)		(0.00)	(0.00)
enrolseconpop		0.005	-0.001		0.004*	0.001
		(0.00)	(0.00)		(0.00)	(0.00)
extdebtGDP		-0.000	-0.001*			
		(0.00)	(0.00)			
GINI index			0.002			0.001*
			(0.00)			(0.00)
_cons	9.162***	8.499***	6.151***	8.922***	8.446***	4.522***
	(0.13)	(1.36)	(2.23)	(0.17)	(0.64)	(1.03)
country fixed effects	X	X	X	X	X	X
year dummies	X	X	X	X	X	X
N	1633	716	314	1633	1185	604
within R²	0.363	0.749	0.879	0.353	0.703	0.835
between R²	0.538	0.212	0.040	0.529	0.009	0.549
overall R²	0.530	0.223	0.021	0.520	0.004	0.611

Notes: [1]Coefficient,[2] Standard errors in parentheses. Significance levels: *p<0.10, **p<0.05, ***p<0.01

Table 10.4 Panel model results classification 3 and 4, 2005–13, 187 countries. Log (GDP per capita) dependent variable

	Classification 3: Non-OECD country			Classification 4: HDI ranking		
	Model 11	Model 12	Model 13	Model 14	Model 15	Model 16
HHDI	-4.912***[1]	-3.167***	-4.125***	-6.513***	-3.917***	-4.529***
	(0.66)	(1.00)	(0.85)	(0.65)	(0.48)	(0.66)
HHDI*NonOECD	5.187***[2]	3.570***	4.364***			
	(0.62)	(0.98)	(0.83)			
HHDI*lowHDI				6.515***	4.452***	4.818***
				(0.61)	(0.49)	(0.66)
HHDI*mediumHDI				7.347***	5.069***	4.926***
				(0.62)	(0.48)	(0.64)
HHDI*highHDI				5.818***	3.352***	3.602***
				(0.62)	(0.45)	(0.56)
Trade (% of GDP)		-0.001***	-0.000		-0.001***	-0.000
		(0.00)	(0.00)		(0.00)	(0.00)
log(Population)		-0.133	0.143		-0.140***	0.195***
		(0.08)	(0.13)		(0.03)	(0.06)
Fertilityrate		-0.015	0.028		-0.001	0.012
		(0.02)	(0.03)		(0.02)	(0.02)
HealtexptotalGDP		-0.068***	-0.080***		-0.072***	-0.077***
		(0.00)	(0.01)		(0.00)	(0.00)
log(Healtexpcapita)		0.422***	0.508***		0.466***	0.541***
		(0.02)	(0.04)		(0.02)	(0.03)
enrolpripop		0.001	-0.006		0.002	-0.009**
		(0.00)	(0.00)		(0.00)	(0.00)
enrolseconpop		0.007**	0.004		0.006***	-0.001
		(0.00)	(0.00)		(0.00)	(0.00)
extdebtGDP		-0.000	-0.000			
		(0.00)	(0.00)			
GINI index			0.003***			0.001*
			(0.00)			(0.00)
_cons	9.668***	8.495***	3.768*	10.500***	10.017***	5.339***
	(0.17)	(1.35)	(2.19)	(0.21)	(0.63)	(1.10)
country fixed effects	X	X	X	X	X	X
year dummies	X	X	X	X	X	X
N	1633	716	314	1633	1172	603
within R^2	0.346	0.752	0.885	0.376	0.711	0.825
between R^2	0.282	0.363	0.305	0.538	0.318	0.390
overall R^2	0.278	0.305	0.119	0.533	0.360	0.467

Notes: [1]Coefficient, [2]Standard errors in parentheses. Significance levels: *$p<0.10$, **$p<0.05$, ***$p<0.01$

this, the result is not very robust, as the other classifications do not show any significance, and goes against our main purpose with regard to changes in health inequality as a propeller for economic growth. Remember, however, that due to data limitation we cannot properly test the hypothesis: the index is available for just one year and we cannot use panel data to enrich our estimation. Although reverse causation rather a single direction causality must be there in any case, and given the already found results – in terms of levels (rather than on variance) – we conclude that further research with new data may be crucial to properly test the initial hypothesis that formed the basis of this chapter. Certainly for shorter subsamples (say OECD) we may account for two inequality adjusted HDI (for years 2010 and 2014), but we judge that the relevance of the hypothesis is better referred to the case of Least Developed Countries (LDCs) for which a higher rank of variations could be observed.

Finally, the rest of the variables follow the same sign and significance as the previous models, except from the Gini index, which is now negative and significant. This result seems to be more reliable for the Gini effect on GDP per capita.

Reassessing the analysis

The problem with the trends in health inequality in different socioeconomic strata is not the improvement among the better off, but the slower rate of improvement among those worse off. For this, the existence and extent of the social protection matters according to its design as an effective income stabiliser and a contributor to improve labour force participation. These relationships used to be curvilinear, which means that the health gains from social policy programmes per euro spent is generally higher at lower levels. This suggests that also modest increases would be of importance in poorer countries in the region. Economic growth funding for education may create a differential impact by investing in special educational groups, with lower educated gaining more, which suggests a clear potential for a reduction of health inequalities. While income inequalities (remember the estimated parameters for the Gini coefficient) may not be a social determinant of health, larger income disparities are usually more directly related to higher relative poverty rates. The relationship between income and health is complicated and certainly not a simple issue of 'more is better', but rather an issue of poverty as well as a gradient (albeit likely with diminishing returns). The links between income and health are commonly formulated at the individual level.

Table 10.5 Cross-section results, 187 countries. Log (GDP per capita) dependent variable

	Model 17	Classification 1		Classification 2	Classification 3	Classification 4
		Model 18	Model 19	Model 20	Model 21	Model 22
ineqadjHHDI	5.148***[1] (0.30)[2]	-0.143 (0.15)	-0.349 (0.25)	-4.036** (1.22)	-0.437 (0.62)	-0.666 (0.63)
poor			-0.246 (0.21)			
ineqadjHHDI*poor			0.243 (0.24)			
quintile1				-4.031*** (1.16)		
quintile2				-3.840*** (1.14)		
quintile3				-3.787** (1.14)		
quintile4				-3.687** (1.14)		
ineqadjHHDI*quintile1				3.872** (1.27)		
ineqadjHHDI*quintile2				3.866** (1.24)		
ineqadjHHDI*quintile3				3.931** (1.24)		
ineqadjHHDI*quintile4				3.870** (1.25)		
NonOECD					-0.271 (0.55)	
ineqadjHHDI*NonOECD					0.316 (0.62)	
lowHDI						-0.510 (0.57)
mediumHDI						-0.450 (0.59)
highHDI						-0.692 (0.55)
ineqadjHHDI*lowHDI						0.588 (0.68)

		Classification 1	Classification 2	Classification 3	Classification 4
ineqadjHHDI*mediumHDI					0.478 (0.68)
ineqadjHHDI*highHDI					0.784 (0.63)
Trade (% of GDP)	-0.000 (0.00)	-0.000 (0.00)	0.000 (0.00)	-0.000 (0.00)	-0.000 (0.00)
log(Population)	-0.000 (0.02)	0.000 (0.02)	-0.002 (0.02)	0.003 (0.02)	0.001 (0.02)
Fertilityrate	0.003 (0.01)	0.005 (0.01)	0.002 (0.01)	0.003 (0.01)	0.003 (0.01)
HealtexptotalGDP	-0.146*** (0.01)	-0.144*** (0.01)	-0.132*** (0.01)	-0.146*** (0.01)	-0.147*** (0.01)
log(Healtexpcapita)	1.023*** (0.02)	1.008*** (0.03)	0.891*** (0.05)	1.025*** (0.03)	1.023*** (0.03)
GINI index	-0.002* (0.00)	-0.002 (0.00)	-0.002 (0.00)	-0.002* (0.00)	-0.002 (0.00)
_cons	5.750*** (0.23)	3.729*** (0.18)	8.231*** (1.19)	3.967*** (0.51)	4.207*** (0.47)
N	175	142	142	142	142
R^2	0.695	0.990	0.993	0.991	0.991

Notes: [1]Coefficient, [2]Standard errors in parentheses. Significance levels: *$p<0.10$, **$p<0.05$, ***$p<0.01$

However the layers of the social context are certainly important and can all be considered as part of the institutional context that will differ across countries, as evidence from survey instruments measuring social capital suggests.

Having said this, we should recognise that to invest in health still should mean more public health spending: education and job creation have a particular beneficial role (see also Chapter Six in this volume). Specifically in developing countries, programmes should ensure that women and children 'go first' to have the minimum income needed for a healthy living given the beneficial external effects that they create on the community and for better long-term human capital investments for the families. Flexible and secure jobs are desperately needed in developed countries since the absence of the right mix of job opportunities and income stability is the main thread for the loss of health for those most vulnerable groups.

Among different countries and over time, health inequalities are the result of a set on interrelated factors with multiple causations. Income appears to be pivotal of all those interactions that affect health inequalities. However, at each moment in time, the weight of those factors on social determined health inequalities may differ and does not only make for a single Income-related Health Inequality (IRHI) problem. It may be not even be only a problem of balancing factors but even of sacrifying one for another. Trade-offs are likely not to appear when actions from universal proportionate programmes benefit the most to the more needed population. However, sometimes these programmes, particularly in developing countries, miss the poor, since their responsiveness to universal actions is lower, due to the lack of information or education.

Given what we now know, despite the observed relationship between income variations and health, more analysis is needed on the epidemiology and macroeconomics of social factors when we move from individual to collective aggregate behaviour of income and health. We need better empirical approaches to deal with the endogenous relationship between health and income by instrumenting adequate variables. The endogeneity is mostly due to the existence of cumulative causation processes related to social conditioning, labour employment/ capital input technologies, and factor interactions. In our estimation, some methodological pitfalls remain. First, we need structural models rather than reduced form equations and fully longitudinal panel data analysis.[5] For instance, Eurostat[6] follows this methodology to determine how income-related health inequalities change in short- and long-term perspectives, using an index of health-related income mobility based on a concentration index (CI).[7] For the EU member states, results indicate the existence of long-term income-related inequalities in health, and low income individuals seem more vulnerable to health limitations. Moreover, the values of the mobility proxies suggest that income dynamics should be taken into account when inequalities are computed in health limitations in order to avoid overestimation. Aware of the drawbacks of the CI,[8] in a further step, the previously mentioned EU report (Eurostat, 2010) uses the 'adjusted' CI (Erreygers, 2009) to compare groups with a different average health.[9] However, as commented, for the purpose of our analysis we need larger samples with wider variation of health and income and checking their differential relevance according to the stage of development of the countries.

Other methodologies that need further improvements include those related to fixed effects estimation (aimed at mitigating unobservable factors), instrumental variables, better matching techniques for quasi-random experiments, and a pseudo panel in order to properly deal with endogeneity decisions. Moreover, in micro econometric approaches, and with individual disaggregate data, reporting bias and sample selection bias should be carefully considered.

In addition, further attention should be paid to non-linearities, adjustment costs, accounting for time in habit formation, unobserved heterogeneity, and changing conditions overtime. Identifying substitution effects is essential, as is the impact of exogenous shocks, technological change, the production model, and more stress and lack of exercise. Otherwise, the result of all this may be a dangerous causative accumulation: poorer, less educated and more addicted. We must therefore disentangle the recursive process for better evidence-based health policies on income and health. For this purpose, we need two main types of economic evidence: the economic burden studies about the human and financial costs of health inequality; and the need of economic evaluation studies about the costs and benefits of specific actions to tackle health inequality.

Conclusion

The result we specifically found for our hypothesis, that more inclusive societies (either in terms of income or health) affects growth positively is reassuring on the one hand, but still puzzling on the other, because even though we find significant correlation we cannot claim causation from our data. Remember, however, that due to data limitations we cannot properly fully test the hypothesis: social progress is assessed by per capita GDP and our best proxy for health inequality for the whole sample is an index that is available for just one year and therefore we cannot use panel data to enrich our estimation. Although even succeeding against data limitation, reverse causality – or rather a single direction causality – must be there in any case. But given the already found expected results in terms of levels (rather than on variance) between better health and higher economic growth, we conclude that further research with new data may be crucial to properly test the initial hypothesis for this chapter. Certainly for shorter subsamples (say OECD) we may account for two inequality-adjusted HHDI (for years 2010 and 2014), but we judge that the relevance of the hypothesis is better referred to the case of LDCs for which a higher rank of variations could be observed.

Notes

[1] On the website, there is a new value for 2014 but it is not standardised with the previous series. As a result, we decided to keep the panel until 2013 in order to have standardised data.

[2] Five countries (Andorra, Argentina, Liechtenstein, Myanmar and Syrian Arab Republic) are not classified because the GDP per capita data is missing.

[3] Idem that in 2.

[4] Tables with the descriptive statistics can be obtained from the authors on request.

[5] Since health policy is concerned with lifetime analysis.

[6] See Eurostat (2010).

[7] The concentration index provides a summary measure of the magnitude of socioeconomic-related inequality in a health variable of interest (source: O'Donnell et al, 2008).

[8] First, the bounds of the CI depend on the mean of the health variable. Second, different rankings are obtained when comparing inequalities in health with inequalities in poor health (Clarke et al, 2002). Third, the index becomes arbitrary if qualitative health variables are used.

[9] The values are in general negative and different from 0. Income-related inequalities in health limitations are suffered particularly by those at the bottom of the income distribution.

References

Bhargava A., D.T. Jamison, L. Lau and C.J.L. Murray (2001) 'Modeling the effects of health on economic growth', *Journal of Health Economics* 20(3): 423–40.

Clarke, P., L. Smith and C. Jenkinson (2002) 'Health inequalities: comparing health inequalities among men aged 18–65 years in Australia and England using the SF-36', *Australian and New Zealand Journal of Public Health* 26: 136–43.

Deaton, A. (2013) *The Great Escape: Health, Wealth, and the Origins of Inequality*, Princeton: Princeton University Press.

Erreygers, G. (2009) 'Correcting the Concentration Index', *Journal of Health Economics* 28(2): 504–15.

Eurostat (2010) 'Methodological issues in the analysis of the socioeconomic determinants of health using EU-SILC data', Methodologies and working papers, https://circabc.europa.eu/sd/a/e16edb50-507e-4938-ad9f-5d7133158e38/KS-RA-10-017-EN-N.pdf (accessed 14 June 2017).

Leigh, A., Jencks, C., Smeeding, T.M. (2009) 'Health and economic inequality', in W. Salverda, B. Nolan and T.M. Smeeding (eds) *The Oxford Handbook of Economic Inequality*, Oxford: Oxford University Press, 384–405.

López-Casasnovas, G., L. Currais and B. Rivera (eds) (2005) *Health and Economic Growth*, Cambridge, MA: MIT Press.

López-Casasnovas, G. (2010) 'La calidad del gasto público y su influencia en el desarrollo económico: una validación empírica para los países de la OCDE 19702005', *Hacienda Pública Española / Revista de Economía Pública* 193: 9–48.

López-Casasnovas, G. and Soley-Bori, M. (2014) 'The Socioeconomic Determinants of Health: Economic Growth and Health in the OECD Countries during the Last Three Decades', *International Journal of Environmental Research and Public Health* 11(1): 815–29.

Marmot, M. (2013) *Interim first report on social determinants of health and the health divide in the WHO European Region*, Copenhagen: World Health Organization.

O'Donnell, O., E. van Doorslaer, A. Wagstaff, M. Lindelow, (2008) *Analyzing Health Equity Using Household Survey Data: A Guide to Techniques and Their Implementation*, Washington, DC: World Bank, https://openknowledge.worldbank.org/handle/10986/6896

United Nations Development Programme (2016) *Human Development Index (HDI)*, http://hdr.undp.org/en/content/human-development-index-hdi and Technical notes http://hdr.undp.org/sites/default/files/hdr2015_technical_notes.pdf (accessed 14 June 2017).

Wilkinson, R. and K. Pickett (2009) *The Spirit Level: Why More Equal Societies Almost Always Do Better*, London: Allen Lane.

ELEVEN

Social protection, social investment and inclusive development

James Midgley

The concept of social investment now features prominently in Western and especially European social policy literature. As discussed earlier in this book, social investment is believed to comprise a new paradigm that offers a dynamic alternative to the traditional 'welfare state' and its emphasis on social services and income benefits. Instead, the new 'social investment state' prioritises interventions that directly link welfare and the economy, promote productive employment and support labour market participation. These interventions include early childhood educational programmes, job training, family leave policies and employment placement services which are usually contrasted with conventional social services and income transfers such as retirement pensions, family welfare services, unemployment benefits and professional social work among others. Catchy epithets such as 'productive' versus 'protective', 'preparing' versus 'repairing', and 'active' versus 'passive' have been invoked to distinguish between social investment and consumption welfare.

In addition to drawing a sharp distinction between investment and consumption, these binary groupings reveal a clear normative preference for the former. This reflects the view that social investment offers a desirable alternative to traditional welfare statism because it enhances capabilities, promotes economic engagement and contributes positively to the economy. Despite their obvious humanitarian impact, traditional welfare programmes are believed to transfer resources from the productive economy to passive welfare recipients. By adopting social investment, governments are better able to deal with economic realities, demographic change and electoral challenges. Also, by recognising that social investments are 'productivist', in that they contribute positively to economic development, neoliberal claims about the deleterious consequences of social spending can be effectively challenged.

On the other hand, concern has been expressed that the switch from welfare statism to social investment will abrogate social policy's historic commitment to social rights and concern with those in need (Morel et al, 2012; Cantillon and Van Lancker, 2013). It is also claimed that the new emphasis on social investment will come at the expense of conventional social services and income transfers and contribute to a rise in poverty and deprivation (Cantillon, 2014). However, it has been pointed out that many governments have not in fact reduced spending on social services or income transfers and these programmes are still widely used to maintain the incomes of those in need (Hudson and Kühner, 2012). To complicate matters, it has been argued that consumption welfare spending can, if properly configured and effectively implemented, have an investment function. This is the position taken in this chapter. These contrasting interpretations reveal that the issues are complex and controversial, and require a more thorough examination.

This chapter hopes to contribute to this goal by showing that social protection programmes function as investments and contribute to inclusive development. It argues that the bifurcation of social investment and consumption welfare creates a false dichotomy, and it rejects the argument that social protection promotes consumption at the expense of economic growth. It identifies four overlapping but contested ways in which social protection policies and programmes generate future rates of return and foster inclusive development. They are:

1. the contribution of social protection benefit payments to poverty reduction – with positive economic effects;
2. the role of these payments in mobilising human capital which is a key ingredient in inclusive development;
3. the importance of benefit payments in promoting labour force participation which is equally important in development; and
4. their role in fostering stability and inclusion.

The chapter concludes by discussing some of the challenges arising from efforts to promote social protection policies that foster social investment and promote development.

The chapter's analysis of social protection's investment function and contribution to development is framed by the wider issue addressed in this book, namely the need for inclusive growth. As explained in Chapter One, it is now widely recognised that in the absence of redistributive policies, economic growth produces a pattern of distorted development in which the benefits of growth accrue primarily to the wealthy and higher income earners and to political and business elites. In this process of distorted or uneven development (Midgley, 2014a), economic growth produces comparatively fewer gains for middle class, lower income and poor people. Although this issue had previously been raised by development scholars like Myrdal (1970) and Seers (1969), it is only recently that it has gained traction in policy circles particularly through a World Bank's Commission (2008) to examine ways in which the population as a whole can benefit from economic growth (Midgley, 2015). Although the Commission's recommendations cover a range of policies affecting employment, decent work, education and healthcare, among others, it is clear that a new commitment to egalitarianism in development is emerging. It is in this regard that social protection plays a key role in fostering the adoption of redistributive policies that promote inclusive growth.

Social protection, social investment and inclusive growth

The term social protection has recently come into vogue to connote a variety of programmes designed to maintain income in times of adversity or to raise standards of living by subsidising incomes. It has largely replaced the previously popular term 'social security' and its various synonyms such as income security, economic security, income protection and income transfers. Conventionally, social protection comprises contributory social insurance schemes, means tested social assistance programmes, universal, non-contributory benefits, statutory employer mandates and transfers through the tax system.

These basic forms of social protection have been augmented by novel initiatives such as matched savings accounts, public works, micro-lending and micro-insurance schemes, food for work and other nutritional projects. These programmatic innovations have been included in the definition of social protection largely because development scholars and practitioners became involved in the field and broadened its definition to encompass interventions that would not have previously been viewed as forming part of social security. Through their involvement, social protection now includes programmes offered by non-profit organisations and grassroots women's and community groups. In addition, commercial providers are also becoming involved by offering a variety of social protection insurance products.

These developments complicate the way social protection has historically been defined and, as Midgley (2014b) points out, this has created a good deal of confusion particularly among Western scholars whose understanding of the field has been shaped by Western social security programmes which provide income transfers through statutory social insurance, social assistance, mandates, universal benefits and tax payments. The involvement of non-profit organisations and grassroots community groups, which sponsor a variety of programmes loosely referred to a social protection, has muddled the field considerably. To focus matters and make the topic more manageable, the term 'social protection' will be used in this chapter to refer to programmes that involve income transfers either in cash or kind and the term 'social protection payments' will be used to characterise these interventions. Nonconventional programmes such as public works, matched savings accounts and micro-insurance will be included since they involve payments of this kind.

It is generally recognised that social protection programmes are concerned with consumption. They raise household incomes and increase spending and are not believed to function as investments that generate future rates of return or contribute to economic growth (Midgley, 2008). Since they transfer resources to 'passive' recipients, they clearly fall within the protective rather than productive category. This is recognised in most academic commentaries. For example, market liberals contend that social protection increases consumption at the expense of production, arguing that this is economically harmful. Writing at a time of severe economic adversity, Bacon and Eltis (1976) claimed that Britain's productive economy was being denuded of workers as well as its vitality as increasing numbers of people relied on benefits rather than employment for their livelihoods. The incompatibility of productive investments and consumption-focused income transfers was also acknowledged by progressive economists such as Okun (1975) who popularised the notion that there is an irreconcilable trade-off between government's egalitarian and productive spending objectives. Even Marxist writers like O'Connor (1973: 7) believe that 'social expenses', as he calls them, are 'not even indirectly productive'. More recently, this idea has been reiterated by social policy scholars concerned with social investment. For example, Morel and her colleagues (2012) clearly distinguish between social policies that promote productive labour force participation and those that de-commodify labour.

Although popular, the productive investment versus consumption dichotomy can be challenged. It is well recognised in Keynesian economics that the distinction between consumption and investment is not clear cut and that consumption creates demand which stimulates production. Cord (2007) notes that this was a key element of Keynes's critique of Say and other neoclassical economists who prioritised production over consumption. As mentioned in the introduction to this chapter, it will be argued that social protection benefit payments do not detract from economic development by fostering wasteful consumption but instead contribute positively to economic development and inclusive growth.

This argument requires that the narrow focus on social protection's consumption function be expanded to recognise that these programmes actually have multiple functions that transcend their conventional concern with income maintenance and poverty reduction. As Midgley (2013) explains, the 'protective' consumption function has characterised much of the literature on the subject but it is clear that social insurance, social assistance and universal benefits are not only concerned with income security. For example, social assistance pensions in South Africa are primarily designed to maintain and supplement the income of poor elders but Patel and Trieghaardt (2008) reveal that they also have a positive impact on family solidarity, educational enrolments, gender relationships and, as will be shown later in this chapter, actually stimulate local economic activities. In addition, the programme also has a political function by attracting electoral support among recipients. This latter function has been widely discussed with reference to Brazil where Hall (2012) points out, the country's *Bolsa Família* cash transfer programme has mobilised considerable political participation. It is by recognising the multiple functions of social protection that its role in promoting development and inclusive growth will be appreciated. The following elaborates.

Social protection, poverty and inclusive growth

Social protection benefit payments raise incomes, reduce poverty and contribute positively to economic development. The proposition that poverty is an impediment to economic growth and that policies designed to reduce poverty are compatible with development can be supported on various grounds. First, prosperous economies rely on adequate levels of consumption among all sections of the population and since poverty limits consumption, it harms development. Second, to maximise inclusive growth, dynamic economies require the participation of people in the productive economy and because those living in poverty are often poorly educated, malnourished or in ill health, their ability to contribute effectively is limited. In addition, inequality, a lack of opportunity and discriminatory practices exclude many poor people from economic participation. This is exacerbated by the segregation of poor people in communities characterised by deprivation, crime, substance abuse and other problems that not only impede development but impose high costs on these communities and societies as a whole. Finally, prosperous economies require creativity and innovation and by denying opportunities to poor people to realise their potential, the economy suffers.

Because social protection benefit payments address these challenges, they promote inclusive development. By directing resources to poor households, their incomes are raised, permitting them to purchase the goods and services they need. By increasing consumption, these benefit payments increase demand for goods and services which in turn stimulates economic production. Increased household income also permits investments in nutrition and health, education and improved housing all of which generate future returns. In principle, most social protection benefit payments have an antipoverty effect but, as mentioned earlier, some like social assistance and tax credits achieve this goal by subsidising incomes. Others such as social insurance prevent poverty when workers are faced with contingencies that jeopardise their wellbeing. Universal child benefits, transfers through the tax system, and minimum and living wage mandates all subsidise incomes and raise standards of living. In the Western countries, where social insurance predominates, social assistance is often used to supplement social insurance and other social protection programmes. Many but not all Western governments have replaced the old Poor Law approach to social assistance (with its meagre and time-limited benefits designed to respond to extreme need) with programmes that subsidise incomes over the long term. These include means tested family benefits, nutritional supplements, fuel subsidies and top-up payments to pensioners whose insurance benefits are too low to meet their needs (Bahle et al, 2011).

Although the situation is improving, Hall and Midgley (2004) report that social insurance schemes in most of the Global South serve a comparatively small proportion of the population and have a limited impact on poverty. To address this problem, many governments have introduced social assistance with the explicit purpose of reducing poverty. This is partly because of their commitment to meet the Millennium Development Goals and, 'just giving money to the poor' (Hanlon et al, 2010) has become an acceptable way of achieving this goal. Transcending the residual, urban based Poor Law measures introduced during colonial times (Midgley, 2011), social assistance programmes now target many more poor people. Some governments have also used social assistance in innovative ways. Food subsidies, employment and public works projects and, of course, conditional cash transfers are just some examples of how governments in the Global South have reformulated conventional approaches to social assistance to address the poverty problem. In addition, Ellis and his colleagues (2009) point out that non-profit organisations supported by international donors are using social assistance to raise the incomes of the people they serve. Their traditional charitable approach has been largely replaced with programmes that combine cash transfers with development initiatives.

A good deal of empirical research has been undertaken to assess social protection's effectiveness as an instrument of poverty reduction and generally positive findings have been reported. Social insurance retirement pensions have practically eradicated poverty among elders in Western countries and their impact is heightened by the use of social assistance to supplement inadequate social insurance benefits. Universal child benefits have made a particularly important contribution in Europe where they help families meet the costs of raising children and particularly of childcare. The absence of child benefits in the US is believed to be a major reason for the country's high level of child poverty. On the other hand, tax credits have reduced poverty in the US, where Gitterman (2010) estimates that the Earned Income Tax Credit (EITC) has raised the incomes of more than 20 million low-paid workers. Kenworthy (2011) observes that similar programmes in the UK and Sweden have been equally effective. Some proactive governments have deliberately used social protection to reduce poverty. In the UK, the Blair government's commitment to decrease child poverty combined cash transfers with other antipoverty measures with positive results (Piachaud, 2013; Waldfogel, 2010).

Social assistance's antipoverty impact in the Global South has been demonstrated by numerous studies that report on their aggregate, national level effects as well as their impact on recipient households. An example of the latter comes from Hulme and Moore (2008) who used a randomised trial to assess the outcome of a cash transfer programme in Bangladesh and concluded that it had raised the incomes of households in the experimental group, improved their nutritional status and eased their vulnerability to crises such as livestock loss. Studies of the impact of social assistance at the national level have reached similar conclusions. For example, Patel (2015) reports that means tested programmes in South Africa, including retirement pensions, child benefits and disability payments have reduced the country's overall poverty rate.

She points out that these schemes have been particularly effective in the rural areas where employment opportunities are scarce and where many households are headed by elders because younger family members have migrated to the cities. Benefits from different schemes are pooled and shared among family members, augmenting total family income. By paying child benefits to directly to carers who are mostly women,

Patel shows that these programmes empower women and have other positive gender effects.

The impact of conditional cash transfers has been extensively researched and numerous studies have reported significant improvements in the nutritional status, health and living standards of beneficiary families. Summarising this research in some detail, Barrientos (2013) concludes that these programmes have positive impacts both on the living standards of recipient families and the overall incidence of poverty in Latin American countries – although in many cases, their aggregate impact is small. However, Papadopolous and Leyer (2016) point out that there are wide differences between different countries and also between geographic areas within countries. Also, they are not, as is often claimed, a quick fix but should, as Barrientos (2013) cautions, be a component of a larger policy mix of poverty reduction efforts including other social protection measures as well as wider development initiatives.

Social protection, human capital and inclusive growth

Social protection benefit payments enhance school enrolments, educational attainment and health and nutrition status and, in this way, contribute positively to human capital investment and to development. Human capital is a critically important determinant of inclusive growth and its role is now widely recognised, augmenting the traditional productive role of land, labour and capital identified by the founders of economics long ago. In the years following the Second World War, human capital was not given the attention it deserved and instead, economists were primarily concerned with mobilising financial capital for industrial investment or post-war reconstruction. Influenced by Keynesian growth models and Soviet economic planning, Midgley (1995) notes that it was generally accepted that the governments of the newly independent nations of the Global South should give priority to industrial investments which economists recommended would create employment, raise incomes and reduce poverty. However, some economists argued that growing economies require workers who are knowledgeable and skilled, well-nourished and healthy. Human resources, they claimed, are as important as financial capital.

Schultz (1959, 1962, 1981) was among the most prominent of these economists stressing the role of what he called 'population quality' in development. If governments wish to achieve national development goals, he argued that they need to improve population quality by allocating resources to education, technical training, nutritional programmes and healthcare. Unlike Becker (1964), his Nobel prize-winning colleague at the University of Chicago, Schultz was interested in the social rather than private rate of return that accrues to human capital investments. Citing research into antimalarial programmes in India, he showed that these programmes not only improved the health of farmers but resulted in significant increases in productivity and aggregate agricultural production. Public investments in education, nutrition and healthcare would, he argued, not only benefit individuals but the economy and society as a whole.

Schultz's work exerted a potent influence on development thinking and human capital became an important element of development policy. In the early 1970s, his ideas were adopted by the World Bank which, under the leadership of Robert McNamara, sought to redirect the Bank's conventional lending policies from large infrastructural projects to poverty alleviation. Staff at the Bank produced a number of sector policy papers which cited many studies to support the contention that improved health and nutrition enhances the productivity of workers in agriculture, construction and industry and that knowledge and skills acquired through appropriate educational investments are needed for development (World Bank, 1975). Subsequently, this research inspired the construction of econometric models by Psacharopoulos (1973) which calculated the social rates of return that accrue to different types of educational investments in countries at different levels of economic development. His work was influential and shaped the Bank's educational lending policies. Abel-Smith (1976) employed a similar approach to advise the World Health Organization that spending on preventive and primary health produced higher rates of return than allocations to hospitals and curative services.

Although the investment and productive functions of education, health and nutrition were generally acknowledged, it was only in the 1990s with the advent of conditional cash transfers that governments began to use social protection purposefully to mobilise human capital for development. As has been extensively documented (Fiszbein and Schady, 2009; Levy, 2006) these programmes were introduced in Brazil and Mexico where, Papadopolous and Leyer (2016) observe, they were designed to promote human capital acquisition by requiring that the children of households receiving cash benefits attend school, are immunised and have health checks. They also imposed other conditionalities such as requiring expecting and lactating mothers to attend clinics. Since then, these programmes have spread all over Latin America and have been adopted in other parts of the world as well, often with technical assistance from the World Bank and other development agencies. Their overall impact on poverty has already been mentioned and, as Barrientos (2013) shows, they have increased school attendance, lowered dropout rates and improved the health and nutritional status of recipient families. However, he cautions that increased school enrolments and clinic attendance does not always result in improvements in knowledge or health status, particularly if schools lack qualified teachers or if clinics are badly managed and poorly supplied. Also, Barrientos points out that most outcome studies focus on the short-term impact of these programmes and their long-term effects still need to be assessed.

Other social protection programmes have also been shown to contribute positively to human capital. Patel (2015) notes that studies of South Africa's child benefit programme reported improved school attendance and nutritional status long before conditionalities were introduced in 2009. Another example comes from India where the government has historically prioritised nutritional schemes for poor families through subsidising the costs of staples, providing school meals and operating in an extensive network of community-based *anganwadi* or childcare centres, all of which Mutatkar (2013) reveals have reduced malnutrition. In addition, he notes that retirement pensions and rural works programmes generate additional income for poor families whose first priority is to improve their nutritional status. Improving nutrition is a preoccupation of many social protection programmes operated by non-governmental organisations in African countries where as Ellis and his colleagues (2009) point out, ameliorating food insecurity is given high priority.

The positive human capital effects of social protection programmes are not limited to the Global South. For example, universal child benefit schemes in Europe and other Western countries are designed to supplement the costs of raising children, helping to increase access to preschool and reduce the costs of food. In addition, many governments have established means tested programmes that improve the nutritional status of poor families. One example is the US where the Supplemental Nutritional Assistance Program (previously referred to as 'food stamps') reaches 46 million low income families, providing an important income subsidy that has improved their food security (Hoefer and Curry, 2012).

In addition to their aggregate impact on the economy, social protection programmes generate private returns and today millions of children and young people benefit from education, better nutrition and healthcare, all of which support their efforts to achieve their career goals and realise their potential. Social protection programmes can also support creative individuals by maintaining their incomes when they are engaged in activities that require their full-time attention. One pointed example of how social protection fosters this goal comes from the popular author J.K. Rowling, who benefited from social assistance payments while she was writing the Harry Potter books. This investment not only produced huge returns to herself and others engaged in the production of her work, but to the state which made the initial investment.

Social protection, labour force participation and inclusive growth

Social protection benefit payments foster labour force participation by promoting employment and self-employment and, in this way, they contribute to inclusive growth. Of course, as Midgley (2008) explained, this contention is hotly disputed by market liberals who have consistently argued that income transfers are a major disincentive fostering dependency and worklessness. Faced with low rates of economic growth and income stagnation during the 1990s, many Western governments appeared to concur with the market liberal critique by introducing labour market 'reforms' which relaxed regulations governing hiring and termination, tightened eligibility requirements for welfare benefits and incentivised employment. Statutory employment regulations were relaxed and welfare to work or 'activation' programmes were widely adopted. In addition, childcare and family leave programmes were strengthened since, it was argued, they would support employment (Bonoli, 2013). What are known as 'flexicurity' policies were introduced by the governments of Denmark and some other European countries (Madden, 2002) to promote labour market participation by combining job training and placement services with income transfers.

These and similar measures, which are collectively referred to as active labour market policies (ALMPs), are often juxtaposed in the social investment literature against direct benefit payments which exemplify what Giddens (1998) famously called 'passive welfare'. However, it can be argued that social protection benefits actually facilitate active labour market participation. For example, the payment of unemployment benefits to workers who have been laid off or made redundant helps them to maintain an acceptable standard of living while they seek work. In the absence of these benefits, they may be reduced to homelessness and destitution, seriously impeding their ability to find employment. Similarly, it can be shown that social protection programmes in developing countries facilitate labour market participation because recipients are no longer surviving on the fringes of the subsistence economy but are able to seek and obtain remunerative work. These programmes also enhance employment by mobilising human capital which helps poor people acquire the knowledge and skills they need to secure employment. In addition, income transfers are used to establish micro-enterprises which also facilitate the involvement of poor people in the productive economy.

Various studied support the claim that social protection enhances labour market participation. Patel (2015) reports increased employment among families and especially women receiving pensions and child benefits and Barrientos and Villa (2016) note that most recipients of conditional cash transfers in Latin American countries engage in productive work. Social assistance has also generated investment funds for micro-enterprises. A study of pensioners in Lesotho by Nyanguru (2008) found that many use a portion of their pension to purchase chickens and other livestock which are then raised and sold at a profit. Patel and Trieghaardt (2008) observe that this is also the case in the rural areas of South Africa where elders gather to receive their pensions at distribution points, known as 'pension day markets' where they trade and sell agricultural and other goods produced from their extra pension income. In addition, a number of governments have established programmes that help social assistance clients establish small businesses. One of the best known is the Self-Employment Assistance Program in the Philippines which was introduced in the 1970s (Queita and Maaliw, 2003). A large number of non-profit organisations, such as the well-documented Grameen Bank in Bangladesh (Yunus and Weber, 2007), have also used micro-enterprise programmes to reduce poverty.

Although public works were not historically regarded as a part of social protection, the situation has changed as these programmes have become prominent in the Global South where they are used primarily to subsidise the incomes of poor families. Of course, they also create employment and contribute a small way to infrastructural development (McCord, 2012). They have also been used in Western countries especially as countercyclical measures which raise the incomes of unemployed workers and stimulate demand during recessions. Among the best known of programmes of this type are the New Deal public works initiatives introduced in the US by the Roosevelt administration in the 1930s. Leighninger (2007) reports that these initiatives increased employment, reduced poverty and left a legacy of parks, museums and other public buildings that many Americans still use and enjoy. Although evaluations of public works programmes in developing countries, and Africa in particular, have not been as positive

(McCord, 2012), some governments are prioritising these programmes. A recent initiative that has attracted international attention is the Indian government's National Rural Employment Guarantee scheme (NREGA), which was established in 2005 to provide work for low income families in the country's rural areas. Mutatkar (2013) reports that the scheme guarantees paid employment for 100 days annually and that if no employment is provided, a cash benefit is paid. He observes that, despite challenges, the programme is effectively targeted at poor families and especially women who generally have a favourable opinion of its impact.

Although widely criticised by social policy writers, welfare to work programmes are widely used in Western countries today to facilitate labour force participation among social assistance beneficiaries and to end their receipt of benefits. However, in many cases, these schemes allow the continuation of benefits for a limited period of time. Sometimes they are known as 'workfare' but this term actually refers to programmes that pay benefit in lieu of wages. This approach has not been widely adopted in Western countries and instead the term 'welfare to work' more accurately captures the intention of schemes that combine benefit payments with regular wages to replace benefits with income derived from regular employment. Peck (2001) notes that these programmes originated in the US in the 1980s reflecting popular disquiet about the alleged abuse of welfare payments by supposedly indolent claimants but they subsequently spread to Europe and other Western countries. However, Moreira and Lødemel (2014) report that many European governments have eased the strict conditionality which originally characterised these programmes by allowing greater flexibility and the gradual phase-out of benefits. Many participants also receive social work counselling and other services. In addition, non-profit and even commercial providers are increasingly responsible for their administration. On the other hand, a more coercive approach has been adopted in the US where many states that are responsible for the Temporary Assistance to Needy Families programme have imposed strict conditionalities and time limits. Accordingly, its impact on poverty has been limited. However, it was noted earlier, the country's EITC has been quite effective in generating employment and raising incomes. Because tax credits and minimum and living wages guarantee a minimally acceptable income, they incentivise employment. Holt (2006) observes that in the US, the tax credit has drawn many low income welfare recipients, and especially women, into the formal labour market

Social protection, stability and inclusive growth

Social protection benefit payments, in combination with other economic and social policies, contribute positively to inclusive growth by promoting stability and social inclusion. Although market liberals seldom recognise the importance of these interventions, many acknowledge that economic volatility has a negative impact. However, they maintain an implacable belief in the ability of market economies to respond through their own, internal adjusting mechanisms and governments, they contend, should not interfere since this is likely to create even greater turmoil. Although Keynes's work is usually associated with countercyclical policies, Skidelsky (1992) points out that he was far more concerned with promoting long-term stability. To achieve this goal, Keynes recommended that governments should adopt monetary and fiscal policies, manage inflation, foster consumption and promote private and public investment. In particular, governments must ensure what Keynes called the 'comprehensive socialisation of investment' (Skidelsky, 2009: 97).

These recommendations shaped economic policy in the Western nations in the years following the Second World War but as the problems of stagnating incomes, high inflation and slow growth, as well as the oil shocks of the 1970s, bedevilled policymakers, they were eventually displaced by market liberal monetarist and supply side prescription which were enthusiastically implemented by radical right-wing governments in the US, the UK and elsewhere. However, as Skidelsky (2009) observes, Keynesianism enjoyed a revival during the Great Recession which began at the end of 2007. For example, in the US, the Obama administration passed the American Recovery and Reinvestment Act in 2009 to introduce a comprehensive Keynesian stimulus package. Although fiercely opposed by Congressional Republicans and their market liberal allies, Grunwald (2012) demonstrates that it slowed the recession and contributed to falling unemployment which is today among the lowest in the Western world. The package allocated more than US$800 billion to infrastructural projects, healthcare, scientific research and education and also included significant allocations to social protection. Although progressive economists like Krugman (2012) believe the stimulus would have been even more effective if substantially more resources were injected into the economy, the Obama package was one of the most ambitious attempts to use Keynesian ideas to revitalise a depressed economy. It also compares favourably with what Blyth (2013) describes as the 'chaotic' approach adopted by most other Western governments.

Social protection benefit payments featured prominently in the Obama administration's stimulus packages by raising unemployment benefits, relaxing conditionalities on means tested programmes, supplementing nutritional and maternal health schemes and even awarding a one-time payment of US$250 to elders receiving retirement pensions. All contributed by increasing consumption, reducing the incidence of poverty and fostering a return to economic normalcy. While these initiatives were based on Keynesian principles, Midgley (2008) points out that Keynes himself paid little attention to social protection's stabilising role and that it was actually Beveridge who, with Keynes's support, popularised the idea that income transfers such as unemployment insurance and family allowances could promote consumption smoothing and contribute to long-term stability. His ideas also informed the now generally accepted Keynesian tenet that social protection serves as an automatic stabiliser with robust countercyclical effects.

It has already been argued that social protection contributes to the inclusion of vulnerable people in the productive economy and, in this way, fosters social solidarity and inclusive growth. Social protection channels resources to poor families, women, minorities, migrants and other groups who have historically derived few benefits from development and in this way it addresses the distortions that characterise development in many parts of the world. Social protection programmes that mobilise assets such as child savings accounts, start-up grants and individual development accounts also promote inclusion. Paxton and his colleagues (2006) point out that these and other programmes foster stakeholding and enhance social solidarity. Inspired by the Singapore government's creative use of the country mandatory provident fund, the Blair government sought to promote stakeholding by introducing a child savings fund as well a matched savings scheme known as the Gateway Account. However, Piachaud (2013) points out that both schemes were abolished by the coalition government after it assumed office in 2010.

Some governments have intentionally used social protection to foster inclusive growth. The governments of Botswana, Costa Rica, Mauritius, Namibia, Singapore and other East Asian developmental states are often mentioned in the literature but recently the government of China has also recognised that social protection can help address the problems of poverty, exclusion, rural–urban disparities and heightened inequality that have impeded the emergence of what the Communist Party leadership calls a 'harmonious society'. Li (2013) observes that although the country's social protection policies have evolved in a haphazard way, attempts are being made to integrate diverse social protection programmes within a more coherent policy framework that achieves this goal. Like Li, Leung and Xu (2015) agree that the country's social protection system is still fragmented, decentralised and challenged by administrative difficulties but they believe that recent efforts to formulate and implement a coherent social protection strategy marks a turning point in the evolution of the country's social policy. Time will tell whether these efforts have succeeded.

Social protection and development

This chapter has produced evidence to support the contention that, if appropriately designed and implemented, social protection benefit payments can function as investments that promote inclusive economic and social development. By reducing poverty, mobilising human capital, facilitating labour force participation and promoting stability and inclusion, social protection benefits do not only transfer resources to 'passive' recipients but have positive economic as well as social welfare effects. However, this conclusion will be challenged, for example by market liberals, who will dismiss the chapter's assertions by insisting that there are sound theoretical as well empirical grounds for arguing that income transfers contribute to consumption spending with negative economic consequences. Many social policy scholars will also contest the chapter's 'economistic' approach arguing that social protection should be a social right and a way of strengthening collective altruistic sentiments, and not a means of achieving economic development. Some social investment writers may be irritated that the chapter challenges their paradigmatic distinction between investment and consumption and undermines normative claims about the benefits of the former.

These concerns require a more extensive discussion than is possible in this chapter but hopefully it will stimulate further debate and a more nuanced understanding of the way social protection benefit payments serve multiple functions which transcend their conventional income maintenance and support goals. In addition, more attention should be given to the challenges that impede the achievement of social protection's commitment to promote inclusive growth. Although arguably of more mundane interest than the normative objections raised by market liberals, welfare statists and social investment writers, social protection's contribution to development is seriously hampered by administrative, funding and political problems.

A major concern is the fragmented nature of social protection programmes and a lack of national policies that effectively integrate these programmes with each other, and more importantly within a comprehensive development framework. Another problem concerns benefit levels and coverage. While Western countries have generally achieved universal coverage, the problems of limited take-up, stigma and exclusion still need to be resolved. In the Global South, enormous progress has been made in extending social protection coverage but many hundreds of millions of people still have limited access to these programmes. Even in countries like Brazil, India and South Africa, where social protection has been given priority, abject poverty and deprivation persist.

The International Labour Organisation (ILO) is giving international leadership in addressing these problems by encouraging its member states to formulate national social protection plans that are integrated with overall economic and social development objectives. Although van Ginneken (2007) reports that some progress has been made, fragmentation as well as administrative inefficiency continues to characterise social protection programmes in many parts of the world. The organisation has also championed the idea of a social protection floor (ILO, 2011) which gives expression to a rights-based approach that ensures that each member state will establish a minimum package of provisions that is accessible to everyone. If implemented, this will contribute further to the achievements of the Millennium Development Goals and the new Sustainable Development Goals. While the idea of giving money to the poor through social protection was previously ridiculed, these efforts suggest that many more governments are committed to using social protection to reduce poverty, invest in people and achieve economic and development goals. The argument that social protection is not a drain on the economy but an instrument of economic and social development which generates positive returns should inspire governments to further action. It should also inspire international donors to support these efforts. As Cichon and Hagemejer (2007) convincingly argued, the cost to the global community of ensuring social protection for all the world's people is comparatively small but will bring huge returns.

References

Abel-Smith, B. (1976) *Value for Money in Health Services*, London: Heinemann.

Bacon, R. and W. Eltis (1976) *Britain's Economic Problems: Too Few Producers*, London: Macmillan.

Bahle, T., V. Hubl and M. Pfeifer (eds) (2011) *The Last Safety Net: A Handbook of Minimum Income Protection in Europe*, Bristol: Policy Press.

Barrientos, A. (2013) *Social Assistance in Developing Countries*, New York: Cambridge University Press.

Barrientos, A. and J.M. Villa (2016) 'Economic and Political Inclusion in Human Development: Conditional Income Transfer Programs in Latin America', *Social Policy and Society* 15(3): 421-33.

Becker, G.S. (1964) *Human Capital: A Theoretical and Empirical Analysis with Special Reference to Education*, New York: Columbia University Press.

Blyth, M. (2013) *Austerity: The History of a Dangerous Idea*, New York: Oxford University Press.

Bonoli, G. (2013) *The Origins of Active Social Policy: Labour Market and Childcare Policies in Comparative Perspective*, New York: Oxford University Press

Cantillon, B. (2014) 'Beyond Social Investment: Which Concepts and Values for Social Policy- making in Europe?' in B. Cantillon and F. Vandenbroucke (eds), *Reconciling Work and Poverty Reduction: How Successful European Welfare States?* New York: Oxford University Press, 286–318.

Cantillon, B. and W. Van Lancker (2013) 'Three Shortcomings of the Social Investment Perspective', *Social Policy and Society* 23(5): 459-68.

Cichon, M. and K. Hagemejer (2007) 'Changing the Development Policy Paradigm: Investing in a Social Security Floor for All', *International Social Security Review* 60(2/3): 169-96.

Cord, R. (2007) *Keynes*, London: Haus Publishing.

Ellis, F., S. Devereux and P. White (2009) *Social Protection in Africa*, Northampton, MA: Edward Elgar.

Fiszbein, R. and N. Schady (2009) *Condition Cash Transfers: Reducing Present and Future Poverty*, Washington, DC: World Bank.

Giddens, A. (1998) *The Third Way: The Renewal of Social Democracy*, Cambridge: Polity Press.

Gitterman, D.P. (2010) *Boosting Paychecks: The Politics of Supporting America's Working Poor*, Washington, DC: Brookings.

Grunwald, M. (2012) *The New New Deal: The Hidden Story of Change in the Obama Era*, New York, NY: Simon & Schuster.

Hall, A. (2012) 'The Last Shall be First: Political Dimensions of Conditional Cash Transfers in Brazil', *Journal of Policy Practice* 11(1–2): 25–41.

Hall, A. and J. Midgley (2004) *Social Policy for Development*, London: Sage Publications.

Hanlon, J., A. Barrientos and D. Hulme (2010) *Just Give Money to the Poor: The Development Revolution from the Global South*, Sterling, VA: Kuamarian Press.

Hoefer, R and C. Curry (2012) 'Food Security and Social Protection in the United States', *Journal of Policy Practice* 11(1/2): 59–76.

Holt, S.D. (2006) *The Earned Income Tax Credit at the Age 30: What We Know*, Washington, DC: Brookings.

Hudson, J. and S. Kühner (2012) 'Analyzing the Productive and Protective Dimensions of Welfare: Looking Beyond the OECD', *Social Policy and Administration* 46 (1), 35–60.

Hulme, D. and Moore, K. (2008) 'Assisting the Poorest in Bangladesh: Learning from BRAC's 'Targeting the Ultrapoor' Programme', in A. Barientos and D. Hulme (eds), *Social Protection for the Poor and the Poorest: Concepts, Policies and Politics*, New York: Palgrave Macmillan, 194–210.

International Labour Organization (2011) *Social Protection Floor for a Fair and Inclusive Globalization* (Report on the Social Protection Floor Advisory Group – Bachelet Report), Geneva: ILO.

Kenworthy, L. (2011) *Progress for the Poor*, New York: Oxford University Press.

Krugman, P. (2012) *End this Depression Now!* New York: Norton.

Leighninger, R. (2007) *Long Range Public Investment: The Forgotten Legacy of the New Deal*, Columbia, SC: University of South Carolina Press.

Leung, J.C.B. and Y. Xu (2015) *China's Social Welfare: The Third Turning Point*, Cambridge, Polity Press.

Levy, S. (2006) *Progress Against Poverty: Sustaining Mexico's Progresa-Oportunidades Program*, Washington, DC: Brookings Institution Press.

Li, B. (2013) 'Future Trajectories for China', in J. Midgley and D. Piachaud (eds), *Social Protection, Economic Growth and Social Change: Goals, Issues and Trajectories in China, India, Brazil and Africa*, Cheltenham: Edward Elgar, 59–71.

Madden, P.K. (2002) 'The Danish Model of Flexicurity: a Paradise with Some Snakes', in H. Sarfati and G. Bonoli (eds), *Labour Market and Social Protection Reforms in International Perspective: Parallel or Converging Tracks?* Aldershot: Ashgate, 243-65.

McCord, A. (2012) *Public Works and Social Protection in Sub-Saharan Africa: Do Public Works Work for the Poor?* Tokyo: United Nations University Press.

Midgley, J. (1995) *Social Development: The Developmental Perspective in Social Welfare*, Thousand Oaks, CA: Sage Publications.

Midgley, J. (2008) 'Social Security and the Economy: Key Perspectives', in J. Midgley and K.L. Tang (eds), *Social Security, the Economy and Development*, New York: Palgrave Macmillan, 51–84.

Midgley, J. (2011) 'Imperialism, Colonialism and Social Welfare', in J. Midgley and D. Piachaud (eds), *Colonialism and Welfare: Social Policy and the British Imperial Legacy*, Cheltenham: Edward Elgar, 36–54.

Midgley, J. (2013) 'Social Protection in Countries Experiencing Rapid Economic Growth: Goals and Functions', in. J. Midgley and D. Piachaud (eds), *Social Protection, Economic Growth and Social Change: Goals, Issues and Trajectories in China, India, Brazil and Africa*, Cheltenham: Edward Elgar, 7–25.

Midgley, J. (2014a) *Social Development: Theory and Practice*, London: Sage Publications.

Midgley, J. (2014b) 'Social Development and Social Protection: New Opportunities and Challenges', in L. Patel, J. Midgley and M. Ulriksen (eds), *Social Protection in Southern Africa: New Opportunities for Social Development*, New York: Routledge, 2–12.

Midgley, J. (2015) 'Social Investment, Inclusive Growth and the State', in R. Hasmath (ed.), *Inclusive Growth, Development and Welfare Policy: A Criticial Assessment*, New York: Routledge, 91–107.

Morel, N., B. Pallier and J. Palme (eds) (2012) 'Beyond the Welfare State as We Knew it?' in N. Morel, B. Pallier and J. Palme (eds), *Towards a Social Investment Welfare State? Ideas, Policies and Challenges*, Bristol: Policy Press, 1–32.

Moreira, A. and I. Lødemel (2014) 'Introduction', in A. Moreira and I. Lødemel (eds), *Activation or Workfare? Governance and the Neo-Liberal Convergence*, New York: Oxford University Press, 1–18.

Mutatkar, R. (2013) 'Social Protection in India: Current Approaches and Issues', in J. Midgley and D. Piachaud (eds), *Social Protection, Economic Growth and Social Change: Goals, Issues and Trajectories in China, India, Brazil and Africa*, Cheltenham: Edward Elgar, 102–16.

Myrdal, G. (1970) *The Challenge of World Poverty*, Harmondsworth, England: Penguin.

Nyanguru, A. (2008) 'Old Age Pensions and the Promotion of the Rights of Older People in Lesotho', *Journal of Social Development in Africa* 22(1): 89–108.

O'Connor, J. (1973) *The Fiscal Crisis of the State*, New York: St. Martin's Press.

Okun, A. (1975) *Equality and Efficiency: The Big Tradeoff*, Washington, DC: Brookings.

Papadopolous, T. and R.V. Leyer (2016) 'Two Decades of Social Investment in Latin America: Outcomes, Shortcomings and Achievements of Conditional Cash Transfers', *Social Policy and Society* 15(3): 435–99.

Patel, L. (2015) *Social Welfare and Social Development in South Africa*, Johannesburg: Oxford University Press.

Patel, L. and J. Trieghaardt (2008) 'South Africa: Social Security, Poverty and Development', in J. Midgley and K.L. Tang (eds), *Social Security, the Economy and Development*, New York: Palgrave Macmillan, 85–109.

Paxton, W. and S. White (2006) 'Introduction: The New Politics of Ownership', in W. Paxton, S. White and D. Maxwell (eds) (2006) *The Citizen's Stake: Exploring the Future of Universal Asset Policies*, Bristol, Policy Press, 1–14.

Peck, J. (2001) *Workfare States*, New York: Guilford Press.

Piachaud, D. (2013) 'Poverty and Social Protection in Britain: Policy Developments Since 1997', in R. Hoefer and J. Midgley (eds) *Poverty, Income and Social Protection: International Policy Perspectives*, New York: Routledge, 92–105.

Psacharopoulos, G. (1973) *Returns to Education: An International Comparison*, Amsterdam: Elsevier.

Queita, R. and A.S. Maaliw (2003) *Self-Employment Assistance Program: Three Decades of Enabling People to Help Themselves*, Quezon City: University of Philippines Press.

Schultz, T.W. (1959) 'Investment in Man: An Economists View', *Social Service Review* 33(2): 209-17.

Schultz, T.W. (1962) 'Reflections on Investments in Man', *Journal of Political Economy* 70(5): 1–8.

Schultz, T.W. (1981) *Investing in People*, Berkeley, CA: University of California Press.

Seers, D. (1969) 'The Meaning of Development', *International Development Review* 11(4): 1–6.

Skidelsky, R. (1992) *John Maynard Keynes: The Economist as Saviour, 1920–1937*, London: Macmillan.

Skidelsky, R. (2009) *Keynes: The Return of the Master*, London: Penguin.

van Ginneken W. (2007) 'Extending Social Security Coverage: Concepts, Global Trends and Policy Issues', *International Social Security Review* 60(2/3): 39–59.

Waldfogel, J. (2010) *Britain's War on Poverty*, New York: Russell Sage.

World Bank (1975) *The Assault on World Poverty: Problems of Rural Development, Education and Health*, Baltimore, MD: Johns Hopkins University Press.

World Bank (2008) *The Growth Report: Strategies for Sustained Growth and Inclusive Development*, Washington, DC: World Bank.

Yunus, M. and Weber, K. (2007) *Creating a World Without Poverty: Social Business and the Future of Capitalism*, New York: Public Affairs Press.

TWELVE

Social politics puzzling: governance for inclusive growth and social investment

Jane Jenson

Policy communities run on ideas as much as interests, on puzzling as much as powering, as Hugh Heclo taught us years ago. This is even more so the case for global social politics where key actors such as international and transnational organisations have few tools for powering – they do not set policy – and they must rely on the force of their propositions to have influence. This force involves not only the production of coherent and convincing quasi-concepts, but also their diffusion across policy communities at the national or other relevant levels of political authority. But national and subnational policy communities also engage in similar 'puzzling over problems of collective action ... [that] occurs in the networks of informed activists and policy middlemen as well as through the learning pathways opened and closed by previous policy decisions' (Heclo, 2010 [1974]: xviii).

As Chapter One of this volume sets out in detail, global social policy in the past decade has engaged in such puzzling by deploying two key concepts: social investment and inclusive growth. Each was developed as a response to what were defined as the excesses of neoliberalism. They provided policy directions for addressing and perhaps halting high and rising rates of poverty and the menacing consequences of social exclusion provoked by the politics of structural adjustment and market fundamentalism, especially after the crisis of 2008. In its Europe 2020 10-year strategy the EU, for example, promised to pursue 'smart, sustainable and inclusive growth', and the strategy was quickly followed in 2013 by the Social Investment Package and a Recommendation for investing in children.

A secondary, and no doubt unintended consequence, of this mobilisation to correct what Chapter One describes as the 'one-sided economism of the neoliberal period' was the 'boundary crossing' that occurred around these two concepts. For example, social investments in human capital to combat child poverty were promoted simultaneously for children in Latin America and Europe, via ideational and organisational cross-boundary work by, among others, UNICEF and the OECD (Jenson, 2010: 74–6). Inclusive growth's conceptual development too involved boundary crossing. Pro-poor policies for development and a global anti-poverty consensus transitioned into an approach to inclusive growth that integrated the social investment perspective as its social policy arm (Jenson, 2015a; Deeming and Smyth, 2015). Consensus emerged about the social policy instruments needed to promote inclusive growth and greater equality. These included the classic instruments of social investment such as early childhood education and care, conditional cash transfers, and activation programmes.

As the social investment perspective moved adjacent to the terrain of inclusive growth and its emphasis on productive policies, however, attention also turned from the *what* of policy propositions – the instruments – towards the *how* – the governance methods. The how of social investment and inclusive growth involves a different model of governance than in the era of the Keynesian welfare state, when public services were most commonly delivered by 'public servants' in accordance with forms of representation centred on national level democratic institutions. It is also different from neoliberals' preference for the voluntary sector, faith-based or charitable forms of community solidarity, and non–governmental organisations, both national and international (Jenson and Levi, 2013). This is a model of cross–sectoral governance, identifying the entrepreneurial possibilities of civil society engaging in service design and delivery, a model that depends less on parliamentary democracy, although it emphasises 'participation', and more on a 'business case' for action.

Increasingly policy communities and learning networks proffer the quasi-concepts of social investment and social entrepreneurship in combination as the appropriate ways to govern financing and delivery of social investments to ensure inclusive growth and to face up to challenges to welfare regimes threatened by crisis as well as the legacies and ideology of neoliberalism. One example that accurately represents this trend in social politics is the report commissioned by the Nordic Council of Ministers, a transnational organisation for regional cooperation. Its members self-identified as 'facing major challenges with regard to maintaining and further developing social welfare', and commissioned a project to map and promote initiatives in support of social entrepreneurship as the form of governance of service provision. The working group defined:

social entrepreneurship to be a type of enterprise with the following characteristics: It is targeted at a social objective/unmet welfare need. It contributes innovative solutions to these challenges. It is driven by the social results, but also by a business model that can make the enterprise sustainable. ... [There is] involvement of the target group, employees (may be the same group) and other key stakeholders [and] cooperation across disciplines and business models (NCM, 2015: 22–3).

The growing popularity of this approach to governance in social politics networks is the product of policy puzzling. This chapter documents this puzzling, with a primary focus on the EU and several welfare regimes housed within it.

Quasi-concepts and social politics

The interlocking of social investment and inclusive growth around a particular notion of governance involved ideational work and linking of quasi-concepts. The conceptualisation of an 'idea', as used by Desmond McNeill (2006: 335), is useful here. For McNeill, an idea is:

> ... a concept which ... is more than simply a slogan or "buzzword" because it has some reputable intellectual basis, but it may nevertheless be found vulnerable on analytical and empirical grounds. What is special about such an idea is that it is able to operate in both academia and policy domains.

This definition makes a gesture towards Antonio Gramsci: '... favoured ideas seem like common sense, and unfavoured ideas as unthinkable' (McNeill, 2006: 335).[1] It is also very close to what Paul Bernard (1999: 48) called a quasi-concept, which he described as a hybrid, making use of empirical analysis and thereby benefiting from 'the legitimising aura of the scientific method', but simultaneously characterised by an indeterminate quality that makes it adaptable to a variety of situations and flexible enough to follow the twists and turns of policy, that everyday politics sometimes makes necessary (also European Commission, 2013; Sabato, Vanhercke and Verschraegen, 2015: 7–8, 46–9). Part of the power of any quasi-concept is its ambiguity, a polysemy that allows it to be used both to analyse the situation and to forge consensus across networks and policy scales (Jenson, 2010: 71–4).[2]

Both social investment and inclusive growth qualify as quasi-concepts, being without stabilised definitions and sometimes hotly disputed, particularly within academic debate (see Chapter One). Yet both serve useful purposes in social politics, defined by Heclo (2010 [1974]: 3) as: 'the political contribution to making and changing collective arrangements of social policy'. This is precisely because of the polysemy characterising them. Nonetheless both quasi-concepts remained somewhat limited in their potential as long as they did not include sufficient guidance about the governance of either social investments (how to make them) or the business practices needed for inclusive growth. To fill this gap, those engaged in the social politics of after-neoliberalism have added an additional quasi-concept to their analytic quiver, that of social entrepreneurship.[3]

This addition comes with the same discursive gesture to a vocabulary of economics as described in Chapter One. Within several worlds of social politics, the quasi-concept provides a novel way to reconfigure market relations in support of social policy initiatives, particularly those that seek to address the new social risks and promote new sources of economic growth. The new social risks include: 'reconciling work and family life, lone parenthood, long-term unemployment, being among the working poor, or having insufficient social security coverage' (Bonoli, 2005: 431). The new locales of growth so as to foster inclusion and combat inequality as well as poverty include the social economy and other sites of social entrepreneurship that create jobs in sectors (such as the environment, culture or social care) underserved by traditional for-profit enterprise or inadequately served by traditional government services. The claim is that effective social investments will be more likely to be correctly identified and properly implemented if they are left to social entrepreneurs of various kinds.

A concrete example comes from city government in Amsterdam, where practices self-identified as those for after-neoliberalism have come from the left of the political spectrum. Local authorities have decentralised neighbourhood budgets so as to do 'welfare new style', via housing and care co-operatives and other initiatives organised by residents of poor and immigrant neighbourhoods. Actions termed 'mutual initiatives' involve public financing of community managed interventions that range from work insertion programmes for youth of immigrant origin to housing coops and even free housing in repurposed buildings in exchange for community service. The model is explicitly intended to overcome the accusations directed towards the Dutch Labour Party (PvdA) 'of being technocratic and alienated from large sections of the electorate ... largely blamed for the bureaucratic tendencies of the "big state"' (Kuitenbrouwer, 2012).

Celebrating and relying on social entrepreneurship in this way marks a profound shift in social policy governance and even social citizenship because it alters the role of the state and patterns of democratic accountability as well as the notion of social rights. The role of the state is no longer to deliver services (as under Keynesianism) or to stand back (as for neoliberals) but to ensure the conditions, including financial support, under which it can ensure their delivery by social entrepreneurs.[4] Such claims rely on longstanding visions of the social economy and community-centred social development (Moulaert and Ailenei, 2005), but their take-up and popularity go much further than the areas in which the social economy has traditionally been an active participant in governance. They involve market-making in the public sector and partnerships with the private and voluntary sectors in ways that multiply the diversity of service choice (BEPA, 2011;[5] NCM, 2015).

Social innovation and entrepreneurship

The move to such governance forms has a history. The modern welfare state's discourse of fostering equality in the face of social inequality flourished in the decades around the Second World War, based on governance via a Weberian-style public administration, with hierarchical decision making and standardisation of access and services.[6] Initial criticisms of such standard services – whether for their lack of choice or their control over vulnerable groups – led to demands for democratisation and bottom-up, often local design and delivery. In this discourse of the 1960s and 1970s, civil society's role was to provide alternative services to break the mould of the top-down, bureaucratic public service. This emphasis on governance by 'voice' then opened the door to another discursive shift. Accompanied by neoliberalism's market fundamentalism, claims for alternatives in social-service provision meant that:

> the various meanings of empowerment shifted from issues of "voice" to issues of "choice"; they now range from giving a group more specifically what it wants or needs to "making the customer satisfied". If a school system, for example, is to be made more responsive to individual talents, preferences, and needs, then why not give parents

more choice over the educational facility and arrangements
to be used? (Evers, 2009, 251)

Just such a commitment to 'voice' characterised, for example, Sweden's decision to open the governance of its health system, schools and childcare to non-public provision. It began with the notion that parents who wanted their children to experience teaching in parent co-operatives or schools with a particular philosophical foundation could develop or patronise 'alternative' educational facilities (Daune-Richard and Mahon, 2001: 160–3). However, Swedish policymakers soon found themselves trapped in the logic their own decisions, as the 'choice revolution' swept through the public sector and social entrepreneurs of all kinds – for profit as well as non-profit – clamoured for their 'right' to receive public funds as well. Sweden was fully engaged in market-making for social services (Blomqvist, 2004: 144–5, passim; see also NCM, 2015, for numerous other examples).

But Sweden was not alone in following this shift from voice to choice.[7] Across the Atlantic, the province of Quebec in the 1960s was designing governance for social services only just wrenched from the control of the Catholic Church. As it did so, it also responded to the ambient ideological claims for community-driven governance and instituted a mixed economy of welfare in which the market activities of the social economy would have a major place (Vaillancourt and Tremblay, 2002: Chapter 2). When neoliberalism arrived in force in the 1990s, the window opened in the governance model by the commitment to non-public provision – albeit by the social economy – made it impossible to resist claims that the new social investments in childcare should also provide public funding of for-profit providers. The market of these private social entrepreneurs alongside the non-profits was thereby constructed (Jenson, 2002: 326–7).

Such an emphasis on market-making is not surprising in this governance model. Much of the policy puzzling about social innovation and entrepreneurship starts with a reference to the work of Joseph Schumpeter (1983 [1934]). As an economist – and as the subtitle of his seminal work said – Schumpeter was most interested in 'profits, capital, credit, interest and the business cycle', the stuff of markets, in other words. Nonetheless, in his discussions of the creative destruction associated with innovation, Schumpeter was careful to consider social as well as economic and institutional factors. Thus a gesture to Schumpeter does not mean a necessarily narrow focus. The EU uses the broad brush definition favoured by the OECD and many foundations and think tanks: 'social innovations are new ideas (products, services and models) that simultaneously meet social needs (more effectively than alternatives) and create new social relationships or collaborations' (BEPA, 2011: 34; see also Caulier-Grice et al, 2012: 18). The report of the Nordic Council of Minister shares this understanding of innovation, using it to:

> ... define social entrepreneurship as creating social value through innovation with a high degree of participant orientation, often with the participation of civil society and often with an economic significance. The innovation often takes place across the three sectors represented by state, market and civil society... (NCM, 2015: 35).[8]

There is a clear emphasis on market-making and market-shaping activities touching public as well as non-profit and for-profit organisations.

States often vaunt social innovation in the form of more market-like behaviour and social entrepreneurship so as to address new social risks.[9] In many cases while states and other public authorities continue to finance interventions to address these risks, they are less willing to design policy that involves them directly in delivery (for the British case see Rees et al, 2017, for example). Instead they turn to other actors to form partnerships or to deliver the service according to a contract with public authorities. Another way that the market is bolstered is by supporting social enterprises of many types because they are seen as more capable of deftly responding to current and changing needs than either the state or the private sector can.

Labour markets are one key domain in which market-building with the support of social policy has occurred, thereby engaging with the social investment perspective and inclusive growth. The social and labour market policy analysis underpinning such interventions rests on the recognition that it is no longer possible to count on traditional firms or the public sector to provide employment for all job seekers. In the Keynesian years when full (male) employment seemed a possibility, private and public sector employers created a supply of jobs that might vary by business cycles but that seemed adequate to absorb the labour force. Policymakers could confine their role in shaping labour markets to regulations about hiring and working conditions. The market also provided an always expanding array of goods and services, appearing to meet all needs. Now, however, and for several decades, growing needs for many kinds of new services as well as job creation and labour market integration have become major preoccupations within social policy communities.

Faced with this puzzle and these challenges, policymakers acting under the influence of the social investment perspective and concerned about widening inequalities and how to generate inclusive growth have turned to fostering and supporting social entrepreneurs and often a social economy that can hopefully and simultaneously achieve two goals. First, to help to train and prepare workers touched by the social risks to enter paid employment; and second, to increase the labour market's need for workers by expanding and better organising markets for goods and services to supply those that the traditional firm does not adequately offer or the state no longer wishes to provide. Advocacy of such shifts frequently evokes mentions of growing needs for social care (including the childcare so important to the social investment perspective). In addition, policy communities concerned with levels and rates of employment in contemporary societies have pinned their hopes on social enterprises that can act as job creators as well as 'work integration enterprises' (Evers et al, 2014: 15–6). Initiatives often coming from the social economy or the voluntary sector may seek to shape either – and sometimes both – the supply and demand structures of labour markets, and this with the support of public authorities. On the supply side, and usually in the name of social inclusion, they work to enable integration into the labour market of young people, women, new immigrants, long-term unemployed – the groups most touched by the new social risks, in other words. These enterprises are an instrument for the achievement of the 'activation' commitment of much social and economic policy which is a pillar of the social investment perspective (Evers and Guillemard, 2012: Chapter 7). On the demand side, social enterprises and the social economy more generally are often tasked with filling gaps in services that do not attract investment by traditional private sector firms. Social entrepreneurship is assumed able to address gaps, and particularly the failure of existing markets adequately to provide work, income and inclusion as well as products and services in areas of social care, health, culture, community development and so on. As this list indicates, these are all areas in which in earlier decades states – whether national or local – were actively engaged in the delivery of services. Now, as demand for such services increases and needs multiply, the state's role is more often one of fostering enterprises, often financing them via contractual arrangements rather than delivering the service directly.

The promotion of social entrepreneurship

This move to social policy governance by social entrepreneurs has been actively promoted by 'puzzling' type organisations. The Nordic Council of Ministers has been cited above. Even more active in the promotion of this model of governance have been the OECD and the EU.

The OECD has long been concerned with promoting higher employment rates but has also increasingly become cognisant of market imperfections (Mahon and McBride, 2008). It was an early convert, along with the World Bank, to the social investment perspective (Mahon, 2010). It has been actively constructing an analysis of how to address social challenges around employment by relying on social innovations (Noya, 2011). While its *Innovation Strategy* still primarily focuses on standard approaches and measures of innovation, social entrepreneurship is discussed as an instrument of response to 'global and social challenges' (OECD, 2010a: 182ff; 2010b: Chapter 5). Deployment of the quasi-concept suggests, in other words, alternative ways of meeting the needs of ageing societies, poverty, rising inequalities and so on (Noya, 2011: 8).

The EU has also been moving in this direction, and even more enthusiastically since the 2008 economic crisis. The EU launched its Social Business Initiative (SBI) in 2011. Initially the potential for 'social business' was broadly cast to include all types of firms from multinationals to social enterprises.[10] Quickly, however, as part of the EU's conversion to promoting 'social innovation', the SBI was retargeted[11] on social entrepreneurs and their businesses, defined and described this way:

> A social enterprise is an operator in the social economy whose main objective is to have a social impact rather than make a profit for their owners or shareholders. It operates by providing goods and services for the market in an entrepreneurial and innovative fashion and uses its profits primarily to achieve social objectives. It is managed in an open and responsible manner and, in particular, involves employees, consumers and stakeholders affected by its commercial activities.

The Commission uses the term 'social enterprise' to cover the following types of business:

- Those for who the social or societal objective of the common good is the reason for the commercial activity, often in the form of a high level of social innovation.
- Those where profits are mainly reinvested with a view to achieving this social objective.
- Those where the method of organisation or ownership system reflects the enterprise's mission, using democratic or participatory principles or focusing on social justice.

There is no single legal form for social enterprises.[12]

Enthusiasm for social enterprise was incorporated into the EU's Europe 2020 strategy, and a series of high profile interventions have signalled that the Union shares the views of those who see a greater role for social entrepreneurship in achieving its targets for social inclusion and poverty reduction via their potential for job creation and innovative services (for example, BEPA, 2014). The EU contributes to encouraging and supporting market actors via actions such as a major conference on 'Empowering social entrepreneurs for innovation, inclusive growth and jobs' (in 2014). At that event workshops focused on the 'potential of social enterprises for job creation and green economy' as well as on the ways that the EU could use its structural funds to support and foster social enterprises.[13] Leverage for jobs, social inclusion and green initiatives were all identified as necessary because inadequately addressed by traditional firms.

To this point we see that social politics networks at the supranational and international level have been actively promoting social policy interventions in a governance model that favours social entrepreneurs. The tools for doing so are varied. The EU has relied on its capacity to distribute valued resources – financial but also knowledge sharing, networking and visibility-enhancing resources – to stimulate its approach to social investment, inclusive growth and social entrepreneurship (Verschraegen and Sabato, 2016). When the EU went public with its promotion of social innovation in 2010, it immediately chose to adopt 'a more "entrepreneurial-oriented" view of social innovation' (Sabato et al, 2015: 19).[14] This entrepreneurial perspective is only one of several ways of parsing the quasi-concept of social innovation (Ilie and During, 2012) but it is the one that has come to dominate EU thinking. It is via this approach that inclusive growth is connected to entrepreneurial innovation, and it supposedly 'growth-building role'. For the EU, the expected economic and social opportunities of entrepreneurship are found in the non-profit sector and social economy, because each contains significant growth potential (BEPA, 2011: 27–9). Indeed, by the time of the second edition of the EU's flagship publication on social innovation, the entrepreneurial orientation was even more visible – as the cover of the publication clearly advertised[15] – and the link to inclusive growth stronger (BEPA, 2014). By then 'inclusive growth' had become one of the Union's goals for 2020.[16] And, the emphasis on social entrepreneurship was weighty:

> social entrepreneurship should be placed in the main "engine room" of European integration: the Single Market raised social innovation to a new level of recognition, allowing major instruments such as public procurement directives or competition policy to engage with the development of this "emerging" sector ... (BEPA, 2014: 19–20).

This perspective had consequences in the realm of social policy and interventions to reduce poverty and increase employment, including those influenced by the social investment perspective. If the place of the public sector – and the need for improvements in its practices – was always mentioned, most enthusiasm went to non-profit and for-profit initiatives, bringing innovative solutions to social needs, creating new markets and representing potential growth and employment. As summarised by the Commissioner of Industry and Entrepreneurship: 'social innovation is both a business and societal opportunity, because the most important sectors for growth in the next decades are linked to the development of human and social capital'.[17] The Social Investment Package published in 2013 called not only for adjustments to policy approaches to achieve the goals of social investment but also encouraged member states to experiment with, adapt, and 'up-scale' ways of financing social investments, whether by Social Impact Bonds or various forms of support for entrepreneurs and the social economy. The Package called on member states to:

> Develop concrete strategies for social innovation, such as public-private-third sector partnerships, ensure adequate and predictable financial support, including microfinance, and provide for training, networking and mentoring in order to support evidence-based policies. Fully take advantage of ... [European programmes'] funding opportunities to do this and to scale up successful projects. ... ; Support social entrepreneurs by providing incentives for start-ups, and their further development, by expanding their knowledge and networks and providing them with an enabling regulatory

environment in line with the Social Business Initiative and the Entrepreneurship 2020 Action Plan... (European Commission, 2013: 12).

These calls for attention to entrepreneurship are accompanied by money; the European Social Funds targeted under the Social Investment Package would be directed towards such partnerships as would those supporting the Employment and Social Innovation Programme. The latter has €919,469,000 in funding available for 2014–20 to promote employment, social inclusion and microcredit, and to support the social economy. Of this total, only 18% was reserved for a network between the European Commission and the national employment services. The rest might go to social partners, civil society organisations, or private business (Sabato et al, 2015: 26–7).

Two sources of the governance model

This focus by the EU and other actors on social entrepreneurship to deliver the programmes of the social investment perspective and other policies generating inclusive growth had at least two sources. Each reflects a tradition that has influenced social policy governance within Europe and beyond in the years of after-neoliberalism. The first is the heritage of neoliberalism offloading to the voluntary or third sector in a number of liberal welfare regimes and the enthusiasm for other forms of service delivery that followed, as efforts were made to recoup losses. The second is longstanding and internationally widespread keenness for the social economy that is present in many continental European countries.

In liberal welfare regimes such as Australia (Phillips, 2006) and Canada, there was an early move to foster 'social entrepreneurship' of the type described here. As Susan Phillips (2001: 182–3) summarised for Canada at the start of the millennium:

> ... how the state develops policy and delivers programmes is changing in fundamental ways. Governance refers to a process of governing through collaboration with voluntary, private or other public sector actors in the planning, design and achievement of government objectives in a manner that shares policy formation, risk and operational planning, and that may replace programme delivery by state employees with those of third parties. It is not a passing fad but an adaptive response to a more diverse population with

differing needs and expectations of the state, and less trust in it, and to a policy environment that is more complex and in which governments are only part of policy solutions.

In the UK as well, the 'third sector' was encouraged to take on a service delivery role in social care, health, housing, education and social inclusion both under the Conservatives and New Labour. In the UK, a strong structuring effect for this form of governance came from New Labour's promotion of a '…Compact between central government and the third sector' that 'signalled intentions to raise the sector's profile, marking a shift in public policy from welfare state hierarchies and marketisation, towards networks and partnership working' (Milbourne, 2009: 279). The market-making enthusiasm that had characterised the Conservative government continued, but the years of New Labour also brought a willingness to spend on services and to promote social entrepreneurship. Thus, Milbourne (2009: 279) could write that:

> For a decade, partnership working and numerous short-term, multi-agency initiatives have characterised state voluntary sector relationships in the UK, entwining public and voluntary services ever more closely and often increasing voluntary sector funding dependency. Such initiatives have included Education and Health Action Zones, Sure Start and New Deal for Communities, while Local Strategic Partnerships (LSPs) established in over 80 deprived local authority areas were charged with co-ordinating local neighbourhood renewal strategies by engaging community representatives alongside private and public sector agencies.

The coalition government's (2010–15) 'Big Society' rhetoric continued this emphasis, stressing even more – in the face of claims about budget crunch and the need for austerity – that it was necessary to outsource service provision to for-profit as well as non-profit providers of services, with increasing emphasis on the former (Milbourne and Cushman, 2015: 463).

This turn to market-based entrepreneurship, albeit led by ideological and public policy preferences, was not simply imposed on civil society in these liberal regimes.

If the first wave of straightforward neoliberalism of the Thatcherist variety left civil society organisations reeling and confused about their role, the last decades have reshaped the practices of social entrepreneurship such that '… many VOs [voluntary organisations] concurred with hegemonic discourse and behaviours, anticipating gains in legitimacy and resources. Many VOs assumed these new cultures apparently by choice ... or in an isomorphic process of imitating, or conforming to, the norms of surrounding organisational arrangements' (Milbourne and Cushman, 2015: 466; for similar argument about the social investment perspective see Jenson and Levi, 2013). As voluntary organisations gained in legitimacy and visibility, they also fostered a community of experts and analysts whose ideological commitment was often to the health of the sector itself and who were able to describe its myriad contributions.[18] At times this meant counterpoising the value of the sector to the old ways of public sector dominance.

Nor, as the leading role of New Labour illustrates, was enthusiasm for other forms of social entrepreneurship confined to the political right. In the UK, so-called mutuals – often in the form of cooperative businesses – have been enthusiastically promoted by both left and right. Writing for the centre-left Policy Network, Todd and Williams (2012) put it this way:

> ... organisations that have "spun out" of the public sector are typically structured as social enterprises with a high degree of employee ownership and sometimes wider community membership. At their best, they are enhancing the relationship between citizens and the providers of public services beyond that which can be delivered either by the traditional "top-down" model of state service provision or by private sector market provision.

Indeed just before becoming leader of the Labour Party, Ed Miliband floated the idea of transforming the BBC into a cooperative,[19] while the Labour government before 2010 '... commenced a process of exploring mutualisation within a range of public services, from cooperative schools to groups of health workers forming employee owned social enterprises' (Todd and Williams, 2012). The trend continued and GOV.UK now provides a how-to website for public sector workers who want to spin out a public service mutual.[20] Successful examples mentioned come from, among other areas, those of the social investment perspective such as childcare.

This enthusiasm from London had a significant influence on Brussels' puzzling and policy propositions about social entrepreneurship. The EU's adoption of the 'entrepreneurial-oriented paradigm' is attributed (by those interviewed by Sabato et al, 2015: 19), to the intellectual influence and lobbying of:

> ... big players in the field of social entrepreneurship or by organisations expert in the application of technological solutions to social issues, such as the Young Foundation and the ICT Company CISCO, with traditional EU players dealing with social policies left somehow at the margins.

There was, however, an additional and significant influence from the continental European tradition of the social economy that had not been completely driven out. While the social economy is another quasi-concept, it is possible to describe its history and identify a trajectory that led to an intersection with growing European enthusiasm for social entrepreneurship. The genealogy performed by Moulaert and Ailenei (2005) dates the progressive movement for a social economy to an earlier period than the forces leading to British mutualism, spin-offs and even downloading to the voluntary sector. In France, it was the crisis of the 1980s with high unemployment and the threat to welfare states that generated proposals by progressives to promote employment by the creation of work integration enterprises and of worker-owned co-operatives (see Evers and Laville, 2004). 'In France, the contemporary (as of the 1980s) re-emergence of the social economy as "social and solidarity economy" is narrowly linked to the reaction against neoliberal principles and individualist ideology' (Moulaert and Ailenei, 2005: 2041). In Sweden there has also been a strong political focus on the social economy and social entrepreneurship. As early as 1997 the Swedish government commissioned a report on the country's social economy, both as a tradition and as a concept to be renewed. Since the 1990s the Swedish government has financially supported, among other things, the development of parents' co-operatives for childcare, staff co-operatives in nursing and care, and work integration social enterprises – all instruments of the social investment perspective. Elsewhere as well entrepreneurship in education has been a focus, one that is 'probably most firmly established and consolidated in Denmark, but is now gaining ground in the other Nordic countries' (NCM, 2015: 58).

The social economy tradition claims a place for varied service providers, experimentation and innovation, but carries less of an anti-state or anti-public provision bias than much of the promotion of social entrepreneurship in the tradition of liberal welfare regimes. The social and solidarity economy is proposed as an alternative to fill gaps more than it is assumed to do things better than the public sector.

Concluding comments

These two positions, and others, arose out of the policy puzzling of the past decade around the need for a governance model for social investment that would engage social entrepreneurs in order to achieve inclusive growth. The social investment perspective gives clear guidance about which types of social policy interventions are to be given priority in after-neoliberalism: early childhood education and care, and activation for employment. Policy work also turned on how to deliver these interventions, but that element of the reform and reworking was often less visible to social policy communities.

This chapter provides an overview of this governance model. In particular, it argues that focusing exclusively on propositions about where to intervene (in the labour market; with child-centred spending) provides only a limited picture of adjustments in social policy thinking since the mid-1990s. Also part of the assemblage is another quasi-concept, also used to invoke promises of wellbeing and inclusive growth. Alongside the propositions about *where* to invest there has been an important change in the emphasis on *who* should provide the service (social entrepreneurs), *how* it should be governed (by non-profits and for-profit enterprises as well as the public sector) and *how* it should be financed (with a mix of public funds, philanthropy and earned revenue).

The social investment perspective mapped onto the narratives of neoliberalism, while reworking them to accommodate a discourse of equity and inclusion (Jenson and Levi, 2013). Enthusiasm for social entrepreneurship also involved a mapping onto the broad cultural narrative of neoliberalism, via a discourse emphasising markets and entrepreneurship, at the same time as moving beyond neoliberalism to call for new services and new public spending if not necessarily public delivery. In this adjustment something has disappeared, of course. This is the expectation of state-designed policy instruments and public services as the best kind of investment, whether for increasing employment or investing in human capital. Instead, states, international organisations and the supranational EU are directing their attention – and their spending – to a myriad of social entrepreneurs that they contract to provide the service, but over which they may retain little policy control or direction.

More generally, this enthusiasm for social investment via social entrepreneurship reflects an emphasis on promoting inclusion and cohesion, which are different goals from equality and social rights. If something is gained with this assemblage, something is also lost.

Notes

[1]   McNeill (2006) used this definition to examine three important ideas that powerfully influenced development policy over several decades: the informal economy, sustainable development and social capital. All three were transferred across space, touching numerous continents, as well as across scale, from the transnational to the local and vice versa. Jenson (2010) applies the notion of quasi-concept to the diffusion of the social investment perspective.

[2]   I will use the notion of quasi-concept rather than 'idea' in this chapter, for several reasons. The first is that it opens space for an analysis of hybridity, ambiguity and polysemy while it enables the task of mapping the biographies of concepts. The second reason to use the term 'quasi-concept' rather than 'idea' is that to employ the latter is almost inevitably to be forced into the intellectual space of 'ideas and politics', a space in which the goal of research has been and continues to be to assess the explanatory weight of ideas, to assess when or how they matter or, alternatively, to identify their generic characteristics. This is not the task this chapter undertakes.

[3]   Among others, Moulaert and Ailenei (2005), Ilie and During (2012), the European Commission (2013) and the NCM (2015: Part 2) all map the polysemy governing the policy deployment of social innovation and social entrepreneurship.

[4]   For example, '… the government in Norway is not themselves providing many activities that encourage social innovation, however it is the largest funder of social innovation activity', https://webgate.ec.europa.eu/socialinnovationeurope/en/social-innovation-norway. The policy paper of the Policy Network, a centre-left think tank in London, has called for the transformation of the UK's National Health Service (NHS) into a mutual funded by taxes but managed by an elected Board of Trustees (Diamond et al, 2015).

[5]   This report from the Bureau of European Policy Advisors (BEPA) is usually dated 2010, but the final version and the one currently available online carries the date 2011.

[6]   This paragraph draws on Evers (2009).

[7]   For other examples, see Evers (2009).

[8]   For a systematised discussion of this appeal to the sectors of the 'welfare diamond', see Jenson (2015b).

[9]   For one recent discussion of such examples see Nicholls and Murdock (2012: especially Chapters 3, 5, 6).

[10] http://ec.europa.eu/internal_market/social_business/index_en.htm. This was intended to be a broad initiative. Other targets were multinationals and SMEs (small and medium sized enterprises), including their involvement with environmental protection and acceptance of corporate responsibility. See the press release at http://europa.eu/rapid/press-release_IP-11-1238_en.htm?locale=en

[11] An internet search for 'social business initiative' leads to a web page titled 'social enterprise'. The multinational corporation and small and medium enterprise are nowhere to be found.

[12] http://ec.europa.eu/growth/sectors/social-economy/enterprises/index_en.htm. This attention to social business with innovative potential is not to be confused with Innovation Union (http://ec.europa.eu/research/innovation-union/index_en.cfm) which focuses on technological innovation and whose new 'innovation indicator' has nothing 'social' about it. See http://europa.eu/rapid/press-release_IP-13-831_en.htm.

13 See the conference report at http://ec.europa.eu/internal_market/ conferences/2014/0116-social-entrepreneurs/workshops/index_en.htm.
14 Sabato et al (2015: 12–8) review the Union's approach to social innovation from the late 1970s and document that many of the elements later explicitly labelled 'social innovation' were already being undertaken, albeit 'between the lines'. They examine the Structural Funds, the Open Method of Coordination and the 7th Framework Programme as examples of such commitments to innovative actions. However, once the quasi-concept was explicitly mobilised, it was often framed along with social entrepreneurship. For a recent mapping of approaches to the quasi-concept, see Pelka and Terstriep (2016).
15 'The illustration of the cover page as well as chapter headings ones [sic] come from a fresco designed live during the Strasbourg's [January 2014] event "Social entrepreneurs, have your say!". All these drawings reflect the highlights of this event and the various forms of exchange tried on during it, organized in a socially innovative way' (BEPA, 2014).
16 The Europe 2020 Strategy announced 'seven flagship initiatives to achieve smart, sustainable and inclusive growth' (http://ec.europa.eu/europe2020/europe-2020-in-a-nutshell/flagship-initiatives/index_en.htm).
17 Antonio Tajani, Commissioner from 2009 to 2014, quoted in Sabato et al (2015: 23).
18 The UK's Voluntary Sector Studies Network was created in the early 2000s, the academic journal *Voluntary Sector Review* has published seven volumes, and the Third Sector Research Centre at the University of Birmingham was 'launched as a Venture Funded ESRC Research Centre, co-funded by the Economic and Social Research Council (ESRC), the UK government Cabinet Office's Office of the Third Sector (renamed the Office for Civil Society in 2010), and the Barrow Cadbury Trust. This funding ran from September 2008 to August 2013' (www.birmingham.ac.uk/generic/tsrc/about/the-centre.aspx).
19 www.thenews.coop/35986/news/co-operatives/miliband-proposes-turning-bbc-mutual
20 www.gov.uk/government/collections/public-service-mutuals

References

BEPA (Bureau of European Policy Advisers) (2011) *Empowering people, driving change. Social innovation in the European Union*, Brussels: European Commission, https://publications.europa.eu/en/publication-detail/-/publication/4e23d6b8-5c0c-4d38-bd9d-3a202e6f1e81

BEPA (2014) *Social Innovation. A decade of changes*, Luxembourg: European Commission.

Bernard, P. (1999) 'La cohésion sociale: critique dialectique d'un quasi-concept', *Lien social et Politiques* 41: 47–59.

Blomqvist, P. (2004) 'The Choice Revolution. Privatization of Swedish Welfare Services in the 1990s', *Social Policy & Administration* 38(2): 139–55.

Bonoli, G. (2005) 'The politics of the new social policies: providing coverage against new social risks in mature welfare states', *Policy & Politics* 33(3): 431–49.

Caulier-Grice, J., A. Davies, R. Patrick and W. Norman (2012) *Defining Social Innovation*, TEPSIE deliverable 1.1, www.tepsie.eu/images/documents/TEPSIE.D1.1.Report.DefiningSocialInnovation. Part%201%20-%20defining%20social%20innovation.pdf

Daune-Richard, A.-M. and R. Mahon (2001) 'Sweden. Models in Crisis', in J. Jenson and M. Sineau (eds), *Who Cares. Women's Work, Child Care and Welfare State Redesign*, Toronto: University of Toronto Press, 146–76.

Deeming, C. and P. Smyth (2015) 'Social Investment after Neoliberalism. Policy Paradigms and Political Platforms', *Journal of Social Policy* 44(2): 297–318.

Diamond, P., F. Field and J. Todd (2015) *Mutual endeavour. Winning support for a 21st century NHS*, Policy Network Paper, 17 February, www.policy-network.net

European Commission (2013) *Social Innovation Research in the European Union. Approaches, Findings and Future Directions*, Policy Review, Brussels: DG Research and Innovation.

Evers, A. (2009) 'Civicness and Civility: Their Meanings for Social Services', *Voluntas, International Journal of Voluntary and Nonprofit Organizations* 20, 239–59.

Evers, A. and A.-M. Guillemard (eds) (2012) *Social Policy and Citizenship*, Oxford: Oxford University Press.

Evers, A. and J.-L. Laville (eds) (2004) *The Third Sector in Europe*, Cheltenham: Edward Elgar.

Evers, A., B. Ewert and T. Brandsen (eds) (2014) *Social Innovations for Social Cohesion*, Liege: EMES.

Heclo, H. (2010 [1974]) *Modern Social Politics in Britain and Sweden. From Relief to Income Maintenance*, Colchester: ECPR Press.

Ilie, E. and R. During (2012) *An Analysis of Social Innovation Discourses in Europe*, http://edepot.wur.nl/197565

Jenson, J. (2002) 'Against the current: Child care and family policy in Quebec', in S. Michel and R. Mahon (eds), *Child care policy at the crossroads. Gender and welfare state restructuring*, New York: Routledge, 309–32.

Jenson, J. (2010) 'Diffusing ideas for after neoliberalism: The social investment perspective in Europe and Latin America', *Global Social Policy* 10(1): 59–84.

Jenson, J. (2015a) 'Broadening the Frame: Inclusive Growth and the Social Investment Perspective', in S. McBride, R. Mahon and G.W. Boychuk (eds), *After '08. Social Policy and the Global Financial Crisis*, Vancouver: University of British Columbia Press, 40–58.

Jenson, J. (2015b) 'The "Social" in Inclusive Growth. The Social Investment Perspective', in R. Hasmath (ed.) *Inclusive Growth, Development, and Welfare Policy. A Critical Assessment*, New York: Routledge, 108–23.

Jenson, J. and R. Levi (2013) 'Narratives and Regimes of Social and Human Rights: The Jackpines of the Neoliberal Era', in P.A. Hall and M. Lamont (eds), *Social Resilience in the Neoliberal Era*, New York: Cambridge University Press, 69–98.

Kuitenbrouwer, M. (2012) 'Mutual Councils as antidotes to populism', Policy Network, 7 June, www.policy-network.net/pno_detail.aspx?ID=4192&title=Mutual+councils+as+antidotes+to+populism

Mahon, R. (2010) 'After-Neoliberalism? The OECD, the World Bank and the Child', *Global Social Policy* 10(2): 172–92.

Mahon, R. and S. McBride (eds) (2008) *The OECD and Transnational Governance*, Vancouver: University of British Columbia Press.

McNeill, D. (2006) 'The Diffusion of Ideas in Development Theory and Policy', *Global Social Policy* 6(3): 334–54.

Milbourne, L. (2009) 'Remodelling the Third Sector: Advancing Collaboration or Competition in Community-Based Initiatives?' *Journal of Social Policy* 38(2): 277–97.

Milbourne, L. and M. Cushman (2015) 'Complying, Transforming or Resisting in the New Austerity? Realigning Social Welfare and Independent Action among English Voluntary Organisations', *Journal of Social Policy* 44(3): 463–85.

Moulaert, F. and O. Ailenei (2005) 'From History to Present Social Economy, Third Sector and Solidarity Relations: A Conceptual Synthesis', *Urban Studies* 42(11): 2037–53.

Nordic Council of Ministers (NCM) (2015) *Social entrepreneurship and social innovation. Initiatives to promote social entrepreneurship and social innovation in the Nordic countries*, Copenhagen: Nordic Council of Ministers, www.norden.org/nordpub

Nicholls, A. and A. Murdock (eds) (2012) *Social Innovation. Blurring Boundaries to Reconfigure Markets*, Basingstoke, Hampshire: Palgrave Macmillan.

Noya, A. (2011) Presentation, at the International Conference on Challenge Social Innovation. Innovating Innovation by Research, Vienna, 19–21 September.

OECD (2010a) *The OECD Innovation Strategy. Getting a Head Start on Tomorrow*, Paris: OECD.

OECD (2010b) *SMEs, Entrepreneurship and Innovation*, OECD: Paris.

Pelka, B. and J. Terstriep (2016) 'Mapping Social Innovation Maps. The State of Research Practice across Europe', *European Public and Social Innovation Review* 1(1): 3–16.

Phillips, S.D. (2001) 'More than stakeholders: Reforming state-voluntary sector relations', *Journal of Canadian Studies* 35(4): 182–202.

Phillips, R. (2006) 'The Role of Nonprofit Advocacy Organizations in Australian Democracy and Policy Governance', *Voluntas: International Journal of Voluntary and Nonprofit Organizations* 17(1): 59–75.

Rees, J., R. Miller and H. Buckingham (2017) 'Commission incomplete: exploring the new model for purchasing public services from the third sector', *Journal of Social Policy*, 46(1): 175–94.

Sabato, S., B Vanhercke, and G. Verschraegen (2015) *The EU framework for social innovation – Between entrepreneurship and policy experimentation*, ImPRovE Working Paper 15/21, http://improve-research.eu

Schumpeter, J. (1983 [1934]) *The Theory of Economic Development. An Inquiry into Profits, Capital, Credit, Interest and the Business Cycle*, New Brunswick, NJ: Transaction Publishers.

Todd, R. and B. Williams (2012) 'Investing in the mutualisation of public services', Policy Network, 6 June, www.policy-network.net

Vaillancourt, Y. and L. Tremblay (eds) (2002) *Social Economy. Health and Welfare in four Canadian provinces*, Montreal: Fernwood and LAREPPS.

Verschraegen, G and S. Sabato (2016) *The integration of place-based social innovations into the EU social agenda*, ImPRovE Working Paper 16/10, http://improve-research.eu

THIRTEEN

Limits to Growth revisited

Tim Jackson and Robin Webster

Anyone who believes that exponential growth can go on forever in a finite world is either a madman or an economist. (Kenneth Boulding, 1973)

[There are] no great limits to growth because there are no limits on the human capacity for intelligence, imagination and wonder. (US President Ronald Reagan, 1983)

Introduction

Inclusive growth is better than non-inclusive growth. Social investment is better than anti-social investment. We are not lacking in examples of either of these less desirable beasts. But neither inclusive growth nor social investment necessarily questions the goal of growth itself. Indeed a leitmotif of social investment has been that social policy can be 'good for growth'; while the inclusive growth framework makes growth the *sine qua non* of human development (World Economic Forum, 2017). Neither approach confronts what is the single most critical question faced by economics on a finite planet. What can prosperity possibly look like in a world of environmental and social limits (Jackson, 2017)?

This question of limits is often left out of social policy discussions. There are reasons for this omission. In a world free of limits, exponential economic growth could continue indefinitely; it is then always possible (in theory) to make the poor better off without in any way denting the expectations of the rich to be better off themselves. Social justice can be approached safely, as it were, behind the canopy of an expanding cornucopia. Introducing limits overturns this convenient fiction. Indeed, as the United Nation's 2030 Agenda for Sustainable Development shows, the links between sustainability and social justice are so deep that we have to develop a more integrated approach. It is worth noting that a strong and growing body of social policy scholarship is now developing these links (Gough, 2016; Dryzek,

2008). But as these authors indicate, the future conversation depends very much on how we understand the environmental perspective and in particular the limits to growth.

Our aim in this chapter is to show how critical the question of limits is for our thinking about social justice and the roles of social policy. We accomplish this by revisiting the book *Limits to Growth* first published in 1972 by the 'Club of Rome' a group of about 30 leading thinkers who were particularly concerned about the potential impacts of exponentially increasing consumption in a finite world (Club of Rome, 2017). The book forecast the pressures the planet would experience if the contemporary growth trends were to continue for the next 100 years. There's little doubt that the publication of *Limits to Growth* sparked a debate. That same debate has been raging now for over 40 years. But what exactly did the original report say? How robust were its findings? And what is the relevance of the limits debate today?

What did Limits to Growth actually say?

In the 1950s and 1960s, Jay Forrester, a professor at the Massachusetts Institute of Technology (MIT), had developed a new approach to understanding the behaviour of nonlinear systems. 'Systems dynamics' uses a computer model to predict how different components of a system interact with each other, often in feedback loops, or circular and interlocking ways, to influence what eventually happens.

Previously, MIT had largely used the technique to analyse patterns in business – the success or failure of different corporations, for example. In the *Limits to Growth* analysis, Forrester and his team applied it to world development patterns (Radzicki and Taylor, 2008).

One simple example is the relationship between population, mortality and food per capita. If a population falls, there may be more food available per head. But the lower population may then also bring down agricultural productivity, reducing the supply of food, increasing mortality and leading to a further fall in population (Meadows et al, 1972). The model included hundreds of causal relationships like this one.

Overall, *Limits to Growth* investigated trends in five major areas: population and industrialisation, pollution, resource depletion and land availability for food.

The MIT team presented and analysed 12 scenarios, each with a different pattern of world development from 1900 to 2100. Every component in the model was linked to mathematical equations informed by the laws of physics and calibrated against empirical data up to 1970.

The 12 scenarios were arranged into three broad groups. The 'standard run' or business-as-usual scenario assumed the same economic, social and physical patterns observed from 1900 to 1970 would continue into the future. Six subsequent 'technological scenarios' started with the same basic pattern, but assumed new advances in technology or that society would increase the amount of resources available, increase agricultural productivity, reduce pollution, or limit population growth. The final set of five 'stabilisation' scenarios looked at what would happen if either population growth, or industrial output, were stabilised.

Only four scenarios avoided overshoot and collapse (Meadows et al, 1972). These scenarios combined stabilising the human population with measures to restrict industrial output per person, as well as technological solutions like resource recycling and pollution control. One scenario which did not introduce these measures until 2000 managed to reached equilibrium, but not permanently.

In the 'standard run' scenario (Figure 13.1), collapse came as a result of resource depletion forcing a slowdown in industrial growth, starting around 2015. The second scenario – the first of the 'technological' scenarios – assumed twice as many resources were available as a result of technological advances. In this projection, population collapse came about as a result of too much pollution.

The majority of the scenarios show industrial output declining in the 2020s and population declining in the 2030s. The researchers did not put precise dates on their projections. In fact, they deliberately left the timeline somewhat vague. They were interested in the general pattern of behaviour, rather than when exactly particular events might happen (Meadows et al, 1972).

Although the inter-dependencies *Limits to Growth* investigated are complex, the dynamics of MIT's model are relatively straightforward to convey. As more and more people achieve higher and higher levels of affluence, they consume more and more of the world's resources. Consumption increases by a certain percentage each year – and population, industrialisation, pollution, food production and resource depletion all follow an exponential growth curve.

Material growth cannot continue indefinitely, argued the book, because planet earth is physically limited. Eventually, the scale of activity passes the carrying capacity of the environment, resulting in a sudden contraction – either controlled or uncontrolled. First the resources supporting humanity – food, minerals, industrial output – begin to decline. This is followed by a collapse in population. The result is a series of bell-shaped curves (Figure 13.1).

Figure 13.1 Overshoot and collapse in the Limits to Growth 'standard run'

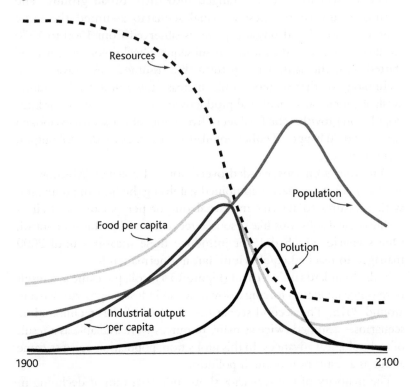

Source: Adapted from Meadows et al (1972; 2004: 169)

The analysis follows a similar logic to predictions made by geoscientist M. King Hubbert in 1956 about world oil supply. Hubbert observed that when oil is extracted from a well, the amount of oil it yields rises exponentially, reaches a point where it stops growing, peaks and enters a terminal decline as the well is exhausted. He suggested that oil production would follow the same pattern globally – a theory that later came to be known as 'peak oil' (Hubbert, 1962).

It is important to note that contraction or collapse does not happen in the model because physical resources supporting humanity disappear entirely. It happens because the quality of a resource declines as more and more of it is extracted. Consequently, it takes more and more investment (both physical and financial) to extract usable high quality resources from raw materials. This diverts resources away from productive industry and from agriculture and eventually the process becomes unsustainable.

When applied to energy, ecologist Charles Hall has called this process of a declining return on resource extraction the 'Energy Return on

Energy Invested' (EROEI). EROEI puts a value on the amount of energy obtained from a fuel like coal or oil, compared to the amount of energy that has to be spent to extract it in the first place (Hall et al, 2014). If this value falls far enough, extraction becomes both financially and energetically unviable. The concept can also be applied to mineral resources like iron, chromium or phosphorous (Sverdrup et al, 2012).

The Limits today

The publication of *Limits* created a furore and it continues to generate debate and analysis more than 40 years later. Many are still dismissive. But on reading the work in 2000 energy analyst Matthew Simmons described himself as amazed. 'The most amazing aspect of the book,' he said, 'is how accurate many of the basic trend extrapolations ... still are some 30 years later' (Simmons, 2000).

In the years since *Limits to Growth* was published, a number of studies have tracked how real world events matched up to its original scenarios. These studies show significant similarities between its projections and what has actually happened.

Limits to Growth's 30 year update, published by the Club of Rome in 2004, and two subsequent modelling studies in 2008 and 2014 from the University of Melbourne concluded that the world is tracking on *Limits to Growth*'s 'standard run' projection (Meadows et al, 2004; Turner, 2008, 2014; Pasqualino et al, 2015). Historical data from publications including the United Nations and the World Resources Institute's Earthwatch database show that the global population and economy has developed according to the patterns the researchers modelled in 1972.

As systems ecologist Charles Hall and a colleague remarked in a paper in 2009, 'We are not aware of any model made by economists that is as accurate over such a long time span' (Hall and Day, 2009).

Is the world already facing resource constraints?

What does this all mean for the future of our economy? In the standard run scenario, natural resources (for example oil, iron and chromium) become harder and harder to obtain. The diversion of more and more capital to extracting them leaves less for investment in industry, leading to industrial decline starting in about 2015. Around 2030, the world population peaks and begins to decrease as the death rate is driven upwards by lack of food and health services (Meadows et al, 2004).

The similarity between *Limits to Growth*'s standard run and the patterns observed over the last 40 years does not necessarily mean that the same trends will continue into the future. Some researchers argue that it is possible, however. The author of the University of Melbourne studies, Dr Graham Turner, asked in 2014 whether global collapse could be 'imminent'. Turner explicitly linked the global financial crisis, high commodity prices and the *Limits to Growth* projections (Turner, 2014).

Another set of studies has modelled the availability of over 40 essential materials using an updated and expanded version of the *Limits to Growth* model. Based on US Geological Survey data, the authors analysed changing patterns of resource extraction. Using earlier work, which suggests there is a time delay of about 40 years between 'peak discovery' and 'peak production' across a wide range of different minerals, the authors aim to forecast when 'peak production' might arrive.

The work, led by Harald Sverdrup from the University of Lund in Sweden and Vala Ragnarsdóttir from the University of Iceland, concluded that most of the resources they studied had either already reached peak production or will do so within the next 50 years (Sverdrup et al, 2012; Sverdrup and Ragnarsdóttir, 2014; Ragnarsdóttir and Sverdrup, 2015). Phosphorous – which is critical to fertilising soil and sustaining agriculture – has already peaked, and will start declining around 2030–40, they said.

Coal production will peak in around 2015–20 and 'peak energy' around the same period. From that point on, they concluded, 'we will no longer be able to take natural-resource fuelled global GDP growth for granted' (Ragnarsdóttir and Sverdrup, 2015).

A book published by the Club of Rome in 2014 also examined the future availability of a wide variety of mined resources, including chromium, copper, tin, lithium, coal oil and gas. The book included specialist contributions from experts across a wide range of fields. It concluded that the rate of production of many mineral commodities is already on the verge of decline (Bardi, 2014).

These analyses are understandably controversial. In a technologically optimistic world, it is often assumed that enough food, water, energy and minerals will be available for the foreseeable future, with the only problems being those of distribution (Stiglitz, 2008). Neo-classical economists also argue that when one resource runs out it can be substituted for another. But this is also controversial. In the case of some key elements (phosphorus is an example), there are no known substitutes (Neumayer, 2000).

Experts themselves are clearly divided on the question of resource limits. In 2014, a World Economic Forum (WEF) survey of hundreds of experts identified resource scarcity as the second most underestimated global issue after financial inequality. But WEF's analysis also highlighted the contested nature of the debate. The WEF concluded that the world has sufficient mineral stocks to 2035, although 'better management of the resource is needed after that point' (World Economic Forum, 2014).

Peak oil: fact or fiction?

Probably the most well-known resource scarcity debate is the one surrounding 'peak oil' – M. King Hubbert's prediction that world oil supply will peak and then start declining. Hubbert's theory and the *Limits to Growth* analysis were developed separately, but they follow the same logic. The resource, in this case oil, becomes harder and harder to extract, eventually forcing a decline in the rate of production (Hubbert, 1962).

Hubbert originally suggested that US oil production would peak in 1970 and world oil production would peak sometime around the year 2000. In fact, US crude oil production did peak in 1970 and started to fall. Global oil production did not peak in 2000, but many considered the possibility that it would a serious concern in the first decade of this century (IEA, 2008; Macalister and Monbiot, 2008). A number of literature reviews now suggest conventional oil production has already peaked, or will do so within the next couple of decades (Miller and Sorrell, 2013).

The expansion of 'unconventional oil' has changed the debate, however. It is now clear that production is rising again. New extraction techniques opened less accessible oil resources up to exploitation. Hydraulic fracturing ('fracking') allowed the expansion of an industry exploiting 'tight oil', most notably in the USA. Canada is now extracting 2.3 million barrels of oil a day from tar sands – in a project labelled 'the largest industrial plan on earth' (Alberta Energy, 2017). Deepwater drilling – for example off the coast of Brazil – also allows companies to access new oil resources (Energy Information Administration, 2015).

As a result, some commentators announced the 'death' of the peak oil theory – putting forward the view that there are huge volumes of oil still to be developed (Maugeri, 2012; Viner, 2013; Wile, 2013). The dramatic fall in oil prices from 2014 appears to further contradict the idea that production could struggle to meet demand in the near future (IEA, 2016a). Instead, argues the International Energy Agency (IEA), we are experiencing low oil prices, low demand and an abundance of resources in the ground as companies seek out new conventional and unconventional supplies (IEA, 2016b).

From an environmental point of view this era of apparent abundance is not without drawbacks. Unconventional oil is difficult, expensive and environmentally destructive to get out of the ground. In fact, as the remaining global oil resources get more and more difficult to extract, less and less energy is gained relative to the energy that needs to be put in to get it in the first place – exactly in line with the principles in *Limits to Growth* (Turner, 2014).

Not everyone is convinced that this era of abundance is here to stay. In the conventional economic view, we should be able to tell something about scarcity from prices. But the price dynamics of oil markets are notoriously difficult to predict. Oil prices rose to a peak of US$147 a barrel in July of 2008. After an extremely volatile period, prices began to collapse through 2014 and 2015, before recovering slightly in 2016 (OilPrice.com, 2017). Low oil price is no more reliable an indicator of abundance, however, than the very high oil price in 2008 was an indicator of immediate scarcity.

There's an interesting theory – called the 'green paradox' – that low oil prices are in part the reaction of an industry fearful of the impacts of climate change policy on its future revenues. The German economist Hans-Werner Sinn has argued that 'if suppliers feel threatened by a gradual greening of economic policies they will extract their stocks more rapidly' thus pushing their prices down (Sinn, 2008).

Low oil prices certainly present a problem for unconventional oils. Getting the oil out of the ground is so difficult that it needs a high price to make the investment financially viable (Arthur, 2015; Crooks, 2016). Weak economic activity, increased energy efficiency, high unconventional production from the USA, and a market decision made by OPEC to keep producing at lower prices in order to maintain its market share all played a part in pushing the price down. The complexity of the market means analysts found it difficult to predict whether oil prices would go on recovering in 2017, or not (for example, Taberner, 2017).

A 2015 analysis of the remaining fossil fuel resources in China, USA, Canada and Australia, which includes unconventional resources, suggests that overall oil production is in fact peaking already. The combination of declining conventional oil with increasing unconventional oil supplies then results in a 'plateau' in supplies to the end of the century, before a decline begins. In a 'high' oil supplies scenario, strong growth continues to 2025, before being replaced to very weak growth to the end of the century, when a decline begins. In a 'low' scenario, the decline begins by 2050 (Mohr et al, 2015).

Overall, the study reaches a striking conclusion. World fossil fuel production is likely to peak in around 2025, it suggests, largely as a result of Chinese coal production peaking. In short, unconventional oil seems to buy us several more decades before resource depletion starts to bite. But if the fear of peak oil has receded slightly, another set of concerns has emerged that was virtually unforeseen in the original *Limits to Growth* work.

Facing up to 'planetary boundaries'

In one respect at least, history has turned out considerably worse than the Club of Rome's projections. The original report made only passing reference to some of the most pressing environmental issues of today. This prompted another set of researchers to take the ideas in *Limits to Growth* one step further. A large cross-disciplinary team led by Dr Johan Rockström of the Stockholm Resilience Centre identified a set of nine ecological processes that regulate the land, ocean and atmosphere.

For each process they identified a series of thresholds beyond which humans would cause unacceptable environmental change. Acknowledging the uncertainty inherent in defining these thresholds, the team also defined a set of 'planetary boundaries' which taken together represent a 'safe operating space' for humanity. This new framing was intended as a shift away from *Limits to Growth*'s approach of analysing the impact of different human activities towards 'the estimation of a safe space for human development' (Rockström et al, 2009).

The nine planetary boundaries relate respectively to: climate change, ocean acidification, biodiversity loss, interference with global nitrogen and phosphorous cycles, ozone depletion, global freshwater use, land system change, atmospheric aerosol loading and chemical pollution.

For each process, the team identified a 'zone of uncertainty' and a 'danger zone'. Crossing over these thresholds could mean 'non-linear, possibly abrupt and irreversible earth system responses' with disastrous consequences for society, the research said.

An update of the work in 2015 found that four of these planetary boundaries had already been crossed. Biodiversity loss, damage to phosphorous and nitrogen cycles, climate change and land use have all slid into or beyond the 'uncertainty zone' (Steffen et al, 2015). Virtually none of this was picked up by the original *Limits to Growth* report.

Climate change

In 1972, the MIT team referred only in passing to the potential impacts of global climate change, concentrating mostly on the local warming effects from burning fossil fuels. Forty years later, climate change is recognised as one of the pre-eminent environmental threats in the world. Scientific evidence gathered by the Intergovernmental Panel on Climate Change (IPCC) suggests that humanity is already in 'overshoot' on our carbon emissions (IPCC, 2014).

In 2015, carbon dioxide levels hit 400 parts per million (ppm). The last time levels were this high was more than a million years ago (NASA, 2015; NOAA, 2015). Humans are pumping carbon into the atmosphere at a rate higher than any point in the last 66 million years – and the effects are being felt (Zeebe et al, 2016). 2015 was the warmest year on record and the first year that temperatures rose 1°C above pre-industrial levels (Met Office, 2016).

The Stockholm researchers set a concentration of 350 parts per million (ppm) of carbon dioxide in the atmosphere as one of the boundaries for climate change (Rockström et al, 2009). This is partially as a result of paleoclimatic data suggesting large polar ice sheets are at risk of collapse at higher carbon dioxide concentrations (Hansen et al, 2008). It is roughly consistent with a temperature rise of 1.5°C above pre–industrial levels.

At the 21st Conference of the Parties to the Climate Change Convention, in Paris in December 2015, the international community agreed to 'pursue efforts' to limit temperature rise to no more than 1.5°C above the pre-industrial average, in order to prevent the dangerous effects of climate change (UNFCCC, 2015).

The challenge of this task is quite extraordinary. The IPCC has identified a range of 'carbon budgets' which define the maximum amount of carbon dioxide that can be emitted for any given likelihood of remaining below a given temperature rise (IPCC, 2014; Schaeffer et al, 2015).

There is a range of estimates of how long it would take us to use up those budgets, if the level of annual emissions were to remain as it is today. To have a two thirds chance of limiting global temperature rise to less than 1.5°C, the available carbon budget would last a maximum of two decades and possibly as little as four years (Carbon Brief, 2017; Millar et al, 2017).

Biodiversity

The term 'biodiversity' – meaning the diversity of plants and animals on the planet – was first used in a publication by biologist E.O. Wilson in 1988. In the same book, Wilson concluded that the extinction rate for the world's species was at that time already 'about 1,000 to 10,000 times more than before human intervention' (Wilson, 1988).

The diversity of vertebrates – which includes mammals, birds, reptiles, amphibians and fish – has declined by 52% in the four decades since *Limits to Growth* was published, according to conservation organisation World Wide Fund For Nature (WWF). The greatest decline was in freshwater species, where the populations WWF monitored for its 'Living Planet Report' declined by three quarters (76%) between 1970 and 2010. Species are affected by habitat loss and degradation and exploitation through hunting and fishing.

WWF calculates that 1.5 earths would be required to meet the demands humanity makes on nature each year. The 'overshoot' is possible because – for now – humanity can destroy forests faster than they grow again, harvest more fish than will be replaced or emit more carbon than the forests or oceans can absorb again. In the long term, however, this is unsustainable, because natural systems cannot renew themselves (WWF, 2014).

Nitrogen and phosphorous

Artificial fertiliser converts nitrogen from the air into a reactive form that plants need to grow. The development of artificial fertiliser has dramatically increased agricultural yields, but excessive nitrogen pollution from fertiliser is upsetting the balance of ecosystems and the global cycle of this element. Phosphorous is also a key element in the soil, critical to food production. According to the planetary boundaries analysis, both of these elements have moved beyond the 'uncertainty zone' and into the 'high risk' zone.

Land use

The amount of land we are converting from one use to another – for example by destroying forests – has also reached a point where it is in the 'uncertainty zone'. This means it also poses a risk to the global climate (Steffen et al, 2015).

Humanity has changed the natural environment so profoundly that we may have created a new – and far more unpredictable – geological epoch, according to recent research. The relatively stable environment of the Holocene, an interglacial period that began about 10,000 years ago, has provided the conditions for human societies to develop and thrive. Now, however, the world has entered a new era known as the Anthropocene, where the activities of humans are the dominant influence on the atmosphere and environment (Lewis and Maslin 2015).

Hundreds of papers have now been published on the Anthropocene. In 2016 an official expert group of scientists recommended to the International Geological Congress that a new geological epoch be formally declared (Carrington, 2016; PhysOrg, 2016).

Responding to the Limits

It is clear enough from this analysis that the economy cannot realistically countenance much more in the way of material growth. Even if more optimistic assumptions about resource availability are adopted, our proximity to several key 'planetary boundaries' is troubling. This is most obviously the case for climate change.

Economic growth is not, however, the same thing as growth in carbon emissions, or growth in the consumption of resources. Economic output is measured in dollars. Material throughput is measured in tonnes. It is clearly sometimes possible to 'decouple' growth in dollars from growth in physical throughputs and environmental impacts.

Between 1980 and 2008, for example, the intensity of material use (per dollar of economic activity) fell by 42% across OECD member countries, and per capita consumption fell by 1.5% over the same period (OECD, 2011).

Since 2014, carbon emissions from burning fossil fuels and industry have flattened, while GDP has increased by around 3.1% to 3.4% a year. This was partly as a result of a global economic slowdown, but also as a result of a shift away from coal and towards renewables – particularly in China (Wales, 2015; IEA, 2017). Across the world, renewables are now being built faster than fossil fuels. Interestingly, the transition to clean energy has largely been taking place faster in poor countries than rich ones (Bloomberg New Energy Finance, 2015; Climatescope, 2015).

This kind of evidence has led the IEA, for example, to argue that greenhouse gas emissions are now 'decoupling from economic growth' (IEA, 2016b). Other commentators have been even more optimistic. 'To the degree to which there are fixed physical boundaries to human consumption,' claims a recently published *Ecomodernist Manifesto*, 'they are so theoretical as to be functionally irrelevant.' (Ecomodernist Manifesto, 2015)

Some argue that we can decouple material throughput from economic output indefinitely, and continue to do so, however much the economy expands. This position is characterised by concepts such as 'green growth', 'clean growth' and 'sustainable growth' and is arguably the dominant response to the *Limits* debate in recent years (NCE, 2014; Krugman, 2014; Füchs, 2015). At its most optimistic it portrays a comforting conclusion that economic growth can continue forever (Harford, 2014).

There are clearly some technological avenues that promise a more efficient, less material society. Digitisation, artificial intelligence and robotisation seem poised to make extraordinary changes both on our working lives and on our lifestyles (EuroCase, 2013).

But assessing the material and environmental impacts of these changes is complex. In the first place, it is essential to distinguish between what is called relative decoupling – a decline in the material intensity of economic output – and absolute decoupling – an absolute fall in material use or emissions. Much of what is celebrated as decoupling is relative rather than absolute decoupling. And where absolute decoupling does occur, it has so far been relatively minor.

There are some clear reasons for this. One of them is that making things more efficient (relative decoupling) tends to make them cheaper and this encourages us to use more of them. This phenomenon is called the 'rebound effect'. Our attempt to reduce consumption or emissions can sometimes even have the perverse effect of increasing them – an effect known as 'backlash' (Sorrell, 2010; Chitnis et al, 2014).

Another difficulty arises from the 'permeability' of trade boundaries. The 'footprint' from our material lives often falls outside the national boundary. Apparent dematerialisation in advanced nations is sometimes just the result of failing to account for the impacts of the production which occur in other countries.

For example, the domestic material consumption measured across the OECD between 1980 and 2008 left out any account of the raw material extraction associated with the manufacture of imported finished and semi-finished goods. Once the inputs from other countries are added in, the 'material footprint' of the OECD nations as a whole rose by almost 50% between 1990 and 2008, according to two studies published in 2015 (Wiedmann et al, 2015; UNEP, 2015).

Similar reservations apply in the climate change debate. Carbon emissions are usually measured on a territorial basis, allowing rich countries to 'export' their emissions elsewhere. This partially explains why, in the first decade of this century, the emissions of emerging economies like China and India increased at such a rapid rate, while those in advanced economies stabilised or declined.

The stabilisation of emissions observed over the past three years has occurred globally, not just in one region. But it is clear that if economic growth continues at predicted rates, the task of fully decoupling emissions from growth is a ferociously difficult one. Since the middle of the 20th century, the global economy has expanded at around 3.65% each year. If it were to continue to expand at the same rate, it would be more than 200 times bigger in 2100 than it was in 1950 (Jackson, 2017).

A world in which everyone around the world achieved the level of affluence currently expected in the west would mean global economic output growing by 30 times by the end of 2100, related to current levels. Meeting carbon targets in such a world would demand quite astonishing rates of decoupling – much higher than anything that has been observed historically (Jackson, 2017).

The heroic nature of conventional assumptions that growth can continue indefinitely without reaching overshoot and collapse has prompted a different kind of reaction to the *Limits* debate. Writing in 1977, former World Bank economist Herman Daly argued that society should move towards a 'steady state economy' (Daly, 1977).

Daly took his inspiration from some surprising sources. As early as 1848, one of the founders of classical economics, John Stuart Mill, had already written of a 'stationary state of population and capital'. He also argued that there would be 'as much scope as ever for all kinds of mental culture, and moral and social progress' within such a stationary state (Mill, 1848).

The idea that economic and material growth is not the same thing as social progress has inspired a wide range of responses to the challenge of *Limits*. Writing in 2015, Pope Francis argued that 'the time has come to accept decreased growth in some parts of the world, in order to provide resources for other places to experience healthy growth' (Pope Francis, 2015)

This call has much in common with the 'degrowth' movement, which has argued that we should aim to simplify lifestyles and reduce material dependencies, irrespective of the impact on conventionally measured growth (D'Alisa et al, 2014; Demaria et al, 2013; Fournier, 2008; Kallis, 2015)

In the words of its proponents, degrowth is a 'missile concept' designed to 'open up a debate silenced by the 'sustainable development' consensus'. It is about 'imagining and enacting alternative visions to modern growth-based development'. Several grassroots movements, most notably the Transition Town movement, have adopted similar ideas (Bardi, 2014; Coke, 2014).

Policy and media have not yet given much credence to these ideas. They are clearly challenging to an economics built around assumptions of continued exponential growth (Jackson, 2017). But in the wake of the financial crisis, degrowth has emerged as a critical challenge to the mainstream orthodoxy.

One of the most frequently encountered objections to degrowth is that it does not offer enough of a positive vision. The terminology of green growth suggests (perhaps falsely) that we can continue to flourish. The terminology of degrowth intimates some kind of decline. 'Instead of a degrowth campaign, I would urge us to develop together a positive narrative,' writes the current Club of Rome Co-Chair, Anders Wijkman, 'where growth and development are discussed in qualitative rather than quantitative terms.' (Wijkman, 2015)

Within the degrowth movement, and indeed outside it, a variety of more positive visions for development do already exist. Some of these are framed around the idea of prosperity. Others are framed around our ability to 'flourish within limits'. Debates about wellbeing and quality of life also contribute to this call for positive narratives (Jackson, 2017; Jørgensen et al, 2015; Raworth, 2012; Skidelsky and Skidelsky, 2013; Victor, 2008).

Some elements within these narratives have considerable traction on both sides of the debate. Addressing social justice, reducing resource dependency, increasing material efficiency, protecting social welfare, investing in low carbon technologies and infrastructures: all of these strategies have a wide appeal.

The key remaining difference between degrowth and green growth is whether or not a strategy of economic growth, as conventionally measured by the GDP, can get us there. Fascinatingly, this may turn out to be a purely academic difference. Secular trends suggest that growth itself may already be declining.

Is economic growth over?

Described by the BBC in 2015 as 'probably the biggest and most important controversy in macroeconomics today', the idea of 'secular stagnation' was first put forward in the 1930s (Weldon, 2015). Economist Alvin Hansen argued that in the wake of the Great Depression, US growth may have stopped permanently (Hansen, 1939).

A subsequent world war and population boom quickly proved Hansen wrong, and the term was forgotten. But at an IMF conference in 2013, former US Treasury secretary Larry Summers suggested it might be time to revive the concept (Summers, 2013). After the 2007–08 financial crisis, Summers argued, the economies of developed countries were failing to recover to their previous levels – and show no prospect of doing so (Summers, 2014).

Summers theorises that from the late 1990s or early 2000s, economic growth in the USA was reliant on a series of financial bubbles – particularly in housing – and a huge expansion of private debt. This generated enough investment and employment to keep growth going, he says, but it was unsustainable. In the aftermath of the crisis, as businesses, households and governments seek to reduce their level of debt, the long-term weakness of the system is becoming visible (Summers, 2015).

This idea is controversial, but no fringe theory. It has prompted debate between Summers, former Federal Reserve chairman Ben Bernanke and Nobel Prize winner Paul Krugman (Weldon, 2015). In 2014, Summers and then UK shadow chancellor Ed Balls co-chaired a commission to explore the idea in depth (Summers and Balls, 2015).

Modelling shows the idea of being 'mired in a recession forever' is possible (Eggertson and Merhrotra, 2014). Although Summers applied the idea to the US, he suggests the 'spectre of secular stagnation' is greater in Europe and Japan (Bernanke, 2015a).

Economist Robert Gordon goes a step further. His 2012 paper 'Is US growth over?' puts forward the 'audacious idea' that rapid economic growth was a one-off event in human history, now coming to an end (Gordon, 2012, 2016)

Before 1750, Gordon points out, there was virtually no economic growth at all. The invention of steam and railroads created a slight increase in living standards from around 1750 to 1830. The USA's second industrial revolution took place as a result of the invention of electricity, the internal combustion engine and indoor plumbing between 1870 to 1900. It drove rapid increases in productivity – in particular, in labour productivity – which continued into the middle of the 20th century.

The third revolution – in computers, the internet and mobile phones – had early benefits, removing the need for repetitive and clerical labour from the 1970s and 1980s onwards. But inventions since 2000 have centred on entertainment and communication devices, altering society but not fundamentally improving working or living standards in the way that electric light, motor cars or indoor plumbing did (Gordon, 2016)

Combined with six 'deflationary headwinds', including an ageing population, rising inequality, and the 'overhang' of consumer and government debt, this slowing down of productivity growth could well account for decline in growth in the USA and elsewhere.

Gordon's analysis comes from a US perspective. The picture for the UK is even more striking (Figure 13.2). A phenomenal slowdown in productivity growth has occurred in just half a century. The trend growth rate rose from less than 1% per year in 1900 to reach 4% per year in 1966. It declined sharply past that point. Digital and information technology slowed (but did not reverse) the decline through the 1980s and 1990s.

Soon after the bursting of the 'dot com' bubble at the turn of the millennium, and long before the financial crisis, the decline began to accelerate. By 2013 trend labour productivity growth was negative. The amount of output produced in each hour of work is currently declining in the UK. The implications for economic growth are profound. In these circumstances, per capita growth is only possible by increasing the labour force or by having everyone work longer hours.

Not all economists accept that the culprit is falling productivity growth (Bernanke, 2015b). At the global level, the economic slowdown is clearly being driven by a variety of changes – not least a change of policy in China – to move away from an export economy and to increase domestic goods and services (Allen, 2015). Nonetheless, it seems relatively clear that, in the advanced economies at least, economic growth is experiencing the law of diminishing returns.

Figure 13.2 The rise and fall of UK labour productivity growth

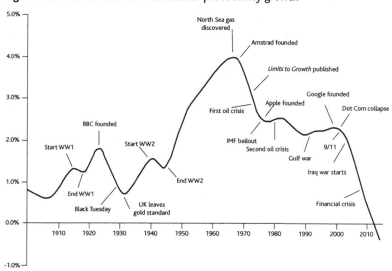

Note: Trend line estimated using the Hodrick-Prescott (HP) filter with the multiplier λ set to 100. Source: Bank of England data (from Hills et al, 2015)

Resource limits and planetary boundaries aside, these factors offer a very real possibility that, as Gordon (2016) puts it, 'future economic growth may gradually sputter out'. In these circumstances, of course, there is an absolute premium on any strategy that will help us to protect human welfare and deliver social progress.

Conclusions

More than four decades after the Club of Rome published its controversial landmark report, debates about the *Limits to Growth* still thrive. These debates remain a vital element in understanding the challenges of economic progress in the 21st century.

If the Club of Rome's projections are right, then the next few decades are decisive. There is unsettling evidence that society is tracking the 'standard run' of the original study – which leads ultimately to collapse. Detailed and recent analyses suggest that production peaks for some key resources may only be decades away.

The evidence of our proximity to planetary boundaries is even more striking. 'Even before we run out of oil,' argues climate change activist Bill McKibben, 'we're running out of planet' (McKibben, 2007). Meeting the Paris Agreement on climate change alone means a radical transformation of our investment portfolios, our technologies and our consumption patterns.

Responses to the *Limits* debate still remain tantalisingly poised between the pessimism of resource constraints and the optimism of technological progress. Kenneth Boulding's warning of the 'madness' of endless exponential growth (cited at the top of this chapter) still resonates. But Ronald Reagan's appeal to human ingenuity is not without foundations. Human creativity has provided for enormous social progress in the space of just a few centuries.

The economy itself is a product both of physical (and therefore limited) processes and of creative (and therefore unlimited) ones. Figuring out an institutional and social balance between the limited and the unlimited is a key challenge for modernity. But this clearly does not mean allowing business-as-usual assumptions about economic growth free rein. The lessons of the original report remain poignant.

Perhaps most striking among those lessons are the dynamics of overshoot and collapse. One of the most important of these dynamics is that collapse comes not from the absolute exhaustion of resources but from a simple and inevitable decline in resource quality. Given that this decline is already visible for many resources, prudency dictates that we take these dynamics seriously.

Another critical lesson from the original report is about the speed and timing of overshoot and collapse. At the point at which peaks in production become obvious and declines are imminent, our options are much more limited than they are while growth is still in progress.

This is sometimes called the Seneca effect. The Roman philosopher Lucius Annaeus Seneca once wrote to his friend Lucilius that 'increases are of sluggish growth, but the way to ruin is rapid' (cited in Bardi, 2014). The critical point is that collapse is a more or less uncontrollable process. Prudency resides in taking action early to transform technological systems, economic institutions and lifestyles. An early policy response matters.

This early response remains conspicuous by its absence, particularly in policy, even 40 years after the Club of Rome's clear warning. Many business leaders are now openly preparing for a world of resource constraints (for example, Jones et al, 2013). But governments are still reticent to think beyond the short term. The demands of *Limits to Growth* suggest an urgent need for policymakers and politicians to take a longer-term perspective: not just on urgent challenges such as climate change but also on resource horizons which are at best a few generations away.

There is another vital issue raised by the *Limits to Growth* debate: namely its implications for social justice. Most of the overshoot, as Anders Wijkman has pointed out, is due to 'wasteful lifestyles in industrialized countries. Poverty is still rampant—more than 3 billion people live on less than 2 US dollars a day' (Wijkman, 2015).

An interesting avenue of progress arises from the body of evidence which suggests that there are also social limits to growth (Hirsch, 1995 [1977]). In the advanced economies at least, economic growth shows diminishing returns in terms of happiness and wellbeing. In some cases, economic expansion undermines the quality of life. This evidence offers the tantalising possibility – reflected by John Stuart Mill's remarks on moral and social progress – that it may be possible to live better and yet to consume less. Limits to growth offer both challenges and opportunities (Inglehart et al, 2008; Jackson, 2009, 2017; Skidelsky and Skidelsky, 2013; Layard, 2005; Blewitt and Cunningham, 2015).

Visions for prosperity which provide the capabilities for everyone to flourish, while society as a whole remains within the safe operating space of the planet are clearly at a premium here. A number of such visions already exist. Developing and operationalising them is vital.

In summary, it is possible to distil a number of key issues which could usefully inform political debate and provide the foundations for an ongoing work programme on the limits to growth. These certainly include the following:

- the economic implications of declining resource quality;
- the financial market implications of low carbon investment strategies;
- the political implications of the need for precautionary, long-term thinking;
- the social implications of inequality in the distribution of available resources;
- the macroeconomic implications of secular stagnation or degrowth.

Perhaps the most important priority of all is to ensure that the *Limits* debate does not become mired in ideological conflict or sidelined by political intractability. The consequences for society as a whole are too important.

References

Alberta Energy (2017) 'Facts and Statistics', www.energy.alberta.ca/oilsands/791.asp

Allen, K. (2015) 'Why is China's stock market in crisis?' *Guardian*, 8 July, www.theguardian.com/business/2015/jul/08/china-stock-market-crisis-explained

Arthur, A. (2015) 'Can Canada's oil sands survive low oil prices?' Christian Science Monitor, 16 September, www.csmonitor.com/Environment/Energy-Voices/2015/0916/Can-Canada-s-oil-sands-survive-low-oil-prices

Bardi, U. (2014) *Extracted: how the quest for mineral wealth is plundering the planet*, White River Junction, VT: Chelsea Green Publishing.

Bernanke, B. (2015a) 'On secular stagnation: Larry Summers responds to Ben Bernanke', 1 April, www.brookings.edu/blogs/ben-bernanke/posts/2015/04/01-larry-summers-response

Bernanke, B. (2015b) 'Why are interest rates so low, part 3: the global savings glut', 1 April, www.brookings.edu/blogs/ben-bernanke/posts/2015/04/01-why-interest-rates-low-global-savings-glut

Blewitt, J. and R. Cunningham (eds) (2015) *The Post-Growth Project: How the End of Economic Growth Could Bring a Fairer and Happier Society*, London: London Publishing Partnership.

Bloomberg New Energy Finance (2015) 'Fossil fuels just lost the race against renewables', 14 April, www.bloomberg.com/news/articles/2015-04-14/fossil-fuels-just-lost-the-race-against-renewables

Boulding, K. (1973) *United States Congress. Energy reorganization act of 1973: Hearings, Ninety-third Congress, first session, on H.R. 11510*, Washington, DC: US Government.

Carbon Brief (2017) 'Analysis: Just four years left of the 1.5C carbon budget', 5 April, www.carbonbrief.org/analysis-four-years-left-one-point-five-carbon-budget

Carrington, D. (2016) 'The Anthropocene epoch: scientists declare dawn of human-influenced age', *Guardian*, 29 August, www.theguardian.com/environment/2016/aug/29/declare-anthropocene-epoch-experts-urge-geological-congress-human-impact-earth

Chitnis, M., S. Sorrel, A. Druckman, S. Firth and T. Jackson (2014) 'Who rebounds most? Estimating direct and indirect rebound effects for different UK socioeconomic groups', *Ecological Economics* 106: 12–32.

Climatescope (2015) 'The clean energy competitiveness index', http://global-climatescope.org/en/download/

Club of Rome (2017) 'History of the Club of Rome', www.clubofrome.org/about-us/history/

Coke, A. (2014) 'Where do we go from here? Transition strategies for a low carbon future', PASSAGE Working Paper 14-03, Guildford: University of Surrey, www.prosperitas.org.uk/assets/wp_14-03_acoke-transition-strategies.pdf

Crooks, E. (2016) 'Investment in Canadian oil and gas to be further slashed', *Financial Times*, 15 January, www.ft.com/content/91fe0582-c388-11e5-b3b1-7b2481276e45

D'Alisa, G., F. Damaria and G. Kallis (eds) (2014) *Degrowth: a vocabulary for a new era*, London: Routledge.

Daly, H. (1977) *Steady-State Economics*, New York: W H Freeman and Co Ltd.

Demaria, F., F. Schneider, F. Sekulova and J. Martinez-Alier (2013) 'What is degrowth? From an activist slogan to a social movement', *Environmental Values* 22(2): 191–215.

Dryzek, J.S. (2008) 'The ecological crisis of the welfare state', JESP symposium: climate change and social policy, *Journal of European Social Policy* 18(4): 334–7.

Ecomodernist Manifesto (2015) www.ecomodernism.org/manifesto-english/

Energy Information Administration (2015) 'Brazil – international energy data and analysis', www.eia.gov/beta/international/analysis_includes/countries_long/Brazil/brazil.pdf

Eggertson, G. and N. Merhrotra (2014) 'A model of secular stagnation', LSE Seminar papers, http://cep.lse.ac.uk/seminarpapers/20-05-14-GE.pdf

Eurocase (2013) 'Transforming Manufacturing: A path to a Smart, Sustainable and Inclusive growth in Europe', EuroCASE Policy Paper, www.euro-case.org/images/stories/pdf/position-paper/Euro-CASE_paper-on-Transforming-manufacturing.pdf

Fournier, V. (2008) 'Escaping from the economy: the politics of degrowth', *International Journal of Sociology and Social Policy* 28(11/12): 528–45.

Füchs, R. (2015) *Green Growth, Smart Growth: A New Approach to Economics, Innovation and the Environment*, London and New York: Anthem Press.

Gough, I. (2016) Welfare states and environmental states: a comparative analysis, *Environmental Politics* 25(1): 24–47.

Gordon, R. (2016) *The Rise and Fall of American Growth: The U.S. Standard of Living since the Civil War*, Princeton: Princeton University Press.

Gordon, R. (2012) 'Is US economic growth over? Faltering innovation confronts the six headwinds', National Bureau of Economic Research: Working Paper 18315, www.nber.org/papers/w18315.pdf

Hall, C. and J. Day (2009) 'Revisiting the Limits to Growth after peak oil', *American Scientist* 97: 230–7, www.esf.edu/efb/hall/2009-05Hall0327.pdf

Hall, C., J. Lambert and S. Balogh (2014) 'EROI of different fuels and the implications for society', *Energy Policy* 64: 141–52, www.sciencedirect.com/science/article/pii/S0301421513003856

Hansen, A. (1939) 'Economic progress and declining population growth', *The American Economic Review* 29(1): 1–15, www.jstor.org/stable/1806983

Hansen, J., M. Sato, P. Kharecha, D. Beerling, R. Berner, V. Masson-Delmotte, M. Pagani, M. Raymo, D.L. Royer, and J.C. Zachos. (2008) 'Target atmospheric CO_2: where should humanity aim?' *Open Atmospheric Science Journal* 2: 217–31, www.columbia.edu/~jeh1/2008/TargetCO2_20080407.pdf

Harford, T. (2014) 'Can economic growth continue forever? Of course!' Freakonomics, http://freakonomics.com/2014/01/24/can-economic-growth-continue-forever-of-course/

Hills, S., R. Thomas and N. Dimsdale (2015) *Three Centuries of Data – Version 2.2*, London: Bank of England, www.bankofengland.co.uk/publications/Documents/quarterlybulletin/threecenturiesofdata.xls

Hirsch, F. (1995 [1977]) *Social Limits to Growth*, Revised edition, London and New York: Routledge.

Hubbert, M.K. (1962) 'Energy Resources: a report to the committee on natural resources', National Academy of Sciences: National Research Council, Publication 1000-D, www.hubbertpeak.com/hubbert/energyresources.pdf

IEA (International Energy Agency) (2008) *World Energy Outlook*, www.worldenergyoutlook.org/media/weowebsite/2008-1994/weo2008.pdf

IEA (2016a) *Medium-term oil market report 2016: overview*, www.iea.org/Textbase/npsum/MTOMR2016sum.pdf

IEA (2016b) 'Decoupling of global emissions and economic growth confirmed', 16 March, www.iea.org/newsroomandevents/pressreleases/2016/march/decoupling-of-global-emissions-and-economic-growth-confirmed.html

IEA (2017) 'IEA finds CO_2 emissions flat for third straight year even as global economy grew in 2016', 17 March, www.iea.org/newsroom/news/2017/march/iea-finds-co2-emissions-flat-for-third-straight-year-even-as-global-economy-grew.html

Inglehart, R., R. Foa, C. Peterson and C. Welzel (2008) 'Development, Freedom and Rising Happiness: a global perspective (1981-2007)', *Perspectives on Psychological Science*, 3(4): 264–85.

IPCC (2014) *Summary for policymakers. Working group III*, www.ipcc.ch/pdf/assessment-report/ar5/wg3/ipcc_wg3_ar5_summary-for-policymakers.pdf

Jackson, T. (2009) *Prosperity without Growth – economics for a finite planet*, London: Earthscan.

Jackson, T. (2017) *Prosperity without Growth – foundations for the economy of tomorrow*, 2nd edition, London: Routledge.

Jones, A., I. Allen, N. Silver, C. Cameron, C. Howarth and B. Caldecott (2013) 'Resource constraints: sharing a finite world Implications of Limits to Growth for the Actuarial Profession', A Report to the Institute and Faculty of Actuaries, www.actuaries.org.uk/sites/default/files/documents/pdf/resourceioareport-print-copy.pdf

Jørgensen, S., B. Fath, S. Nors Nielsen, F. Pulselli, D. Fiscus and S. Bastianoni (2015) *Flourishing within limits to growth*, London: Routledge.

Kallis, G. (2015) 'The Degrowth Alternative', Essay for the Great Transition Initiative, www.greattransition.org/publication/the-degrowth-alternative

Krugman, P. (2014) 'Could fighting global warming be cheap and free?' *New York Times*, 18 September, www.nytimes.com/2014/09/19/opinion/paul-krugman-could-fighting-global-warming-be-cheap-and-free.html

Layard, R. (2005) *Happiness*, London: Penguin.

Lewis, S. and M. Maslin (2015) 'Defining the Anthropocene', *Nature* 519: 171–80.

Macalister, T. and G. Monbiot (2008) 'Global energy supply will peak in 2020, says energy agency', *The Guardian*, 15 December, www.theguardian.com/business/2008/dec/15/global-oil-supply-peak-2020-prediction

Maugeri, L. (2012) 'Oil: the next revolution. The unprecedented surge of oil production capacity and what it means for the world', Harvard Kennedy School, Geopolitics of Oil Project, Discussion paper 2012-10.

McKibben, B. (2007) *Deep Economy: the wealth of communities and the durable future*, New York, NY: Henry Holt and Company.

Meadows, D., D. Meadows, J. Randers and W. Behrens III (1972) *The Limits to Growth*, Club of Rome, New York, NY: Universe Books.

Meadows, D., J. Randers and D. Meadows (2004) *Limits to Growth: the thirty year update*, London: Earthscan.

Met Office (2016) '2015: the warmest year on record, say scientists', 20 January, www.metoffice.gov.uk/news/releases/archive/2016/2015-global-temperature

Mill, J.S. (1848) *Principles of Political Economy with some of their Applications to Social Philosophy*. Book IV, Chapter VI 'Of the Stationary State'. London: Longman's Green and Co.

Miller, B. and Sorrell, S. (2013) 'The future of oil supply', *Philosophical Transactions of the Royal Society A* 372(206), http://rsta.royalsocietypublishing.org/content/372/2006/20130179

Millar, R., J. Fuglestvedt, P. Friedlingstein, J. Rogelj, M. Grubb, H.D. Matthews, R. Skeie, P. Forster, D. Frame and M. Allen (2017) 'Emission budgets and pathways consistent with limiting warming to 1.5°C', *Nature Geoscience*, 10: 741–47, Doi:10.1038/ngio3031.

Mohr, W., J. Wang, G. Ellem, J. Ward and D. Giurco (2015) 'Projection of fossil fuels by country', *Fuel* 141: 120–35.

NASA (2015) 'NASA scientists react to 400ppm milestone', 21 May, http://climate.nasa.gov/400ppmquotes/

NCE (2014) *Better Growth, Better Climate*, The New Climate Economy Report, The Synthesis Report, Global Commission on the Economy and the Climate, Washington, DC: World Resources Institute, http://2014.newclimateeconomy.report/wp-content/uploads/2014/08/BetterGrowth-BetterClimate_NCE_Synthesis-Report_web.pdf

Neumayer, E. (2000) 'Scarce or abundant? The economics of natural resource availability', *Journal of Economic Surveys* 14(3): 307–35.

National Oceanic and Atmospheric Administration (NOAA) (2015) 'Greenhouse benchmark reached', 6 May, http://research.noaa.gov/News/NewsArchive/LatestNews/TabId/684/ArtMID/1768/ArticleID/11153/Greenhouse-gas-benchmark-reached-.aspx

OECD (2011) *Resource Productivity in the G8 and the OECD*, Paris: Organization for Economic Cooperation and Development, www.oecd.org/env/waste/47944428.pdf

OilPrice.com (2017) 'Crude Oil Brent – Monthly OHLC Chart', http://oilprice.com/commodity-price-charts

Pasqualino, R., A. Jones, I. Monasterolo and A. Phillips (2015) 'Understanding Global Systems Today—A Calibration of the World3 Model between 1995 and 2012', *Sustainability* 7(8): 9864–89.

PhysOrg (2016) 'The Anthropocene is here: scientists', 29 August, https://phys.org/news/2016-08-anthropocene-scientists.html

Pope Francis (2015) 'Encyclical letter Laudato Si' of the Holy Father Francis on care for our common home', The Vatican, http://w2.vatican.va/content/francesco/en/encyclicals/documents/papa-francesco_20150524_enciclica-laudato-si.html

Radzicki, M., and Taylor, R. (2008) 'Origin of System Dynamics: Jay W. Forrester and the History of System Dynamics', in U.S. Department of Energy, 'Introduction to System Dynamics', www.systemdynamics.org/DL-IntroSysDyn/start.htm

Ragnarsdóttir, K.V. and H. Sverdrup (2015) 'Limits to Growth revisited', The Geological Society, www.geolsoc.org.uk/Geoscientist/Archive/October-2015/Limits-to-growth-revisited

Raworth, K. (2012) 'A safe and just space for humanity. Can we live within the doughnut?' Oxfam Discussion Paper, Oxford: Oxfam, www.oxfam.org/sites/www.oxfam.org/files/file_attachments/dp-a-safe-and-just-space-for-humanity-130212-en_5.pdf

Reagan, R. (1983) 'Remarks at Convocation Ceremonies at the University of South Carolina in Columbia', 20 September 1983, www.presidency.ucsb.edu/ws/?pid=40486

Rockström, J., W. Steffen, K. Noone, Å. Persson, F.S. Chapin, III, E. Lambin, T.M. Lenton, M. Scheffer, C. Folke, H. Schellnhuber, B. Nykvist, C.A. De Wit, T. Hughes, S. van der Leeuw, H. Rodhe, S. Sörlin, P.K. Snyder, R. Costanza, U. Svedin, M. Falkenmark, L. Karlberg, R.W. Corell, V.J. Fabry, J. Hansen, B. Walker, D. Liverman, K. Richardson, P. Crutzen, and J. Foley (2009) 'Planetary boundaries: exploring the safe operating space for humanity', *Ecology and Society* 4(2): 32.

Schaeffer, M., J. Rogelj, N. Roming, F. Sferra, B. Hare and O. Serdeczny (2015) 'Feasibility of limiting warming to 1.5C and 2°C', Climate Analytics, Briefing Note, http://climateanalytics.org/files/feasibility_1o5c_2c.pdf

Simmons, M. (2000) 'Revisiting The Limits to Growth: Could the Club of Rome have been correct, after all?' An energy white paper, www.mudcitypress.com/PDF/clubofrome.pdf

Sinn, H. W. (2008) 'Public policies against global warming', *International Tax and Public Finance* 15(4): 360–94.

Skidelsky, E. and Skidelsky, R. (2013) *How much is enough? Money and the Good Life*, London: Penguin.

Sorrell, S. (2010) 'Mapping Rebound Effects from Sustainable Behaviours: Key Concepts and Literature Review', Sussex Energy Group, SPRU, University of Sussex, Brighton.

Steffen, W., K. Richardson, J. Rockström, S. Cornell, I. Fetzer, E. Bennett, R. Biggs, S. Carpenter, W. Vries, C. de Wit, C. Folke, D. Gerten, J. Heinke, G. Mace, L. Persson, V. Ramanathan, B. Reyers and S. Sörlin (2015) 'Planetary boundaries: guiding human development on a changing planet', *Science* 347(6223), http://science.sciencemag.org/content/early/2015/01/14/science.1259855

Stiglitz, J. (2008) 'Scarcity in an age of plenty', *Guardian*, 15 June, www.theguardian.com/commentisfree/2008/jun/15/economics.food

Summers, L. (2013) 'IMF Fourteenth annual research lecture in honor of Stanley Fischer', 8 December, http://larrysummers.com/imf-fourteenth-annual-research-conference-in-honor-of-stanley-fischer/

Summers, L. (2014) 'US economic prospects: secular stagnation, hysteresis and the zero lower bound', *Business Economics* 49: 65–73.

Summers, L. (2015) 'On secular stagnation: a response to Bernanke', 1 April, http://larrysummers.com/2015/04/01/on-secular-stagnation-a-response-to-bernanke/

Summers, L. and Balls, E. (2015) 'Report of the Commission on Inclusive Prosperity', Center for American Progress, 15 January, www.americanprogress.org/issues/economy/report/2015/01/15/104266/report-of-the-commission-on-inclusive-prosperity/

Sverdrup, H., and K.V. Ragnarsdóttir (2014) 'Natural resources in a planetary perspective', *Geochemical Perspectives* 3(2), www.geochemicalperspectives.org/wp-content/uploads/2015/09/v3n2.pdf

Sverdrup, H., D. Koca and K.V. Ragnarsdóttir (2012) 'Peak metals, minerals, energy, wealth, food and population; urgent policy considerations for a sustainable society', *Journal of Environmental Science and Engineering* B 1.(5):499–533.

Taberner, P. (2017) 'Where Will Oil Prices Go This Year?' oilprice.com, 13 January, http://oilprice.com/Energy/Energy-General/Where-Will-Oil-Prices-Go-This-Year.html

Turner, G. (2008) 'A comparison of The Limits to Growth with 30 years of reality', *Global Environmental Change* 18: 397–411.

Turner, G. (2014) 'Is global collapse imminent?' Melbourne Sustainable Society Initiative, research paper no.4, Melbourne University.

UNFCCC (2015) 'Adoption of the Paris Agreement', United Nations Framework Convention on Climate Change, https://unfccc.int/resource/docs/2015/cop21/eng/l09.pdf

UNEP (2015) 'International Trade in Resources – a biophysical assessment', Paris: United Nations Environment Programme, www.resourcepanel.org/file/351/download?token=bGPFr8hN

Victor, P. (2008) *Managing without Growth: slower by design not by disaster*, Cheltenham: Edward Elgar.

Viner, B. (2013) 'Why the world isn't running out of oil', *Daily Telegraph*, 19 February, www.telegraph.co.uk/news/earth/energy/oil/9867659/Why-the-world-isnt-running-out-of-oil.html

Wales, K. (2015) 'Global greenhouse gas emissions set to fall in 2015', *Nature*, www.nature.com/news/global-greenhouse-gas-emissions-set-to-fall-in-2015-1.18965

Weldon, D. (2015) 'Why 'secular stagnation' matters', BBC News, 2 April, www.bbc.co.uk/news/business-32163541

Wiedmann, T., H. Schandl, M. Lenzen, D. Moran, Sangwon Suh, J. West and Keiichiro Kanemoto (2015) 'The Material Footprint of Nations', *Proceedings of the National Academy of Sciences* 112(20): 6271–6.

Wijkman, A. (2015) 'Commentary on the Degrowth Alternative', Great Transition Initiative, www.greattransition.org/commentary/anders-wijkman-the-degrowth-alternative-giorgos-kallis

Wile, R. (2013) 'Peak oil is dead', Business Insider, 29 March, www.businessinsider.com/death-of-peak-oil-2013-3?IR=T

Wilson, E.O. (1988) *BIodiversity*. Washington, DC: National Academy Press.

World Economic Forum (2014) *The future availability of natural resources: a new paradigm for global resource availability*, World Scenario Series, Geneva: WEF, www3.weforum.org/docs/WEF_FutureAvailabilityNaturalResources_Report_2014.pdf

World Economic Forum (2017) *The inclusive growth and development report 2017*, Geneva: WEF.

World Wide Fund For Nature (WWF) (2014) *Living Planet Report*, http://wwf.panda.org/about_our_earth/all_publications/living_planet_report/

Zeebe, R., A. Ridgwell and J. Zachos (2016) 'Anthropogenic carbon release rate unprecedented during the past 66 million years', *Nature Geoscience* 9: 325–9.

FOURTEEN

Conclusion: towards a new global social policy framework?

Paul Smyth and Christopher Deeming

Introduction

The origin of this book was our sense of a growing convergence between the leading edge social policy agenda of social investment and the development policy agenda of inclusive growth, especially among international organisations. This sense of convergence has been magnified hugely by the 2015 launch of the UN's 2030 Agenda on Sustainable Development which, as Koehler (2016) observes, was conceptualised as 'universal, in the sense of being applicable to all countries' meaning that 'the decades-old dichotomy of "developed" versus "under-developed" is cast aside'. As our contributed chapters suggest, the impetus for a new 'universal' whole world approach to social policy has come very much from the developing countries. There, often stellar growth rates have been accompanied by that explosion of social policy initiatives associated with inclusive growth; while in much of the OECD, the prospects for welfare reform through social investment remain constrained by austerity economics. But in spite of their very different origins and current policy challenges our volume concludes that social investment and inclusive growth do provide two key conceptual stepping stones towards a new universal global social policy framework in the making.

From the outset we observe just how relatively recent and dynamic has been the development of the two policy approaches. As Anton Hemrijck reminds us in Chapter Two, at the turn of the century social investment was little more than a 'metaphorical' gesture towards the productive value of social policy while by now it has become a systematic and fundamental rethink of the role of social policy in responding to the new social risks of the 21st century through social investment in human capital 'stocks' and 'flows', with the 'buffers' of social security. It has quite radically refocused policy attention away from a too exclusive emphasis on the role of taxes and transfers in moderating market inequalities to a focus on the role of social investment and services generally in enabling citizens to realise their capabilities amid the various 'transitions' encountered across the life course, described by Jon Kvist in Chapter Nine. As Hemrijck rightly claims this is based on a robust multidimensional understanding of growth, or development that looks to more inclusive, less siloed, forms of governance and far more sophisticated forms of programme evaluation and analysis which can capture the complex benefits flowing from social investments. The challenge to the model – in Europe at least – has been the lack of a complementary 'grand economic theory' to displace neoliberal thought informing austerity economics. Reflecting perhaps its 'third way' origins, the social investment approach has been less a direct critique of the neoliberal economic model and more a renewal of the welfare system in response to the labour market, family and demographic changes of the preceding decades.

As Sarah Cook indicates in Chapter Three, the idea of inclusive growth is more recent and is part of a complex set of policy influences associated with the development of the UN 2030 Agenda. The concept of inclusive and sustainable development embraces more than inclusive growth and, indeed, problematises the goal of growth itself. Moreover, the differing constructions placed on inclusive growth or shared prosperity by key agencies such as the World Bank, the Asian Development Bank and the UN indicate that as yet its role still remains more 'metaphorical' than that of the now systematically developed social investment perspective in social policy. Nevertheless, we agree with de Haan (2015) that despite 'a certain degree of fad-ism' the idea remains important for progressive social policy development. Its importance for the future of global social policy is that it has provided an economic critique of the neoliberal economic model or Washington Consensus; a critique that has rapidly escalated into a new consensus among the international development agencies that market-led development is not pro-poor and too much inequality can be detrimental to sustainable growth. It is this foundation in economic policy which most differentiates inclusive growth from social investment.

Cook shows how the social policy implications of inclusive growth have begun to be elaborated. This involves a transformation from the residual, safety net approach to social policy of the Washington Consensus to 'universal', 'rights based' models of 'social protection' (Kabeer, 2014, 2015; Barrientos, 2016). Here, as Midgley suggests in Chapter Eleven, 'social protection' does not have the negative connotations of waste and dependency that it had acquired in the OECD countries in the neoliberal period. Protection is understood to involve state spending on education, health and welfare – all of which is designed to produce a more inclusive pattern of economic and social development. At the same time 'social protection' has been increasingly understood as about more than income maintenance and rather involving a multidimensional understanding of human development – and thus also requiring more integrated, inclusive forms of governance. To this extent it increasingly resembles the thematic structure of the social investment approach to social policy.

As we remarked earlier in this book it is not long since scholars bewailed the separate research worlds of social policy and development studies. From our chapters we can see just how rapidly the different worlds are converging. Economic transformations in the developing economies are bringing comparable social policy transformations and with that an increasingly shared policy universe with the mature welfare state nations. As developed and developing countries extricate themselves from their once common neoliberal policy environment and as the boundaries between developed and developing economies disappear it should only be expected that a common global social policy 'one world' framework will emerge. It is with that in mind that we have set the two policy perspectives of social investment and inclusive growth side by side in this book for the first time and here we conclude with some reflections on what our expert contributors have pointed to as key points for future dialogue. Following the structure of the book we begin with the more theoretical issues before moving to the more operational. Of the former we begin with the most vexed issue of how the relationship between economic and social policy is understood; followed by a reflection on what is meant by social policy as 'investment' and 'protection' and how the relationship between the two is to be conceived. This leads us to a reflection on Klasen's overview of the emerging science of definition and measurement of inclusive growth which frames our conclusions on the central role of social services in shaping the development process. Following Jenson's chapter we highlight the challenge this poses for more inclusive forms of governance before highlighting two of the biggest issues facing the new global social policy framework: the future of work and environmental sustainability.

Understandings of the relationship between economic and social policy

The biggest conundrum facing a new global social policy model is that, while both social investment and inclusive growth have emerged as policy designs for a post-neoliberal economic order, the transition from that order has been distinctly uneven. Economic neoliberalism remains very strong in the EU where the contradictions between a social investment approach in welfare and a neoliberal economic policy stance are stark. Meanwhile the inclusive growth approach is premised upon a post-neoliberal order. As Hibben (2016: 152) writes of the approach to inclusive growth at the IMF: the '2008 crisis delegitimised three decades of macroeconomic policy consensus that drew from monetarism, new classical economics, and New Keynesianism. This was supplanted by an ideological environment more open to Keynesian ideas supportive of countercyclical monetary and fiscal response' – including the role of social protection as an automatic fiscal stabiliser. However, as Cook observes in Chapter Three, this new premise is not always apparent in practice. How these macroeconomic policy questions are eventually settled remains of great importance for the future development of global social policy. Here we simply note some of the key similarities and differences in the way the social investment and inclusive growth models frame the relationship between economic and social policy.

For all its emphasis on the productive value of social policy, social investment has had a rather specific, carefully limited engagement with economic policy. At its turn of the century origin, neoclassical fundamentalism seemed well established in Europe in an era of continuous economic growth. The social policy challenge was seen less as showing that the economic model was flawed and more demonstrating how the free market approach in the economy might be made more compatible with a more 'inclusive society' through social investment. As Hemrijck shows in Chapter Two this lack of engagement with 'grand' economic theory has left it open to the charge of being a 'fair weather' agenda only. Nevertheless, as he points out, at the level of microeconomics there is now a robust empirical base for claims made for the productive value of welfare and social services. On the terrain of microeconomic reform, then, an excellent case has been made as to why social policy interventions are likely to produce better overall outcomes than would the neoliberal reliance on purely market mechanisms. The problem for the social investment approach then has rather been its silence in relation to other key economic issues. The European experience obviously highlights the importance of more flexible macroeconomic settings. But its rather exclusive focus on supply side factors also creates a silence on how markets might be managed to produce the broad-based, employment centred pattern of economic demand which the inclusive growth approach sees as the foundation of a sustainable social policy regime. Further its genesis pre-2008 meant that the economic problems created by inequality have not been such a priority issue. Overall then, the recovery of the productive value of social policy has been a very positive achievement of the social investment approach but one which does point to the need for greater integration into a broader policy framework geared to sustainability and economic development discussed by Tim Jackson and Robin Webster in Chapter Thirteen.

In thinking through such integration it is useful to reflect on the prehistory of social policy and economic thought. Most accounts place the welfare state within or, alongside, a Keynesian economic framework. While this can be useful shorthand it does overlook the fact that the post-war consensus in economics is more accurately understood as the 'neoclassical synthesis'. In this synthesis Keynesian theory was stripped of its more radical critique of neoclassical theory and its policy contribution confined to the macroeconomic policy settings necessary for full employment. Thus, a more flexible macroeconomic policy was justified to the extent of achieving full (male) employment but once that was achieved the economy was best left to work in terms of the neoclassical model. This meant that with the demise of Keynesian macroeconomic management in the 1980s there was no longer that flexible monetary and fiscal economic policy framework which had accommodated the rise of social spending in the welfare state and 'reform' became a matter of generalising neoclassical microeconomic reform across the entire economy. As Jordan (2006) noted, this left social welfare without any economic justification. This should remind us just how novel and important the kind of microeconomic analysis of social investment put forward in Hemericjk's chapter is for any future global policy framework.

This needs emphasis because, as both Midgley and Hemerijck discuss in this book, there remains considerable confusion within social policy scholarship around economic value being placed on social policies. There has been a tenacious view among some that social policy ought to be 'against' and not 'for' markets. We have recently shown how this can be linked to the ideological welfare wars of the 1970s and 1980s when the state and market were pitted against each other with a vanishing middle ground (Smyth and Deeming, 2016). By contrast for pre-welfare state thinkers like Tawney and Polanyi and even the classic welfare state theorists such as T.H. Marshall the equation was better thought of in terms of 'social policy and markets'. Here the welfare state was understood to rest on the foundation not of a pure market economy but rather a 'mixed economy' wherein welfare state social policies were complemented by an active economic state correcting for market failure, especially in the area of unemployment but also for unacceptable extremes of inequality. For social policy a key feature was the enlarged fiscal space created by the Keynesian model which allowed society scope to influence the pattern of economic development which otherwise would have been left to private decision making in the market.

For the development of a new coherent global social policy framework, then, it will be important to value not discard the rediscovery of the productive value of social policy in the social investment model. At the same time it will be necessary to link it to considerations of compatible macroeconomic policies as well as those economic policies designed to influence the kind of broad-based pattern of economic development proposed in the inclusive growth approach. In the latter approach there has not been that rather tortuous legacy of a welfare state period with which to contend and certainly social and economic thought today appears more ready to embrace a social policy *and* markets model. This has no doubt been facilitated by the fact that here it has been leading economists themselves who have helped critique neoliberalism (see Chapter One), thus creating a theoretical space for that new convergence of new economic and social policy thinking which characterises ideas about inclusive growth. First we illustrate this complementarity in economic policy before looking at the more distinctive social policy features of the inclusive development model.

The report on inclusive growth for the World Economic Forum by Samans et al (2015) was important in asking how to translate the emerging goal of inclusive growth into an operational framework. As might be anticipated, they present the challenge as one of growth not automatically translating into an 'end of poverty' and into a broad-based or societal 'prosperity' but often into excessive inequality, social discontent and issues of legitimation. So, how is inclusive growth to be achieved? Characteristically of this approach they emphasise that the policy instruments for achieving inclusion must go 'well beyond the two areas most commonly featured', namely education and redistribution. Rather they say the 'journey towards a new, more socially inclusive, growth paradigm' needs to focus on a wide range of social and economic institutions upon which a 'broad based advancement of living standards depends' (Samans et al, 2015: 7–8). Beyond the appropriate macroeconomic, trade and regulatory policy settings they propose seven 'pillars' as key to an inclusive development pattern. These are: education and skills; employment and labour compensation; asset building and entrepreneurship; financial intermediation of real economy investment; corruption and rents; basic services and infrastructure; and fiscal transfers. We do not reproduce these here as definitive but rather as an illustration of the economic approach to inclusion in which those factors which shape 'the distribution of opportunity and outcomes within the market' are seen to be as important for achieving social goals as the more traditional instruments of education and welfare. Indeed, these authors stress that 'the essential measure of the inclusiveness of a society's growth model is the extent to which it produces broad gains in living standards before fiscal transfers are taken into account' (Samans et al, 2015: 9). Here then appropriate economic management in what we used to term a 'mixed economy' re-emerges as an economic foundation of an inclusive social policy regime.

The inclusive growth economic model appeals to pragmatism and the importance of 'getting the institutions right' rather than to a new 'grand theory'. While this can be frustrating for those seeking to redefine the economic and social policy roles of government in a new global framework it should not disguise the fact that the agenda does imply a shift to a positive role for government intervention in the economy (North, 1990; World Bank, 1993; Rodrik et al, 2004; Acemoglu and Robinson, 2012). The report by Samans et al is representative of this view when it references a key body of 'institutional' economic theory which developed in response to the experience of the East Asian 'miracle' in the late 20th century and which emphasised the active roles of states in steering the pattern of economic growth. But it is here that we reach the limits of what the international organisations and agencies can contribute to the development of a global social policy. The question, 'what is an inclusive economic policy?' inevitably takes us to the heart of social policy itself. What kind of society is intended? How are social and economic goals to be balanced? What should be the roles of government, market and civil society? In pursuing these questions it is notable that the East Asian model – set out by Kwon in Chapter Four – has become a central focus not only for economists but also social policy scholars seeking to articulate the social dimension of inclusive growth in terms of a 'developmental welfare state model'.

There are two major points to be observed in Kwon's contribution. The first is the way we might begin to think of the social investment approach in terms of a developmental welfare state. Thus, Kwon begins his chapter with the observation that the very proposition that social policy might be considered an investment 'is not an entirely new idea'. He looks back to its origins in Bismarckian welfare before showing how it underpinned the early development of the South Korean 'developmental welfare state'. His account is especially relevant to the inclusive growth model's emphasis on establishing a broad-based pattern of economic development as the basis of a sustainable social policy regime. Thus, while states such as Korea were accused of 'subordinating welfare to the economy' they actually developed as highly egalitarian societies. He explains that this came about principally through what were considered the 'economic' policies of land redistribution together with public health and human capital investment. These were indeed 'economic' policies but they were egalitarian by design. And, we might add, the success of these policies required in turn a wider economic development strategy pursued by highly effective bureaucracies promoting industrialisation through industry policies, tax arrangements, state investments and so on. Today we might wonder at the way in which this 'productive' function of the East Asian welfare state model ever came to be regarded as novel, exceptional and outside the normal framing of comparative social policy in terms of 'social protection'.

Subsequent scholarship has queried how distinctive was the mix of 'productive' and 'protective' social policy in the East Asian regime; while, also showing how exceptional OCED thinking was in the late 20th century that social policy was only about protection (Goodin, 2001; Kuhnle and Hort, 2004; Hwang, 2011; Hudson and Kuhner, 2012, 2013; Smyth and Deeming, 2016). Nevertheless, unlike Europe and unlike Latin America, the East Asian countries – as Gyu-Jin Hwang (2011) writes – displayed a strong 'resilience against the powerful force of economic liberalization' maintaining a positive role for government in social policy and economic management. It is for this reason that a number of development studies scholars engaging with the welfare state literatures have turned to the idea of a 'developmental welfare state' as able to capture the economic as well as the social functions required of an inclusive development regime (Riesco, 2007; Lau and Mok, 2013; Koehler, 2014; Kwon and Koo, 2014). For social policy researchers recovering the productive value of the welfare state, it suggests the kinds of complementary linkages which need to be established with economic policy in any inclusive new global social policy framework.

While Kwon emphasises the productive value of the 'social investment' approach he is equally concerned to show how for growth to be inclusive there must also be a complementary, universal approach to 'social protection for citizens'. The limits of the so-called Bismarckian model of 'social investment' was the selective way in which social benefits were assigned to those who were of strategic importance for growth. In South Korea's transition to industrialisation, the social benefits went to the new industrial workforce while 'the poor, the disabled, the elderly and children were supposed to be taken care of by their families'. In that model, it was a case of the 'economy first'. The limits of the model became critical with the turn of the century Asian financial crisis leading to the transition to a universal rights based approach to social protection. This timing, he notes, makes an extraordinary contrast with the way in which in Europe the global financial crisis led rather to welfare austerity. In a variation on the theme of 'flexicurity', the South Korean move to universal protection was designed in part to facilitate major economic reforms including greater labour market flexibility. He concludes that 'the extension of the developmental welfare state made itself more inclusive but still developmental'. Kwon's account of the contemporary challenges facing South Korean social policy is quite similar to the new social risks scenario developed by Hemerijck as are the suite of policy responses proposed. What is most notable about the South Korean experience is the way which the productive and protective goals are seen as what Kwon calls a 'dual imperative for Korean society' rather than being a source of conflict as in Europe.

This idea of a 'dual imperative' might be seen as critical for bringing together the ideas of social investment and inclusive growth in a new global social policy framework. It is also a key concern in the chapters by Hemerijck and Midgley. As the former indicates, a strong counterpoint to the emergence of the 'social investment state' was criticism that it privileged the economy while subordinating or downgrading 'passive', or protective welfare. He shows that while there may have been some such tendency in the early developmental phase of the social investment approach today we find rather a strong emphasis on that 'virtuous circle' where protection supports investments and vice versa. Something of a reverse process is revealed in the case of the development literature. Thus, it is very noticeable that the social policy renaissance leading up to the UN2030 Agenda was carried out very much under the banner of 'social protection' and not social investment. This is a big story that cannot be taken up here but as we can see from Deacon's (2013) account of 'global social policy in the making' the idea of a universal, rights based 'Social Protection Floor' long galvanised United Nations focused reformers campaigning against the residual 'safety net' welfare models associated with the Washington Consensus at the World Bank and IMF.

But as Midgley shows us, here the term 'social protection' does not have the narrow connotation of 'taxes and transfers' and 'passive welfare' that it acquired in the mature welfare states. It certainly includes them but so also most of what the social investment approach would cover such as 'payments in mobilising human capital', matched savings accounts and micro insurance, labour market programmes, payments in mobilising human capital and fostering stability and inclusion in general. It can also include public employment programmes such as India's National Rural Employment Guarantee scheme. And while he acknowledges that his rejection of 'binary groupings' like protection versus investment will antagonise some, his chapter suggests to us that 'properly configured and effectively implemented' virtually everything we call 'social policy' can be both productive and protective.

What is important for the future development of a global social policy strategy is the way in which, in development policy, the UN 'social protection' agenda has now converged with the post-Washington Consensus economics of inclusive growth. As the World Bank Group (2016) states, its goals are now 'fully aligned with the SDGs [Sustainable Development Goals]: end poverty, promote prosperity and improve people's wellbeing while protecting the environment'. Its new 'shared prosperity' framework adds to previous concern with 'the poor': however, the aim of raising the wellbeing of the 'bottom 40%' understood in multidimensional terms while enhancing the 'voice and participation' of citizens. The social policy agenda is expressed in terms of 'investment in human development' including education, health, water and sanitation, social assistance and insurance'.

Of course the critiques and caveats raised by this policy turn are manifold but it is not our purpose to address these here. What we emphasise are the shifts in thinking about the relationship between economic and social policy which have accompanied the rise of the social investment and inclusive growth agendas in the shadow of the global SDGs. Together our authors make a compelling case that it is time to move beyond what Midgley called 'binary groupings'. His and Hemericjk's work exemplify the convergence of development policy's social protection perspective with the welfare state perspective on social investment. And if the 'developmental welfare state' has emerged as a model among development scholars, Kwon shows us why its economic development and universal social protection goals must be a 'dual imperative'.

Inclusive development: the 'process', the labour market and the third imperative

If the chapters above suggest a convergence of thinking between social investment and inclusive growth which might supply the overarching goals for a coherent universal global social policy framework, our other contributions map some of the key issues in terms of its implementation. Of topmost importance is the switch of emphasis from 'outcomes' to 'processes'. The former focus is associated with the residual, 'safety net' model of welfare under neoliberalism whereby social policy was not to alter the market processes of production but to rather provide limited forms of post hoc redistribution. The new emphasis does not ignore outcomes but also factors in the contributions of social policies to the process of production itself. This has raised some important issues in terms of definition and measurement while bringing centre stage the role of services such as education, health and 'social protection' in shaping the development process. We identify some common themes in the social investment and inclusive growth approaches to these issues while also highlighting the pivotal role of labour markets and environmental sustainability in the new global policy framework.

As Klasen shows in Chapter Five, an emphasis on both the productive and protection roles of social policy has been at the forefront of development policy scholarship concerned with the definition and measurement of inclusive growth. While his overview of the variety of definitions concludes that it remains 'ill-defined', it is clear that it is establishing an important research agenda that is overshadowing earlier approaches to definition and measurement developed in the period of the welfare state (Ranieri and Ramos, 2013; Asia Development Bank, 2014; Gupta et al, 2015; World Bank Group, 2016). While the OECD itself has put forward a measurement framework for inclusive growth, Klasen finds that it is really just 'another multidimensional wellbeing indicator' that remains wedded to the primacy of income, translating the non-income aspects of development into income equivalents. This maintains the emphasis on the role of social services in terms of protection without incorporating their roles in shaping the 'processes' of inclusive development. According to Klasen, development scholars and international development agencies such as the Asian Development Bank and the World Bank are much further advanced in developing measures that capture both the outcomes and processes of inclusive development. These frameworks have emphasised the importance of broad-based pattern of economic development as the foundation of social policy. He notes, for example, that the World Bank emphasises the process of inclusion as very much about economic participation rather than redistribution via taxes and transfers. In keeping with our emphasis on the 'dual imperative', Klasen wants broader measures that capture an understanding of inclusive growth reflected in a pre-tax and transfer pattern of income growth which is non-discriminatory against disadvantaged groups, together with non-income dimensions which act to reduce existing disadvantage.

While Klasen's critique of the OECD inclusive growth measures as lagging the international development agencies is well made, this volume overall would suggest that the evolution of the newer social investment approach actually looks to close that gap. As noted above, Hemerijck's chapter shows how an early aspiration to identify the productive value of welfare has developed into a comprehensive framework for mapping the productive and protective functions of social policy across the life course understood in terms of stocks, flows and buffers. It identifies the 'chain of temporal and transversal complementarities' involved in the development process and suggests how this needs to be managed in order to achieve inclusive outcomes. Importantly this shifts the social policy focus from moderating market outcomes via the tax and transfer system to an examination of the complementing roles of the social services and income support systems in both reducing inequality and enabling participation in economic development. Several chapters in our book explore aspects of this approach.

Thus, Busmeyer notes how the early 'canonical texts' of the social investment literature focused very much on the role of investment in early childhood education and care. He shows how this has evolved into a more comprehensive account of the role of learning and skills across the life course. Such investment can both raise productivity and contribute to a more inclusive society. But they may not depending on a range of factors. Busmeyer examines two policy areas to demonstrate how 'processes' can influence 'outcomes'. First he considers the public and private mix in education funding, finding that higher proportions of private spending are associated with higher levels of inequality. Second, he shows that countries with a more coordinated variety of capitalism place a higher value on vocational education and training, resulting in greater protection against unemployment in periods of economic downturn.

Turning to the other major social service, health, we find in Chapter Ten by López-Casanovas and Maynou that the relationship between health policy and the economy is much less clear cut. While there have indeed been major studies by Marmot (2103) and others which show positive growth outcomes associated with reductions in health inequalities, our authors show that it is extremely difficult to establish whether or not the 'health and growth nexus truly reflects a causal relationship'. They emphasise the problem of 'reverse causality'. Are people more economically productive because they are healthier or are they healthier because they are more economically productive? Nevertheless, with such caveats, López–Casanovas and Maynou conclude that the main challenges in addressing health inequalities relate to improving the position of those who are worse off. Here, they say, policy should recognise the need for an integrated response sensitive to the links between health, income, education, skills and employment. In developing economies they propose this means a women and children 'go first' approach in terms of income support which is critical for the health and education of the next generation; while in developed economies it is 'flexible and secure jobs' which can do the most to maintain the health of the most vulnerable groups.

Together these chapters suggest how the 'supply side' analyses of the social investment approach have indeed begun to address that neglect of 'process' in older welfare state measurement frameworks identified by Klasen. They capture the temporal or life course aspects as well as the complementarities between dimensions of health, education, income support and so on. While the contexts of developed and developing economies vary greatly, the clear thematic resemblance between the social investment approach outlined here and that of the inclusive growth framing of development as a multidimensional, socioeconomic 'process' suggests a possible common theoretical foundation for the consideration of issues of definition and measurement in the emerging new global policy framework. It is also clear that this work is still at an early stage. Our chapter on health for example reminds us how complex are the chains of causality between social and economic dimensions of development; while Hemerijck says bluntly that the work of 'conjecturing and testing social investment returns ... is still in its infancy'.

Inclusive governance

A final reflection on the question of process flows from this identification of the importance of capturing the 'complementarities' or synergies between the different dimensions of development. As Jenson writes in Chapter Twelve, it is one thing to recognise the '*what*' of policy propositions – the instruments' and another to understand the '*how*'. If we are to have inclusive development we will need 'after-neoliberal' forms of inclusive governance. She sees the precursors of inclusive governance as first, the Keynesian style hierarchical model staffed commonly by public servants and organised around social equality and rights. The second was neoliberalism privileging markets and promoting 'civil society' organisations in place of state delivery (see also OECD, 2016).

The inclusive governance model, according to Jenson, is more triadic or cross sectoral and emphasising 'the entrepreneurial possibilities of civil society engaging in service design and delivery, a model that depends less on parliamentary democracy, although it emphasises "participation", and more on a "business case" for action'. She notes that this Schumpeterian style promotion of the 'social entrepreneur' at first mapped onto the broader narrative of neoliberalism before reasserting a role for 'new public spending if not service delivery'. She also notes how this latter emphasis on the role of the 'social sector' augmenting rather than displacing the role of government is deeply rooted in continental European traditions of the 'social economy'. From other literatures we can see just how important the related idea of the 'social and solidarity economy' has become in development thinking (Utting, 2015; UNRISD, 2016). Moreover, we can see from Klasen's account of the UN approach to inclusive growth that there is now a renewed emphasis on the role of state and voluntary sector partnerships in giving citizens a greater 'voice' over the development process, an emphasis laid out in detail in the UNRISD (2016) flagship report, *Policy Innovations for Transformative Change*. Indeed, if through inclusive development we are witnessing a rebalancing of the 'what' of social policy towards a universal approach then ideas about 'how' will need to address those gaps in governance identified by Jenson in Chapter Twelve.

Two key challenges: employment and the environment

In this attempt to show how concepts of social investment and inclusive growth might help define a coherent new global social policy framework two issues have presented as of fundamental importance: the labour market and the environment. Here it is significant that our chapter on health ended with an emphasis on the importance of paid employment. Indeed, as Klasen observed for the major international organisations, inclusive growth has been very much about managing economic growth in a way which offers economic opportunity for all. This brings us to one of two major questions facing a new global social policy framework: is this a realistic ambition?

Our two chapters on employment scope some of the major issues. In Chapter Seven Bonoli writes that active labour market programmes have often been presented as a signature social investment policy contrasting with passive social protection. While he understands that in a 'balanced labour market' such investments in human capital can contribute to more inclusive growth, the emergence of 'unbalanced labour markets' in most OECD countries has largely nullified this role. He canvasses the variety of programmes – upskilling, improving labour market matching, putting pressure and preserving human capital – to show their minimal impact in polarised labour markets brought about by globalisation, technological change and mass migration. Without an economic strategy to rebalance labour markets he believes that the best social policy can offer is 'intelligent redistribution' which does not undermine work incentives such as through tax credits and a progressive VAT. While Bonoli's focus is the OECD, it clearly has implications for any attempt to develop a global framework for labour market policy.

In Chapter Six, Schmid takes up this challenge, boldly linking the issue of informal labour in the OECD to that of the developing economies while proposing a 'common ground of social policy' at the global level. He states from the outset that the 'standard employment contract' cannot be the basis of such a global policy. His wide ranging inquiry emphasises that the rise of non-standard forms of employment in Europe can be a 'curse' but might also be a 'blessing'. Indeed, he shows that there is a very strong correlation between productivity increase and voluntary part-time work (but not involuntary). The challenge is to have labour market regulations and wage/welfare combinations that protect not particular jobs but the employability of the worker across the life course. His account of the developing economies showcases the roles of conditional cash transfers in Brazil and the NEGRA in India which guarantees up to 100 days work each year to rural populations. He suggests that globally a social policy paradigm of inclusive growth premised on 'standard employment' is completely unrealistic and a recipe for failure. An inclusive labour contract will need to be based on 'the idea of a right to a decent income beyond formal employment'. It should include 'all forms of work' and would require the adoption of a new system of social rights and obligations.

The qualified support of Bonoli and Schmid for the role of employment as the key mechanism for inclusion contrasts with the central emphasis of agencies like the World Bank on managing broad-based, employment centred growth as the foundation of inclusive social policy. While this is too large a topic to be canvassed here it does lead us to reflect on the future of growth itself. In Chapter Thirteen, Jackson and Webster consider the theory of secular stagnation whereby the economic slowdown in many developed economies might be a sign that growth is 'over'. While this may appear pessimistic, they show how our thinking about development must engage with the environmental limits to growth. Here, ideas of decoupling growth from these limits appears unrealistic, meaning that we may have to consider policy goals closer to that of 'steady state' or 'degrowth'. As international organisations and policy communities begin to construct these policy alternatives it is clear that the environmental issues converge inextricably with the social and the economic. As Jackson and Webster note, rebalancing growth or development between countries is very much a matter of social justice. For these reasons, sustainability needs to be seen as the 'third imperative' of a strategy for a global social policy.

Conclusion

While our book has had the rather modest aim of exploring the similarities and differences of the concepts of social investment and inclusive growth deployed by policy actors we do believe that our contributed chapters have produced a significant resource for thinking about a new global social policy framework in the making. From our experience as editors we have discovered what an exciting and important exchange is developing at the disciplinary borders of social policy and development studies. As recently as 2013, Surender (2013) took up the question of how relevant Western social policy thinking is to the developing country experience. She canvassed the reasons why many major authors had thought not (such as Gough and Wood et al, 2004; Wood and Gough, 2006; Collier, 2007; Yeates, 2014). From her account of colonial history and the development models of the 20th century including the neoliberal turn from the 1980s we can track the separate paths of disciplinary development. But she found that with the end of the Washington Consensus and a new emphasis on the role of the state in the economy and in social protection a new chapter appeared to be beginning, one in which the East Asian experience of the developmental state appeared to be bridging the old disciplinary divide. Our book speaks very much to that new shared social policy experience which Surender saw emerging.

Klasen also notes how advanced the development research communities were on many of the big questions of a more integrated approach to development. This was very much the case in terms of their emphasis on the importance of effective economic management for broad-based economic development as the basis of a social policy regime. It was also the case in terms of the high degree of positive support for 'social protection' in the new development model. At the same time we did find that the social investment approach had accomplished a highly sophisticated albeit 'supply side' integration of the productive and protective roles of social policy as adapted to the new social risks of the Western societies. Both in terms of policy goals, instruments and governance we found much convergence. In terms of goals there is the 'triple imperative'; in terms of means there is a shared emphasis on the multidimensional process as much as outcomes of development with a resultant emphasis on the core social services such as education and health as much as welfare; while in terms of governance there is the after-neoliberal emphasis on positive and effective state institutions and markets alongside a more 'entrepreneurial' civil society. We believe such ideas can furnish the raw materials of a new global social policy framework.

We also identified key challenges to the global framework in terms of developing the 'inclusive labour contract' and the integration of the third imperative, environmental sustainability. Only in one area did we find not just a challenge but an obstacle to convergence: that is the European austerity economic agenda which was shown to be simply inimical to the social investment and inclusive growth approaches.

Finally, we remain very aware of the limitations of this exploration of policy ideas. It says nothing about how influential these ideas will be in the real world of politics, or, whether they will actually coalesce into collective action shaping a new global social policy architecture. But we have shown that they are actually reframing a global discussion of the role of social policy, which is of immense importance in-itself. This is the language through which the United Nations is calling for a new 'social contract' to replace that which emerged in the mid 20th century. It is the language informing debates among the increasingly influential regional social policy bodies such as Union of South American Nations, Association of Southeast Asian Nations, South African Development Community, and the European Union (see GSP Forum, 2015). And while the ideas and policy logics will be taken up in different ways across nations, reflecting different historical and cultural experiences, we think the social contracts of the future will indeed reflect these converging perspectives of social investment and inclusive growth that is sustainable.

References

Acemoglu, D. and Robinson, J.A. (2012) *Why Nations Fail: The Origins of Power, Prosperity and Poverty*, London: Profile Books.

Asian Development Bank (2014) 'ADB' Support for Inclusive Growth', Thematic Evaluation Study, Reference Number: SES: REG 2014-03, www.adb.org/sites/default/files/evaluation-document/36217/files/tes-ig.pdf (accessed 14 June 2017).

Barrientos, A. (2016) 'Justice-based social assistance', *Global Social Policy* 16(2): 151–65.

Collier, P. (2007) *The Bottom Billion: Why the Poorest Countries are Failing and What Can Be Done About It*, Oxford: Oxford University Press.

Deacon, B. (2013) *Global Social Policy in the Making: The Foundations of the Social Protection Floor*, Bristol: Policy Press.

de Haan, A. (2015) 'Inclusive Growth: Beyond Safety Nets?', *European Journal of Development Research* 27(4): 606–22.

Global Social Policy (GSP) Forum (2015) *Global Social Policy*, 15(3): 329–54. http://journals.sagepub.com/toc/gspa/15/3 (accessed 14 June 2017).

Goodin, R.E. (2001) 'Work and welfare: towards a post-productivist welfare regime', *British Journal of Political Science* 31(1): 13–39.

Gough, I., G. Wood, A. Barrientos, P. Bevan, P. Davis and G. Room (eds) (2004) *Insecurity and Welfare Regimes in Asia, Africa and Latin America: Social Policy in Development Contexts*, Cambridge: Cambridge University Press.

Gupta, J., N. Pouw and M. Ros-Tonen (2015) 'Towards an Elaborated Theory of Inclusive Development', *European Journal of Development Research* 27(4): 541–59.

Hibben, M. (2016) *Poor States, Power and the Politics of IMF Reform*, London: Palgrave.

Hudson J. and S. Kuhner (2012) 'Analyzing the Productive and Protective Dimensions of Welfare: Looking Beyond the OECD', *Social Policy & Administration* 46(1): 35–60.

Hudson, J. and A. Kuhner (2013) 'Analysing the productivist dimensions of welfare: looking beyond the Greater China Region', in Maggie K.W. Lau and M.G. Koo (eds), *Managing Social Change and Social Policy in Greater China*, Abingdon: Routledge, 217–38.

Hwang, G.-J. (ed.) (2011) *New Welfare States in East Asia*, Cheltenham: Edward Elgar.

Jordan, B. (2006) *Social Policy for the Twenty-First Century*, Cambridge, Polity Press.

Kabeer, N. (2014) 'The Politics and Practicalities of Universalism: Towards a Citizen-Centred Perspective on Social Protection', *European Journal of Development Research* 26: 338–54.

Kabeer, N. (2015) 'Evolving meanings of "the social" in the international development agenda', *Journal of International and Comparative Social Policy* 31(2): 114–31.

Koehler, G. (2014) 'Some preliminary reflections on development, public policy and welfare states', in D. Chopra and G. Koehler (eds), *Development and Welfare Policy in South Asia*, Abingdon: Routledge, 9–24.

Koehler, G. (2016) 'Assessing the SDGs from the standpoint of eco-social policy: using the SDGs subversively', *Journal of International and Comparative Social Policy* 32(2): 149–64.

Kuhnle, S. and S. Hort (2004) 'The Developmental Welfare State in Scandinavia', Social Policy and Development programme Paper Number 17, Geneva: UNRISD.

Kwon, H. and M.G. Koo (eds) (2014) *The Korean Government and Public Policies in a Developmental Nexus*, Switzerland: Springer.

Lau, Maggie K.W. and Ka-Ho Mok (eds) (2013) *Managing Social Change and Social Policy in Greater China*, Abingdon: Routledge.

North, D.C. (1990) *Institutions, Institutional Change and Economic Performance*, New York: Cambridge University Press.

OECD (2016) *The Governance of Inclusive Growth*, Paris: OECD Publishing.

Ranieri, R. and R. Ramos (2013) *Inclusive Growth: Building Up A Concept*, Working Paper number 104, Brasília: International Policy Centre for Inclusive Growth (IPC-IG), www.ipc-undp.org/pub/IPCWorkingPaper104.pdf (accessed 14 June 2017).

Riesco, M. (ed.) (2007) *Latin America: A New developmental Welfare State Model in the Making?*, Basingstoke: Palgrave.

Rodrik, D., A. Subramanian and F. Trebbi (2004) 'Institutions Rule: The Primacy of Institutions Over Geography and Integration in Economic Development', *Journal of Economic Growth* 9(2): 131–65.

Samans, R., J. Blanke, G. Corrigan and M. Drzeniek (2015) *The Inclusive Growth and development Report 2015*, Geneva: World Economic Forum.

Smyth, P. and C. Deeming (2016) 'The "Social Investment Perspective" in Social Policy: A Longue Durée Perspective', *Social Policy and Administration*, 50(6): 675–90.

Surender, R. (2013) 'The role of historical contexts in shaping social policy in the global South', in R. Surender and R. Walker (eds), *Social Policy in a Developing World*, Cheltenham: Edward Elgar, 14–34.

United Nations Research Institute for Sustainable Development (UNRISD) (2016) *Policy Innovations for Transformative Change Implementing the 2030 Agenda for Sustainable Development*, UNRISD Flagship Report, Geneva.

Utting, P. (ed.) (2015) *Social and Solidarity Economy: Beyond the Fringe*, London: ZED Books.

Wood, G. and I. Gough (2006) 'A comparative welfare regime approach to global social policy', *World Development* 34(10): 1696–712.

World Bank (1993) *The East Asian Miracle*, Washington, DC: World Bank.

World Bank Group (2016) *Global Monitoring report 2015/2016: Development Goals in an Era of Demographic Change*, Washington, DC: World Bank.

Yeates, N. (2014) *Understanding Global Social Policy*, Second Edition, Bristol: Policy Press.

Index

Notes: Page numbers in *italics* indicate figures, boxes and tables.